THE
BEST
OF
Gourmet

THE
BEST
OF
Gourmet

1994 EDITION

FROM THE EDITORS OF GOURMET

Food Photographs by Romulo A. Yanes

CONDÉ NAST BOOKS • RANDOM HOUSE, NEW YORK

LIBRARY OF CONGRESS
CATALOGING-IN-PUBLICATION DATA

(Revised for vol. 9)
Main entry under title:

The Best of Gourmet
    Includes Indexes
    1. Cookery, International. I. Gourmet.
TX 723-B4686   1993   641.5945-dc20   92-36723
ISBN 0-679-43347-3 (v. 9)
ISSN 1046-1760

Most of the recipes in this work were published previously in *Gourmet* Magazine.

Manufactured in the United States of America

98765432   24689753   23456789
First Edition

All the informative text in this book was written by Diane Keitt and Judith Tropea.

Grateful acknowledgment is made to the following for permission to reprint recipes previously published in *Gourmet* Magazine:

Laurie Colwin: ''Corn Fritters'' (page 89); ''Classic Shortbread'' (page 220). Copyright © 1993 by Laurie Colwin. Reprinted by permission of Donadio and Ashworth, Inc.

Kemp Minifie: ''Strawberry Shortcake'' (page 216); ''Cream Biscuits'' (page 216); ''Buttermilk Biscuits'' (page 217). Copyright © 1993 by Kemp Miles Minifie. Reprinted by permission of the author.

Elizabeth Schneider: ''Berry and Farmer Cheese Tart'' (page 226). Copyright © 1993 by Elizabeth Schneider. Reprinted by permission of the author.

Zanne Early Zakroff: ''Goat Cheese Mashed-Potato Gratin'' (page 180). Copyright © 1993 by Zanne Early Zakroff. Reprinted by permission of the author.

The following photographers have generously given their permission to use the photographs listed below. Ray Cranbourne's photograph has been published previously in *Gourmet* Magazine:

Shao Zi Bai/China Tourism Photo Library: ''Terraced Fields, Yunnan'' (page 252). Copyright © 1986. Printed by permission of the China Tourism Photo Library.

Zenon Christodoulou: ''Beijing'' (page 7). Copyright © 1990. Printed by permission of the photographer.

Ray Cranbourne: ''Guangzhou (Canton)'' (page 284). Copyright © 1987. Reprinted by permission of Black Star.

Charles Offerman: ''Summer Palace, Beijing'' (page 266). Copyright © 1992. Printed by permission of the photographer.

United Nations: ''Chengdu, Sichuan Province'' (Photo #156178), (page 276). Copyright © 1982. Printed by permission of the United Nations Photo Library.

For Condé Nast Books

Jill Cohen, Vice President
Ellen Maria Bruzelius, Direct Marketing Manager
Kristine Smith-Cunningham, Advertising Promotion Manager
Lisa Faith Phillips, Fulfillment Manager
Diane Pesce, Composition Production Manager
Serafino J. Cambareri, Quality Control Manager

For *Gourmet* Books

Diane Keitt, Editor
Judith Tropea, Associate Editor

For *Gourmet* Magazine

Gail Zweigenthal, Editor-in-Chief

Zanne Early Zakroff, Executive Food Editor
Kemp Miles Minifie, Senior Food Editor
Alexis M. Touchet, Associate Food Editor
Leslie Glover Pendleton, Food Editor
Amy Mastrangelo, Food Editor
Lori Longbotham, Food Editor
Jennifer G. Wehrle, Assistant Food Editor

Romulo A. Yanes, Photographer
Marjorie H. Webb, Stylist
Nancy Purdum, Stylist

Produced in association with **Media Projects Incorporated**

Carter Smith, Executive Editor
Anne Wright, Project Director
Kate Hartnick, Project Editor
Martina D'Alton, Associate Project Editor
Marilyn Flaig, Indexer
Michael Shroyer, Art/Production Director

The text of this book was set in Times Roman by the Composition Department of Condé Nast Publications Inc. and U.S. Lithograph Typographers. The four-color separations were done by The Color Company, Seiple Lithographers, and Applied Graphic Technologies. The book was printed and bound at R.R. Donnelley and Sons. Stock is Citation Web Gloss, Westvāco.

Front Jacket: ''Grilled Teriyaki Shrimp and Vegetable Brochettes'' (page 127).

Back Jacket: ''Nectarine Blueberry Cobbler'' (page 242).

Frontispiece: ''Berry and Farmer Cheese Tart'' (page 226).

ACKNOWLEDGMENTS

The editors of *Gourmet* Books would like to thank the colleagues and free-lancers whose shared ideas and skills are all a part of *The Best of Gourmet, 1994*.

This year our Cuisines of the World section highlights the Flavors of China. Zanne Early Zakroff carefully developed a flavorful Dim Sum menu and Alexis M. Touchet devised a very festive Lunar New Year's Buffet feast as well as a *nouvelle*-style Harvest Moon Dinner. All menus were photographed by Romulo A. Yanes and styled by Jeannie Oberholtzer. Food stylists were Amy Mastrangelo, Leslie Glover Pendleton, and Alexis M. Touchet. *Gourmet*'s Wine Editor, Gerald Asher, selected the beverages for each menu. Charming line illustrations by Jim Saucier, and regional photography by Shao Zi Bai, Zenon Christodoulou, Ray Cranbourne, and Charles Offerman give us a closer look at this fascinating country. Special thanks goes to Nina Simonds for sharing so much of her time and invaluable expertise on Chinese cooking with us, and to Guy Thom and Lily Thom who answered our many questions about China.

We would also like to thank Kemp Minifie who created and styled the colorful (and very tasty) Grilled Teriyaki Shrimp and Vegetable Brochettes that appear on the front jacket. Also, we are grateful to Georgia Chan Downard whose practical and delicious recipes appear in this year's addendum, Cooking from a Basic Pantry. Lovely country drawings by Vicky Harrison complement this section.

We are indebted to the artists who provided the line drawings that appear throughout the book. They are: Edgar Blakeney, Carla Borea, Jean Chandler, Beverly Charlton, Suzanne Dunaway, Barbara Fiore, Kathy Grimm, Maria Harkis, Vicky Harrison, Suzie Howard, Lauren Jarrett, Laura Hartman Maestro, Zoe Mavridis, Jeanne Meinke, Jenni Oliver, Monique Faith Parry, Agni Saucier, Jim Saucier, Alexandra Schultz, and Margaret Shields.

Michael Shroyer, our book designer, continues to put his stamp on this series and we thank him for keeping its rushed schedule. Also, thank you to Elaine Richard and Kathleen Duffy-Freud, for their careful proofreading, and to Toni Rachiele and Rebecca Ynocencio, who answered our editorial queries.

ᘱᗂ

CONTENTS

INTRODUCTION   9

PART ONE: THE MENU COLLECTION   11

INTRODUCTION

ads come and go, but true classics are cherished forever. There is something about the understated nature of simple foods and designs that says *good taste* and *good living*, and that is what *Gourmet* magazine is all about. As I reviewed this ninth annual volume, which beautifully showcases all the menus and the best recipes from the twelve issues that appeared in 1993, I was struck by the fact that we depend on these favorites now as much as ever. After all, there really is no substitute for the best.

Before a food can be considered a "classic" it must be universally loved. America has been blessed with plentiful crops and livestock, bountiful oceans and streams, and, most important, vast numbers of international emigrants who have brought their own recipes to our shores. Last April, for the first time ever, we ran an entire issue, *Gourmet's America*, filled with our country's most prized foods. The volume you now hold includes one of my favorite menus from that issue—Celebrating America's Heritage (page 31)—which highlights our national treasures and includes scrumptious Seafood Canapés with Lemon-Chive Butter, a comforting Garlic Roast Pork, creamy Potato, Spinach, and Feta Gratin, and an incredibly good Boston Cream Pie. As a matter of fact, our America issue was so successful we have decided to do another in 1994.

Speaking of classics, our Gastronomie sans Argent column has appeared in the magazine for almost 30 years, offering a monthly collection of recipes for seasonally appropriate fruits, vegetables, or other food items. Last year we decided to expand the possibilities of this column, and now it is presented in many guises. During peak harvest months, for example, we offered recipes for several different foods in our newly named columns Pick of the Crop and From the Farm Stand. The result is a larger variety of recipes in each issue,

and for this volume we have selected many of the best ones, including Arugula Pesto, Wild Blueberry Pie, Grilled Chicken Salad with Mangoes and Greens, and Parchment-Baked Minted Potatoes.

Other timeless dishes also appeared throughout the year in a series of articles written by our dear friend Laurie Colwin, who died unexpectedly in late 1992. Laurie was dedicated to great American foods and never tired of praising them in her casual, relaxed style. We have added a few of her recipes to this book, including my new favorites for Classic Shortbread (page 220) and Corn Fritters (page 89).

It is fitting that our addendum this year, Cooking from a Basic Pantry (page 293), is filled with classic dishes. This informative section tells you exactly what you need to stock a basic pantry, where and how to store these goods in your kitchen, and how long you can expect them to keep fresh. Then we present 24 delicious recipes for breakfasts, lunches, dinners, desserts, and snacks that all can be made from your plentiful shelves. Puffed Apple Pancake, Cheddar Bread Pudding with Roasted Red Peppers and Chilies, Spaghetti Carbonara, and Apple Brown Betty are just a sampling.

And, our Cuisines of the World section this year turns to The Flavors of China (page 251). Here you will find beautiful photographs of this fascinating land as well as helpful information on Chinese ingredients, cooking methods, and equipment. Three menus follow—A Lunar New Year's Buffet, Harvest Moon Dinner, and Dim Sum (the beloved assortment of Chinese snacks)—to test your newfound skills.

As you can see, *The Best of Gourmet, 1994 Edition* has much to offer. We hope that you will enjoy it to the fullest—and learn a little along the way.

Gail Zweigenthal
Editor-in-Chief

THE MENU COLLECTION

he most memorable meals are often not only filled with favorite dishes but enjoyed with family and friends in a relaxed atmosphere. Ideally, the cook has a cache of special recipes on hand to meet everyone's desires, and the setting is comfortable and inviting. The following 70 pages of outstanding full-color photographs offer just such a collection of fine menu ideas. Here you will find all 24 menus from the 1993 columns, *Gourmet*'s Menus and Cuisine Courante, with food and table settings that are classic *Gourmet*—stylish and welcoming.

Life in the 1990s is demanding enough without complicated meals! And, as you will notice, *Gourmet* offers more easy picnics, lunches, and dinners than ever before. Eating out of doors usually means less preparation time, and a number of our menus are designed to be served alfresco. For your next winter outing turn to our Picnic in the Snow, a fun little meal boasting a make-ahead Barbecue Bean Soup filled with warming spices, special Prosciutto, Münster, and Cumin Corn-Bread Sandwiches, and delectable Chocolate Wafer and Graham Cracker Brownies. Later in the year, as the sun turns up the heat, look for A Blueberry-Picking Picnic, a simple summer repast of cooling dishes—Chilled Tomato Yogurt Soup bursting with puréed vine-ripened tomatoes, two easy *Gourmet* sandwiches made with specialty goods from the delicatessen, and mouth-puckering Gingered Lemon Almond Squares. There is even a lovely hors d'oeuvres party for Toasting the Bride and Groom at poolside (or anywhere under warm, friendly skies) that is designed to impress without fuss. Substantial Fillet of Beef, Arugula, and Artichoke Crostini, cooling Salmon Mousse with Salmon Roe and Crudités, spicy Chicken Satés with Peanut Dipping Sauce . . . and these are just a sampling.

Even our elegant celebratory meals are filled with easy favorites. Our Thoroughly Modern Mother's Day

menu, for example, offers classic simplicity and outstanding taste that any mother would love. Fragrant Fino Sherry and savory Lemon-Pepper Parmesan Crackers make a tasty combination to begin the festivities. (The dough for these delicious tidbits can be made two days ahead.) Then, succulent Grilled Salmon with Fennel Orange Salsa quickly cooks over glowing coals while tender Asparagus with Scallion Butter and a young herb salad with flavorful cassis (black-currant) vinaigrette take but a few minutes to prepare. And, for dessert, an ever-so-light Rosewater Angel Food Cake with a sugar glaze and fresh raspberries makes a beautiful finale.

Simple elegance continues throughout the holidays. In November we offer a Holiday Weekend Brunch, an ideal way to extend the celebration of turkeyday, especially if you have out-of-town guests. Pretty Cranberry Champagne Cocktails, a rich Maple Walnut Coffeecake, and delicious Cream Cheese and Chive Scrambled Eggs are just a few of the gems that await. And as the holiday season becomes more hectic, you will enjoy A Casual Christmastime Dinner. Here, *everything* can be prepared ahead. From the crispy, wreath-shaped Cucumber Tapenade Canapés, to the rich-tasting Baked Polenta with Shiitake Ragout, to the sensational Cranberry Swirl Ice-Cream Cake, this menu is a dream.

As in the past, Gerald Asher, *Gourmet*'s wine editor, suggests complementary beverages for the menus. Whether it's Harpoon Ale for our Fourth of July Cookout, or Champagne Cuvée William Deutz '85 to toast An Intimate New Year's Eve feast, you can feel confident that his selections are always perfectly matched to the occasion.

Let this volume of *The Best of Gourmet* show you how to entertain in style without the worry. With the following menus in hand, you will find that your next gathering will be enjoyed by all, *especially* you!

NEW YEAR'S DAY
FIRESIDE LUNCHEON

Herbed Oxtail Terrine, p. 144

Shellfish Stew Provençale, p. 128

Parsleyed Garlic Bread, p. 106

*Mixed Greens with
Tarragon Vinaigrette, p. 196*

St. Clement Vineyards Napa Valley Chardonnay '90

---

*Orange Flans with
Candied Zest, p. 244*

Anise Pine-Nut Cookies, p. 217

Shellfish Stew Provençale;
Parsleyed Garlic Bread

Orange Flans with Candied Zest;
Anise Pine-Nut Cookies

AN INTIMATE NEW YEAR'S EVE

Caviar Puff-Pastry Stars, *p. 87*

Champagne Cuvée William Deutz '85

Filets Mignons with Mustard Port Sauce, *p. 130*

Red Onion Confit, *p. 130*

Pommes Anna, *p. 179*

Buttered Snow Peas and Carrots, *p. 179*

Nuits-Saint-Georges, Domaine Daniel Rion, Les Vignes Rondes '90

---

*Chocolate Profiteroles
with Caramel Coffee Ice Cream
and Bittersweet Chocolate Sauce*, *p. 234*

De Loach Russian River Valley Late-Harvest Gewürztraminer '91

Filets Mignons with Mustard Port Sauce; Red Onion Confit;
Pommes Anna; Buttered Snow Peas and Carrots

A CARIBBEAN
BUFFET

Fried Green Plantains, p. 93

Sauce Chien, p. 93

Salt Cod Fritters, p. 88

Jamaican Sorrel Rum Punch, p. 246

Piña Colada Punch, p. 247

———————

Jerk Chicken, p. 147

Curried Red Snapper, p. 121

Yellow Rice, p. 171

Black Beans, p. 174

Squash Purée with Olive Oil and Lime, p. 183

Wilted Cucumber Salad, p. 197

Josmeyer Riesling d'Alsace, Le Kottabe '90

Cold lager

———————

Banana Coconut Cream Pie, p. 222

Spiced Caramel Oranges, p. 243

Salt Cod Fritters; Fried Green Plantains; Sauce Chien;
Piña Colada Punch; Jamaica Sorrel Rum Punch

Jerk Chicken; Yellow Rice;
Curried Red Snapper;
Black Beans; Squash Purée
with Olive Oil and Lime;
Wilted Cucumber Salad

CUISINE COURANTE

PICNIC
IN THE SNOW

Barbecue Bean Soup, p. 108

Prosciutto, Münster, and
Cumin Corn-Bread Sandwiches, p. 139

Pickled Carrots, Turnips,
and Peppers, p. 176

Chocolate Wafer and
Graham Cracker Brownies, p. 222

Barbecue Bean Soup; Prosciutto,
Münster, and Cumin Corn-Bread Sandwiches;
Pickled Carrots, Turnips, and Peppers

22

A SOUTHWESTERN
DINNER

Roasted Yellow Pepper Soup and
Roasted Tomato Soup with Serrano Cream, p. 114

———

Grilled Pork Kebabs with
Manchamantel Sauce, p. 137

Corn Cakes, p. 102

Herbed Orzo with Toasted Pine Nuts, p. 163

Hearts of Romaine with
Creamy Lime Vinaigrette, p. 193

Château d'Aquéria Tavel Rosé '91

———

Mexican Chocolate Torte, p. 214

Roasted Yellow Pepper Soup and
Roasted Tomato Soup with Serrano Cream

Grilled Pork Kebabs with Manchamantel Sauce;
Corn Cakes; Herbed Orzo with Toasted Pine Nuts

Mexican Chocolate Torte

Cream Cheese and Jam Turnover

CUISINE COURANTE

A BREEZE OF A LUNCH

Minestrone, p. 108

Garlic Bruschetta, p. 105

Assorted Dry-Cured Italian Sausages

Escarole and Radicchio Salad, p. 192

*Santino Grandpère Vineyard Zinfandel
Shenandoah Valley of California '89*

Cream Cheese and Jam Turnovers, p. 228

Minestrone; Garlic Bruschetta; Escarole and Radicchio Salad;
Assorted Dry-Cured Italian Sausages

CELEBRATING
AMERICA'S HERITAGE

Seafood Canapés with Lemon-Chive Butter, p. 97

A favorite ice-cold vodka

———————

Escarole Soup, p. 111

———————

Garlic Roast Pork, p. 138

Potato, Spinach, and Feta Gratin, p. 181

Beets with Horseradish, p. 175

Dandelion and Sorrel Salad with Paprika Stars, p. 191

De Loach Russian River Valley Zinfandel '90

———————

Boston Cream Pie, p. 224

Heitz Cellars California Angelica '74

Dandelion and
Sorrel Salad with
Paprika Stars

Escarole Soup

Garlic Roast Pork; Potato, Spinach, and
Feta Gratin; Beets with Horseradish

32

Spring Onion Soup with Garlic Croutons

CUISINE COURANTE

MEANWHILE...
BACK AT THE RANCH

Spring Onion Soup with Garlic Croutons, p. 112

Bacon and Sage Panfried Trout, p. 122

Grilled Chili-Rubbed Lamb Chops, p. 142

Hot Pepper Jelly, p. 142

Wild Rice and Toasted Pecan Pilaf, p. 172

*Spinach and Mushroom Salad
with Orange Vinaigrette, p. 194*

Simi Mendocino County Chenin Blanc '90

Sterling Vineyards Napa Valley Merlot '89

Pinto Raisin Bread Pudding with Apples and Cheese, p. 229

Bacon and Sage Panfried Trout; Grilled Chili-Rubbed Lamb Chops;
Spinach and Mushroom Salad with Orange Vinaigrette;
Wild Rice and Toasted Pecan Pilaf

A
THOROUGHLY MODERN
MOTHER'S DAY

Lemon-Pepper Parmesan Crackers, p. 104

La Ina Fino Sherry

Grilled Salmon with
Fennel Orange Salsa, p. 120

Asparagus with Scallion Butter, p. 174

Herb Salad with
Cassis Vinaigrette, p. 192

Kunde Magnolia Lane Vineyard
Sonoma Valley Sauvignon Blanc '91

Rosewater Angel Food Cake, p. 210

Asti Spumante Fontanafredda

Grilled Salmon with Fennel Orange Salsa;
Asparagus with Scallion Butter

38

Rosewater Angel Food Cake

A NEW ENGLAND BREAKFAST

Stir-Fried Red Flannel Hash, p. 158

Fried Eggs, p. 156

Raspberry Corn Muffins, p. 103

Orange Juice

Coffee

Fried Eggs; Stir-Fried Red Flannel Hash;
Raspberry Corn Muffins

A GREEK LUNCHEON

Herbed Olives, p. 91   *Cucumber Yogurt Dip, p. 98*

Marinated Squid and Fennel, p. 122

White Bean and Vegetable Salad, p. 196   *Eggplant Spread, p. 99*

Green Olive and Coriander Relish, p. 205

Pita Wedges

Boutari Kretikos '91

Grilled Lemon Prawns, p. 128

Watercress and Radish Salad, p. 195

Feta Cumin Corn Bread, p. 102

Apricot Yogurt Cake with Orange Honey Syrup, p. 212

Halvah Vanilla Ice Cream, p. 236

Patriaki Muscat

Grilled Lemon Prawns;
Watercress and
Radish Salad;
Feta Cumin Corn Bread

Cucumber Yogurt Dip; Herbed Olives; Marinated Squid and Fennel;
Pita Wedges; White Bean and Vegetable Salad;
Green Olive and Coriander Relish; Eggplant Spread

TOASTING THE
BRIDE AND GROOM

*Fillet of Beef, Arugula,
and Artichoke Crostini, p. 96*

*Salmon Mousse with
Salmon Roe and Crudités, p. 94*

*Chicken Satés with
Peanut Dipping Sauce, p. 88*

*Pasta Salad with
Tomatoes and Peas, p. 200*

Tropical Sparkling Sangría, p. 247

*León Beyer
Pinot Blanc de Blancs d'Alsace '90*

Saintsbury Carneros Pinot Noir '91

Rolling Rock Extra Pale Premium Beer

---

*Gingersnap and Lemon
Ice Cream Sandwiches, p. 236*

Fillet of Beef, Arugula, and Artichoke Crostini;
Salmon Mousse with Salmon Roe and Crudités; Chicken Satés with
Peanut Dipping Sauce; Pasta Salad with Tomatoes and Peas

FOURTH OF JULY COOKOUT

Spiced Walnuts, p. 96

Tomato Bacon Sandwiches, p. 95

———————

Maple-Barbecued Chicken, p. 149

*Potato, Corn, and
Cherry Tomato Salad
with Basil Dressing, p. 198*

*Romaine and Cucumber Salad
with Garlic Vinaigrette, p. 193*

Black Pepper Pita Toasts, p. 106

———————

*Red, White, and Blue Cheesecake
with Chocolate Cookie Crust, p. 212*

Watermelon Slices

———————

Seghesio Winery Sonoma County Zinfandel '90

Harpoon Ale

Lemonade

Maple-Barbecued Chicken; Potato, Corn, and Cherry Tomato Salad
with Basil Dressing; Black Pepper Pita Toasts; Romaine and
Cucumber Salad with Garlic Vinaigrette

Eggplant,
Roasted Pepper,
and Goat Cheese
Terrine with
Parsley Sauce

CUISINE COURANTE

DINNER IN THE GREAT INDOORS

Eggplant, Roasted Pepper, and
Goat Cheese Terrine
with Parsley Sauce, p. 177

Radici di Lapio '91 Fiano di Avellino, Mastroberardino

Roast Rack of Lamb, p. 140

Herbed Tomato Chutney, p. 140

Basil Couscous with
Summer Squash, p. 169

Château Grand-Puy-Lacoste Grand Cru Classé Pauillac '83

Dark Chocolate Mint Velvets, p. 230

Sugar Crisps, p. 221

Quinta da Ervamoira 10-Year-Old Porto

Roast Rack of Lamb; Herbed Tomato Chutney;
Basil Couscous with Summer Squash

LUNCH
FOR A LAZY DAY

Yellow Tomato Salad
with Lemongrass, p. 200

————————

Crab Cakes, p. 124

Tarragon Tartar Sauce, p. 125

Red Cabbage and Carrot Slaw, p. 200

Burgess Cellars Napa Valley Triere Vineyard Chardonnay '91

————————

Ricotta Gelato with
Blackberry Sauce, p. 238

Crab Cakes; Tarragon Tartar Sauce;
Red Cabbage and Carrot Slaw

Ricotta Gelato with Blackberry Sauce

A
BLUEBERRY-PICKING
PICNIC

Chilled Tomato Yogurt Soup, p. 116

Olive and Jarlsberg Salad Sandwich, p. 157

Corned Beef and Coleslaw Sandwich, p. 134

Ockfener Bockstein Kabinett '89 Weingut Dr. Fisher

Gingered Lemon Almond Squares, p. 219

Chilled Tomato Yogurt Soup;
Olive and Jarlsburg Salad Sandwich;
Corned Beef and Coleslaw Sandwich

A POLO PICNIC

Pickled Shrimp, *p. 95*

Stilton and Hazelnut Spread, *p. 101*

Stuffed Eggs with Caviar, *p. 89*

Saffron Vichyssoise, *p. 114*

Pimm's Cups, *p. 246*

Gimlets, *p. 246*

———

Cold Roast Fillet of Beef, *p. 131*

Cucumber Horseradish Sauce, *p. 131*

Curried Yogurt Sauce, *p. 131*

Assorted Breads

Tomato, Potato, and
Mustard Green Salad, *p. 199*

Cumin and Coriander Spiced
Chick-Pea Salad, *p. 197*

Joseph Phelps Vineyards Vin du Mistral Grenache Rosé '92

Taj Mahal Beer

———

Orange Caraway Seed Cakes, *p. 215*

Port and Honey Poached Pears
with Lemon Curd Mousse, *p. 243*

Pimm's Cups; Gimlets; Stilton and Hazelnut Spread;
Stuffed Eggs with Caviar; Pickled Shrimp

Saffron Vichyssoise;
Cold Roast Fillet
of Beef; Cucumber
Horseradish Sauce;
Curried Yogurt Sauce;
Assorted Breads;
Cumin and Coriander
Spiced Chick-Pea Salad;
Tomato, Potato, and
Mustard Green Salad

BACK-TO-SCHOOL SEND-OFF

Caesar Salad, p. 192

---

*Cornmeal-Crusted
Oven-Fried Chicken, p. 146*

*Mashed Potatoes with
Garlic and Shallots, p. 180*

Minted Sugar Snap Peas, p. 179

MacRostie Carneros Chardonnay '90

Nectarine Blueberry Cobbler, p. 242

Cornmeal-Crusted Oven-Fried Chicken; Mashed Potatoes with
Garlic and Shallots; Minted Sugar Snap Peas

A MEXICAN FIESTA

*Guacamole with Scallion
and Coriander, p. 100*

*Black Bean, Green Pepper,
and Red Onion Dip, p. 98*

———————

Caldo Tlalpeño, p. 110

Tamales, p. 185

*Jícama, Pineapple, and
Watercress Salad with
Orange Chili Vinaigrette, p. 195*

Dos Equis beer

———————

*Mexican Floating Island with
Kahlúa Custard Sauce and
Sesame Pumpkin-Seed Brittle, p. 232*

Fresh Figs

Black Bean, Green Pepper, and Red Onion Dip;
Guacamole with Scallion and Coriander

Caldo Tlalpeño; Tamales;
Jícama, Pineapple, and Watercress Salad
with Orange Chili Vinaigrette

Mexican Floating Island with Kahlúa Custard Sauce and
Sesame Pumpkin-Seed Brittle; Fresh Figs

Black and White Chocolate Macaroon Tart with Raspberry Sauce

CUISINE COURANTE

AN ELEGANT AUTUMN DINNER

Eggplant Ravioli with
Lemon Sage Oil and Fried Onions, p. 164

Hattenheimer Wisselbrunnen Riesling Kabinett Weingut
Freiherr zu Knyphausen '91

Orange Duck Breasts on Braised Chicory, p. 152

Gorgonzola and Pear Millet Pilaf, p. 170

Roasted Cauliflower with Rosemary, p. 176

''BB'' Riesling Auslese Trocken Weingut Dr. Bürklin-Wolf '90

Black and White
Chocolate Macaroon Tart
with Raspberry Sauce, p. 228

Eggplant Ravioli with Lemon Sage Oil and Fried Onions

A SHAKER THANKSGIVING

Creamed Oysters on Toasted Corn Bread, p. 92

---

*Roast Turkey with Chestnut Stuffing
and Cider Gravy, p. 153*

Cranberry Fruit Relish, p. 204

Scalloped Onions, Leeks, and Shallots, p. 178

Maple Squash Purée, p. 184

Herbed Buttered Parsnips, p. 178

Warm Green Bean Salad with Dill, p. 196

Sanford Santa Barbara County Chardonnay '91

Ohio Shaker Lemon Pie, p. 224

Cranberry Raisin Tart, p. 226

*Beringer California Special Select Late Harvest
Johannisberg Riesling '89*

Creamed Oysters on Toasted Corn Bread

Roast Turkey with Chestnut Stuffing and Cider Gravy;
Cranberry Fruit Relish;
Scalloped Onions, Leeks,
and Shallots; Maple Squash Purée;
Herbed Buttered Parsnips; Warm Green Bean Salad with Dill

Maple Walnut Coffeecake

HOLIDAY WEEKEND BRUNCH

Maple Walnut Coffeecake, p. 214

Cream Cheese and Chive Scrambled Eggs, p. 156

Shredded Potato Pancakes with Smoked Salmon, p. 158

Watercress Salad with Warm Vinaigrette, p. 194

Cranberry Champagne Cocktails, p. 246

Honey Vanilla Rice-Pudding Crème Brûlée, p. 231

Cranberry Champagne Cocktails; Cream Cheese and Chive
Scrambled Eggs; Watercress Salad with Warm Vinaigrette;
Shredded Potato Pancakes with Smoked Salmon

CHRISTMAS DINNER

Oxtail Bouillon with Parmesan Puffs, p. 112

Oxtail Pâté, p. 92

Blandy's 5-Year-Old Dry Sercial Madeira

———

*Roasted Rack of Venison and Shallots
with Dried-Cranberry Gravy, p. 144*

*Brown-and Wild-Rice Pilaf
with Porcini and Parsley, p. 172*

Purée of Three Root Vegetables, p. 184

*Mixed Greens
with Honey Vinaigrette and Gorgonzola, p. 195*

Barbaresco Santo Stefano Bruno Giacosa '88

———

Chocolate Linzertorte, p. 227

Vin Santo Badia a Coltibuono '87

Oxtail Bouillon with Parmesan Puffs

Chocolate Linzertorte

Roasted Rack of Venison and Shallots with Dried-Cranberry Gravy;
Brown-and Wild-Rice Pilaf with Porcini and Parsley; Purée of Three Root Vegetables

Prosciutto-Wrapped
Breadsticks
with Fig;
Cucumber
Tapenade Canapés

CUISINE COURANTE

A CASUAL CHRISTMASTIME DINNER

Prosciutto-Wrapped Breadsticks with Fig, p. 87

Cucumber Tapenade Canapés, p. 97

*Jekel Vineyards Arroyo Seco
Johannisberg Riesling '91*

———————

Baked Polenta with Shiitake Ragout, p. 170

Arugula, Radicchio, and Endive Salad, p. 190

Cosimo Taurino Salice Salentino Rosso '88

———————

Cranberry Swirl Ice-Cream Cake, p. 235

Clear Creek Distillery Pear Brandy

Baked Polenta with Shiitake Ragout;
Arugula, Radicchio, and Endive Salad

A RECIPE COMPENDIUM

n this section you will find a collection of the best recipes that appeared in *Gourmet* magazine during 1993. Here we have gathered all the recipes from *Gourmet*'s Menus and Cuisine Courante columns that are pictured in Part One, The Menu Collection, as well as the finest dishes from all the magazine's other regular food columns—In Short Order, Twice as Good, The Last Touch, Gastronomie sans Argent, and Forbidden Pleasures—plus additional recipes from special articles that appeared throughout the year. Whether you are looking for one of your own favorites, searching for a particular type of dish, or merely browsing, here you will find organized chapters that will help you locate whatever you need.

Because today's busy lifestyles often leave little time for cooking, we have included many In Short Order recipes, versatile dishes for two that can be made in 45 minutes or less. Chilled Curried Carrot Soup, Fettuccine with Red Pepper and Basil Sauce, and Stir-Fried Chicken with Yellow Peppers and Snow Peas, for example, are ideal luncheon *or* light dinner entrées. Add an Artichoke Heart, Fennel, and Parmesan Salad, or Iceberg Lettuce Wedges with Stilton Dressing and Radishes, or perhaps a Romaine and Mushroom Salad with Garlic Caper Vinaigrette, and you have a more substantial meal. And, if time permits, you can make an irresistible quick dessert—Ice Cream with Raspberry Sauce and Praline Bits, Bing Cherry Clafouti, or Warm Upside-Down Cheesecakes with Pineapple Sauce . . . all are as wonderful as they sound.

There are also many appropriate dishes from In Short Order for those intimate occasions when you want to pamper a very special guest. Anchovy-Stuffed Mushrooms, a zestful hors d'oeuvre, followed by tender Rib-Eye Steaks with Bell Pepper and Olives, refreshing Herbed Couscous with Lemon, and colorful Minted Cherry Tomatoes and Zucchini, for example, would make a simple, yet memorable, meal. For dessert, Iced Coffee Mousse served in long-stemmed glasses would be an elegant choice. (To easily find any of our quick dishes, use the 45-Minute Index.)

To further help you save time in the kitchen we have included some recipes from the Twice as Good column. Now, with a bit of planning, you can make and enjoy a delicious, easy meal and, a few days later, transform it into another that is equally exciting. Succulent Roast Cod with Potatoes, Onions, and Olives, accompanied by Swiss Chard with Roasted Pepper, is bound to become a family favorite. Then, we show you how to make *even more* of a good thing; the leftover cod and Swiss chard makes an excellent filling for robust Cod Cannelloni with Swiss Chard and Roasted Pepper. With recipes like these, we guarantee that your family will never complain about leftovers again.

And, of course, everyone looks for little recipes that turn an ordinary meal into something extraordinary. Many of these recipes come from The Last Touch, a thematic column filled with easy ideas that make a difference. Begin a winter gathering around the fire with some hot spirited drinks, such as Warm Beaujolais Kir or Hot Apricot Buttered Rum. Wake up simple meats or fish with salsas and relishes such as Spicy Fruit Salsa or Orange, Fig, and Pine Nut Relish. You'll even find flavored vinegars that enliven dressings and marinades: Chili Vinegar; Opal-Basil Cinnamon Vinegar; Tarragon Green-Peppercorn Vinegar; and more.

Naturally, you will always need recipes for the freshest foods of the season. After all, when baskets of luscious red tomatoes, deep green zucchini, and bright yellow corn appear at the farm stand, capitalizing on their peak flavor is key. Gastronomie sans Argent has always been the source for seasonal recipes; each month a particular food is featured and numerous recipes are offered. During 1993 *Gourmet* expanded the scope and theme of this marvelous column. Over a dozen items

Curried Grilled Chicken Salad

were highlighted in the newly named Pick of the Crop, and From The Farm Stand columns, with a wide variety of recipes for many newly harvested fruits, vegetables, and herbs. Honeydew in Rosemary Syrup, Cherry Almond Cake, Parchment-Baked Minted Potatoes, Peach Crumb Cake, Basil Tabbouleh, Summer Vegetable Stew, Zucchini Frittata with Blossoms, and Chilled Tomato Yogurt Soup are just a sampling.

We have also included many recipes from feature articles that showcase a particular type of food. Fall Fruit Desserts offers delightful recipes for apples, pears, cranberries, and persimmons. And from an informative Asian Noodle article come Stir-Fried Rice Noodles with Shrimp; Curried Chicken Coconut Noodle Soup; Cold Sesame Noodles; and more. As an added bonus, many of these recipes can be made in 45 minutes or less.

Everyone's entitled to a splurge now and then, and our Forbidden Pleasures column is *the* source for sinfully good fare. What could be more inviting than crisp-topped, fluffy Goat Cheese Mashed-Potato Gratin enriched with lots of butter, cream, and cheese? Or, if naughty desserts are more tempting and you happen to have the summer's best strawberries on hand, try our unbeatable Strawberry Shortcake. Light-as-air cream or buttermilk biscuits are filled with gently mashed ripe berries swimming in their own juices and dollops of lightly beaten fresh whipped cream.

Go ahead! Indulge yourself with the Recipe Compendium as you would any unbelievably good treat. Leaf through its pages and let your mind conjure up wonderful recipe combinations. Jot down favorite titles and then, someday soon, gather your family and friends and share your dreams.

HORS D'OEUVRES, CANAPÉS, DIPS AND SPREADS

HORS D'OEUVRES

Prosciutto-Wrapped Breadsticks with Fig

For the fig spread
¼ cup finely chopped stemmed dried black
   Mission figs
2 tablespoons Port
¼ cup water
1½ teaspoons sugar
½ teaspoon Dijon-style mustard
¼ teaspoon fresh lemon juice, or to taste

18 very thin slices of prosciutto
   (about 6 ounces)
18 *grissini* (long thin breadsticks)

Make the fig spread: In a small saucepan simmer the figs in the Port and the water with the sugar, covered, for 20 minutes and simmer the mixture, uncovered, until the liquid is reduced to about 1 tablespoon. In a food processor (preferably small) purée the fig mixture with the mustard and the lemon juice and transfer the spread to a small bowl. *The fig spread may be made 1 week in advance, kept covered and chilled, and allowed to return to room temperature.*

Working with 1 slice at a time, spread one side of each prosciutto slice with ½ teaspoon of the fig spread, fold the slice lengthwise into a thin strip, and wrap it in a spiral around 1 of the breadsticks. *The breadsticks may be wrapped no more than 30 minutes in advance.* Makes 18 hors d'oeuvres.

PHOTO ON PAGE 83

Caviar Puff-Pastry Stars

½ pound frozen puff pastry, thawed
an egg wash made by beating together 1 large
   egg and 1 teaspoon water
⅓ cup sour cream or *crème fraîche*
1 ounce black caviar
3 tablespoons minced fresh chives

Preheat the oven to 400° F. On a floured surface roll out the puff pastry ⅛ inch thick and with a 3-inch star-shaped cutter cut out 8 pastry stars. Transfer the stars to a lightly greased baking sheet, brush the tops with the egg wash, being careful not to let the wash drip down the sides, and bake the stars in the middle of the oven for 12 to 15 minutes, or until they are puffed and golden. Transfer the stars to a rack and let them cool completely. With a sharp small knife carefully split the stars in half horizontally to form a total of 16 stars, leaving the bottoms cut sides up and the tops cut sides down. Just before serving, spoon about 1 teaspoon of the sour cream onto each star, divide the caviar among the stars, and sprinkle the hors d'oeuvres with the chives. Makes 16 hors d'oeuvres.

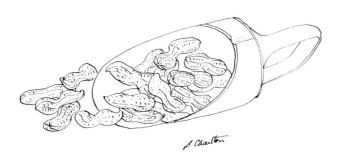

J. Charlton

sauce, the sugar, the cayenne, the water, and salt and pepper to taste until the mixture is smooth and transfer the sauce to a bowl. *The sauce may be made 2 days in advance and kept covered and chilled.*

Grill the chicken with the marinade clinging to it on an oiled rack set 5 to 6 inches over glowing coals for 1½ minutes on each side, or until it is cooked through, and serve the *satés* with the dipping sauce. Makes about 32 *satés*.

PHOTO ON PAGE 47

Chicken Satés with Peanut Dipping Sauce

2 whole skinless boneless chicken breasts
    (about 1¼ pounds)
about thirty-two 7-inch bamboo skewers,
    soaked in water to cover for 15 minutes
For the marinade
¾ cup sweetened flaked coconut
2 teaspoons chopped peeled fresh gingerroot
2 teaspoons curry powder
2 tablespoons fresh lime juice
½ cup hot water
For the dipping sauce
⅓ cup smooth peanut butter
1 garlic clove
2 tablespoons fresh lime juice
2 tablespoons soy sauce
1 teaspoon sugar
⅛ teaspoon cayenne, or to taste
⅓ cup water

Cut the chicken lengthwise into ¼-inch-thick slices, thread the slices lengthwise onto the skewers, and season them with salt and pepper.

Make the marinade: In a blender blend together the coconut, the gingerroot, the curry powder, the lime juice, and the hot water until the mixture is smooth, strain the mixture through a fine sieve into a bowl, pressing hard on the solids, and let the marinade cool. *The marinade may be made 2 days in advance and kept covered and chilled.*

In a large shallow dish pour the marinade over the chicken, coating the chicken well, and let the chicken marinate, covered and chilled, for at least 1 hour and up to 3 hours. (Do not let the chicken marinate longer or the meat will break down.)

Make the dipping sauce: In a blender blend together the peanut butter, the garlic, the lime juice, the soy

Curried Pine Nut and Coconut Chips

1 coconut without any cracks and
    containing liquid
2 large egg whites
1½ teaspoons curry powder
1 teaspoon sugar
⅛ teaspoon cayenne, or to taste
1½ teaspoons salt, or to taste
½ cup pine nuts (about 3 ounces), minced

Preheat the oven to 400° F. Pierce the softest eye of the coconut with an ice pick or a skewer and drain the liquid. Bake the coconut in the oven for 15 minutes, break it with a hammer on a work surface, and with the point of a strong small knife pry the flesh out of the shell carefully. With a vegetable peeler peel off the dark skin and peel the coconut into thin 1-inch-long strips. Spread the coconut in a jelly-roll pan, bake it in the middle of the oven for 8 minutes, or until it is dried slightly but not browned, and let it cool.

Reduce the oven temperature to 350° F. In a bowl whisk together the egg whites, the curry powder, the sugar, the cayenne, and the salt, add the coconut and the pine nuts, and toss the mixture well. Spread the mixture evenly in the jelly-roll pan, bake it in the middle of the oven, stirring occasionally, for 15 to 20 minutes, or until it is crisp and golden, and let it cool. The chips keep in an airtight container for 1 week. Makes about 4 cups.

Accras de Morue
(Salt Cod Fritters)

½ pound skinless boneless salt cod, cut into
    2-inch pieces and rinsed
1 cup all-purpose flour
¼ cup milk
1 large egg

¾ teaspoon double-acting baking powder
a rounded ¼ teaspoon ground allspice
2 garlic cloves, minced
a 4-inch-long fresh hot red or green chili,
    seeded and minced (wear rubber gloves)
3 scallions, chopped fine
1 tablespoon finely chopped fresh coriander
    if desired
vegetable oil for deep-frying
sauce chien (page 93) as an accompaniment

In a large bowl let the salt cod soak in enough cold
water to cover it by 3 inches, changing the water several
times, for at least 8 hours or overnight. Drain the salt
cod well in a sieve and in a food processor purée it. Add
the flour, the milk, the egg, the baking powder, the allspice, and the garlic and blend the mixture well. Transfer the mixture to a bowl and stir in the chili, the
scallions, and the coriander. In a deep fryer or large
deep skillet heat 1½ inches of the oil to 360° F. on a
deep-fat thermometer and in it fry teaspoons of the mixture in batches, stirring and turning them occasionally,
for 1 to 2 minutes, or until they are golden and cooked
through. Transfer the fritters as they are fried with a
slotted spoon to paper towels to drain. *The fritters may
be made 2 days in advance and kept covered and
chilled. Reheat the fritters on a rack in a shallow roasting pan in a preheated 450° F. oven for 5 minutes.* Serve
the fritters with the sauce. Makes about 70 fritters.

PHOTO ON PAGE 19

Corn Fritters

2 cups water
¼ cup olive oil plus additional olive oil or
    light sesame oil for frying the fritters
2 cups all-purpose flour
1 large egg, separated
3⅓ cups uncooked fresh corn
    (cut from about 6 large ears)
1 garlic clove
salsa as an accompaniment if desired

In a bowl stir the water and ¼ cup of the olive oil, a
little at a time, into the flour seasoned with salt, stir in
the egg yolk, and stir the batter until it is smooth. In another bowl with an electric mixer beat the egg white until it is just stiff, fold it into the batter, and let the batter
stand for 1 hour.

Stir the corn into the batter. In a large deep skillet heat
about 1 inch of the additional oil with the garlic clove
over moderately high heat until the garlic turns golden
and discard the garlic with a skimmer. Heat the oil until
it registers 375° F. on a deep-fat thermometer, stir the
batter to distribute the corn evenly, and in the oil fry
rounded tablespoons of the batter, about 6 at a time, for
2 to 2½ minutes on each side, or until the fritters are
golden. Transfer the fritters as they are cooked to paper
towels to drain and serve them with the *salsa*. Makes
about 20 fritters.

Deviled Eggs

10 hard-boiled large eggs
¼ cup spicy brown mustard
3 tablespoons mayonnaise
1 teaspoon white-wine vinegar
¼ teaspoon Tabasco
3 tablespoons minced fresh parsley leaves
1 tablespoon drained bottled capers
2 to 3 tablespoons water

Halve the eggs lengthwise, force the yolks through a
sieve into a bowl, and stir in the mustard, the mayonnaise, the vinegar, the Tabasco, the parsley, and the capers. Stir in enough of the water to reach the desired
consistency, add salt and pepper to taste, and mound the
filling in the egg whites. Makes 20 deviled egg halves.

Stuffed Eggs with Caviar

12 hard-boiled large eggs
2 tablespoons mayonnaise
2 tablespoons sour cream
2 teaspoons fresh lemon juice,
    or to taste
2 ounces black caviar

Cut a paper-thin slice off the ends of each egg and
halve the eggs crosswise. Force the yolks through a
sieve into a bowl and stir in the mayonnaise, the sour
cream, the lemon juice, and salt and pepper to taste.
Transfer the filling to a pastry bag fitted with a large
decorative tip and pipe it into the egg whites, mounding
it. *The stuffed eggs may be made 1 day in advance and
kept covered and chilled.* Just before serving, top the
eggs with the caviar. Makes 24 stuffed eggs.

PHOTO ON PAGE 61

Goat Cheese, Date, and Bacon Strudels

six 18- by 14-inch sheets of *phyllo*, stacked
   between 2 sheets of wax paper and covered
   with a dampened kitchen towel
¾ stick (6 tablespoons) unsalted butter,
   melted
4 tablespoons sesame seeds, toasted lightly
10 ounces mild goat cheese, softened
   (about 1 cup)
26 pitted dates, cut crosswise into thirds
8 slices of crisp-cooked bacon, crumbled
2 tablespoons minced scallion

Preheat the oven to 400° F. On a work surface arrange a 20-inch-long sheet of wax paper with a long side facing you. Put 1 sheet of the *phyllo* on the wax paper, brush it with some of the butter, and sprinkle it with about 2 teaspoons of the sesame seeds. On this, layer, brush, and sprinkle 1 more sheet of the *phyllo* in the same manner and lay a third sheet of *phyllo* on top. Spread ½ cup of the goat cheese along the pastry in a 1-inch strip about 2 inches above the near long side, leaving a 2-inch border at each end. Arrange half the date pieces on the cheese and sprinkle them with half the bacon, half the scallion, and 2 teaspoons of the remaining sesame seeds. Using the wax paper as a guide, lift the bottom 2 inches of the pastry over the filling, fold in the ends, and roll up the strudel tightly. Transfer the strudel carefully, seam side down, to a lightly buttered baking sheet and brush it with some of the remaining butter. Make another strudel with the remaining ingredients in the same manner.

Bake the 2 strudels in the lower third of the oven for 15 to 20 minutes, or until they are golden, and let them cool to warm on the baking sheet on a rack. *The strudels may be made 1 day in advance and kept covered loosely and chilled. Reheat the strudels in a preheated 375° F. oven for 10 minutes.* Serve the strudels warm, cut into 1-inch pieces with a serrated knife. Makes about 36 hors d'oeuvres.

Goat Cheese with Herbed Olive Oil

1 small bay leaf
4 garlic cloves, cut into thin slivers
1 tablespoon fresh rosemary leaves
¼ teaspoon coriander seeds, crushed lightly
¼ teaspoon fennel seeds, crushed lightly
10 whole black peppercorns

¼ teaspoon dried thyme leaves, crumbled
¼ cup extra-virgin olive oil
a ½-pound log of soft mild goat cheese such
   as Montrachet, cut into 8 pieces
toasted French or Italian bread slices as an
   accompaniment

In a small saucepan simmer the bay leaf, the garlic, the rosemary, the coriander seeds, the fennel seeds, the peppercorns, and the thyme in the oil for 5 minutes. Arrange the goat cheese on a platter, spoon the oil mixture over it, and serve the goat cheese with the toasted bread. Serves 4 to 6.

*Melon and Prosciutto with
Balsamic Vinegar and Mint*

2 tablespoons balsamic vinegar
2 tablespoons minced fresh mint leaves plus
   mint sprigs for garnish
1 tablespoon sugar
twelve ¼-inch-thick wedges of seeded and
   peeled honeydew melon or cantaloupe
4 thin slices of prosciutto (about 2 ounces)

In a small bowl stir together the vinegar, the minced mint, and the sugar, let the mixture stand for 30 minutes, and force it through a fine sieve set over a bowl, pressing hard on the solids. Arrange 3 wedges of the melon on each of 4 chilled plates and drizzle each serving with some of the vinegar mixture. Drape each serving of melon with a slice of the prosciutto and garnish the plates with the mint sprigs. Serves 4 as a first course.

Anchovy-Stuffed Mushrooms

6 small white mushrooms, the stems removed
   and minced and the caps left whole
2 tablespoons fresh white bread crumbs
2 teaspoons freshly grated Parmesan
2 teaspoons olive oil
1 teaspoon minced fresh parsley leaves
1 teaspoon red-wine vinegar, or to taste
1 anchovy fillet, mashed to a paste
small flat-leafed parsley leaves for garnish

Preheat the oven to 350° F. In a small bowl stir together the minced mushroom stems, the bread crumbs, the Parmesan, the oil, the parsley, the vinegar, the anchovy paste, and salt and pepper to taste until the stuffing is combined well. Arrange the mushroom caps, stemmed sides up, on a baking sheet, with a teaspoon fill the cavities with the stuffing, mounding it slightly, and bake the mushrooms in the middle of the oven for 15 minutes. Garnish each mushroom with a parsley leaf. Serves 2 as an hors d'oeuvre.

Herbed Olives

1 pound Kalamata or other brine-cured black
    olives, drained and patted dry
2 teaspoons dried rosemary, crumbled
2 teaspoons dried thyme, crumbled
1 tablespoon fresh lemon juice
five 2-inch strips of lemon zest, removed with
    a vegetable peeler
¾ cup extra-virgin olive oil

In a bowl stir together the olives, the herbs, the lemon juice, the zest, and the oil and let the olives marinate, covered and chilled, for 3 days. *The marinated olives may be made 2 weeks in advance and kept covered and chilled.* Serve the olives at room temperature. Makes about 3 cups.

PHOTO ON PAGE 44

Pickled Onion and Monteréy Jack Quesadillas

2 small red onions, sliced thin
⅔ cup cider vinegar
4 garlic cloves, halved
½ teaspoon whole black peppercorns, crushed
½ teaspoon coriander seeds, crushed
½ teaspoon cuminseed, crushed
½ teaspoon salt
eight 7-inch flour tortillas
2 cups grated Monterey Jack
¼ cup minced fresh coriander plus sprigs
    for garnish
2 scallions, minced
dried hot red pepper flakes to taste

In a saucepan boil the onions in just enough salted water to cover for 1 minute, drain them, discarding the water, and return them to the pan with the vinegar, the garlic, the peppercorns, the coriander seeds, the cuminseed, and the salt. Add just enough water to cover the onions and boil the mixture for 3 minutes. Transfer the onion mixture to a glass bowl and let it stand for at least 3 hours and up to 24 hours.

In a dry 8-inch skillet arrange 1 of the tortillas, sprinkle it with ½ cup of the Monterey Jack, ¼ cup of the pickled onions, 1 tablespoon of the minced coriander, one fourth of the scallions, and red pepper flakes to taste, and top the mixture with another tortilla. Cook the *quesadilla* over moderate heat for 4 minutes on each side, or until the cheese is melted and the tortilla is browned lightly. Cut the *quesadilla* into 8 wedges and garnish it with about 2 tablespoons of the pickled onions and a coriander sprig. Make 3 more *quesadillas* in the same manner with the remaining tortillas and ingredients. Makes 32 hors d'oeuvres.

Oxtail Pâté

5 pounds oxtails, cooked (reserved from the
    oxtail bouillon, page 112)
1 onion, chopped
¾ stick (6 tablespoons) unsalted butter,
    softened
⅓ cup fresh orange juice
2 teaspoons drained bottled green peppercorns
2 tablespoons oxtail bouillon (page 112) or
    beef broth
⅛ teaspoon ground cloves
1 teaspoon salt
crusty peasant bread as an accompaniment

Discard the fat and bones from the oxtails and transfer the meat to a food processor. In a skillet cook the onion in 2 tablespoons of the butter over moderate heat,
stirring occasionally, until it is golden, add it to the meat
with the remaining 4 tablespoons butter, the orange
juice, the peppercorns, the bouillon or broth, the
cloves, and the salt, and pulse the motor until the pâté is
minced but not puréed. Pack the pâté into a crock. *The
pâté may be made 3 days in advance and kept covered
and chilled*. Serve the pâté at room temperature with the
bread. Makes about 2½ cups.

Creamed Oysters on Toasted Corn Bread

½ cup minced shallot
½ cup minced celery plus 3 tablespoons finely
    chopped celery leaves
½ stick (¼ cup) unsalted butter
3 tablespoons all-purpose flour
32 shucked oysters, reserving 1¼ cups of the
    liquor, strained
¼ cup milk
¼ cup heavy cream
2 teaspoons Worcestershire sauce
1 teaspoon ground celery seeds
¼ teaspoon cayenne, or to taste
8 squares of corn bread (recipe follows), split,
    toasted, and buttered

In a large heavy saucepan cook the shallot and the
minced celery in the butter over moderate heat, stirring,
until the vegetables are softened, add the flour, and
cook the mixture over moderately low heat, stirring, for
3 minutes. Stir in the reserved oyster liquor, the milk,
and the cream, bring the mixture to a boil, stirring, and

simmer it, stirring, for 3 minutes. Stir in the Worcestershire sauce, the celery seeds, the cayenne, the oysters,
and salt to taste, simmer the mixture for 1 to 2 minutes,
or until the edges of the oysters curl, and stir in the
celery leaves.

Arrange a bottom half of a corn bread square on each
of 8 heated plates, spoon the creamed oysters over the
bottom halves, and top them with the remaining halves.
Serves 8 as a first course.

PHOTO ON PAGES 72 AND 73

Corn Bread

1 cup yellow cornmeal
1 cup all-purpose flour
1½ teaspoons double-acting baking powder
½ teaspoon baking soda
½ teaspoon salt

2 large eggs
1¼ cups buttermilk
½ stick (¼ cup) unsalted butter, melted
  and cooled

Preheat the oven to 425° F. Grease a 9-inch-square pan generously. In a bowl whisk together the cornmeal, the flour, the baking powder, the baking soda, and the salt. In a small bowl whisk together the eggs, the buttermilk, and the butter, add the buttermilk mixture to the cornmeal mixture, and stir the batter until it is just combined. Heat the greased pan in the oven for 3 to 5 minutes, or until it is very hot, add the batter, spreading it evenly, and bake the corn bread in the middle of the oven for 15 minutes, or until the top is pale golden and the sides begin to pull away from the edges of the pan. Let the corn bread cool for 5 minutes, turn it out onto a rack, and let it cool completely. Cut the corn bread into 9 squares. Makes nine 3-inch squares.

Tostones
(Fried Green Plantains)

3 green (unripe) plantains* (available at
  Hispanic markets and some specialty
  produce markets)
vegetable oil for deep-frying
sauce chien (recipe follows) as an
  accompaniment

*the plantains should be fried the day they
  are purchased, but they can be kept,
  wrapped well in a plastic bag
  and chilled, for 2 or 3 days.

With a small sharp knife cut the ends from each plantain and cut a lengthwise slit through the skin along the inside curve. Beginning in the center of the slit, pry the skin from the plantain and cut the flesh crosswise into 1-inch-thick pieces. In a deep fryer or large deep skillet heat 1½ inches of the oil to 375° F. on a deep-fat thermometer, in it fry a batch of the plantain pieces for 1½ to 2 minutes, or until they are pale golden, and transfer them with a slotted spoon to paper towels to drain briefly. Working quickly, using a tortilla press or the flat bottom of a glass, flatten each piece, cut side up, between sheets of wax paper to a thickness of no less than ¼ to ⅓ inch. Refry the flattened pieces in the 375° F. oil, turning them occasionally, for 2 to 3 minutes, or until

they are golden, transfer them with a slotted spoon to paper towels to drain, and season them with salt. (The *tostones* should be crisp on the outside and chewy on the inside.) Fry the remaining plantain pieces in batches in the same manner. *The* tostones *are best served immediately, but they can be made up to 1 day in advance, wrapped well in plastic bags, and reheated on a rack in a shallow baking pan in a preheated 450° F. oven for 3 to 5 minutes, or until they are heated through.* Serve the *tostones* with the sauce. Makes about 24 *tostones*.

PHOTO ON PAGE 19

Sauce Chien
(Caribbean Spicy Dipping Sauce)

1 small onion, minced
3 scallions, minced
⅓ cup minced red bell pepper
2 garlic cloves,
  minced
1 Scotch bonnet or *habañero* chili, seeded and
  minced (wear rubber gloves), or 1 teaspoon
  Scotch Bonnet Pepper Sauce*
1 teaspoon salt
¼ teaspoon dried thyme,
  crumbled
⅞ cup water
2 tablespoons white-wine vinegar
¼ cup fresh lime juice
2 tablespoons vegetable oil
2 tablespoons chopped fresh coriander,
  or to taste, plus a coriander sprig for
  garnish if desired

*available by mail order from Mo Hotta–Mo
  Betta, P.O. Box 4136, San Luis Obispo,
  CA 93403, tel. (800) 462-3220

In a heatproof bowl combine the onion, the scallions, the bell pepper, the garlic, the chili, the salt, and the thyme. In a small saucepan bring the water to a boil with the vinegar, pour the vinegar mixture over the vegetable mixture, and let the mixture cool. Stir in the lime juice and the oil. *The sauce may be made 2 days in advance and kept covered and chilled.* Let the sauce come to room temperature, stir in the chopped coriander, and garnish the sauce with the coriander sprig. Makes about 2 cups.

PHOTO ON PAGE 19

*Roasted Potatoes with Cream Cheese and
Sun-Dried Tomato Filling*

a ½-pound russet (baking) potato
1 tablespoon olive oil
3 tablespoons cream cheese,
 softened
2 tablespoons minced drained bottled
 sun-dried tomatoes in oil
1 tablespoon minced scallion greens

Preheat the oven to 500° F. Cut twelve ¼-inch-thick
rounds from the middle of the potato, discarding the
ends, pat them dry with paper towels, and brush them on
both sides with the oil. Roast the potato slices on a baking sheet in the upper third of the oven for 6 minutes, or
until the undersides are golden. Turn the slices, roast
them for 6 minutes more, or until the undersides are
golden and crisp, and let them cool until they can be
handled.

While the potatoes are roasting, in a small bowl stir
together the cream cheese, the tomatoes, the scallion,
and salt and pepper to taste. Spread the filling on half
the potato slices, top it with the remaining potato
slices, pressing the slices together to form sandwiches,
and halve the sandwiches. Makes 12 hors d'oeuvres,
serving 2.

Gingered Sweet-Potato Fritters

a ½-pound sweet potato
1½ teaspoons minced peeled fresh gingerroot
2 teaspoons fresh lemon juice
¼ teaspoon dried hot red pepper flakes
¼ teaspoon salt
1 large egg
5 tablespoons all-purpose flour
vegetable oil for deep-frying

Peel and grate coarse the sweet potato. In a food processor chop fine the grated sweet potato with the gingerroot, the lemon juice, the red pepper flakes, and the salt,
add the egg and the flour, and blend the mixture well. In
a large saucepan heat 1½ inches of the oil over moderately high heat to 360° F. on a deep-fat thermometer,
drop tablespoons of the sweet-potato mixture into the
oil in batches, and fry the fritters, turning them, for 2
minutes, or until they are golden. Transfer the fritters to
paper towels to drain. Makes about 18 small fritters,
serving 2 as an hors d'oeuvre.

Salmon Mousse with Salmon Roe and Crudités

fresh coriander leaves for garnish
2 tablespoons cold water plus ⅓ cup
 boiling water
1 tablespoon fresh lemon juice
1 envelope (about 1 tablespoon) of
 unflavored gelatin
½ pound thinly sliced smoked salmon
a 7¼-ounce can salmon, drained and the
 skin discarded
1½ cups sour cream
¼ teaspoon Tabasco, or to taste
¼ cup finely chopped scallion
1 cup heavy cream
¼ cup salmon roe
celery leaves for garnish
assorted *crudités* such as cucumber, celery,
 jícama, *daikon*, and blanched snow peas

Line the bottom of an oiled 5-cup charlotte mold or
soufflé dish with a round of wax paper, oil the paper,
and press the coriander leaves face down onto the paper
decoratively. In a small bowl combine the cold water
and the lemon juice, sprinkle the gelatin over the mixture, and let it soften for 2 minutes. Add the boiling water and stir the mixture until the gelatin is dissolved. In a
food processor blend together the smoked salmon, the
canned salmon, the sour cream, and the Tabasco until
the mixture is smooth, add the gelatin mixture, the scallion, and salt and pepper to taste, and blend the mixture
until it is combined well. In a large bowl beat the heavy
cream until it holds soft peaks, add it to the salmon mixture, and pulse the motor until the mousse is just combined. Pour the mousse into the prepared mold and chill
it, covered, for at least 8 hours or overnight.

Dip the mold into a large pan of hot water for 2 seconds and run a thin knife around the edge. Invert a platter over the mold and invert the mousse onto the platter. (If the coriander leaves stick to the wax paper, replace them on top of the mousse.) Spoon the salmon roe around the edges of the mousse, garnish the platter with the celery leaves, and serve the mousse with the *crudités*. Serves 12 to 14 as an hors d'oeuvre.

PHOTO ON PAGE 47

Sesame Sticks

1½ tablespoons unsalted butter, melted
3 slices of homemade-type white bread,
    crusts discarded and the bread cut into
    ½-inch-wide sticks
½ cup sesame seeds

Preheat the oven to 350° F. Season the butter with salt and pepper, brush it on the bread sticks, and roll the sticks in the sesame seeds. Bake the sesame sticks on a baking sheet in the middle of the oven for 15 minutes, or until they are golden. Makes about 15 sesame sticks.

Pickled Shrimp

¾ cup cider vinegar
1½ teaspoons coarsely ground black pepper
2 teaspoons salt
½ teaspoon sugar
¾ teaspoon English-style dry mustard
¼ teaspoon dried hot red pepper flakes,
    or to taste
¼ teaspoon mustard seeds, crushed
¼ teaspoon coriander seeds, crushed
1 cup olive oil
3 large garlic cloves, crushed
1 bay leaf
1½ pounds (24 to 30) large shrimp, shelled
    and deveined
1 medium onion, halved lengthwise and
    sliced thin
1 lemon, sliced thin
2 tablespoons minced fresh dill or parsley
    leaves, or to taste, plus a dill sprig
    for garnish

In a bowl whisk together the vinegar, the pepper, the salt, the sugar, the mustard, the red pepper flakes, the mustard seeds, and the coriander seeds and add the oil in a stream, whisking. Whisk the marinade until it is emulsified and stir in the garlic and the bay leaf. In a large saucepan of salted boiling water cook the shrimp for 1 minute, or until they are just cooked through, drain them well, and add them to the marinade. Let the mixture cool, stir in the onion and the lemon, and let the shrimp mixture marinate, covered and chilled, stirring occasionally, for at least 12 hours and up to 1 day. Stir in the minced dill, transfer the pickled shrimp to a serving bowl, and garnish it with the dill sprig. Serves 8.

PHOTO ON PAGE 61

Swiss Cheese with Walnuts and Mustard

3 tablespoons Dijon-style mustard
3 tablespoons sour cream
¼ teaspoon dried tarragon,
    crumbled
½ cup thinly sliced scallion
2½ cups coarsely grated Swiss cheese
    (about ½ pound)
½ cup chopped walnuts, toasted lightly and
    cooled
crackers as an accompaniment

In a bowl whisk together the mustard, the sour cream, the tarragon, the scallion, and pepper to taste, add the Swiss cheese and the walnuts, and combine the mixture well. Serve the mixture with the crackers. Makes about 2½ cups.

Tomato Bacon Sandwiches

8 slices of bacon, chopped
1½ cups mayonnaise
3 tablespoons Dijon-style mustard
30 slices of homemade-type white bread,
    crusts removed
15 thick large tomato slices

In a large heavy skillet cook the bacon over moderate heat, stirring, until it is crisp, transfer it to paper towels to drain, and chop it fine. In a bowl stir together the bacon, the mayonnaise, and the mustard. Spread the bacon mayonnaise on one side of each bread slice, sandwich the tomatoes between the slices, and cut each sandwich into 4 triangles. Makes 60 hors d'oeuvre sandwiches.

Spiced Walnuts

¾ stick (6 tablespoons) unsalted butter
1½ teaspoons Chinese five-spice powder
¼ teaspoon cayenne, or to taste
2¼ teaspoons dried thyme, crumbled
6 cups walnuts

Preheat the oven to 350° F. In a large heavy saucepan melt the butter with the five-spice powder, the cayenne, the thyme, and salt to taste, stirring, add the walnuts, and toss them to coat them well. Bake the walnuts in batches in a shallow baking pan in the middle of the oven for 10 minutes and let them cool until they are warm. Makes 6 cups.

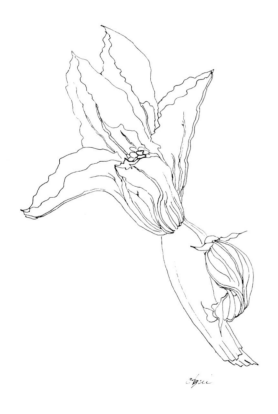

Curried Fried Zucchini Blossoms

1 cup all-purpose flour
2 teaspoons curry powder
¼ teaspoon salt
1 to 1⅛ cups chilled seltzer or club soda
¼ pound mozzarella, grated coarse
  (about 1 cup)

1 tablespoon finely chopped fresh coriander
16 zucchini blossoms, pistils removed
  if desired
vegetable oil for deep-frying

In a bowl whisk together the flour, the curry powder, and the salt, add 1 cup of the seltzer, and whisk the batter until it is smooth. Let the batter stand for 10 minutes and, if desired, thin it with enough of the remaining seltzer to reach the consistency of crêpe batter. In a small bowl toss together the mozzarella and the coriander and divide the mixture among the blossoms, stuffing it inside them and pressing the ends of the blossoms closed.

In a deep skillet heat 1 inch of the oil to 375° F. on a deep-fat thermometer. Working quickly in batches, dip the blossoms, 1 at a time, in the batter, coating them completely, and fry them in the oil, turning them, for 1½ to 2 minutes, or until they are golden and crisp. (Make sure the oil returns to 375° F. before adding each new batch.) Transfer the blossoms as they are fried with a slotted spoon to paper towels to drain, sprinkle them with salt, and serve them warm. Makes 16 fried zucchini blossoms, serving 4 as an hors d'oeuvre.

CANAPÉS

Fillet of Beef, Arugula, and Artichoke Crostini

a 2½-pound trimmed fillet of beef, tied
two 6-ounce jars marinated artichoke hearts,
  rinsed and drained
1 garlic clove
¼ cup white-wine vinegar
½ cup olive oil
thirty-six ½-inch-thick diagonal slices
  of Italian bread (about 2 long loaves),
  toasted lightly
2 bunches of *arugula*, coarse stems discarded
  and the leaves washed well, spun dry, and
  cut into shreds (about 4 cups)
36 Parmesan curls formed with a
  vegetable peeler

Preheat the oven to 500° F. Pat the fillet dry, season it with salt and pepper, and in a small roasting pan roast it in the middle of the oven for 23 minutes, or until it registers 125° F. on a meat thermometer for rare meat. Transfer the fillet to a cutting board and let it cool. *The fillet may be roasted 1 day in advance and kept covered and chilled.*

In a blender purée the artichoke hearts and the garlic with the vinegar, the oil, and salt and pepper to taste and transfer the purée to a bowl. *The purée may be made 3 days in advance and kept covered and chilled.*

Spread each slice of toast with some of the artichoke purée, top the purée with some of the *arugula*, and divide the fillet, sliced very thin, among the *crostini*. Top the *crostini* with the Parmesan curls. Makes 36 *crostini*.

PHOTO ON PAGES 46 AND 47

Cucumber Tapenade Canapés

sixteen ¼-inch-thick slices of seedless
    cucumber
8 teaspoons *tapenade*, *olivada*, or other black
    olive paste (available at specialty foods
    shops and some supermarkets)
32 julienne strips of drained bottled roasted
    red pepper, each about 1 inch long
16 flat-leafed parsley leaves

In the center of each cucumber slice put ½ teaspoon of the *tapenade*, drape 2 of the pepper strips in an X over it, and garnish each canapé with a parsley leaf. *The canapés may be made 30 minutes in advance and kept covered and chilled.* Makes 16 canapés.

PHOTO ON PAGE 83

Radishes with Chive Butter

¾ stick (6 tablespoons) unsalted butter,
    softened
2 tablespoons cream cheese, softened
1 tablespoon minced fresh chives
¼ teaspoon freshly grated lemon zest
Tabasco to taste
18 radishes (about 2 bunches), the leaves
    trimmed, leaving 1 inch of the stem, and
    the radishes halved lengthwise
36 fresh flat-leafed parsley leaves for garnish

In a small bowl with a fork combine well the butter, the cream cheese, the chives, the zest, the Tabasco, and salt to taste and transfer the mixture to a pastry bag fitted with a medium-sized open-star tip. Arrange the radishes, cut sides up, on a platter, put a parsley leaf on each radish half, and pipe the chive butter onto it. Makes 36 hors d'oeuvres.

Seafood Canapés with Lemon-Chive Butter

¼ pound marinated herring, rinsed, drained,
    and cut into 16 pieces
½ red onion, sliced thin
3 tablespoons fresh orange juice
For the lemon-chive butter
¾ stick (6 tablespoons) unsalted butter,
    softened
3 tablespoons sour cream
2 teaspoons fresh lemon juice
1 tablespoon minced fresh chives

16 slices of rye bread
2 ounces smoked salmon, chopped fine
2 tablespoons finely chopped red onion
1 ounce black caviar
For the garnish
fresh parsley leaves
thin crosswise slices of orange sections
fresh chives
½-inch-long fine julienne of orange zest

In a small bowl combine well the herring, the onion, the orange juice, and pepper to taste and let the herring marinate, covered and chilled, for at least 3 hours or overnight.

Make the lemon-chive butter: In a bowl with an electric mixer cream the butter and beat in the sour cream and the lemon juice gradually. Beat the mixture until it is light and smooth and beat in the chives and salt and pepper to taste.

Toast the bread until it is just pale golden, cut out 3 decorative shapes from each piece, and spread one side of each shape with some of the lemon-chive butter. In a small bowl toss together the salmon and the red onion and divide the mixture among 16 of the toasts. Drain the herring, discarding the onion, and divide it among 16 of the toasts. Divide the caviar among the remaining 16 toasts. Garnish the salmon canapés with the parsley leaves, garnish the herring canapés with the orange slices, the chives, and the zest, and arrange the canapés on a platter. *The canapés may be prepared 1 hour in advance and kept covered and chilled.* Makes 48 canapés.

DIPS AND SPREADS

Black Bean, Green Pepper, and Red Onion Dip

1½ cups dried black beans, picked over
   and rinsed
2 quarts plus ¼ cup water
1 large green bell pepper, chopped fine,
   reserving about 1 teaspoon for garnish
1 small red onion, chopped fine, reserving
   about 1 teaspoon for garnish
3 tablespoons vegetable oil
1½ teaspoons ground cumin, or to taste
2 tablespoons cider vinegar, or to taste
tortilla chips as an accompaniment
cherry peppers for garnish if desired

In a large saucepan let the beans soak in cold water to cover for 1 hour, drain them, and in the pan combine them with 2 quarts of the water. Bring the water to a boil and cook the beans at a slow boil for 1 hour, or until they are tender.

While the beans are cooking, in a large heavy skillet cook the bell pepper and the onion in the oil over moderate heat, stirring, until the vegetables are softened. Drain the beans, reserving ½ cup of them, add the beans to the bell pepper mixture with the remaining ¼ cup water, and simmer the mixture, covered tightly, for 15 minutes, or until the beans are very tender. In a food processor blend the mixture with the vinegar and salt to taste, pulsing the motor until the mixture is combined well but not puréed smooth. Transfer the dip to a bowl and stir in the reserved ½ cup beans. *The dip may be made 2 days in advance and kept covered and chilled.* Garnish the dip with the reserved bell pepper and onion and serve it with the tortilla chips. Makes about 3 cups.

PHOTO ON PAGE 66

Chile con Queso y Cerveza
(*Cheese and Chili Beer Dip*)

2 cups grated sharp Cheddar (about ¼ pound)
2 cups grated Jarlsberg (about ¼ pound)
2 tablespoons all-purpose flour
1 small onion, minced
1 tablespoon unsalted butter
¾ cup beer (not dark)
½ cup drained canned tomatoes, chopped fine

1 bottled pickled *jalapeño* chili, minced
   (wear rubber gloves)
tortilla chips as an accompaniment

In a bowl toss the cheeses with the flour and reserve the mixture. In a large heavy saucepan cook the onion in the butter over moderately low heat, stirring, until it is softened, add the beer, the tomatoes, and the *jalapeño*, and simmer the mixture for 5 minutes. Add the reserved cheese mixture by ½ cupfuls to the beer mixture, stirring after each addition until the cheeses are melted, and serve the dip with the chips. Makes about 4½ cups.

Cucumber Yogurt Dip

two 8-ounce containers plain yogurt
1 pound cucumbers, peeled, seeded, and
   chopped fine
2 teaspoons finely chopped fresh dill plus
   dill sprigs for garnish
3 garlic cloves, minced
1 tablespoon extra-virgin olive oil
1 tablespoon fresh lemon juice
pita loaves, cut into wedges, as an
   accompaniment

Let the yogurt drain in a fine sieve set over a bowl, covered and chilled, for 6 hours. Pour the liquid from the bowl and in the bowl stir together the drained yogurt, the cucumber, squeezed dry between paper towels, the chopped dill, the garlic, the oil, the lemon juice, and salt to taste. Let the dip stand, covered and chilled, for at least 2 hours and up to 8 hours to allow the flavors to develop. Stir the dip, garnish it with the dill sprigs, and serve it with the *pita* wedges. Makes about 2 cups.

PHOTO ON PAGE 44

Pine Nut Yogurt Dip

½ cup pine nuts (about 3 ounces), toasted lightly
1 garlic clove, chopped
1 tablespoon fresh lemon juice
1 tablespoon olive oil
1 tablespoon water
⅛ teaspoon cayenne
½ cup plain yogurt
1½ tablespoons finely chopped fresh coriander
toasted *pita* triangles or *crudités* as an
   accompaniment

In a blender or food processor blend together the pine nuts, the garlic, the lemon juice, the oil, the water, and the cayenne until the mixture is smooth. Transfer the mixture to a small bowl, stir in the yogurt, the coriander, and salt to taste, and serve the dip with the *pita* triangles or the *crudités*. Makes about 1 cup.

Spinach Dip

¾ pound spinach (about 1 bunch), coarse
    stems discarded and the leaves washed well
    and drained
1 cup plain yogurt
¼ cup mayonnaise
½ cup peeled, seeded, and finely chopped
    cucumber
½ cup finely chopped radish
¼ cup minced onion
2 scallions, minced
1 large garlic clove, minced and mashed to a
    paste with ½ teaspoon salt
2 teaspoons minced fresh tarragon or
    ¼ teaspoon dried, crumbled
1 teaspoon white-wine vinegar,
    or to taste
pita toasts or *crudités* as an accompaniment

In a large heavy saucepan cook the spinach in the water clinging to the leaves, covered, over moderate heat, stirring once or twice, for 3 to 4 minutes, or until it is wilted, refresh it under cold water, and drain it well in a colander. Squeeze the spinach dry by handfuls and chop it fine. In a bowl stir together well the spinach, the yogurt, the mayonnaise, the cucumber, the radish, the onion, the scallions, the garlic paste, the tarragon, the vinegar, and salt and pepper to taste. Serve the dip with the *pita* toasts or the *crudités*. Makes about 2 cups.

Eggplant Spread

two 1½-pound eggplants
1 medium onion, minced
1 garlic clove, minced
2 tablespoons minced fresh flat-leafed parsley
    leaves plus parsley sprigs for garnish
1 teaspoon minced fresh thyme leaves
2 teaspoons minced fresh basil leaves
3 tablespoons extra-virgin olive oil
2 tablespoons red-wine vinegar

2 tablespoons drained bottled capers,
    chopped fine
pita loaves, cut into wedges, as an
    accompaniment

Pierce the eggplants in several places with a fork and grill them on a rack set about 4 inches over glowing coals for 30 to 35 minutes, or until they are very soft. (Alternatively, the eggplants may be broiled on the rack of a broiler pan under a preheated broiler about 6 inches from the heat, turning them, for 30 to 35 minutes, or until they are soft.) Let the eggplants cool until they can be handled, halve them, and discard as many seeds as possible. Scrape the flesh away from the skin and squeeze the eggplant gently between paper towels to remove as much excess liquid as possible. In a bowl mash the eggplant coarse, stir in the onion, the garlic, the minced herbs, the oil, the vinegar, the capers, and salt and pepper to taste, and let the spread stand, covered and chilled, for 3 hours to allow the flavors to develop. *The eggplant spread may be made 1 day in advance and kept covered and chilled.* Garnish the eggplant spread with the parsley sprigs and serve it with the *pita* wedges. Makes about 2 cups.

PHOTO ON PAGE 44

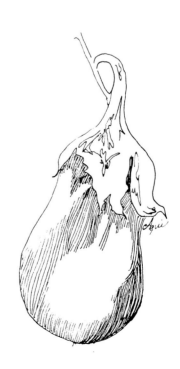

Guacamole with Scallion and Coriander

3 avocados (preferably California)
¼ cup finely chopped scallion, or to taste
¼ cup finely chopped fresh coriander
2 tablespoons fresh lemon juice, or to taste
tortilla chips as an accompaniment
cherry peppers for garnish if desired

Halve and pit the avocados and scoop the flesh into a bowl. Mash the avocados coarse with a fork, stir in the scallion, the coriander, the lemon juice, and salt to taste, and combine the mixture well. *The guacamole may be made 1 day in advance and kept chilled, its surface covered with plastic wrap.* Serve the *guacamole* with the tortilla chips. Makes about 3 cups.

PHOTO ON PAGE 66

b. Charlton

Deviled Ham

¾ pound cooked ham, cut into pieces
¼ cup Dijon-style mustard
½ stick (¼ cup) unsalted butter, softened
1 tablespoon honey
¼ teaspoon ground cloves
3 tablespoons minced onion
3 tablespoons minced sweet pickle

In a food processor grind the ham until it is minced, add the mustard, the butter, the honey, and the cloves, and blend the mixture until it is smooth. Transfer the mixture to a bowl and stir in the onion, the pickle, and pepper to taste. Serve the deviled ham with crackers or as a sandwich filling. Makes about 2 cups.

Brandade de Saumon
(Salmon and Potato Purée)

½ pound skinless salmon fillet
a ½-pound russet (baking) potato
4 garlic cloves
½ cup extra-virgin olive oil
¼ cup heavy cream
a large pinch of dried thyme, crumbled
1 tablespoon fresh lemon juice, or to taste
imported black olives as an accompaniment
toasted French bread slices as an
   accompaniment

In a saucepan of simmering water poach the salmon for 5 minutes, or until it is just cooked through, transfer it with a slotted spoon to a plate, and keep it warm, covered. In the water in the pan boil the potato, peeled and cut into ½-inch pieces, with the garlic for 10 minutes, or until the potato is tender. While the potato and garlic are cooking, in a saucepan heat the oil, the cream, and the thyme over low heat until the mixture is hot, remove the pan from the heat, and keep the mixture warm, covered. Drain the potato and garlic, return them to the pan, and cook them over high heat, shaking the pan, for 30 seconds, or until any excess liquid is evaporated.

In a bowl with an electric mixer beat the potato and the garlic on medium-low speed until the mixture is smooth, add the salmon, and beat the mixture until it is combined well. Add the cream mixture gradually, beating, and add the lemon juice and salt and pepper to taste. Transfer the *brandade* to a bowl and serve it warm with the olives and the toasted bread. *The* brandade *may be* made 1 day in advance, kept covered and chilled, and reheated over low heat, stirring constantly. Makes about 2 cups.

Stilton and Hazelnut Spread

½ pound Stilton, crumbled (about 2 cups)
  and softened
4 ounces cream cheese,
  softened
3 tablespoons Tawny Port or medium-dry
  Sherry, or to taste
⅓ cup chopped toasted and skinned hazelnuts
  (procedure on page 219) plus additional for
  garnish if desired
Melba toast as an accompaniment

In a food processor blend the Stilton, the cream cheese, the Port, and salt and pepper to taste until the mixture is smooth, add the ⅓ cup hazelnuts, and pulse the motor a few times, until the nuts are incorporated. Transfer the spread to a crock or ramekin and chill it, covered, until it is firm. *The spread may be made 3 days in advance and kept covered and chilled.* Garnish the spread with the additional nuts and serve it with the Melba toast. Makes about 2 cups.

PHOTO ON PAGE 60

Muhammara
(Turkish Walnut, Red Bell Pepper, and Cumin Spread)

a 7-ounce jar of roasted red peppers, drained
⅔ cup fine fresh bread crumbs
⅓ cup walnuts, toasted lightly and
  chopped fine
2 to 4 garlic cloves, minced and mashed to a
  paste with ½ teaspoon salt
1 tablespoon fresh lemon juice, or to taste
2 teaspoons pomegranate molasses*
1 teaspoon ground cumin
½ teaspoon dried hot red pepper flakes
¾ cup extra-virgin olive oil
toasted *pita* triangles as an accompaniment

*available at Middle Eastern markets or
  by mail order from Adriana's Bazaar,
  2152 Broadway, New York, NY 10023,
  tel. (212) 877-5757.

In a food processor blend together the peppers, the bread crumbs, the walnuts, the garlic, the lemon juice, the pomegranate molasses, the cumin, the red pepper flakes, and salt to taste until the mixture is smooth and with the motor running add the oil gradually. Transfer the *muhammara* to a bowl and serve it at room temperature with the *pita* triangles. Makes about 1¾ cups.

BREADS

QUICK BREADS

Beer, Sun-Dried Tomato, and Olive Quick Bread

3½ cups all-purpose flour
1 teaspoon salt
½ teaspoon baking soda
1 teaspoon double-acting baking powder
1 large egg, beaten lightly
a 12-ounce bottle of beer (not dark)
½ cup chopped drained sun-dried tomatoes
    packed in oil, reserving 1 tablespoon
    of the oil
⅓ cup chopped pimiento-stuffed olives

Preheat the oven to 350° F. and grease and flour a loaf pan, 9 by 5 by 3 inches. In a large bowl whisk together the flour, the salt, the baking soda, and the baking powder, add the egg, the beer, the tomatoes with the reserved oil, and the olives, and stir the batter until it is just combined. Turn the batter into the pan and bake the bread in the middle of the oven for 40 minutes, or until a tester comes out clean. Turn the bread out onto a rack and let it cool. Makes 1 loaf.

Corn Cakes

1 cup stone-ground yellow cornmeal
    (available at specialty foods shops and
    many supermarkets)
½ cup all-purpose flour
1 teaspoon salt
¾ teaspoon baking soda
½ teaspoon freshly ground pepper
2 teaspoons sugar
2 tablespoons unsalted butter, melted and
    cooled, plus additional melted butter for
    brushing the griddle
1 large egg

1 cup buttermilk
1 cup thawed frozen corn, chopped coarse
¼ cup finely chopped onion
¼ cup finely chopped, rinsed, drained, and
    patted-dry bottled roasted red peppers
1 fresh *jalapeño* or *serrano* chili, or to taste,
    seeded and minced (wear rubber gloves)
1 cup coarsely grated Monterey Jack

In a bowl whisk together the cornmeal, the flour, the salt, the baking soda, the pepper, and the sugar. In another bowl whisk together 2 tablespoons of the butter, the egg, and the buttermilk, stir in the corn, the onion, the roasted pepper, the chili, and the Monterey Jack, and stir in the cornmeal mixture, stirring until the batter is just combined. Heat a griddle over moderately high heat until it is hot, brush it lightly with some of the additional butter, and working in batches drop the batter by a ¼-cup measure onto the griddle. Spread the batter slightly to form 3½- to 4-inch cakes, cook the cakes for 2 to 3 minutes on each side, or until they are golden, transferring them as they are cooked to a platter, and keep them warm. Makes about 12 corn cakes.

PHOTO ON PAGE 26

Feta Cumin Corn Bread

1½ cups yellow cornmeal
1 cup all-purpose flour
2 teaspoons double-acting baking powder
½ teaspoon baking soda
1 teaspoon salt
2 teaspoons ground cumin
1½ cups crumbled Feta
1 cup thinly sliced scallion
2 large eggs
1 cup milk
2 tablespoons sugar
¼ cup olive oil

Preheat the oven to 350° F. Into a large bowl sift together the cornmeal, the flour, the baking powder, the baking soda, the salt, and the cumin, add the Feta and the scallion, and toss the mixture well. In a bowl whisk together the eggs, the milk, the sugar, and the oil, add the milk mixture to the cornmeal mixture, and stir the batter until it is just combined. Pour the batter into a greased loaf pan, 9 by 5 by 3 inches, and bake the corn bread in the middle of the oven for 45 to 50 minutes, or until a tester comes out clean. Let the corn bread cool in the pan on a rack for 5 minutes and run a thin knife around the edges of the pan. Turn the corn bread out onto the rack and let it cool completely. *The corn bread may be made 2 days in advance and kept wrapped tightly in foil and chilled.*

PHOTO ON PAGE 45

Raspberry Corn Muffins

1 cup yellow cornmeal
1 cup all-purpose flour
½ cup sugar
1 teaspoon double-acting baking powder
1 teaspoon baking soda
¼ teaspoon salt
2 large eggs
1¼ cups plain yogurt
½ stick (¼ cup) unsalted butter,
    melted and cooled
1 cup fresh raspberries

Preheat the oven to 375° F. and butter well twelve ½-cup muffin tins. In a bowl whisk together the cornmeal, the flour, the sugar, the baking powder, the baking soda, and the salt. In another bowl whisk together the eggs, the yogurt, and the butter, add the flour mixture, and stir the batter until it is just combined. Fold in the raspberries gently, divide the batter among the muffin tins, and bake the muffins in the middle of the oven for 20 minutes, or until a tester comes out clean. Let the muffins cool in the tins on a rack for 3 minutes, turn them out onto the rack, and let them cool completely. *The muffins may be made 1 day in advance and kept in an airtight container.* Makes 12 muffins.

PHOTO ON PAGES 40 AND 41

Zucchini Raisin Bran Muffins

⅔ cup all-purpose flour
⅔ cup whole-wheat flour
⅔ cup miller's bran (available at natural foods
    stores and some supermarkets)
2 teaspoons double-acting baking powder
¾ teaspoon salt
1 teaspoon cinnamon
¼ teaspoon ground cloves
1 stick (½ cup) unsalted butter, softened
⅔ cup sugar
2 large eggs
1 teaspoon vanilla
¼ cup milk
½ cup raisins
½ cup chopped walnuts
2 cups coarsely grated zucchini

Preheat the oven to 375° F. In a bowl whisk together the flours, the bran, the baking powder, the salt, the cinnamon, and the cloves. In a large bowl with an electric mixer cream the butter with the sugar until the mixture is light and fluffy, add the eggs, 1 at a time, beating well after each addition, and beat in the vanilla. Beat the flour mixture into the butter mixture, beat in the milk, and stir in the raisins, the walnuts, and the zucchini. Divide the batter among 12 well-buttered or paper-lined ½-cup muffin tins and bake the muffins in the middle of the oven for 25 to 30 minutes, or until a tester comes out clean. Turn the muffins out onto a rack and let them cool. Makes 12 muffins.

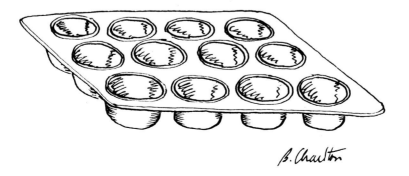

B. Charlton

Cheddar Cornmeal Scones

¾ cup all-purpose flour
½ cup yellow cornmeal
1¼ teaspoons double-acting baking powder
1 teaspoon sugar
½ teaspoon salt
a pinch of cayenne
3 tablespoons cold unsalted butter,
  cut into bits
¾ cup plus 2 tablespoons coarsely grated
  sharp Cheddar
1 large egg, separated
⅓ cup milk

Preheat the oven to 425° F. In a bowl whisk together the flour, the cornmeal, the baking powder, the sugar, the salt, and the cayenne, blend in the butter until the mixture resembles coarse meal, and stir in ¾ cup of the Cheddar. In a small bowl stir together the egg yolk and the milk, add the mixture to the flour mixture, and stir the mixture with a fork until it just forms a soft dough. Turn the dough out onto a lightly floured surface, knead it gently 8 to 10 times, and pat it into a 6-inch round. Cut the round with a sharp knife into 6 equal wedges, arrange the scones about 2 inches apart on a lightly greased baking sheet, and brush the tops lightly with some of the egg white, beaten lightly. Sprinkle each scone with about 1 teaspoon of the remaining Cheddar and bake the scones in the middle of the oven for 15 to 17 minutes, or until they are golden and cooked through. Makes 6 scones.

Three-Cheese Pizza with Onion and Sage

For the dough
about 1¼ cups unbleached all-purpose flour
1¼ teaspoons (half a ¼-ounce package)
  fast-acting yeast
½ cup hot water (130° F.)
1 tablespoon olive oil
1 teaspoon honey
½ teaspoon salt
½ cup cornmeal

cornmeal for sprinkling the baking sheet
6 large fresh sage leaves, halved, or
  1 teaspoon dried sage, crumbled
¾ cup finely diced Danish Fontina
¼ cup crumbled blue cheese
½ red onion, sliced thin into rings
¼ cup freshly grated Parmesan

Make the dough: In a food processor combine ½ cup of the flour and the yeast, with the motor running add the hot water, and turn the motor off. Add the oil, the honey, the salt, the cornmeal, and ½ cup of the remaining flour, blend the dough until it forms a ball, and if necessary blend in enough of the remaining ¼ cup flour to form a soft but not sticky dough. Process the dough for 30 seconds, turn it out onto a lightly floured surface, and knead it 10 times. Form the dough into a ball and let it rest, covered with an inverted bowl, in a warm place for 20 minutes.

Preheat the oven to 500° F. On a lightly floured surface roll out the dough into a 12-inch circle and transfer it to an oiled baking sheet (preferably black steel), sprinkled lightly with the cornmeal. (If using the dried sage sprinkle it evenly over the dough.) Scatter the Fontina and the blue cheese evenly over the dough, leaving a ½-inch border, and arrange the onion rings and the fresh sage leaves over the cheese. Sprinkle the pizza with the Parmesan and bake it on the bottom rack of the oven for 10 minutes, or until the crust is golden and the cheese is bubbling. Serves 2.

CRACKERS AND TOASTS

Lemon-Pepper Parmesan Crackers

1½ cups finely grated fresh Parmesan
  (about ¼ pound)
¾ cup all-purpose flour
1 teaspoon freshly grated lemon zest
¾ teaspoon coarsely ground black pepper plus
  additional for sprinkling the crackers
½ stick (¼ cup) cold unsalted butter,
  cut into bits
1 tablespoon plus 2 teaspoons water
1 teaspoon fresh lemon juice

In a bowl stir together the Parmesan, the flour, the zest, and ¾ teaspoon of the pepper and with a pastry blender blend in the butter until the mixture resembles coarse meal. Make a well in the center, add the water and the lemon juice, and combine the mixture with a fork until it just forms a dough. On a work surface knead the dough until it is just combined, transfer it to a sheet of wax paper, and using the wax paper as a guide form it into an 11- by 1½-inch squared-off log. Chill the dough, wrapped in the wax paper, for 1 hour, or until it is firm enough to slice. *The dough may be made 2 days in advance and kept wrapped well and chilled.*

Preheat the oven to 375° F. Cut the dough log into ¼-inch-thick slices, arrange the slices 1 inch apart on baking sheets, and bake them in batches in the middle of the oven for 10 minutes, or until they are golden around the edges. Transfer the crackers carefully with a spatula to a rack, let them cool, and sprinkle them with the additional pepper. Makes about 44 crackers.

Tapenade Crackers

¼ cup *tapenade* (Provençal black olive and
    caper spread, available at specialty foods
    shops and some supermarkets)
½ teaspoon fennel seeds, crushed
½ teaspoon freshly grated lemon zest
1½ cups all-purpose flour
¼ teaspoon cayenne
1 stick (½ cup) cold unsalted butter,
    cut into bits
1 cup finely grated Fontina (about ¼ pound)
1 tablespoon ice water
1 large egg, beaten

Preheat the oven to 450° F. In a small bowl stir together the *tapenade*, the fennel seeds, and the zest. In a medium bowl blend the flour, the cayenne, the butter, the Fontina, and a pinch of salt until the mixture resembles coarse meal, add the ice water, and toss the mixture until it just forms a stiff dough. On a lightly floured surface roll out the dough into a ⅛-inch-thick rectangle, spread half of it with the *tapenade* mixture, and fold the remaining half over the *tapenade*. Brush the dough with the egg and with a cookie cutter or sharp knife cut it into squares. Bake the crackers on a baking sheet in the middle of the oven for 8 minutes, or until they are golden, transfer them to a rack, and let them cool slightly. Serve the crackers warm.

Garlic Bruschetta

eight ¾-inch-thick slices of crusty peasant
    bread (preferably from a large round loaf)
3 garlic cloves, halved crosswise

6 tablespoons olive oil
    (preferably extra-virgin)

Preheat the broiler. On a baking sheet toast the bread slices in batches under the broiler about 3 inches from the heat for about 1 minute on each side, or until they are golden, transferring them as they are toasted to a work surface. Rub one side of each toast slice with the cut side of a garlic clove, brush it with some of the oil, and season it with salt. Serves 8.

PHOTO ON PAGES 28 AND 29

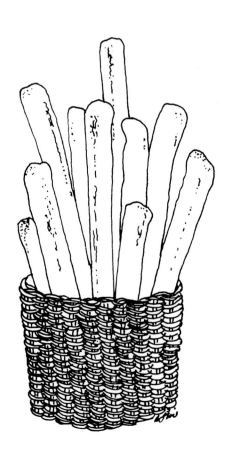

Parsleyed Garlic Bread

2 garlic cloves
¼ teaspoon salt, or to taste
2 tablespoons unsalted butter,
  softened slightly
¼ cup olive oil
1 tablespoon minced fresh parsley leaves
a 12-inch whole-wheat *baguette*
a 12-inch white *baguette*

Preheat the oven to 375° F. In a small food processor or a blender purée the garlic with the salt, the butter, and the oil until the mixture is smooth, transfer the mixture to a bowl, and stir in the parsley. Cut each *baguette* crosswise with a serrated knife into 1-inch sections without cutting all the way through to the bottom, spread some of the garlic mixture in each cut, and spread the remaining mixture on the tops of the *baguettes*. Wrap each *baguette* loosely in foil and bake the bread in the oven for 10 minutes. Open the foil to expose the tops of the *baguettes* and bake the bread for 5 minutes more, or until it is hot and crusty. Makes 2 loaves.

PHOTO ON PAGE 14

Black Pepper Pita Toasts

1 stick (½ cup) unsalted butter,
  cut into pieces
2 teaspoons freshly ground black pepper
8 *pita* loaves, each loaf quartered and
  separated to form 8 triangles

Preheat the oven to 400° F. In a small saucepan melt the butter with the pepper and salt to taste, brush the butter on the rough sides of the *pita* triangles, and bake the triangles on baking sheets in batches in the middle of the oven for 8 to 10 minutes, or until they are golden. Makes 64 *pita* toasts.

SOUPS

Arugula Vichyssoise

¾ cup finely chopped white and pale green
  part of leek, washed well (about 1 leek)
2 tablespoons olive oil
1 garlic clove, chopped
1 small russet (baking) potato, peeled, grated
  coarse (about ¾ cup), and reserved in water
  to cover
2 cups low-salt chicken broth
2 cups packed *arugula*, washed well and
  spun dry
3 tablespoons half-and-half or heavy cream
1 slice of homemade-type white bread, cut
  into ½-inch cubes
1 small plum tomato, seeded and diced,
  for garnish

In a small heavy saucepan cook the leek with salt and
pepper to taste in 1 tablespoon of the oil over moderate
heat, stirring, until it is softened, add the garlic, the potato, drained, and the broth, and simmer the mixture,
covered, for 8 to 10 minutes, or until the potato is very
soft. Stir in the *arugula*, simmer the mixture, covered,
for 1 minute, and in a blender purée it in batches for 2
minutes, or until it is completely smooth. Transfer the
purée to a metal bowl set in a larger bowl of ice and cold
water, stir in the half-and-half, and chill the soup, stirring occasionally, for 10 minutes, or until it is cold.

While the soup is chilling, in a small heavy skillet
cook the bread cubes in the remaining 1 tablespoon oil
over moderate heat, stirring, until they are browned,
transfer the croutons to paper towels, and season them
with salt. Divide the soup between 2 bowls and top it
with the croutons and the tomato. Makes about 2½
cups, serving 2.

Chilled Avocado and Zucchini Soup

1 medium zucchini, cut into
  ½-inch slices
1 California avocado
1 cup buttermilk
¾ cup ice cubes plus additional to
  thin the soup if desired
2 tablespoons fresh lemon juice
¼ teaspoon ground cumin
1½ teaspoons minced fresh chives

In a steamer set over boiling water steam the zucchini, covered, for 10 minutes, or until it is very tender. In
a blender purée the zucchini with the avocado, halved,
peeled, and chopped, the buttermilk, ¾ cup of the ice
cubes, the lemon juice, and the cumin and add enough
of the additional ice cubes to reach the desired consistency. Divide the soup between 2 bowls and sprinkle it
with the chives. Makes about 2¼ cups, serving 2.

Barbecue Bean Soup

3 cups chopped onion
3 garlic cloves, minced
¼ cup vegetable oil
2 tablespoons chili powder
2 tablespoons ground cumin
1 teaspoon ground allspice
¼ teaspoon ground cloves
two 32-ounce cans tomatoes including the
   juice, chopped
three 16-ounce cans pink beans or pinto
   beans, drained and rinsed
two 7-ounce bottles roasted red peppers,
   rinsed, drained, and chopped
3½ cups beef broth
¼ cup molasses
1 tablespoon Tabasco
2 teaspoons cider vinegar, or to taste

In a kettle cook the onion and the garlic in the oil over moderate heat, stirring, until the onion is softened, stir in the chili powder, the cumin, the allspice, and the cloves, and simmer the mixture for 1 minute. Add the tomatoes with the juice, the beans, the roasted peppers, the broth, the molasses, the Tabasco, and salt and pepper to taste and simmer the soup, covered partially and stirring occasionally, for 1½ hours. Stir the vinegar into the soup and simmer the soup until it is heated through. *The soup may be made 2 days in advance, cooled completely, uncovered, and kept covered and chilled. Reheat the soup and ladle it into thermoses.* Makes about 13 cups, serving 8.

PHOTO ON PAGES 22 AND 23

Pasta e Fagioli
(White Bean and Pasta Soup)

2 slices of bacon, chopped
1 small onion, chopped fine
1 garlic clove, minced
1 small rib of celery, chopped fine
1 carrot, sliced thin
1½ cups chicken broth
a 16-ounce can white beans, rinsed well
   and drained
a 16-ounce can tomatoes, drained and chopped
⅓ cup *tubetti* or other small tubular pasta
2 tablespoons minced fresh parsley leaves
freshly grated Parmesan as an accompaniment

In a heavy saucepan cook the bacon over moderate heat, stirring, until it is crisp, pour off all but 1 tablespoon of the fat, and in the remaining fat cook the onion and the garlic, stirring, until the onion is softened. Add the celery, the carrot, and the broth and simmer the mixture, covered, for 5 minutes. In a bowl mash ⅓ cup of the beans, stir them into the bacon mixture with the remaining whole beans and the tomatoes, and simmer the mixture, covered, stirring occasionally, for 5 minutes. Stir in the *tubetti*, simmer the soup, covered, for 10 minutes, or until the pasta is *al dente*, and if desired thin the soup with water. Let the soup stand off the heat, covered, for 5 minutes, stir in the parsley, and serve the soup in bowls sprinkled with the Parmesan. Makes about 3 cups, serving 2 as a main course.

Minestrone

½ pound (about 1¼ cups) dried white beans
   such as Great Northern, picked over
   and rinsed
½ teaspoon salt
¼ pound *pancetta* (Italian cured pork belly,
   available at Italian markets and specialty
   foods shops) or sliced lean bacon, chopped
⅓ cup olive oil
1 onion, chopped
1 large carrot, cut into ½-inch dice
1 rib of celery, cut into ½-inch dice
3 garlic cloves, chopped fine
2 zucchini, scrubbed and cut into ½-inch dice
¼ pound green beans, trimmed and cut into
   ½-inch pieces
½ pound boiling potatoes
4 cups shredded green cabbage
   (preferably Savoy)
½ pound kale, rinsed, drained, stems
   discarded, and the leaves chopped
   (about 6 cups)
a 28-ounce can tomatoes, chopped coarse and
   drained well
4½ cups chicken broth (preferably low-salt)
freshly grated Parmesan, garlic *bruschetta*
   (page 105), and dry-cured sausages
   as accompaniments

In a large bowl let the white beans soak in enough water to cover them by 2 inches overnight or quick-soak them (procedure follows). Drain the white beans, in a saucepan combine them with enough water to cover them by 2 inches, and simmer them, uncovered, adding more water if necessary to keep them barely covered, for 45 minutes to 1 hour, or until they are tender. Add the salt and simmer the white beans for 5 minutes more. Remove the pan from the heat and let the white beans stand, uncovered.

In a heavy kettle cook the *pancetta* in the oil over moderate heat, stirring, until it is crisp and pale golden, add the onion, and cook the mixture, stirring, until the onion is softened. Add the carrot, the celery, and the garlic and cook the mixture, stirring, for 4 minutes. Add the zucchini, the green beans, and the potatoes, peeled and cut into ¾-inch dice, and cook the mixture, stirring, for 4 minutes. Add the cabbage and the kale and cook the mixture, stirring, until the cabbage is wilted. Add the tomatoes and the broth and simmer the soup, covered, for 1 hour.

Drain the white beans, reserving the liquid, in a blender or food processor purée half of them with 1 cup of the reserved liquid, and stir the purée and the remaining white beans into the soup. Simmer the soup, uncovered, for 15 minutes, thin it if desired with some of the remaining reserved liquid, and season it with salt and pepper. *The soup may be made 3 days in advance and kept covered and chilled. Reheat the soup, thinning it with water as desired.* Serve the soup with the Parmesan, the *bruschetta*, and the sausages. Makes about 10 cups, serving 6 to 8.

PHOTO ON PAGES 28 AND 29

To Quick-Soak Dried Beans

In a large saucepan combine dried beans, picked over and rinsed, with triple their volume of cold water. Bring the water to a boil and cook the beans, uncovered, over moderate heat for 2 minutes. Remove the pan from the heat and let the beans soak for 1 hour.

Cream of Broccoli Soup

¾ cup chopped onion
1 carrot, sliced thin
2 teaspoons mustard seeds
2 tablespoons unsalted butter
¾ pound broccoli, chopped coarse
2 cups chicken broth
1 cup water
1½ teaspoons fresh lemon juice, or to taste
¼ cup sour cream

In a heavy saucepan cook the onion, the carrot, the mustard seeds, and salt and pepper to taste in the butter over moderate heat, stirring, until the onion is soft, add the broccoli, the broth, and the water, and simmer the mixture, covered, for 15 to 20 minutes, or until the broccoli is very tender. In a blender purée the soup in batches until it is smooth, transferring it as it is puréed to another heavy saucepan. Whisk in the lemon juice and salt and pepper to taste, heat the soup over moderately low heat, and whisk in the sour cream (do not let the soup boil). Makes about 4 cups, serving 2.

ture, stirring, for 1 minute. Add the broth, the water, and salt and pepper to taste and simmer the mixture, covered, for 15 minutes, or until the carrots are very tender. In a blender purée the mixture in batches with the ice cubes, the lemon juice, and salt to taste for 1 minute, or until it is smooth, transferring the soup as it is puréed to a metal bowl set in a larger bowl of ice and cold water. Chill the soup, stirring occasionally, for 10 minutes, or until it is cold, divide it between 2 chilled bowls, and sprinkle it with the coriander and the peanuts. Makes about 3 cups, serving 2.

Caldo Tlalpeño
(Spicy Chicken Broth with Chicken, Vegetables, and Chick-Peas)

8 cups chicken broth
a 1¼-pound whole chicken breast with
 skin and bones
1 onion, halved lengthwise and sliced
 thin lengthwise
1½ tablespoons vegetable oil
2 carrots, cut into ⅛-inch-thick slices
1 zucchini, cut into ¼-inch-thick slices
a 19-ounce can chick-peas, rinsed and drained
 (about 2 cups)
2 drained canned whole *chipotle* chilies in
 adobo (available at Mexican and Hispanic
 markets and some specialty foods shops),
 rinsed, seeded, and cut into strips
 (wear rubber gloves)
1 avocado (preferably California) for garnish
8 lime wedges for garnish

In a large saucepan bring the broth just to a boil and in it poach the chicken at a bare simmer for 15 minutes, or until the chicken is just cooked through. Remove the pan from the heat and let the chicken cool in the broth. Transfer the chicken to a cutting board, reserving the broth, and discard the skin and bones. Shred the chicken and reserve it, covered and chilled. In a large heavy saucepan cook the onion in the oil over moderate heat, stirring, until it is softened, stir in the carrots and the zucchini, and cook the mixture, stirring, for 1 minute. Add the reserved broth to the vegetable mixture with the chick-peas and simmer the soup for 8 minutes, or until the carrots are just tender. *The soup and the chicken may be prepared up to this point 1 day in advance and kept covered and chilled.* Stir the reserved chicken into the

Chilled Curried Carrot Soup

1 small onion, sliced thin
1 tablespoon vegetable oil
4 carrots (about ¾ pound),
 peeled and sliced thin
1 teaspoon curry powder
1 tablespoon Major Grey's chutney,
 chopped fine
1 cup chicken broth
1 cup water
1 cup ice cubes
1½ teaspoons fresh lemon juice, or to taste
1 tablespoon minced fresh coriander
1 tablespoon minced peanuts

In a saucepan cook the onion in the oil over moderately low heat, stirring, until it is softened. Add the carrots, the curry powder, and the chutney and cook the mix-

soup with the chilies and salt and pepper to taste, simmer the soup gently until the chicken is heated through, and divide it among 8 bowls. Garnish each serving with some of the avocado, peeled, pitted, and sliced, and a lime wedge. Makes about 11 cups, serving 8.

PHOTO ON PAGE 68

Hearty Corn Chowder

10 cups water
6 ears of corn, shucked
¼ pound lean bacon, chopped fine
the white and pale green parts of 2 leeks,
    washed well and chopped
1 russet (baking) potato (about ½ pound)
1 red bell pepper, chopped fine
2 fresh *jalapeño* chilies, or to taste, seeded
    and chopped fine (wear rubber gloves)
1½ cups half-and-half
pistou (recipe follows) as an accompaniment
    if desired

In a kettle bring the water to a boil and in it boil the corn, covered, for 10 minutes. Transfer the corn to a colander and pour the cooking water into a large heatproof bowl. In the kettle cook the bacon over moderate heat, stirring, until it is crisp and golden and with a slotted spoon transfer it to paper towels to drain. Pour off all but 2 tablespoons of the fat from the kettle and in the remaining fat cook the leeks over moderate heat, stirring, for 5 minutes. Add the potato, peeled and diced fine, and cook the mixture, stirring, for 10 minutes. Add the corn, cut from the cobs, the reserved cooking water, the bell pepper, the *jalapeños*, and salt and pepper to taste and simmer the chowder for 1 hour. In a blender purée 2 cups of the chowder, return it to the kettle, and stir in the half-and-half. Heat the corn chowder over moderate heat, stirring, until it is hot, ladle it into bowls, and top each serving with a dollop of the *pistou* and some of the bacon. Makes about 12 cups, serving 6 to 8.

Pistou
(Provençal Basil Sauce)

8 cups packed fresh basil leaves, rinsed and
    spun dry
2 garlic cloves, chopped fine
½ cup olive oil
¼ cup freshly grated Parmesan

In a food processor purée the basil and the garlic, add the oil, the Parmesan, and salt and pepper to taste, and blend the *pistou* until it is smooth. Stir the *pistou* into soups or toss it with cooked pasta or vegetables. *The pistou may be made 1 week in advance and kept, chilled, in an airtight container*. Makes about 1 cup.

Escarole Soup

2 large garlic cloves, minced
2 tablespoons olive oil
1 cup chopped onion
12 cups chicken broth (preferably low-salt)
½ teaspoon dried orégano, crumbled
½ cup tiny pasta shapes, such as egg flakes
    or *pastina*
1 head (about 1 pound) of escarole, washed
    well and cut into ½-inch-wide strips
3 hard-boiled eggs, sliced thin lengthwise
about 1 cup coarsely grated Parmesan

In a kettle cook the garlic in the oil over low heat, stirring, until it is pale golden, add the onion, and cook the mixture, stirring, until the onion is softened. Add the broth and the orégano, bring the mixture to a boil, and add the pasta. Simmer the soup for 5 minutes, add the escarole and salt and pepper to taste, and simmer the soup for 5 minutes more. Ladle the soup into soup plates, top it with the egg slices, and sprinkle it with the Parmesan. Makes about 3 quarts, serving 8.

PHOTO ON PAGE 32

Garlic and Potato Soup

3 large garlic cloves, chopped fine
1 pound unpeeled red potatoes, cut into
    ½-inch pieces (about 3 cups)
1 tablespoon vegetable oil
4 cups water
½ cup thinly sliced scallion greens

In a heavy saucepan cook the garlic and the potatoes in the oil over moderate heat, stirring occasionally, until the vegetables are pale golden, add the water and salt to taste, and simmer the mixture for 20 minutes, or until the potatoes are very soft. In a blender purée the soup in batches until it is smooth, transferring it as it is puréed to a bowl, and stir in the scallion and salt and pepper to taste. Makes about 4 cups, serving 2.

Mushroom Soup

10 ounces mushrooms, chopped fine
1 tablespoon unsalted butter
1¾ cups beef broth
¾ cup water
1½ tablespoons cornstarch
1 tablespoon soy sauce
1 tablespoon wine vinegar or fresh lemon
    juice, or to taste
2 scallions, sliced thin

In a saucepan sauté the mushrooms in the butter over high heat, stirring, until the liquid the mushrooms give off is evaporated and stir in the broth and the water. In a small bowl whisk together the cornstarch, the soy sauce, and the vinegar until the cornstarch is dissolved and stir the mixture into the soup. Bring the soup to a boil, stirring, and simmer it for 5 minutes. Stir in the scallions and salt and pepper to taste and simmer the soup for 1 minute more. Makes about 3 cups, serving 2.

Spring Onion Soup with Garlic Croutons

For the garlic croutons
1 loaf of Italian bread
4 garlic cloves, sliced
⅓ cup olive oil
For the soup
2 pounds large onions (preferably white),
    chopped fine
3 tablespoons unsalted butter
2 tablespoons vegetable oil
4 large garlic cloves, minced
¾ cup dry vermouth or dry white wine
7 cups chicken broth
1½ tablespoons Angostura bitters
3 cups finely chopped scallion
    (about 3 bunches)

Make the garlic croutons: Preheat the oven to 325° F. With a serrated knife remove the crust from the bread, discarding it, and cut the bread into ¾-inch cubes. In a shallow baking pan arrange the bread cubes in one layer, bake them in the middle of the oven, stirring occasionally, for 10 to 15 minutes, or until they are golden, and transfer the croutons to a large bowl. In a skillet cook the garlic in the oil over moderately low heat, stirring, until it is golden and with a slotted spoon discard the garlic. Drizzle the oil over the croutons,

tossing to coat them well, and sprinkle the croutons with salt to taste.

Make the soup: In a kettle cook the onions in the butter and the oil over moderate heat, stirring occasionally, for 25 to 30 minutes, or until they are soft and pale golden, add the garlic, and cook the mixture for 3 minutes. Stir in the vermouth and boil the mixture until most of the liquid is evaporated. Add the broth, the bitters, and salt and pepper to taste and simmer the soup for 5 minutes. *The soup may be made up to this point 2 days in advance, kept covered and chilled, and reheated.* Stir in the scallion.

Serve the soup topped with the croutons. Makes about 12 cups, serving 8.

PHOTO ON PAGE 35

Onion and Garlic Beer Soup

4 pounds onions (about 10), sliced thin
4 large garlic cloves, minced
2 tablespoons olive oil
a 12-ounce bottle of beer (not dark)
5¼ cups beef broth
2 tablespoons sugar
2 tablespoons unsalted butter
4 slices of day-old rye bread, crusts discarded
    and the bread cut into ½-inch cubes
freshly grated Parmesan as an accompaniment

In a heavy kettle cook the onions and the garlic in the oil over moderate heat, stirring occasionally, until the mixture is browned. Stir in the beer and the broth, simmer the mixture, covered, for 45 minutes, and stir in the sugar and salt and pepper to taste. While the soup is simmering, in a heavy skillet melt the butter over moderate heat, add the bread cubes, and cook them, stirring, until they are golden. Divide the soup among 6 bowls and top it with the Parmesan and the croutons. Makes about 12 cups, serving 6.

Oxtail Bouillon with Parmesan Puffs

5 pounds oxtails
3 onions, peeled and quartered
3 carrots, cut into 1-inch sections
the zest of 1 orange removed in strips with a
    vegetable peeler
1 cup dry white wine
4 quarts water

⅓ cup fresh cranberries
10 ounces mushrooms, chopped coarse
3 ribs of celery, cut into 1-inch sections
4 sprigs of thyme or ½ teaspoon dried thyme
1 bay leaf
4 cloves
1 teaspoon peppercorns
Parmesan puffs (recipe follows) as an
   accompaniment

Preheat the oven to 450° F. In a large roasting pan combine the oxtails, patted dry and seasoned with salt and pepper, the onions, the carrots, and the zest, roast the mixture in the middle of the oven, turning the oxtails occasionally, for 45 minutes, or until the oxtails are browned, and transfer it to a large stockpot. Deglaze the pan with the wine over high heat, scraping up the brown bits, and add the deglazing liquid to the stockpot with the water, the cranberries, the mushrooms, the celery, the thyme, the bay leaf, the cloves, and the peppercorns. Bring the liquid to a boil, skimming the froth, and simmer the mixture gently, uncovered, for 3 hours.

Ladle the liquid through a sieve lined with a rinsed and squeezed kitchen towel into a large bowl, reserving the oxtails for another use such as oxtail pâté (page 92) and discarding the remaining solids. *The bouillon can be made 3 days in advance and kept chilled.* Discard the fat, bring the bouillon just to a boil, and ladle it into heated bowls. Top the bouillon with the Parmesan puffs. Makes about 8 cups, serving 6 to 8.

PHOTO ON PAGE 79

Parmesan Puffs

1 large egg yolk
1 tablespoon water
⅓ cup freshly grated Parmesan
2 teaspoons all-purpose flour
2 large egg whites
¼ teaspoon vinegar
2 tablespoons fine dry bread crumbs
vegetable oil for deep-frying

In a small bowl whisk together the egg yolk, the water, the Parmesan, and the flour. In a bowl with an electric mixer beat the egg whites with the vinegar until they hold soft peaks, stir half the whites into the yolk mixture with the bread crumbs, and fold in the remaining whites gently but thoroughly. In a skillet heat ¼ inch of the oil until it registers 350° F. on a deep-fat thermometer, into it drop the batter in batches by ¼ teaspoons, and fry the puffs, turning them, for 1 minute, or until they are browned and crisp. Transfer the puffs as they are cooked with a slotted spoon to paper towels to drain. *The puffs may be made 3 days in advance and kept in an airtight container.* Makes about 1½ cups.

J. Savin

Roasted Yellow Pepper Soup and Roasted Tomato Soup with Serrano Cream

For the pepper soup
3 tablespoons finely chopped shallot
½ teaspoon dried thyme, crumbled
1 tablespoon unsalted butter
6 yellow bell peppers, roasted (procedure follows) and chopped coarse (about 6 cups)
1½ cups low-salt chicken broth plus additional to thin the soup
¼ cup heavy cream
fresh lemon juice to taste

For the tomato soup
3 pounds plum tomatoes, quartered lengthwise
3 unpeeled large garlic cloves
3 tablespoons finely chopped shallot
½ teaspoon dried orégano, crumbled
1 tablespoon unsalted butter
1½ cups low-salt chicken broth plus additional to thin the soup
¼ cup heavy cream
fresh lemon juice to taste

For the serrano cream
3 fresh *serrano* chilies or *jalapeños*, seeded and chopped fine (wear rubber gloves)
1 large garlic clove, minced and mashed to a paste with ½ teaspoon salt
½ cup *crème fraîche* or sour cream

Make the pepper soup: In a heavy saucepan cook the shallot, the thyme, and salt and pepper to taste in the butter over moderately low heat, stirring, until the shallot is soft, add the bell peppers and 1½ cups of the broth, and simmer the mixture, covered, for 12 to 15 minutes, or until the peppers are very soft. In a blender purée the soup in batches until it is very smooth, forcing it as it is puréed through a fine sieve set over the pan, cleaned, and whisk in the cream, enough of the additional broth to reach the desired consistency, the lemon juice, and salt and pepper to taste. *The soup may be made 1 day in advance, kept covered and chilled, and reheated.*

Make the tomato soup: Preheat the oven to 350° F. Spread the tomatoes, skin side down, in one layer on 2 foil-lined jelly-roll pans, add the garlic to 1 of the pans, and bake the tomatoes and the garlic in the oven for 45 minutes to 1 hour, or until the tomatoes are very soft and their skin is dark brown. Let the tomatoes and the garlic

cool in the pans on racks. In a heavy saucepan cook the shallot, the orégano, and salt and pepper to taste in the butter over moderately low heat, stirring, until the shallot is soft, add the tomatoes, the garlic (skins discarded), and 1½ cups of the broth, and simmer the mixture, covered, for 15 minutes. In a blender purée the soup in batches until it is very smooth, forcing it as it is puréed through a fine sieve set over the pan, cleaned, and whisk in the cream, the additional broth if necessary (both soups should have the same consistency), the lemon juice, and salt and pepper to taste. *The soup may be made 1 day in advance, kept covered and chilled, and reheated.*

Make the *serrano* cream: In a blender blend together the chilies, the garlic paste, and the *crème fraîche* until the mixture is combined well. (Be careful not to over-blend the mixture or the cream may curdle.) Force the mixture through a fine sieve set over a small bowl. *The serrano cream may be made 1 day in advance, kept covered and chilled, and brought to room temperature before serving.*

To serve the soup: For each serving ladle ½ cup of each soup into 2 glass measuring cups, pour the soups simultaneously into a shallow soup bowl from opposite sides of the bowl, and drizzle some of the *serrano* cream over each serving. Makes about 3 cups of each soup, serving 6.

PHOTO ON PAGES 24 AND 25

To Roast Peppers

Using a long-handled fork char the peppers over an open flame, turning them, for 2 to 3 minutes, or until the skins are blackened. (Or broil the peppers on the rack of a broiler pan under a preheated broiler about 2 inches from the heat, turning them every 5 minutes, for 15 to 25 minutes, or until the skins are blistered and charred.) Transfer the peppers to a bowl and let them steam, covered, until they are cool enough to handle. Keeping the peppers whole, peel them starting at the blossom end, cut off the tops, and discard the seeds and ribs. (Wear rubber gloves when handling chilies.)

Saffron Vichyssoise

4 cups finely chopped white and pale green part of leek, washed well and drained
1 cup finely chopped onion
3 ribs of celery, sliced thin (about 1 cup)

114

3 carrots, sliced thin (about 1 cup)
¾ teaspoon dried thyme,
    crumbled
1 bay leaf
½ stick (¼ cup) unsalted butter
2 large russet (baking) potatoes
    (about 1 pound)
½ teaspoon saffron threads,
    crumbled
⅔ cup dry white wine
4 cups chicken broth
2 cups water
¾ cup half-and-half

In a heavy kettle cook the leek, the onion, the celery, the carrots, the thyme, the bay leaf, and salt and pepper to taste in the butter over moderate heat, stirring, until the vegetables are softened. Add the potatoes, peeled and cut into 1-inch pieces, the saffron, the wine, the broth, and the water and simmer the mixture, covered, for 20 minutes, or until the vegetables are very tender. Discard the bay leaf and in a blender purée the soup in batches, transferring the soup as it is puréed to a large bowl. Stir in the half-and-half and salt and pepper to taste, let the soup cool, and chill it for at least 8 hours or overnight. Makes about 11 cups, serving 8 to 10.

PHOTO ON PAGE 62

Soba Soup with Spinach and Tofu

For the broth
7 cups water
a 6-inch length of *kombu** (dried kelp), wiped
    with a dampened cloth
1 ounce (about 2 cups) dried bonito flakes*
½ cup soy sauce
3 tablespoons *mirin** (syrupy rice wine)
1 tablespoon sugar

½ pound dried *soba** (buckwheat noodles)
2 carrots, sliced thin
½ pound spinach, coarse stems discarded and
    the leaves washed well, spun dry, and cut
    crosswise into 1½-inch-wide strips
8 to 10 ounces firm tofu (preferably silken),
    cut into ½-inch cubes
3 to 4 tablespoons *miso** (fermented bean
    paste), or to taste, if desired
2 scallions, minced

*available at Japanese markets, natural foods stores, and by mail order from Adriana's Bazaar, tel. (212) 877-5757

Make the broth: In a saucepan bring the water to a boil with the *kombu*, simmer the *kombu* for 2 minutes, and remove it with tongs, discarding it. Stir in the bonito flakes and simmer the mixture, stirring occasionally, for 3 minutes. Stir in the soy sauce, the *mirin*, and the sugar and simmer the broth for 5 minutes. Strain the broth through a fine sieve into a heatproof bowl and pour it back into the pan.

In a kettle of salted boiling water cook the noodles for 3 to 5 minutes, or until they are *al dente*, being careful not to overcook them, drain them in a colander, and rinse them under cold water.

Add the carrots to the broth and simmer them, covered, for 5 minutes. Stir in the spinach and the tofu and simmer the soup for 1 minute. In a small bowl stir together well ½ cup of the soup broth and the *miso* and pour the mixture back into the pan. Divide the noodles among 6 large bowls, ladle the soup over them, and sprinkle each serving with some of the minced scallions. Serves 6.

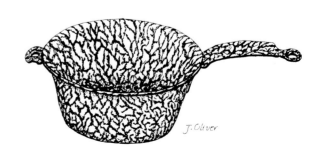

J. Oliver

Spinach Fennel Soup

2 pounds fennel bulb (sometimes called anise, available at most supermarkets), chopped (about 5 cups)
1 onion, chopped
2 tablespoons olive oil
2 cups chicken broth
2 cups water
1 teaspoon fennel seeds
¾ pound spinach (about 1 bunch), coarse stems discarded and the leaves washed well and drained

In a heavy kettle cook the fennel bulb and the onion in the oil, covered, over moderately low heat, stirring occasionally, for 10 minutes, add the broth, the water, and the fennel seeds, and simmer the mixture, covered, for 10 to 15 minutes, or until the fennel bulb is tender. Stir in the spinach and simmer the soup for 1 minute, or until the spinach is wilted. In a blender purée the soup in batches. The soup may be served hot or chilled. Makes about 8 cups, serving 6 to 8.

Gingered Butternut Squash Soup

1 onion, chopped fine
2 teaspoons olive oil
1½ cups chopped peeled butternut squash
2½ cups water
2 garlic cloves, minced and mashed to a paste with ½ teaspoon salt
¾ teaspoon grated peeled fresh gingerroot
3 tablespoons minced fresh parsley leaves

In a heavy saucepan cook the onion in the oil over moderately low heat, stirring, until it is softened, add the squash and 2 cups of the water, and simmer the mixture for 15 minutes, or until the squash is very tender. Stir in the garlic paste and the gingerroot and simmer the

soup for 1 minute. In a blender purée the soup with the remaining ½ cup water and stir in the parsley and salt and pepper to taste. Makes about 2 cups, serving 2.

Icy Dilled Tomato Soup

1 pound tomatoes, cored and quartered
1 tablespoon thinly sliced scallion
1 tablespoon fresh lime juice
½ teaspoon sugar
1 cup ice cubes
1½ tablespoons minced fresh dill
1 tablespoon mayonnaise thinned with ½ teaspoon water

In a blender purée the tomatoes and the scallion with the lime juice, the sugar, the ice cubes, and salt and pepper to taste and force the purée through a fine sieve set over a bowl, pressing hard on the solids. Stir in the dill, divide the soup between 2 bowls, and drizzle some of the mayonnaise over each serving. Makes about 2½ cups, serving 2.

Chilled Tomato Yogurt Soup

3 pounds tomatoes (about 6), cored and cut into chunks
1 cup plain yogurt
1 teaspoon curry powder
1 cup packed fresh basil leaves, chopped fine

In a food processor or blender purée the tomatoes in batches, force the purée through a fine sieve set over a bowl, and whisk in the yogurt, the curry powder, the basil, and salt and pepper to taste. Chill the soup, covered, until it is cold. *The soup may be made 1 day in advance and kept covered and chilled.* Makes about 5 cups, serving 4.

PHOTO ON PAGE 59

FISH AND SHELLFISH

FISH

Crisp Red-Cooked Bass Fillets

1½ tablespoons soy sauce
1 tablespoon Scotch or medium-dry Sherry
1 teaspoon minced peeled fresh gingerroot
½ teaspoon sugar
1 tablespoon cornstarch
¼ teaspoon aniseed, crushed with a rolling pin
⅛ teaspoon cinnamon
¾ cup water
two ½-pound black bass, snapper, or other
    white fish fillets with skin
1 tablespoon vegetable oil
1 scallion, minced

In a small saucepan whisk together the soy sauce, the Scotch, the gingerroot, the sugar, ½ teaspoon of the cornstarch, the aniseed, the cinnamon, and the water, bring the mixture to a boil, whisking, and simmer it, covered, for 5 minutes.

While the sauce is simmering, pat the fillets dry between paper towels and rub both sides with the remaining 2½ teaspoons cornstarch, shaking off the excess. In a large non-stick skillet heat the oil over moderately high heat until it just begins to smoke, add the fillets, skin sides down, and sear them, pressing them with a metal spatula to flatten them, for 4 minutes. Turn the fillets, strain the soy sauce mixture through a fine sieve into the skillet, and simmer the mixture for 3 minutes, or until the fish just flakes. Transfer the fillets, skin sides

up, with a slotted spatula to plates and simmer the sauce, stirring, for 1 minute, or until it is thickened slightly. Spoon the sauce around the fillets and sprinkle the fillets with the scallion. Serves 2.

Spicy Blackened Catfish

2 teaspoons sweet paprika
½ teaspoon dried orégano, crumbled
½ teaspoon dried thyme, crumbled
¼ teaspoon cayenne, or to taste
½ teaspoon sugar
½ teaspoon salt
¼ teaspoon freshly ground black pepper
2 catfish fillets (about 1 pound)
1 large garlic clove, sliced thin
1 tablespoon olive oil
1 tablespoon unsalted butter
lemon wedges as an accompaniment

In a small bowl combine the paprika, the orégano, the thyme, the cayenne, the sugar, the salt, and the black pepper, pat the catfish dry, and sprinkle the spice mixture on both sides of the fillets, coating them well. In a large skillet sauté the garlic in the oil over moderately high heat, stirring, until it is golden brown and discard the garlic. Add the butter, heat it until the foam subsides, and in the fat sauté the catfish for 4 minutes on each side, or until it is cooked through. Transfer the catfish fillets with a slotted spatula to 2 plates and serve them with the lemon wedges. Serves 2.

Sautéed Cod Provençale

1½ tablespoons olive oil
two ½-inch-thick pieces of cod fillet
  (about 6 ounces each)
2 plum tomatoes, peeled, seeded, and diced
2 Kalamata or other brine-cured black olives,
  pitted and sliced thin
¼ teaspoon fresh thyme leaves or a pinch of
  dried, crumbled
2 fresh large basil leaves, sliced thin

In a non-stick skillet heat 1 tablespoon of the oil over moderate heat until it is hot but not smoking and in it sauté the cod, seasoned with salt and pepper, for 30 seconds. Sprinkle the cod with the tomatoes, the olives, and the thyme, reduce the heat to moderately low, and cook the mixture, covered, for 2 minutes. Scatter the basil over the fish, drizzle it with the remaining ½ tablespoon oil, and cook it, covered, for 1 minute, or until it just flakes. Serves 2.

The following recipe and its accompaniment have been designed to produce leftovers that can be used to make the Cod Cannelloni with Swiss Chard and Roasted Pepper below.

Roast Cod with Potatoes, Onions, and Olives

1 pound (about 3) onions, cut into
  ½-inch-thick slices
3 large garlic cloves, minced
¼ cup olive oil
⅓ cup vegetable oil
1 pound (about 2 large) boiling potatoes
¾ cup Kalamata or other brine-cured black
  olives, pitted and quartered
½ teaspoon dried rosemary, crumbled
¼ cup minced fresh parsley leaves
a 2½-pound piece of center-cut cod fillet
Swiss chard with roasted pepper as an
  accompaniment (recipe follows)

Preheat the oven to 450° F. In a large skillet cook the onions and the garlic in the olive oil over moderate heat, stirring occasionally, until the mixture is pale golden. While the onion mixture is cooking, in another large skillet heat the vegetable oil over moderately high heat until it is hot but not smoking and in it sauté the pota-

toes, peeled and cut into ¼-inch-thick slices, in batches, turning them, for 5 to 8 minutes, or until they are pale golden, transferring them as they are cooked to a bowl. Add the onion mixture to the potatoes with the olives, the rosemary, the parsley, and salt and pepper to taste and combine the mixture well.

Put the cod in the center of a large shallow baking dish, season it with salt and pepper, and arrange the potato mixture around it. Roast the mixture in the middle of the oven for 20 to 25 minutes, or until the fish just flakes. (If planning to make the cod cannelloni, recipe below, flake 2 cups of the cod and reserve it, covered and chilled.) Serve the roast cod with the Swiss chard with roasted pepper. Serves 4 with leftovers for the cannelloni.

Swiss Chard with Roasted Pepper

2½ pounds Swiss chard, washed well, the
  coarse stems removed and chopped coarse,
  and the leaves chopped coarse separately
1 red bell pepper, roasted (procedure on
  page 114) and chopped coarse
2 tablespoons extra-virgin olive oil

In a kettle cook the chard stems in about ½ cup water, covered, over high heat for 5 minutes, add the chard leaves, and cook the chard, covered, stirring occasionally, for 5 minutes. Drain the chard well and in a bowl toss it with the roasted pepper, the oil, and salt and pepper to taste. (If planning to make the cod cannelloni, recipe follows, reserve 1½ cups of the chard mixture, covered and chilled.) Serves 4 with leftovers for the cannelloni.

Cod Cannelloni with Swiss Chard and Roasted Pepper

2 cups spicy tomato sauce (recipe follows)
3 tablespoons unsalted butter
¼ cup all-purpose flour
1 cup milk
4 large square or 8 small rectangular sheets
  of instant (no-boil) lasagne (available
  at specialty foods shops and some
  supermarkets)
2 cups flaked cooked cod
  (such as roast cod, recipe above)
1½ cups Swiss chard with roasted pepper
  (preceding recipe)

⅓ cup chopped fresh basil leaves plus basil
   sprigs for garnish
freshly grated Parmesan as an accompaniment

Preheat the oven to 350° F. Spread the tomato sauce
in the bottoms of 4 individual gratin dishes or in the bottom of a shallow baking dish just large enough to hold
8 cannelloni in one layer. In a saucepan melt the butter
over moderately low heat, whisk in the flour, and cook
the *roux*, whisking, for 3 minutes. Add the milk in a
stream, whisking, simmer the béchamel, whisking constantly, for 2 minutes, and season it with salt and pepper. Transfer the béchamel to a bowl and let it cool,
covered. In a pan of hot water let the sheets of lasagne
soak for 10 to 15 minutes, or until they are softened. To
the béchamel add the cod, the Swiss chard with roasted
pepper, the chopped basil, and salt and pepper to taste
and combine the mixture well.

If using the square lasagne sheets halve each sheet to
form 2 rectangles. Working with 1 rectangle at a time,
spread about ⅓ cup of the cod mixture lengthwise down
the center of each sheet, beginning with a long side roll
up the sheet to enclose the filling, leaving both ends
open, and arrange 2 cannelloni, seam sides down, in
each dish, spooning some of the tomato sauce over
them. Bake the cannelloni, covered with foil, in the
middle of the oven for 20 to 25 minutes, or until they are
heated through, garnish them with the basil sprigs, and
serve them with the Parmesan. Makes 8 cannelloni,
serving 4.

Spicy Tomato Sauce

1 small onion, chopped fine
2 large garlic cloves,
   minced
2 tablespoons olive oil
a 28- to 32-ounce can plum tomatoes
   including the juice, chopped
1 teaspoon sugar
¼ teaspoon dried hot red pepper flakes

In a heavy saucepan cook the onion and the garlic in
the oil over moderate heat, stirring, until they are gold-
en, add the tomatoes with the juice, the sugar, the red
pepper flakes, and salt to taste, and simmer the sauce,
stirring occasionally, for 30 minutes, or until it is thickened. *The tomato sauce may be made 1 day in advance
and kept covered and chilled.* Makes about 2 cups.

Sweet-and-Sour Halibut

¼ cup water
1½ tablespoons red-wine vinegar
1 whole scallion, sliced thin, plus the green
   parts of 2 scallions, sliced thin
1½ teaspoons minced peeled fresh gingerroot
1½ teaspoons sugar
1 tablespoon soy sauce
1 tablespoon ketchup
¼ teaspoon Asian (toasted) sesame oil
   (available at Asian markets and some
   specialty foods shops and supermarkets)
1 teaspoon cornstarch dissolved in
   2 tablespoons water
a 1-inch-thick halibut steak (about 1 pound),
   the skin and bone discarded and the fish cut
   into ¾-inch pieces
all-purpose flour seasoned with salt and
   pepper for dredging the fish
vegetable oil for frying the fish
cooked rice as an accompaniment

In a saucepan simmer the water and the vinegar with
the sliced whole scallion, the gingerroot, the sugar, the
soy sauce, and the ketchup, stirring occasionally, for 5
minutes, add the sesame oil and the cornstarch mixture,
stirred, and simmer the sauce, stirring, for 2 minutes.
Keep the sauce warm, covered.

In a bag shake the halibut in the flour, transfer it to a
large sieve or colander, and shake it to remove the excess. In a large deep skillet heat ¼ inch of the vegetable
oil over moderately high heat until it is hot but not smoking and in it fry the halibut in 2 batches, turning it, for 2
to 3 minutes, or until it is cooked through, transferring it
as it is cooked with a slotted spoon to paper towels to
drain. Add the halibut to the sauce, stirring to coat it
well, and serve it over the rice and sprinkled with the
scallion greens. Serves 2.

Grilled Salmon with Fennel Orange Salsa

For the salsa

1 cup finely diced fennel bulb (sometimes
    called anise) plus 1 tablespoon minced
    fennel leaves
½ cup finely diced orange sections
10 *picholine* olives (available at specialty
    foods shops) or other green olives, pitted
    and minced
2 tablespoons drained bottled small capers
1 tablespoon fresh orange juice
1 teaspoon fresh lemon juice, or to taste

¼ cup olive oil
4 teaspoons fresh lemon juice
eight ¼-pound pieces of skinned salmon fillet
32 *radicchio* leaves (about 3 or 4 heads)

Make the *salsa*: In a bowl stir together the fennel bulb
and leaves, the diced orange, the olives, the capers, the
juices, and salt and pepper to taste.

In a small bowl stir together the oil, the lemon juice,
and salt and pepper to taste. Put the salmon on a large
platter, pour the oil mixture over it, and let the salmon
marinate, turning it once, for 10 minutes.

Grill the salmon, skinned sides down, on an oiled
rack set 5 to 6 inches over glowing coals or in a hot well-
seasoned ridged grill pan over moderately high heat for
5 minutes, turn it, and grill it for 3 minutes more, or until it is just cooked through. Arrange 4 of the *radicchio*
leaves on each of 8 heated plates, put a piece of salmon
in the center, and top it with some of the *salsa*. Serves 8.

PHOTO ON PAGE 38

Poached Ginger Salmon Steaks

a 1-inch piece of peeled fresh gingerroot,
    sliced thin, plus 1 teaspoon minced
    peeled fresh gingerroot
1 large garlic clove, mashed with the
    flat side of a knife
2 lemon slices
2 tablespoons soy sauce
1 cup water
two ½-inch-thick salmon steaks
    (each about 6 ounces)
1 tablespoon unsalted butter,
    cut into bits
1 tablespoon minced fresh parsley leaves

In a 2-quart microwave-safe casserole with a lid combine the sliced gingerroot, the garlic, the lemon, the soy
sauce, and the water and microwave the mixture, uncovered, at high power (100%) for 5 minutes. Add the
salmon in one layer and sprinkle it with the minced gingerroot. Microwave the mixture, covered, at medium
power (50%) for 5 minutes, or until the salmon just
flakes, and transfer the salmon with a slotted spatula
to 2 plates. In a bowl whisk together 2 tablespoons of
the cooking liquid, the butter, the parsley, and salt and
pepper to taste and spoon the sauce over the salmon.
Serves 2.

Salmon and Spinach Strudel

two 10-ounce packages frozen
    chopped spinach
1 cup chopped onion
¾ cup chopped fennel bulb
    (sometimes called anise)
2 teaspoons fennel seeds
1 stick (½ cup) unsalted butter
2 tablespoons all-purpose flour
½ cup milk
2 tablespoons Ricard or other
    anise-flavored spirit
½ cup plus 2 tablespoons freshly grated
    Parmesan
two ¾-inch-thick salmon steaks
    (about ½ pound each)
2 tablespoons water
2 tablespoons fine dry bread crumbs

six 18- by 14-inch sheets of *phyllo*, stacked
between 2 sheets of wax paper and covered
with a dampened kitchen towel
lemon wedges as an accompaniment

In a saucepan cook the spinach according to the package instructions, drain it, and let it cool. When the spinach is cool enough to handle, squeeze it dry by handfuls, transferring it as it is squeezed to a bowl. (The spinach should be very dry.) In the saucepan cook the onion and the fennel bulb and seeds in 2 tablespoons of the butter over moderate heat, stirring, until the vegetables are softened, stir in the flour, and cook the mixture, stirring, for 1 minute. Add the milk and the Ricard and cook the mixture, stirring, for 3 minutes. (The mixture will be extremely thick.) Stir the fennel mixture into the spinach with ½ cup of the Parmesan and salt and pepper to taste. *The filling may be made 1 day in advance and kept covered and chilled.*

In a non-stick skillet melt 1 tablespoon of the remaining butter over moderately high heat until the foam subsides and in it sauté the salmon steaks, patted dry and seasoned with salt and pepper, for 1 minute on each side. Add the water to the skillet and cook the salmon, covered, over moderately low heat for 5 to 6 minutes, or until it is just cooked through. Remove the skillet from the heat and let the salmon cool. Discard the skin from the salmon, halve the steaks, and discard the bones. In a small bowl stir together the remaining 2 tablespoons Parmesan and the bread crumbs.

Preheat the oven to 425° F. In a small saucepan melt the remaining 5 tablespoons butter. On a work surface arrange two 20-inch-long sheets of wax paper with the long sides slightly overlapping and facing you. Put 1 sheet of the *phyllo* on the wax paper, brush it with some of the butter, and sprinkle it with about 2 teaspoons of the Parmesan crumbs. On this, layer, brush, and sprinkle 4 more sheets of the *phyllo* in the same manner and lay the sixth sheet of *phyllo* on top.

Spread the spinach filling in a 3-inch-wide strip, mounding it on the *phyllo* 4 inches above the near long side, leaving a 2-inch border at each end, and arrange the salmon on top, pressing it gently into the filling. Using the wax paper as a guide, lift the bottom 4 inches of the pastry over the filling, fold in the ends, and roll up the strudel tightly. Transfer the strudel carefully, seam side down, to a lightly buttered baking sheet, brush it with the remaining butter, and bake it in the lower third of the oven for 25 minutes, or until it is golden. Let the strudel cool to warm on the baking sheet on a rack. *The strudel may be made 1 day in advance and kept covered loosely and chilled. Reheat the strudel in a preheated 400° F. oven for 15 minutes.* Serve the strudel warm, cut into 1-inch slices with a serrated knife, with the lemon wedges. Serves 6.

Curried Red Snapper

For the sauce
2 onions, chopped fine
¼ cup vegetable oil
a 1-inch cube of peeled fresh gingerroot, minced
4 garlic cloves, minced
1 green bell pepper, chopped fine
1 red bell pepper, chopped fine
3 tablespoons curry powder
¼ cup all-purpose flour
3 cups low-salt chicken broth
a 28-ounce can plum tomatoes, drained well
and chopped fine
2 tablespoons fresh lime juice

a 4- to 4½-pound red snapper, cleaned,
leaving the head and the tail intact
fresh coriander sprigs for garnish if desired

Make the sauce: In a large heavy saucepan cook the onions in the oil over moderate heat, stirring, until they are softened, add the gingerroot and the garlic, and cook the mixture, stirring, for 1 minute. Add the bell peppers and cook the mixture, stirring, until the peppers are softened. Add the curry powder and the flour and cook the mixture over moderately low heat, stirring, for 3 minutes. Add the broth, bring the mixture to a boil, whisking, and stir in the tomatoes. Simmer the sauce, stirring occasionally, for 5 minutes and stir in the lime juice and salt and pepper to taste. *The sauce may be made 3 days in advance and kept covered and chilled. Reheat the sauce before continuing with the recipe.*

Preheat the oven to 350° F. Arrange the snapper on a deep ovenproof platter, ladle about 2 cups of the sauce over it, keeping the remaining sauce covered and warm, and cover the platter tightly with oiled foil, oiled side down. Bake the snapper in the middle of the oven for 45 to 55 minutes, or until it just flakes. Garnish the snapper with the coriander sprigs and serve the remaining sauce separately. Serves 10 as part of a buffet.

PHOTO ON PAGE 21

Red Snapper with Sherry Beurre Blanc

¼ cup medium-dry Sherry
1 large shallot, minced (about ¼ cup)
2 tablespoons dry white wine or water
1 tablespoon Sherry vinegar (available at
    specialty foods shops) or white-wine vinegar
3 tablespoons cold unsalted butter,
    cut into 4 pieces
two ½-inch-thick red snapper fillets
    (about 10 ounces total), seasoned
    with salt and pepper

In a small saucepan cook the Sherry, the shallot, the white wine, the vinegar, and salt and pepper to taste over moderately high heat until the liquid is reduced to about 2 tablespoons, remove the pan from the heat, and whisk in the butter, 1 piece at a time, adding each new piece before the previous one has melted completely. (The sauce should not get hot enough to liquefy. It should be the consistency of thin hollandaise.)

Preheat the broiler. On a foil-covered broiler pan broil the fillets about 4 inches from the heat for 4 to 5 minutes, or until they just flake, divide them between 2 plates, and spoon the sauce over them. Serves 2.

Orange and Fennel Poached Sole

¼ cup fresh orange juice
¼ cup dry white wine
1 tablespoon white-wine vinegar
2 shallots, chopped fine
½ teaspoon fennel seeds
2 strips of orange zest, removed with a
    vegetable peeler
½ cup water
2 sole or orange roughy fillets (about 1 pound)
1 tablespoon unsalted butter

In a skillet boil the orange juice, the wine, and the vinegar with the shallots, the fennel seeds, and the zest, shaking the skillet, until most of the liquid is evaporated. Add the water, bring the mixture to a boil, and in it poach the sole, covered, at a bare simmer for 10 minutes. Transfer the sole with a slotted spatula to 2 plates and keep it warm, covered. Boil the poaching liquid until it is reduced to about ⅓ cup, remove the skillet from the heat, and swirl in the butter. Season the sauce with salt and pepper and pour it through a fine sieve over the sole. Serves 2.

Marinated Squid and Fennel

1½ pounds squid, cleaned (procedure
    follows), the body sacs cut into
    ⅓-inch-rings, the flaps sliced thin,
    and the tentacles halved
2 tablespoons fresh lemon juice
⅓ cup red-wine vinegar
1 tablespoon minced fresh orégano
    leaves or 1 teaspoon dried,
    crumbled
½ teaspoon fennel seeds
2 garlic cloves, minced
¾ cup olive oil
2 small fennel bulbs (sometimes called anise),
    trimmed, quartered, and sliced thin, or
    6 ribs of celery, sliced thin on the diagonal
pita loaves, cut into wedges, as an
    accompaniment

In a large saucepan of boiling water cook the squid with the lemon juice for 45 seconds (the water probably will not return to a boil in this time), drain it in a colander, and refresh it under cold water. In a large bowl whisk together the vinegar, the orégano, the fennel seeds, the garlic, and salt and pepper to taste, add the oil in a stream, whisking, and whisk the dressing until it is emulsified. Add the squid and the fennel or celery, combine the mixture well, and let it marinate, covered and chilled, for at least 4 hours to allow the flavors to develop. *The marinated squid may be made 1 day in advance and kept covered and chilled.* Serve the marinated squid with the *pita* wedges. Serves 8 as a first course.

PHOTO ON PAGE 44

To Clean Squid

Pull the head and body of the squid apart, cut off the tentacles just below the eyes, and reserve the tentacles and body sac. Discard the transparent quill from inside the body sac, rinse the body sac well, and peel off the purple membrane covering it. Pull off the flaps gently from the body sac to avoid tearing it and reserve them.

Bacon and Sage Panfried Trout

24 slices of bacon
3 tablespoons minced fresh sage
    leaves or 1 tablespoon dried, crumbled,
    plus fresh sage sprigs for garnish

8 trout (about 10 ounces each), cleaned and
    boned, leaving the head and tail intact
about 2 cups yellow cornmeal for
    coating the trout
⅓ cup olive oil
lemon wedges for garnish

In a large heavy skillet cook 8 of the bacon slices over moderate heat, turning them occasionally, until they are crisp, transfer them to paper towels to drain, and pour off the fat. Crumble the cooked bacon into a small bowl and stir in the minced sage. In the skillet cook the remaining 16 bacon slices in 2 batches until the bacon just becomes translucent and the edges begin to curl, transfer them to paper towels to drain, and pour off the fat.

Preheat the oven to 375° F. Rinse the trout under cold water and pat them dry inside and out. Sprinkle the cavity of each trout with one eighth of the crumbled bacon mixture and salt and pepper to taste. Wrap 2 of the whole bacon slices around each trout, using wooden picks to secure the bacon and close the cavities. Mound the cornmeal on a sheet of wax paper and roll each trout in it, coating it completely and gently shaking off the excess cornmeal.

Heat the skillet over moderately high heat until it is hot, add the oil, and heat it until it is hot but not smoking. In the oil fry the trout, not touching each other, in batches for 3 minutes on each side, or until they are just firm and the bacon is golden, transferring them as they are fried with long spatulas to a shallow baking pan. When all the trout have been fried, bake them in the oven for 5 minutes, or until they just flake and are heated through. Discard the wooden picks, arrange the trout carefully on a platter, and garnish them with the sage sprigs and the lemon wedges. Serves 8.

PHOTO ON PAGE 34

Sautéed Tuna with Warm Olive Vinaigrette

4 tablespoons olive oil
two 1-inch-thick tuna steaks
5 Kalamata or other brine-cured black olives,
    pitted
2 teaspoons drained bottled capers
1 garlic clove, minced
1 teaspoon Dijon-style mustard
2 teaspoons balsamic vinegar, or to taste
1 plum tomato, seeded and chopped
1 tablespoon water
2 tablespoons finely chopped drained bottled
    roasted red peppers plus additional for
    garnish if desired
1 tablespoon finely chopped white and green
    parts of scallion plus additional for garnish
    if desired
lemon wedges as an accompaniment

In a heavy skillet, preferably non-stick, heat 1 tablespoon of the oil over moderately high heat until it is hot but not smoking and in it sauté the tuna steaks, patted dry and seasoned with salt and pepper, for 4 to 5 minutes on each side, or until they are just cooked through. While the tuna is cooking, in a blender or small food processor blend together the olives, the capers, the garlic, the mustard, the vinegar, the tomato, the water, and salt and pepper to taste and with the motor running add the remaining 3 tablespoons oil, blending the dressing until it is emulsified. Transfer the tuna to plates and wipe the skillet clean. Pour the dressing into the skillet, heat it over moderate heat until it is hot, and stir in 2 tablespoons of the roasted peppers and 1 tablespoon of the scallion. Spoon the dressing over the tuna, garnish the tuna with the additional roasted peppers and scallion, and serve it with the lemon wedges. Serves 2.

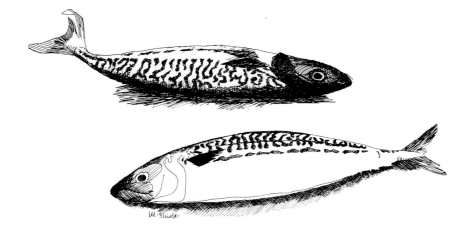

SHELLFISH

Crab Cakes

½ stick (¼ cup) unsalted butter, melted
   and cooled
4 large eggs, beaten lightly
6 tablespoons sour cream
¼ cup minced fresh parsley leaves
   (preferably flat-leafed)
2 tablespoons fresh lemon juice
1 teaspoon Worcestershire sauce
1 teaspoon paprika
½ teaspoon salt, or to taste
¼ teaspoon cayenne, or to taste
2 pounds lump crab meat, picked over
2 cups fine fresh bread crumbs
⅓ cup cornmeal
½ cup vegetable oil

tarragon tartar sauce (recipe follows) as an
   accompaniment
lemon wedges as an accompaniment

In a bowl whisk together the butter, the eggs, the sour cream, the parsley, the lemon juice, the Worcestershire sauce, the paprika, the salt, and the cayenne and stir in the crab meat and the bread crumbs gently. Form ½-cup measures of the mixture into twelve ¾-inch-thick cakes and transfer the crab cakes as they are formed to a baking sheet sprinkled with half the cornmeal. Sprinkle the crab cakes with the remaining cornmeal and chill them, covered with plastic wrap, for at least 1 hour or overnight.

Preheat the oven to 200° F. In a large heavy skillet heat the oil over moderately high heat until it is hot but not smoking and in it sauté the crab cakes in batches, turning them once, for 3 to 4 minutes on each side, or until they are golden, transferring them as they are cooked to paper towels to drain. Keep the crab cakes warm on another baking sheet in the oven. Serve the crab cakes with the tarragon tartar sauce and the lemon wedges. Makes 12 crab cakes, serving 6.

PHOTO ON PAGE 56

Tarragon Tartar Sauce

1½ cups mayonnaise
3 shallots, minced
4 *cornichons* (French sour gherkins, available at specialty foods shops and some supermarkets), minced
18 green olives (preferably brine-cured), pitted and chopped
1½ tablespoons minced fresh tarragon leaves
1 tablespoon cider vinegar, or to taste
Tabasco to taste

In a small bowl whisk together the mayonnaise, the shallots, the *cornichons*, the olives, the tarragon, the vinegar, and the Tabasco until the tartar sauce is combined well. *The sauce may be made 1 day in advance and kept covered and chilled.* Makes about 2 cups.

PHOTO ON PAGE 56

Mussels Steamed in Spiced Beer

a 12-ounce bottle of beer (not dark)
2 bay leaves
4 whole cloves
1 teaspoon coriander seeds
1 teaspoon mustard seeds
¼ teaspoon cayenne, or to taste
½ teaspoon salt
2 lemon wedges
36 mussels, preferably cultivated, scrubbed well in several changes of water and the beards scraped off if necessary
minced fresh parsley leaves for garnish

In a kettle bring the beer to a boil with the bay leaves, the cloves, the coriander seeds, the mustard seeds, the cayenne, the salt, and the lemon wedges and boil the mixture, covered partially, for 2 minutes. Add the mussels, steam them, covered, over moderately high heat, stirring once or twice, for 4 to 7 minutes, or until they are opened, discarding any unopened ones. Sprinkle the mussels with the parsley. Serves 6 as a first course.

Grilled Scallops with Coriander Butter Sauce

2 tablespoons minced onion
1 tablespoon white-wine vinegar
¼ cup water
1 teaspoon ground coriander
½ stick (¼ cup) cold unsalted butter, cut into 4 pieces
¾ pound sea scallops
vegetable oil for brushing the scallops
2 tablespoons minced fresh coriander

In a small heavy saucepan simmer the onion, the vinegar, the water, and the ground coriander until the liquid is reduced to about 1 tablespoon and whisk in the butter, 1 piece at a time, lifting the pan from the heat occasionally to let the mixture cool and adding each new piece of butter before the previous one has melted completely. (The sauce should not get hot enough to liquefy. It should be the consistency of thin hollandaise.) Season the sauce with salt and pepper, transfer it to a small bowl set in a larger bowl of warm water, and keep it warm.

Brush the scallops with the oil, heat a ridged grill pan over high heat until it is hot and just begins to smoke, and in it grill the scallops, covered, for 5 minutes on each side, or until they are cooked through. Whisk the fresh coriander into the butter sauce, spoon the sauce onto 2 plates, and arrange the scallops on it. Serves 2.

Sautéed Scallops with Ginger

1 tablespoon vegetable oil
1 tablespoon unsalted butter
¾ pound sea scallops, halved horizontally
2 teaspoons minced peeled fresh gingerroot
1 shallot, minced
2 tablespoons minced scallion greens
1 teaspoon fresh lemon juice, or to taste

In a large heavy skillet heat the oil and the butter over moderately high heat until the foam subsides, in the fat sauté the scallops, patted dry, for 30 seconds on each side, or until they are cooked through, and transfer them to a bowl. In the fat remaining in the skillet cook the gingerroot and the shallot over moderately low heat, stirring, until the shallot is softened and stir in the scallion, the scallops with any juice that has accumulated in the bowl, the lemon juice, and salt and pepper to taste. Serves 2.

Scallops and Saffron Couscous Strudel

1¼ cups water
¾ cup couscous
2 tablespoons vegetable oil
½ teaspoon salt
½ teaspoon crumbled saffron threads
1 cup mayonnaise
2 large garlic cloves, crushed
lemon juice to taste
1 small red bell pepper, chopped
1 small green bell pepper, chopped
6 ounces sea scallops, quartered
½ cup thawed frozen peas
six 18- by 14-inch sheets of *phyllo*, stacked
    between 2 sheets of wax paper and covered
    with a dampened kitchen towel
5 tablespoons unsalted butter, melted
10 teaspoons fine dry bread crumbs

In a saucepan bring the water to a boil, stir in the couscous, 1 tablespoon of the oil, and the salt, and remove the pan from the heat. Let the couscous stand, covered, for 5 minutes. Set a rack over another saucepan of boiling water, put the saffron in a heatproof saucer on the rack, and let it steam for 3 to 4 minutes, or until it is brittle. In a blender or small food processor blend the mayonnaise, the saffron, the garlic, and the lemon juice. In a non-stick skillet heat the remaining tablespoon oil over moderately high heat until it is hot but not smoking and in it sauté the bell peppers, stirring, until they begin to brown. Add the scallops and sauté the mixture, stirring once or twice, for 1 minute, or until the scallops are just cooked through. Remove the skillet from the heat and stir in the peas and salt and pepper to taste. In a large bowl fluff the couscous with a fork, stir in well the scallop mixture and ½ cup of the saffron-garlic mayonnaise, and let the filling cool.

Preheat the oven to 425° F. On a work surface arrange two 20-inch-long sheets of wax paper with the long sides overlapping slightly and facing you. Put 1 sheet of the *phyllo* on the wax paper, brush it with some of the butter, and sprinkle it with about 2 teaspoons of the bread crumbs. On this, layer, brush, and sprinkle 4 more sheets of the *phyllo* in the same manner and lay the sixth sheet of *phyllo* on top.

Spread the filling in a 3-inch-wide strip, mounding it on the *phyllo* 4 inches above the near long side, leaving a 2-inch border at each end. Using the wax paper as a guide, lift the bottom 4 inches of the pastry over the fill-

ing, fold in the ends, and roll up the strudel tightly. Transfer the strudel carefully, seam side down, to a lightly buttered baking sheet, brush it with the remaining butter, and bake it in the lower third of the oven for 25 minutes, or until it is golden. Let the strudel cool to warm on the baking sheet on a rack. *The strudel may be made 1 day in advance and kept covered loosely and chilled. Reheat the strudel in a preheated 400° F. oven for 15 minutes.* Serve the strudel warm, cut into 1-inch slices with a serrated knife, with the remaining saffron-garlic mayonnaise. Serves 6.

Crispy Noodle Cake with Shrimp and Snow Peas

¾ pound fresh* or dried** thin Asian egg
    noodles or *capellini*
1 tablespoon vegetable oil
2 teaspoons Asian (toasted) sesame oil**
For marinating the shrimp
two ⅛-inch-thick slices of fresh gingerroot,
    flattened with the flat side of a heavy knife
1½ tablespoons Scotch
2 teaspoons cornstarch
1 pound medium shrimp (about 25), peeled,
    deveined, rinsed, and squeezed dry gently
    in a kitchen towel

10 dried *shiitake* mushrooms**, soaked in
    1½ cups hot water for 20 minutes
2½ tablespoons cornstarch
1 cup chicken broth
3 tablespoons soy sauce
2 tablespoons Scotch
1 teaspoon sugar
1 teaspoon Asian (toasted) sesame oil**
8 tablespoons vegetable oil
3 tablespoons minced scallion
1½ tablespoons minced peeled fresh
    gingerroot
½ pound snow peas, each trimmed and cut
    diagonally into 3 pieces

*available at some Asian markets
**available at Asian markets, some specialty
    foods shops and supermarkets, and by mail
    order from Adriana's Bazaar, (212) 877-5757

In a kettle of salted boiling water cook the noodles until they are *al dente*, drain them well, and in a bowl toss them with the oils. Spread the noodles evenly in an oiled 13- by 9-inch metal baking pan, smoothing the top, and let them cool, uncovered.

Marinate the shrimp: In a small bowl pinch the gingerroot in the Scotch, stir in the cornstarch, the shrimp, and a pinch of salt, and let the shrimp marinate for 20 minutes. Discard the gingerroot.

Drain the mushrooms, reserving the soaking liquid, discard the stems, and quarter the caps. Let the soaking liquid settle, pour 1 cup of it into a bowl, discarding the remaining liquid, and stir in the cornstarch, the broth, the soy sauce, the Scotch, the sugar, and the sesame oil.

Preheat the broiler. Brush the top of the noodle cake lightly with 1 tablespoon of the vegetable oil and broil it under the broiler as close to the heat as possible for 5 to 7 minutes, or until it is crisp. Invert the noodle cake onto an oiled baking sheet, brush it lightly with 1 tablespoon of the remaining vegetable oil, and broil it for 5 to 7 minutes more, or until it is crisp. Keep the noodle cake warm in a 250° F. oven.

In a wok heat 4 tablespoons of the remaining vegetable oil over high heat until it just begins to smoke and in it stir-fry the shrimp mixture for 1 to 2 minutes, or until the shrimp are just cooked through. Transfer the shrimp with a slotted spoon to a sieve set over a bowl to drain and discard the oil in the wok.

In the wok heat the remaining 2 tablespoons vegetable oil over high heat until it is hot but not smoking and in it stir-fry the scallion and the minced gingerroot for 15 seconds. Add the mushrooms and stir-fry the mixture for 30 seconds. Stir the broth mixture, add it to the wok, and simmer the mixture, stirring, for 1 minute. Add the shrimp and the snow peas and simmer the mixture, stirring, for 1 minute, or until the shrimp are heated through. Slide the noodle cake onto a platter, cut it into 6 servings, and pour the shrimp mixture over it. Serves 6.

Grilled Teriyaki Shrimp and Vegetable Brochettes
For the teriyaki marinade
⅓ cup soy sauce
2 tablespoons chopped peeled
    fresh gingerroot
3 tablespoons sugar
2 tablespoons *mirin* (sweet Japanese rice
    wine, available at Asian markets, specialty
    foods shops, and some supermarkets)
2 tablespoons water

12 large shrimp, shelled, leaving the tail and
    the first joint intact, and deveined if desired
four 12-inch bamboo skewers
2 zucchini, each about 7- to 8-inches long,
    trimmed
sixteen ½-inch slices of red bell pepper
16 scallion brushes (procedure on page 128)
vegetable oil for brushing the brochettes

Make the teriyaki marinade: In a small saucepan combine the soy sauce, the gingerroot, the sugar, the *mirin*, and the water and bring the mixture to a boil, stirring until the sugar is dissolved. Let the marinade cool to room temperature and transfer it to a bowl or a resealable plastic bag. Add the shrimp to the marinade and let it marinate, covered and chilled, for 2 hours or overnight. Drain the shrimp, discarding the marinade.

In a shallow dish let the skewers soak in water to cover for 30 minutes.

Using a mandoline or similar slicing device cut the zucchini lengthwise into thin slices, about ⅛ inch thick, discarding the end slices. In a steamer set over boiling water steam the zucchini slices in 2 batches for 2 to 3 minutes, or until they are just tender and pliable (do not overcook them), and transfer them to a bowl of ice and cold water to stop the cooking.

Assemble the brochettes: Working with 1 skewer at a time, thread the skewer with a bell pepper slice, a scallion brush, one end of a zucchini slice, and a shrimp. Wrap the zucchini slice over one side of the shrimp and thread it back onto the skewer. Continue to weave the zucchini slice around the vegetables and shrimp, using 4 bell pepper slices, 4 scallion brushes, and 3 shrimp per skewer and as many zucchini slices as necessary to complete each skewer (see photograph on front jacket).

Brush the brochettes with the oil and grill them on an oiled rack set 5 to 6 inches over glowing coals, for 3 minutes on each side, or until the shrimp are just cooked through. Serves 2.

PHOTO ON FRONT JACKET

To Make Scallion Brushes

Trim the roots and the green parts from scallions, leaving about 3½ inches of stalk. Make crisscross cuts about 1 inch deep at both ends of each stalk and spread the cut ends gently. Put the scallions in a bowl, add ice water to cover, and chill the scallions for 1 hour, or until the fringed ends have curled like flower petals. Drain the scallions well.

Grilled Lemon Prawns

1 cup olive oil
1 tablespoon dried orégano, crumbled
1 tablespoon dried thyme, crumbled
2 teaspoons freshly grated lemon zest
2 teaspoons coarse salt
2 teaspoons freshly ground black pepper
24 prawns or jumbo shrimp
3 tablespoons fresh lemon juice
lemon wedges as an accompaniment

In a large bowl stir together the oil, the herbs, the zest, the salt, and the pepper, add the prawns, and toss them to coat them well. Let the prawns marinate, covered and chilled, for at least 1 hour or overnight. Stir in the lemon juice, let the mixture stand at room temperature for 30 minutes, and drain the prawns in a fine sieve.

Grill the herb-coated prawns on a rack set about 4 inches over glowing coals for 3 minutes on each side, or until they are cooked through. (Alternatively, the prawns may be broiled on the rack of a broiler pan under a preheated broiler about 4 inches from the heat for 4 minutes on each side.) Divide the prawns among 8 plates and serve them with the lemon wedges. Serves 8.

PHOTO ON PAGE 45

Shellfish Stew Provençale

1 large onion, chopped
2 pounds fennel bulb (sometimes called anise, available at most supermarkets), trimmed and sliced thin
1 red bell pepper, sliced thin lengthwise
¼ cup olive oil
the zest of 1 orange, removed in strips with a vegetable peeler
2 teaspoons minced fresh thyme leaves or 1 teaspoon dried, crumbled, plus thyme sprigs for garnish
1 bay leaf
¼ teaspoon cayenne
½ teaspoon crumbled saffron threads
2 cups dry white wine
4 cups white fish stock (recipe follows) or bottled clam juice
a 28- to 32-ounce can tomatoes, drained and chopped
2 large garlic cloves, minced
16 small shrimp, shelled and deveined
16 small hard-shelled clams, cleaned (procedure on page 129)
1 pound King crab legs, thawed, shelled, and the cartilage discarded
8 large sea scallops, halved, or 16 small sea scallops

In a kettle cook the onion, the fennel, and the bell pepper in the oil over moderate heat, stirring, until the vegetables are softened. Stir in the zest, the minced thyme, the bay leaf, the cayenne, and the saffron, cook the mixture, stirring, for 30 seconds, and add the wine, the stock, the tomatoes, and salt and pepper to taste. Simmer the mixture, uncovered, for 15 minutes, add the garlic, and simmer the mixture for 5 minutes. *The stew may be prepared up to this point 2 days in advance, cooled, uncovered, and kept covered and chilled.* Stir in the shrimp and the clams and simmer the mixture, covered, for 5 minutes. Add the crab legs and the scallops, simmer the stew, covered, for 3 minutes, or until the scallops are just cooked through and the clams are opened, and discard the bay leaf and any unopened clams. Divide the stew among 8 heated bowls and garnish it with the thyme sprigs. Serves 8.

PHOTO ON PAGE 14

White Fish Stock

2 pounds bones and trimmings of any
   white fish such as sole or whiting, chopped
2 cups sliced onion
24 long parsley sprigs
4 tablespoons fresh lemon juice
1 teaspoon salt
7 cups cold water
1 cup dry white wine

In a well-buttered heavy saucepan combine the fish bones and trimmings, the onion, the parsley, the lemon juice, and the salt and steam the mixture, covered, over moderately high heat for 5 minutes. Add the water and the wine, bring the liquid to a boil, skimming the froth, and simmer the stock for 20 minutes. Strain the stock through a fine sieve into a bowl, let it cool to warm, and chill it, covered. The stock keeps, covered and chilled, for 1 week if it is brought to a boil every 2 days and then allowed to cool to warm, uncovered, before being chilled again. The stock keeps, frozen, for 3 months. Makes about 6 cups.

To Clean Hard-Shelled Clams

Scrub the clams thoroughly with a stiff brush under cold water, discarding any that have cracked shells or that are not shut tightly.

MEAT

BEEF

Filets Mignons with Horseradish Crumbs

3 tablespoons fine dry bread crumbs
1½ tablespoons drained bottled horseradish
1 teaspoon Dijon-style mustard
½ tablespoon unsalted butter
1½ tablespoons vegetable oil
two 1½-inch-thick filets mignons
    (about ½ pound each)
1 small onion, sliced thin
¼ cup dry red wine

In a small heavy skillet cook the bread crumbs, the horseradish, and the mustard with salt and pepper to taste in the butter over moderate heat, stirring, until the crumbs are golden brown and transfer the horseradish crumbs to a bowl.

Wipe the skillet clean, in it heat the oil over moderately high heat until it is hot but not smoking, and in it sauté the filets, patted dry and seasoned with salt and pepper, for 1 minute on each side. Reduce the heat to moderately low and cook the filets for 5 minutes more on each side for medium-rare meat. Transfer the filets to plates and pour off the fat from the skillet. In the skillet cook the onion over moderate heat, stirring, until it is golden, add the wine, and boil the mixture, scraping up the brown bits, until the liquid is reduced to a glaze. Spoon the onion mixture over the filets and top the filets with the horseradish crumbs. Serves 2.

Filets Mignons with Mustard Port Sauce

2 tablespoons olive oil
four 5- to 6-ounce filets mignons
    (each about 1½ inches thick)
3 tablespoons minced shallot
⅓ cup Tawny Port
⅔ cup dry red wine

1 cup beef broth
1½ teaspoons Dijon-style mustard
a *beurre manié* made by kneading together
    1 tablespoon softened unsalted butter and
    1 tablespoon all-purpose flour
flat-leafed parsley sprigs for garnish
red onion *confit* (recipe follows) as an
    accompaniment

In a heavy skillet heat the oil over moderately high heat until it is hot but not smoking and in it brown the filets mignons, patted dry and seasoned with salt and pepper to taste, for 2 minutes on each side. Sauté the filets mignons, turning them on both sides and the edges, for 4 to 6 minutes more for medium-rare meat, transfer them to a cutting board, and let them stand, covered loosely with foil, while making the sauce.

In the fat remaining in the skillet cook the shallot over moderately low heat, stirring, until it is softened, add the Port and the red wine, and boil the mixture until it is reduced by two thirds. Add the broth, boil the mixture until it is reduced by half, and strain the mixture through a fine sieve into a small saucepan. Whisk in the mustard, bring the mixture to a boil, and add the *beurre manié*, a little at a time, whisking until the sauce is smooth. Simmer the sauce, whisking occasionally, for 2 minutes, whisk in any juices that have accumulated on the board, and season the sauce with salt and pepper.

Cut the filets mignons into ¼-inch-thick slices, divide the slices among 4 plates, and spoon the sauce over them. Garnish the filets mignons with the parsley and serve them with the red onion *confit*. Serves 4.

PHOTO ON PAGES 16 AND 17

Red Onion Confit

1 tablespoon minced garlic
¼ cup minced shallot
½ teaspoon dried thyme, crumbled
1 tablespoon olive oil

2½ cups thinly sliced red onion
¼ cup Tawny Port
½ cup dry red wine
1 teaspoon sugar, or to taste
1 tablespoon balsamic vinegar, or to taste
3 tablespoons minced fresh parsley leaves

In a heavy skillet cook the garlic and the shallot with the thyme and salt and pepper to taste in the oil over moderately low heat, stirring, until the shallot is softened. Add the red onion and cook the mixture, stirring, for 5 to 10 minutes, or until the onion is very soft. Add the Port, the red wine, the sugar, and the vinegar and simmer the mixture, uncovered, for 5 to 10 minutes, or until almost all the liquid is evaporated. Stir in the parsley and salt and pepper to taste and cook the mixture, stirring, for 1 minute. *The* confit *may be made 1 day in advance, kept covered and chilled, and reheated.* Makes about 1 cup.

PHOTO ON PAGE 17

Cold Roast Fillet of Beef
a trimmed 3- to 3½-pound fillet of beef, tied,
    at room temperature
parsley sprigs for garnish if desired
cucumber horseradish sauce and curried
    yogurt sauce (recipes follow) as
    accompaniments

Preheat the oven to 500° F. Pat dry the fillet and season it with salt and pepper. In an oiled roasting pan roast the fillet in the middle of the oven for 20 to 25 minutes, or until a meat thermometer registers 130° F. for medium-rare meat, and let it cool to room temperature. *The fillet may be roasted 2 days in advance and kept wrapped and chilled.* Slice the fillet crosswise, arrange it on a cutting board or platter, and garnish it with the parsley. Serve the beef with the sauces. Serves 8.

PHOTO ON PAGES 62 AND 63

Cucumber Horseradish Sauce
1 cucumber, peeled, seeded, and diced fine
    (about ¾ cup)
¾ cup sour cream
3 tablespoons drained bottled horseradish,
    or to taste
1 teaspoon white-wine vinegar, or to taste

2 teaspoons minced fresh tarragon leaves, or
    to taste, plus a tarragon sprig for garnish

In a bowl whisk together the cucumber, the sour cream, the horseradish, the vinegar, the minced tarragon, and salt and pepper to taste and chill the sauce, covered, for at least 2 hours and up to 1 day. Transfer the sauce to a serving dish and garnish it with the tarragon sprig. Makes about 1½ cups.

PHOTO ON PAGE 63

Curried Yogurt Sauce
¾ cup plain yogurt
2 tablespoons Major Grey's mango chutney
1 teaspoon fresh lime juice, or to taste
½ cup mayonnaise
1 tablespoon curry powder, or to taste
2 tablespoons minced red onion plus
    additional for garnish

In a blender or small food processor blend together ½ cup of the yogurt, the chutney, and the lime juice until the mixture is smooth, transfer the mixture to a bowl, and whisk in the remaining ¼ cup yogurt, the mayonnaise, the curry powder, the 2 tablespoons onion, and salt and pepper to taste. Chill the sauce, covered, for at least 8 hours and up to 3 days. Transfer the sauce to a serving dish and sprinkle it with the additional onion. Makes about 1½ cups.

PHOTO ON PAGE 63

Rib-Eye Steaks with Bell Pepper and Olives

1 tablespoon vegetable oil
two 1-inch-thick rib-eye steaks
1 large garlic clove, minced
1 small red bell pepper, chopped fine
½ cup Kalamata or other brine-cured black
    olives, pitted and chopped fine
1 tablespoon red-wine vinegar

In a heavy skillet heat the oil over moderately high heat until it is hot but not smoking and in it brown the steaks, patted dry and seasoned with salt and pepper, for 1 minute on each side. Reduce the heat to moderate, cook the steaks for 2 minutes more on each side for medium-rare meat, and transfer them to 2 plates.

In the fat remaining in the skillet cook the garlic over moderately low heat, stirring, for 30 seconds, or until it is fragrant, add the bell pepper, and cook the mixture, stirring occasionally, for 3 minutes, or until the bell pepper is softened. Stir in the olives, the vinegar, and salt and pepper to taste and cook the mixture, stirring, for 1 minute. Spoon the olive mixture over the steaks. Serves 2.

Sesame Beef and Scallion Kebabs

¼ cup soy sauce
2 garlic cloves, forced through a garlic press
1 tablespoon Asian (toasted) sesame oil
    (available at Asian markets and some
    specialty foods shops and supermarkets)
1 teaspoon minced fresh gingerroot
1½ tablespoons sugar
2 teaspoons wine vinegar
2 teaspoons sesame seeds
1 teaspoon black pepper
¾ pound boneless shell steak, cut into
    1-inch cubes
five 7-inch bamboo skewers
8 scallions, trimmed

In a small bowl whisk together the soy sauce, the garlic, the oil, the gingerroot, the sugar, the vinegar, the sesame seeds, and the pepper. Thread the steak cubes loosely onto 4 of the skewers and thread the remaining skewer crosswise through the middle of each scallion so that the scallions stand parallel to one another. Put the beef and scallion kebabs in a shallow dish just large enough to hold them, pour the marinade over them,

coating them well, and let the kebabs marinate, chilled, turning them frequently, for at least 25 minutes and up to 4 hours. Grill the kebabs on an oiled rack set about 6 inches over glowing coals, turning them, for 10 minutes. (Alternatively the kebabs may be broiled under a preheated broiler about 4 inches from the heat in the same manner.) Divide the beef and the scallions, both removed from the skewers, between 2 plates. Serves 2.

Grilled Skirt Steak with Coriander Garlic Sauce

½ cup minced fresh coriander (about 1 bunch)
2 garlic cloves, minced and mashed to a paste
    with ¼ teaspoon salt
¼ cup minced *pepperoncini* (about 8 whole
    with the stems discarded)
3 tablespoons olive oil
2 teaspoons fresh lemon juice
½ teaspoon freshly ground black pepper
a 1-pound skirt steak

In a small bowl combine the coriander, the garlic paste, the *pepperoncini*, the oil, the lemon juice, the pepper, and salt to taste. On a plate rub the steak with about half the sauce and let it marinate at room temperature for 15 minutes. Grill the steak on a rack set about 6 inches over glowing coals for 4 minutes on each side for medium-rare meat, transfer it to a cutting board, and cut it on the diagonal into thin slices. Serve the steak with the remaining sauce. Serves 2 generously.

Meatballs in Lemon Caper Sauce

3 tablespoons fresh white bread crumbs
1 large egg, beaten lightly
1 tablespoon minced onion
3 teaspoons drained bottled capers
6 ounces ground chuck
½ cup plus 1 teaspoon water
½ cup beef broth
2 teaspoons fresh lemon juice
1 bay leaf
a 2- by ½-inch strip of lemon zest, removed
    with a vegetable peeler, plus ¼ teaspoon
    grated lemon zest
½ teaspoon mixed pickling spice
1 teaspoon cornstarch
2 tablespoons sour cream
1 tablespoon chopped fresh parsley leaves

cooked egg noodles or rice as an
accompaniment if desired

In a bowl stir together the bread crumbs, the egg, the onion, 2 teaspoons of the capers, minced, and salt and pepper to taste, add the beef, and combine the mixture gently but thoroughly (do not overmix). Form the beef mixture into small meatballs, about 1 inch in diameter.

In a flameproof casserole just large enough to hold the meatballs in one layer simmer ½ cup of the water, the broth, and the lemon juice with the bay leaf, the zest strip, and the pickling spice, covered, for 10 minutes, add the meatballs, and cook them, covered, at a gentle simmer for 20 minutes. Transfer the meatballs with a slotted spoon to a plate and keep them warm. In a small bowl stir together the remaining 1 teaspoon water and the cornstarch, stir the cornstarch mixture into the broth mixture, and boil the sauce, stirring, until it is thickened. Remove the casserole from the heat and stir in the sour cream, the remaining 1 teaspoon capers, the grated zest, and 2 teaspoons of the parsley, stirring until the sauce is combined. Return the meatballs to the casserole and cook the mixture over low heat, stirring, for 1 minute. Discard the bay leaf and the zest strip and serve the meatballs and sauce, sprinkled with the remaining 1 teaspoon parsley, over the noodles. Serves 2.

Alexandra Schulz

Short Ribs with Rye Berries
1 cup rye berries (available at natural
foods stores)
2½ pounds boneless beef short ribs from the
chuck, cut into 3-inch sections
3 tablespoons olive oil

the white part of 4 small leeks, halved
lengthwise, sliced crosswise, washed well,
and drained (about 2 cups)
6 medium carrots, halved lengthwise and cut
on the diagonal into 1-inch slices
(about 2 cups)
4 outer ribs of celery, trimmed and sliced
thick on the diagonal (about 1½ cups)
6 garlic cloves
five 2½- by 1-inch strips of lemon zest,
removed with a vegetable peeler
1 bay leaf
a 14- to 16-ounce can tomatoes, drained
2 cups beef broth plus additional if desired
2 cups water
1 cup dry red wine
4 tablespoons minced fresh parsley leaves

In a kettle of boiling water cook the rye berries for 40 minutes and drain them. While the rye berries are cooking, arrange the ribs in one layer on the rack of a broiler pan, season them with salt and pepper, and broil them under a preheated broiler about 2 inches from the heat for 4 to 6 minutes on each side, or until they are browned.

Preheat the oven to 350° F. In a large flameproof casserole heat the oil over moderately high heat until it is hot but not smoking and in it sauté the leeks, the carrots, the celery, 4 of the garlic cloves, sliced thick, 3 strips of the zest, and the bay leaf, stirring occasionally, for 5 minutes, or until the vegetables are softened slightly. Stir in the rye berries, the tomatoes, 2 cups of the broth, the water, and the wine, add the ribs with their juices, making sure they are covered with the liquid, and bring the liquid to a boil. Cook the mixture, covered, in the oven, stirring every 30 minutes and adding the additional broth or water if necessary to keep the ribs covered with liquid, for 2 hours, or until the meat is tender. (The liquid should be simmering; reduce the temperature if it boils vigorously.) Simmer the mixture, uncovered, on top of the stove for 1 hour more, or until the sauce is thickened and the rye berries are cooked through. Discard the bay leaf and the lemon zest.

Mince together the remaining 2 strips zest and the remaining 2 garlic cloves, sliced thick, stir them into the rib mixture with 3 tablespoons of the parsley, and season the mixture with salt and pepper. Serve the mixture sprinkled with the remaining 1 tablespoon parsley. Serves 6.

Corned Beef and Coleslaw Sandwich

2 tablespoons white-wine vinegar
1½ tablespoons Dijon-style mustard plus
   additional for spreading on the bread
1½ tablespoons drained bottled horseradish
¼ cup olive oil
3 cups thinly sliced cabbage
1 cup thinly sliced red onion
1 cup coarsely grated carrots
a 16-inch-long loaf of Italian or French bread,
   halved horizontally with a serrated knife
½ pound thinly sliced corned beef

In a large bowl whisk together the vinegar, 1½ table-spoons of the mustard, the horseradish, and salt and pepper to taste, add the oil in a stream, whisking, and whisk the dressing until it is emulsified. Add the cabbage, the onion, and the carrots, toss the coleslaw well, and chill it, covered, overnight.

Spread the bread with the additional mustard, arrange the coleslaw and the corned beef on the bottom half of the bread, and fit the top half on the filled bottom, pressing the loaf together firmly. Quarter the sandwich with a serrated knife and wrap it tightly in plastic wrap. *The sandwich may be made 6 hours in advance and kept wrapped and chilled.* Serves 4.

PHOTO ON PAGE 59

VEAL

Veal Scallops with Mushrooms and Herbs

¼ cup finely chopped shallot
1 garlic clove, minced
½ teaspoon dried sage, crumbled
2½ tablespoons olive oil
¼ pound fresh *shiitake* mushrooms, stems
   discarded and the caps sliced
¼ pound white mushrooms, sliced
¾ cup dry white wine
½ pound veal scallops
   (each about ⅛ inch thick)
all-purpose flour seasoned with salt and
   pepper for dredging the veal
⅔ cup chicken broth
¼ cup heavy cream
2 tablespoons minced fresh parsley leaves
   (preferably flat-leafed)

In a heavy skillet cook the shallot, the garlic, and the sage in 1 tablespoon of the oil over moderately low heat, stirring, until the shallot is softened, add the mushrooms and salt and pepper to taste, and cook the mixture over moderate heat, stirring, until the mushrooms are tender and all the liquid they give off is evaporated. Add ¼ cup of the wine, simmer it until it is evaporated, and transfer the mixture to a bowl. Dredge the veal in the seasoned flour, shaking off the excess. In the skillet, cleaned, heat the remaining 1½ tablespoons oil over moderately high heat until it is hot but not smoking and in it sauté the veal for 1 minute on each side, or until it is golden. Transfer the veal to a platter and keep it warm.

Add the remaining ½ cup wine to the skillet and deglaze the skillet over moderately high heat, stirring and scraping up the brown bits, until the wine is reduced to a glaze. Add the broth, boil the liquid until it is reduced by half, and stir in the cream, the mushroom mixture, and salt and pepper to taste. Simmer the sauce until it is thickened slightly, stir in the parsley, and pour the sauce over the veal. Serves 2.

PORK

The following recipe has been designed to produce leftovers that can be used to make Indian-Style Red Curry with Pork (page 136).

Pork Tenderloin Roulade with Herb Filling

4 pork tenderloins (about 3 pounds total)
1½ cups minced fresh flat-leafed
   parsley leaves
⅔ cup minced fresh lovage or
   celery leaves
1 tablespoon minced fresh
   thyme leaves
4 garlic cloves, minced
1½ teaspoons minced fresh lemon zest,
   removed with a vegetable peeler
1 cup freshly grated Parmesan
2 tablespoons vegetable oil
1 cup chopped white part of scallion
⅓ cup dry white wine
1⅓ cups water
couscous with pecans and scallions (recipe
   follows) as an accompaniment

Preheat the oven to 350° F. Butterfly 2 of the pork tenderloins and flatten them, cut sides up, between 2 sheets of plastic wrap until they are about ⅓ inch thick. Overlap 2 of the long edges by 1 inch, flatten the tenderloins together to form an even thickness, and discard the top piece of plastic wrap. In a bowl stir together the herbs, the garlic, the zest, and the Parmesan and spread the mixture evenly on the pork, leaving a 1-inch border on the long edges. Using the plastic wrap as a guide and beginning with a long side, roll the pork up jelly-roll fashion and tie the *roulade* tightly at 1-inch intervals with kitchen string. Tuck under the tails of the 2 remaining tenderloins to form an even thickness.

In a skillet heat the oil over moderately high heat until it is hot but not smoking and in it brown the *roulade* and the tenderloins, patted dry and seasoned with salt and pepper, in batches, transferring them as they are browned to a roasting pan. Roast the *roulade* and the tenderloins in the middle of the oven for 30 minutes, or until the tenderloins register 160° F. on a meat thermometer. Transfer the tenderloins to a cutting board, let them cool completely, and reserve them, covered and chilled, up to 4 days, for making the pork curry (page 136). Roast the *roulade* for 10 minutes more, or until it registers 160° F. on the thermometer, transfer it to the cutting board, and let it stand, covered loosely, for 10 minutes.

Add the scallion to the roasting pan and cook it over moderate heat, stirring, until it is softened. Add the wine and deglaze the pan over high heat, scraping up the brown bits. Add the water, bring the gravy to a boil, and boil it until it is reduced to about 1 cup. Reserve ½ cup of the gravy for making the pork curry. Discard the strings from the *roulade* and slice the *roulade* into ½-inch-thick pieces. Spoon the gravy onto a platter, arrange the *roulade* on it, and serve it with the couscous. Serves 4 with leftovers for the pork curry.

Couscous with Pecans and Scallions

2¼ cups water
3 tablespoons vegetable oil
1½ cups couscous
½ cup pecans, toasted lightly
    and chopped
½ cup chopped scallion greens

In a heavy saucepan bring the water and the vegetable oil to a boil, stir in the couscous and salt and pepper to taste, and remove the pan from the heat. Let the couscous mixture stand, covered, for 5 minutes, fluff it with a fork, and stir in the pecans and the scallion greens. Serves 4.

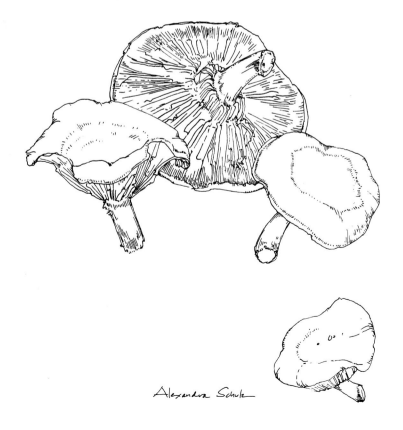

Alexandra Schultz

Indian-Style Red Curry with Pork

3 onions, sliced thin
2 tablespoons vegetable oil
1 tablespoon minced peeled fresh gingerroot
4 garlic cloves, minced and mashed to a paste
    with ½ teaspoon salt
1½ teaspoons ground cumin
1½ teaspoons ground coriander
1 tablespoon paprika
¼ teaspoon cayenne
2 small bay leaves
½ cup pork gravy (reserved from the pork
    tenderloin *roulade*, page 134)
¼ cup plain yogurt
1½ cups water
3 red bell peppers, cut into short strips
2 roasted pork tenderloins (reserved from the
    pork tenderloin *roulade*, page 134), cut
    into ¾-inch pieces
¼ cup minced fresh parsley leaves
spiced basmati rice (page 172) and sesame
    carrot salad (page 197) as accompaniments

In a large shallow flameproof casserole cook the onions in the oil over moderate heat, stirring, until they are
golden, add the gingerroot and the garlic paste, and
cook the mixture, stirring, for 30 seconds. Add the
spices and the bay leaves, cook the mixture, stirring, for
30 seconds, and stir in ¼ cup of the gravy. Add the yogurt, 1 tablespoon at a time, stirring after each addition
until it is incorporated, stir in the remaining ¼ cup gravy
and the water, and simmer the mixture, covered, for 5
minutes. Stir in the bell peppers, simmer the mixture,
covered, for 5 minutes, or until the bell peppers are
crisp-tender, and stir in the pork and salt and pepper
to taste. Simmer the mixture until the pork is heated
through, discard the bay leaves, and stir in the parsley.
Serve the pork curry with the basmati rice and the carrot
salad. Serves 4 to 6.

Pork Medallions with Spiced Tomato Pan Gravy

1½ tablespoons vegetable oil
1 pork tenderloin (about ¾ pound), cut
    crosswise into 1-inch-thick medallions
1 medium onion, chopped
1 garlic clove, minced
½ cup canned tomato purée
½ cup water

¼ teaspoon freshly grated nutmeg
½ teaspoon ground coriander
⅛ teaspoon ground cloves
buttered noodles as an accompaniment

In a large heavy skillet heat the oil over moderately
high heat until it is hot but not smoking and in it brown
the pork, patted dry, transferring it as it is browned to a
plate. In the fat remaining in the skillet cook the onion
and the garlic over moderate heat, stirring, until the onion is golden, add the tomato purée, the water, the nutmeg, the coriander, and the cloves, and simmer the
mixture for 10 minutes. Stir in the pork and any juices
that have accumulated on the plate and simmer the mixture, covered, for 5 minutes, or until the pork is cooked
through. Season the pan gravy with salt and pepper and
serve it with the pork over the noodles. Serves 2.

Grilled Pork Kebabs with Manchamantel Sauce
eight 12-inch bamboo skewers
1 dried *ancho* chili*, stemmed and seeded
  (wear rubber gloves)
1 cup water
4 garlic cloves, chopped
1 onion, chopped
1½ tablespoons ground cumin
2 tablespoons chopped fresh thyme leaves or
  2 teaspoons dried thyme, crumbled
2 tablespoons chopped fresh orégano leaves or
  2 teaspoons dried orégano, crumbled
2 teaspoons salt, or to taste
2 teaspoons black peppercorns,
  crushed
⅓ cup olive oil
⅓ cup fresh lemon juice
3 pork tenderloins (about 2¼ pounds), each
  trimmed and cut crosswise into 8 pieces
twenty-four 1-inch chunks of fresh pineapple
twenty-four 1-inch chunks of red onion
manchamantel sauce (recipe follows) as an
  accompaniment

*available at Hispanic markets, some
  specialty foods shops, and some
  supermarkets or by mail order from Los
  Chileros de Nueva Mexico, Santa Fe, NM
  87502, tel. (505) 471-6967 or Adriana's
  Bazaar, New York, NY 10023, tel.
  (212) 877-5757

Let the skewers soak in water to cover for 1 hour. Preheat the oven to 250° F. Toast the chili on a baking sheet in the middle of the oven for 5 minutes and transfer it to a heatproof bowl. Pour enough boiling water over the chili to cover, let the mixture stand for 30 minutes, and drain the chili. In a blender blend together the chili, the 1 cup water, the garlic, the onion, the cumin, the thyme, the orégano, the salt, the peppercorns, the oil, and the lemon juice until the marinade is smooth.

In a large heavy-duty resealable plastic bag combine the pork and the marinade and let the pork marinate, chilled, for at least 6 hours or overnight.

Drain the pork, pat it dry lightly, and thread each skewer loosely with 3 pieces of the pork, 3 chunks of the pineapple, and 3 chunks of the red onion. Grill or broil the kebabs on an oiled rack set about 4 to 5 inches from the heat for 8 to 10 minutes on each side, or until the

pork is cooked through but still slightly pink. Serve the kebabs with the *manchamantel* sauce. Makes 8 kebabs, serving 6 to 8.

PHOTO ON PAGE 26

Manchamantel Sauce
(Ancho Chili Fruit Sauce)

2 ounces dried *ancho* chilies* (about 5),
  stemmed and seeded (wear rubber gloves)
1 tablespoon minced garlic
1 cup finely chopped onion
3½ tablespoons vegetable oil
1 tablespoon sugar plus additional to taste
1½ tablespoons cider vinegar plus additional
  to taste
1 cup low-salt chicken broth
½ cup water
1 cup chopped fresh pineapple
¾ cup sliced banana (about 1 small banana)
½ teaspoon cinnamon
a pinch of ground cloves

*available at Hispanic markets, some
  specialty foods shops, and some
  supermarkets or by mail order from Los
  Chileros de Nueva Mexico, Santa Fe, NM
  87502, tel. (505) 471-6967 or Adriana's
  Bazaar, New York, NY 10023, tel.
  (212) 877-5757

Preheat the oven to 250° F. Toast the chilies on a baking sheet in the middle of the oven for 5 minutes and transfer them to a heatproof bowl. Pour enough boiling water over the chilies to cover, let the mixture stand for 30 minutes, and drain the chilies. In a heavy skillet cook the garlic, the onion, and salt and pepper to taste in 2 tablespoons of the oil over moderately low heat, stirring, until the onion is soft and pale golden, add 1 tablespoon of the sugar and 1½ tablespoons of the vinegar, and cook the mixture, stirring, for 1 minute. Transfer the onion mixture to a blender, add the chilies, the broth, the ½ cup water, the pineapple, the banana, the cinnamon, the cloves, the additional sugar and vinegar if desired, and salt and pepper to taste, and blend the sauce until it is very smooth. In the skillet heat the remaining 1½ tablespoons oil over moderately high heat until it is hot but not smoking, add the sauce, and simmer it, stirring, for 5 minutes. Makes about 3 cups.

Garlic Roast Pork

an 8- to 10-pound fresh ham (½ leg of pork)
6 garlic cloves, chopped coarse
2 tablespoons fresh orange juice
1 tablespoon vegetable oil
1 tablespoon wine vinegar
1 teaspoon salt
1 teaspoon black pepper
½ teaspoon dried orégano,
    crumbled
1 large onion, sliced
For the gravy
4 cups water
¼ cup all-purpose flour
⅓ cup fresh orange juice
2 tablespoons wine vinegar
2 tablespoons sugar

fresh flat-leafed parsley leaves for garnish
strips of orange zest for garnish

Preheat the oven to 350° F. With a sharp knife score the skin and fat of the ham deeply in a diamond pattern. In a blender purée the garlic with the orange juice, the oil, the vinegar, the salt, the pepper, and the orégano and rub the mixture all over the ham. Put the onion in the middle of a roasting pan, arrange a rack on top of it, and put the ham on the rack. Roast the ham in the oven for 4 hours, or until a meat thermometer registers 170° F., and let it stand in the pan at room temperature for 15 minutes. Transfer the ham to a carving board, pull off the cracklings (crisp pieces of skin), reserving them, and remove and discard the remaining fat. Slice the meat thin across the grain, arrange it on a platter, and keep it warm with the reserved cracklings, covered.

Make the gravy: Transfer 2 tablespoons of the fat from the roasting pan to a saucepan and pour off the remaining fat from the pan juices. Add the water to the roasting pan and deglaze the pan over high heat, scraping up the brown bits. Add the flour to the fat in the saucepan, cook the *roux* over low heat, whisking, for 2 minutes, and strain the mixture from the roasting pan through a sieve into the *roux*, pressing hard on the solids. Whisk in the orange juice, the vinegar, and the sugar, simmer the gravy, whisking, for 5 minutes, and season it with salt and pepper.

Serve the pork with the gravy and garnish it with the parsley and the zest. Serves 8.

PHOTO ON PAGE 33

Pork Chops in Beer Teriyaki Marinade

⅔ cup soy sauce
¼ cup *mirin* (syrupy rice wine, available at
    Asian markets and some supermarkets)
    or sweet Sherry
¼ cup cider vinegar
⅓ cup sugar
2 tablespoons chopped fresh gingerroot
⅔ cup beer (not dark)
six 1-inch-thick rib or loin pork chops

In a saucepan combine the soy sauce, the *mirin*, the vinegar, the sugar, the gingerroot, and the beer, simmer the mixture until it is reduced to about 1⅓ cups, and let the marinade cool until it is room temperature. In a shallow baking dish large enough to hold the pork chops in one layer combine the pork chops and the marinade, turning the chops to coat them thoroughly, and let the chops marinate, covered and chilled, turning them several times, overnight.

Pour the marinade into a saucepan and boil it for 5 minutes. Grill the pork chops on an oiled rack set about 4 inches over glowing coals, basting them with the marinade during the last 5 minutes of the cooking time, for 8 minutes on each side, or until they are just cooked through. Alternatively the pork chops may be broiled on the rack of a broiler pan under a preheated broiler in the same manner. Serves 6.

Grilled Pork Chops with Sour Cherry Sauce

3 tablespoons balsamic vinegar
3 tablespoons sugar
¾ cup dry red wine
¼ cup minced shallot
a 3-inch cinnamon stick
1 cup chicken broth
1 pound sour cherries (about 3 cups), pitted
1 tablespoon cornstarch dissolved in
    1 tablespoon cold water
2 teaspoons fresh lime juice,
    or to taste
eight 1-inch-thick boneless pork chops
vegetable oil for rubbing the chops

In a heavy saucepan boil the vinegar with the sugar over moderate heat until the mixture is reduced to a glaze. Add the wine, the shallot, and the cinnamon stick and boil the mixture until it is reduced to about ¼ cup.

138

Add the broth and the cherries and simmer the sauce for 5 minutes. Stir the cornstarch mixture, add enough of it to the sauce, stirring, to thicken the sauce to the desired consistency, and simmer the sauce for 2 minutes. Discard the cinnamon stick, stir in the lime juice and salt and pepper to taste, and keep the sauce warm, covered.

Pat the chops dry with paper towels, rub both sides of each chop with the oil, and season the chops with salt and pepper. Grill the chops on an oiled rack set 5 to 6 inches over glowing coals for 6 to 8 minutes on each side, or until they are just cooked through. Transfer the pork chops to a platter and spoon the sauce over them. Serves 8.

Spicy Pork with Bean-Thread Noodles
For marinating the pork
¾ pound ground pork
2 teaspoons rice vinegar
2 teaspoons soy sauce
1 teaspoon Asian (toasted) sesame oil*

6 ounces bean-thread (cellophane) noodles*
2 tablespoons vegetable oil
½ cup thinly sliced scallion
1 tablespoon minced garlic
1 tablespoon minced peeled fresh gingerroot
2 teaspoons Asian chili paste* or ½ teaspoon
   dried hot red pepper flakes
1½ cups chicken broth
3 tablespoons Scotch
1 tablespoon soy sauce
1 tablespoon rice vinegar
1 teaspoon sugar
1 teaspoon Asian (toasted) sesame oil
3 tablespoons chopped fresh coriander, or to
   taste, if desired

*available at Asian markets, some specialty
   foods shops and supermarkets, and by mail
   order from Adriana's Bazaar, (212) 877-5757

Marinate the pork: In a small bowl combine the pork gently with the rice vinegar, the soy sauce, and the sesame oil and let it marinate at room temperature for 20 minutes.

In a bowl soak the noodles in warm water to cover for 15 minutes, drain them, and cut them into 3- to 4-inch lengths.

In a wok or large heavy skillet heat the vegetable oil over moderately high heat until it just begins to smoke and in it stir-fry ¼ cup of the scallion, the garlic, and the gingerroot for 30 seconds. Add the pork and the chili paste and stir-fry the mixture, breaking up the lumps, until the meat is no longer pink. Add the noodles, the broth, the Scotch, the soy sauce, the vinegar, and the sugar and simmer the mixture, stirring occasionally, for 3 to 5 minutes, or until the noodles have absorbed the liquid. Transfer the mixture to a platter, drizzle it with the sesame oil, and sprinkle it with the coriander and the remaining ¼ cup scallion. Serves 4 to 6.

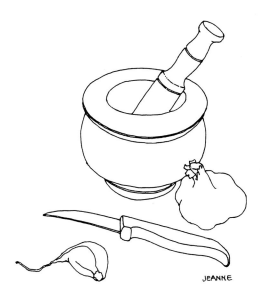

JEANNE

Prosciutto, Münster, and
Cumin Corn-Bread Sandwiches

1 recipe cumin corn bread (page 140), cooled
   to room temperature
3 tablespoons honey mustard*
½ pound thinly sliced prosciutto*
½ pound thinly sliced Münster

*available at specialty foods shops and
   some supermarkets

Cut the corn bread in half and cut each half crosswise into 4 pieces (each about 4 by 2 inches). Halve each piece horizontally with a serrated knife and spread the bottom halves of the corn bread with some of the mustard. Layer the bottom halves with the prosciutto and the Münster and cover the sandwiches with the top halves of the corn bread. Makes 8 sandwiches.

PHOTO ON PAGE 23

Cumin Corn Bread

¾ cup all-purpose flour
1 cup yellow cornmeal
1 tablespoon sugar
1½ teaspoons double-acting baking powder
½ teaspoon salt
1 cup milk
1 large egg, beaten lightly
1 tablespoon unsalted butter, melted and
    cooled
2 teaspoons cuminseed

Preheat the oven to 425° F. In a bowl stir together the flour, the cornmeal, the sugar, the baking powder, and the salt, add the milk, the egg, the butter, and the cuminseed, and stir the mixture until it is combined. Spread the batter in an even layer in a greased 8-inch-square baking pan, bake the corn bread in the middle of the oven for 20 to 25 minutes, or until it pulls away from the sides of the pan and the top is golden, and invert it onto a cutting board.

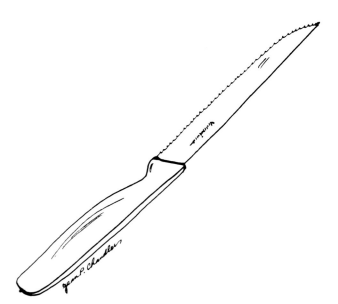

LAMB

Roast Rack of Lamb

1 teaspoon vegetable oil
two 1¼-pound trimmed and frenched racks of
    lamb (each with 7 or 8 ribs)
herbed tomato chutney (recipe follows) as an
    accompaniment

Preheat the oven to 450° F. In a heavy skillet heat the oil over moderately high heat until it is hot and in it brown the racks of lamb, seasoned with salt and pepper, 1 at a time, turning them, for 3 to 4 minutes, or until all sides are browned evenly. Transfer the racks as they are browned to a roasting pan, fat and meat side up, and roast them in the middle of the oven for 15 to 20 minutes, or until a meat thermometer registers 130° F. for medium-rare meat. Transfer the lamb to a cutting board, let it stand, uncovered, for 10 minutes, and slice it into chops. Divide the chops among 4 heated plates and spoon dollops of the chutney on each plate. Serves 4.

Herbed Tomato Chutney

1½ pounds plum tomatoes, peeled, seeded,
    and quartered
1½ cups chopped onion
⅓ cup sugar
⅓ cup white-wine vinegar
a 1-inch piece of peeled fresh gingerroot,
    minced
1 bottled pickled *jalapeño*, seeded and
    chopped fine (wear rubber gloves)
1 teaspoon coriander seeds
1 teaspoon mustard seeds
¾ teaspoon salt
1 tablespoon chopped fresh rosemary leaves
    or ¼ cup shredded fresh mint leaves

In a heavy saucepan toss together gently the tomatoes, the onion, and the sugar and let the mixture stand for 2 hours.

Stir in the vinegar, the gingerroot, the *jalapeño*, the coriander seeds, the mustard seeds, and the salt and simmer the mixture for 10 minutes. Transfer the solids with a slotted spoon to a bowl, pouring any accumulated liquid back into the pan, and boil the liquid until it is reduced to about ½ cup. Stir in the rosemary or the mint and pour the liquid over the tomato mixture. Stir the chutney gently and chill it, covered, for 2 hours, or until it is cold. *The chutney may be made 5 days in advance and kept covered and chilled.* Serve the chutney chilled or at room temperature. Makes about 2 cups.

The following recipe has been designed to produce leftovers that can be used to make Lamb-Stuffed Cabbage (page 142).

Herbed Roast Leg of Lamb

2½ pounds (about 15) plum tomatoes,
    sliced thick
10 ounces mushrooms, quartered
1 red bell pepper, chopped
1 yellow onion, halved, with the skin left on
2 shallots with the skin intact
2 heads of garlic, the outer skin removed,
    leaving the cloves attached at the root end
¼ pound red pearl onions (available at
    specialty produce markets) or white pearl
    onions, blanched in boiling water for
    3 minutes, drained, and peeled
2 fresh rosemary sprigs
2 fresh orégano sprigs
2 fresh thyme sprigs
6 tablespoons olive oil
a 6-pound leg of lamb, trimmed of excess fat
mixed baby vegetables (recipe follows) as an
    accompaniment
fresh mint sprigs for garnish

Preheat the oven to 450° F. In a large roasting pan stir together the tomatoes, the mushrooms, the bell pepper, the yellow onion, the shallots, the garlic, the pearl onions, the rosemary, orégano, and thyme sprigs, ¼ cup of the oil, and salt and pepper to taste. Arrange the lamb, patted dry, on top of the vegetable mixture, drizzle it with the remaining 2 tablespoons oil, and season it with salt and pepper. Roast the lamb and the vegetables in the middle of the oven for 15 minutes, reduce the temperature to 350° F., and roast the lamb and the vegetables, basting the lamb and stirring the vegetables every 20 minutes, for 1 hour and 20 minutes more, or until the lamb registers 145° F. on a meat thermometer for medium-rare meat.

Transfer the lamb to a cutting board and let it stand, covered loosely with foil, for 15 minutes. Reserve the pearl onions for the mixed baby vegetables (recipe follows). If planning to make the stuffed cabbage (page 142), reserve the yellow onion, the shallots, and the garlic in one bowl and the tomatoes, the bell pepper, and the mushrooms, discarding the herbs, in another bowl, both mixtures covered and chilled. Transfer the lamb to a platter, spoon the baby vegetables around it, and garnish the lamb with the mint sprigs. If planning to make the stuffed cabbage (page 142), reserve 1 pound of the lamb. Serves 4 (or 6 to 8 if not reserving lamb for the stuffed cabbage).

Mixed Baby Vegetables

¼ pound baby zucchini and/or baby
    yellow squash*
¼ pound baby yellow and/or green
    pattypan squash*
6 ounces baby carrots,
    trimmed and peeled
¼ pound *haricots verts** (thin green beans),
    trimmed
1 small potato (about ¼ pound)
1 tablespoon olive oil
the pearl onions reserved from the herbed
    roast leg of lamb (preceding recipe)
1 tablespoon minced fresh dill and/or mint
    leaves, or to taste

*available at specialty produce markets

In a kettle of boiling salted water cook separately the zucchini, the pattypan squash, the carrots, and the *haricots verts* until each vegetable is crisp-tender and cook the potato, peeled and cut into ½-inch dice, until it is cooked through, transferring the vegetables as they are cooked with a slotted spoon to a bowl of ice and cold water to stop the cooking. Drain the vegetables and pat them dry. *The vegetables may be prepared up to this point 1 day in advance and kept covered and chilled.*

In a large skillet heat the oil over moderately high heat until it is hot but not smoking and in it sauté the zucchini, the pattypan squash, the carrots, the *haricots verts*, and the onions for 3 minutes, or until they are heated through. Stir in the potato, the herbs, and salt and pepper to taste and sauté the mixture for 1 minute. Serves 4.

Lamb-Stuffed Cabbage

the tomato mixture reserved from the herbed
    roast leg of lamb (page 141)
6 large outer leaves from a head of Savoy
    cabbage, reserving the remaining
    cabbage for another use
6 tablespoons olive oil
2 cups finely chopped peeled eggplant
1 pound lamb reserved from the herbed roast
    leg of lamb (page 141), chopped fine
2 tablespoons dry red wine
the yellow onion mixture reserved from the
    herbed roast leg of lamb (page 141), peeled
    and chopped fine
¼ cup minced fresh parsley leaves
2 tablespoons minced fresh dill
¼ teaspoon cinnamon
⅛ teaspoon ground allspice
1½ cups fresh bread crumbs
2 large eggs, beaten lightly

Strain the tomato mixture in a sieve set over a bowl, reserve the liquid, and in a food processor purée the solids. In a kettle of boiling salted water blanch the cabbage leaves in batches for 1 to 2 minutes, or until they are softened slightly but are still bright green, transferring them as they are blanched with a slotted spoon to a bowl of ice and cold water to stop the cooking. Remove the cabbage leaves from the ice water and pat them dry.

In a large heavy skillet heat 4 tablespoons of the oil over moderately high heat until it is hot but not smoking, in it sauté the eggplant, stirring, for 3 minutes, or until it is browned, and transfer it with the slotted spoon to paper towels to drain. In the skillet heat the remaining 2 tablespoons oil until it is hot but not smoking and in it sauté the lamb, stirring, for 2 to 3 minutes, or until it is no longer pink. Add the wine and cook the mixture for 1 to 2 minutes, or until the liquid is evaporated. Stir in 1 cup of the tomato purée, the yellow onion mixture, the eggplant, the parsley, the dill, the cinnamon, and the allspice and cook the mixture for 2 minutes. Transfer the mixture to a bowl, let it cool, and stir in the bread crumbs, the eggs, and salt and pepper to taste.

Preheat the oven to 350° F. Arrange 1 of the blanched cabbage leaves on the bottom of an oiled 1½-quart charlotte mold and line the side of the mold with 3 or 4 of the blanched leaves, overlapping the leaves slightly. Fill the cabbage-lined mold with the lamb mixture, smoothing the top, and top the mixture with another blanched cabbage leaf. Bake the stuffed cabbage in the middle of the oven for 1 hour, or until it is firm to the touch.

While the stuffed cabbage is baking, force the remaining tomato purée through a fine sieve into a small saucepan, stir in enough of the reserved tomato liquid to make a thick sauce, and heat the sauce over moderate heat until it is warm. Serve the stuffed cabbage, cut into wedges, with the sauce. Serves 4 to 6.

Grilled Chili-Rubbed Lamb Chops

3 tablespoons medium-hot pure chili powder*
1 tablespoon ground cumin
2 teaspoons dried thyme, crumbled
2 teaspoons sugar
1½ teaspoons salt
¾ teaspoon ground allspice
1 teaspoon freshly ground black pepper
16 rib lamb chops (each about 1½ inches
    thick), trimmed of excess fat
about 2 cups hot pepper jelly (recipe follows,
    or available at specialty foods shops and
    some supermarkets) as an accompaniment

*available at some specialty foods shops and
    by mail order from Los Chileros de Nuevo
    Mexico, P.O. Box 6215, Santa Fe, NM
    87502, tel. (505) 471-6967, or Adriana's
    Bazaar, 2152 Broadway, New York, NY
    10023, tel. (212) 877-5757

In a small bowl stir together the chili powder, the cumin, the thyme, the sugar, the salt, the allspice, and the black pepper. Sprinkle the spice mixture over the chops, rub it evenly all over the meat, and chill the chops, covered, for at least 4 hours or overnight.

Prepare a grill with glowing coals or preheat the broiler. On the oiled rack of the grill or on a broiler pan in the broiler grill or broil the chops 4 inches from the heat for 5 to 7 minutes on each side for medium-rare meat. Serve the chops with the pepper jelly. Serves 8.

PHOTO ON PAGE 34

Hot Pepper Jelly

1 pound red bell peppers
½ pound green bell peppers
6½ cups sugar
1½ cups cider vinegar

2 teaspoons dried hot red pepper flakes
9 ounces liquid pectin

Cut the bell peppers into 1-inch pieces and in a food processor chop them very fine. Transfer the chopped peppers to a deep kettle, add the sugar, the vinegar, and the red pepper flakes, and bring the mixture to a boil, stirring until the sugar is dissolved. Stir in the pectin and boil the mixture over moderately high heat, stirring, until it reaches the jelly stage (222° F. on a candy thermometer). Transfer the jelly to sterilized Mason-type jars (sterilizing procedure follows), filling the jars to within ¼ inch of the tops, wipe the rims with a dampened towel, and seal the jars. The jelly keeps, sealed, in a cool dark place indefinitely. Serve the jelly as a condiment with grilled meats or with cream cheese on crackers. Makes about 7 cups.

To Sterilize Jars and Glasses for Pickling and Preserving

Wash the jars in hot suds and rinse them in scalding water. Put the jars in a kettle and cover them with hot water. Bring the water to a boil, covered, and boil the jars for 15 minutes from the time that steam emerges from the kettle. Turn off the heat and let the jars stand in the hot water. Just before they are to be filled invert the jars onto a kitchen towel to dry. (The jars should be filled while they are still hot.) Sterilize the jar lids for 5 minutes, or according to the manufacturer's instructions.

Garlic Rosemary-Marinated Lamb Chops

1 teaspoon finely chopped lemon zest
1 garlic clove, minced and mashed to a paste
    with ½ teaspoon salt
1½ teaspoons chopped fresh rosemary or
    ½ teaspoon dried, crumbled
1 tablespoon olive oil
four 1¼-inch-thick loin lamb chops

In a small bowl stir together the zest, the garlic paste, the rosemary, the oil, and pepper to taste, rub the chops with the marinade, and let them marinate on a plate for 20 minutes. Preheat the broiler and broil the lamb chops on the rack of a broiler pan about 4 inches from the heat for 4 to 5 minutes on each side for medium-rare meat. Serves 2.

Alexandra Schulz

Lamb Chops with Mushroom Wine Sauce

1 tablespoon olive oil
two ½-inch-thick lamb shoulder chops
    (about 1 pound total), patted dry
2 large garlic cloves, minced
½ small onion, chopped fine (about ¼ cup)
¼ pound mushrooms, sliced
1 tablespoon soy sauce
1 tablespoon red-wine vinegar
½ cup dry red wine
¼ teaspoon dried thyme, crumbled
1 teaspoon cornstarch dissolved in
    ½ cup water
1 tablespoon minced fresh parsley leaves

In a skillet heat the oil over moderately high heat until it is hot but not smoking and in it sauté the chops, seasoned with salt and pepper, flattening them occasionally with a metal spatula, for 4 minutes on each side for medium meat. Transfer the chops with a slotted spatula to a small platter and keep them warm, covered loosely with foil.

Pour off all but 1 tablespoon of the fat and in the remaining fat cook the garlic over moderate heat, stirring, until it is pale golden. Add the onion and cook the mixture, stirring, for 1 minute. Add the mushrooms and the soy sauce and cook the mixture over moderately high heat, stirring, until the liquid the mushrooms give off is evaporated. Add the vinegar and boil the mixture until the liquid is evaporated. Add the wine and the thyme and boil the mixture until almost all the liquid is evaporated. Stir the cornstarch mixture, add it to the skillet, and bring the sauce to a boil, stirring. Season the sauce with salt and pepper, spoon it over the chops, and sprinkle the chops with the parsley. Serves 2.

OTHER MEATS

Herbed Oxtail Terrine

For the terrine

5 pounds meaty oxtails, trimmed of excess fat
¼ cup vegetable oil
9 cups beef broth
1½ cups dry red wine
a 14- to 16-ounce can tomatoes including
   the juice
2 onions, chopped coarse
2 carrots, chopped coarse
4 garlic cloves, crushed
1 bay leaf
1⅓ cups chopped scallion
½ cup minced fresh parsley leaves
3 tablespoons fresh lemon juice
½ teaspoon black pepper

For the sauce

⅓ cup sour cream
¼ cup mayonnaise
2 tablespoons drained bottled capers,
   chopped
1 tablespoon Dijon-style mustard
2 teaspoons drained bottled horseradish,
   or to taste

soft-leafed lettuce for lining the plates
bottled pickled onions and *cornichons* (French
   sour gherkins, available at specialty foods
   shops and some supermarkets) for garnish

Make the terrine: Preheat the oven to 325° F. Pat the oxtails dry, season them with salt and pepper, and in a heavy kettle brown them in batches in the oil over moderately high heat, transferring them as they are browned to a platter or shallow baking pan. To the kettle add the broth, the wine, the tomatoes with the juice, the onions, the carrots, the garlic, the bay leaf, and the oxtails with any juices that have accumulated on the platter, bring the liquid to a boil, and braise the oxtails, covered, in the middle of the oven for 4 hours. Transfer the oxtails with a slotted spoon to a bowl, reserving the liquid, let them cool, and remove the meat, discarding the bones and fat. Strain the reserved cooking liquid through a sieve into a large bowl. In another large bowl stir together the meat, the scallion, the parsley, the lemon juice, the pepper, and 2 cups of the cooking liquid until the mixture is combined well, reserving the remaining cooking liquid. Rinse a loaf pan, 9 by 5 by 3 inches, with cold water (do not dry it), spoon the oxtail mixture into it, and add some of the reserved cooking liquid if necessary to just cover the oxtail mixture. Chill the terrine, covered, for 4 hours, or until it is set. *The terrine may be prepared up to this point 2 days in advance and kept covered and chilled.* Let the terrine stand at room temperature for 20 minutes. Run a thin knife around the edge of the terrine to loosen it, dip the pan in hot water for 20 seconds, and invert a chilled platter over it. Invert the terrine with a sharp rap onto the platter and with an electric knife or a very sharp knife cut it into ½-inch-thick slices.

Make the sauce: In a bowl whisk together the sour cream, the mayonnaise, the capers, the mustard, and the horseradish until the sauce is combined well.

Line each of 8 plates with some of the lettuce, arrange a slice of the terrine on the lettuce, and spoon a dollop of the sauce over a corner of the slice. Garnish each serving with some of the pickled onions and *cornichons* and serve the remaining sauce separately. Serves 8 generously.

Roasted Rack of Venison and Shallots with Dried-Cranberry Gravy

an 8- to 11-rib (3- to 4-pound) rack of
   farm-raised venison*, halved to form
   two 4- to 6-rib racks or a 2½-pound beef fillet
2 pounds shallots, trimmed and peeled
2 tablespoons vegetable oil plus additional for
   rubbing the venison
½ cup beef broth
½ cup red wine
½ cup water
1 tablespoon juniper berries (available in
   the spice section of supermarkets),
   crushed lightly
2 teaspoons cornstarch dissolved in
   2 tablespoons water
⅓ cup dried cranberries (available at specialty
   foods shops)
1 tablespoon balsamic vinegar

*available by mail order from D'Artagnan,
   tel. (800) 327-8246 or, in New Jersey,
   (210) 792-0748; and from Specialty World
   Foods, tel. (800) 233-0193

Preheat the oven to 425° F. In a roasting pan large enough to hold the venison racks without crowding them, toss the shallots with 2 tablespoons of the vegetable oil and salt and pepper to taste and roast them in the middle of the oven, stirring occasionally, for 25 to 30 minutes, or until they are golden. Pat the venison dry, season it with salt and pepper, and rub it generously with the additional vegetable oil. Heat a large heavy skillet over high heat until it is hot and in it sear the venison on all sides. Push the shallots to the sides of the roasting pan, stand the venison racks in the middle of the pan, allowing the bones to rest together, and roast the mixture in the middle of the oven for 23 minutes or until a meat thermometer registers 125° F. for rare meat. Transfer the racks with the shallots to a platter and let them stand, covered loosely with foil, for 15 minutes. To the roasting pan add the beef broth, the red wine, the water, and the juniper berries and simmer the mixture, scraping up the brown bits, for 5 minutes. Strain the mixture through a fine sieve set over a small saucepan, whisk the cornstarch mixture, and add it to the saucepan with the cranberries, the balsamic vinegar, and salt and pepper to taste. Simmer the gravy, whisking, for 5 minutes. Cut the venison into individual chops and serve it with the shallots and the gravy. Serves 6.

PHOTO ON PAGE 80

POULTRY

CHICKEN

Chicken with Whole-Oat Stuffing

1¼ cups whole oats (sometimes called oat
    groats, available at natural foods stores)
4 shallots, minced
1 cup finely diced fennel bulb (sometimes
    called anise, available at most
    supermarkets)
1 stick (½ cup) unsalted butter, softened
1 cup finely diced scrubbed zucchini
1 cup finely diced mushroom caps
¼ cup heavy cream
2 tablespoons finely chopped fresh chives
2 tablespoons minced fresh parsley leaves
a pinch of dried tarragon, crumbled
a pinch of freshly grated lemon zest
a 5-pound roasting chicken, giblets reserved
    for another use

In a kettle of boiling water cook the whole oats for 30 minutes and drain them. While the oats are cooking, in a skillet cook the shallots and the fennel in 2 tablespoons of the butter over moderate heat, stirring, until the vegetables are softened, add the zucchini and the mushrooms, and sauté the mixture over moderately high heat, stirring, until the zucchini and mushrooms are softened. Stir in the cooked oats, the cream, the chives, the parsley, the tarragon, the zest, and salt and pepper to taste and remove the skillet from the heat.

Preheat the oven to 450° F. Rinse the chicken and pat it dry completely. Pack the cavity with some of the stuffing and transfer the remaining stuffing to a small baking dish. Truss the chicken, rub it all over with 4 tablespoons of the remaining butter, and season it with salt and pepper. Arrange the chicken, breast side down, on a rack set in a shallow roasting pan and roast it in the lower third of the oven for 50 minutes. Turn the chicken breast side up, baste it with the remaining 2 tablespoons butter, melted, and the pan juices, and roast it for 20

minutes more, or until a meat thermometer inserted in the fleshy part of a thigh registers 180° F. During the last 30 minutes of roasting, cook the remaining stuffing, covered with foil, in the 450° F. oven. Let the chicken stand for 10 minutes before carving. Serve the chicken with the stuffing. Serves 6.

Cornmeal-Crusted Oven-Fried Chicken

¾ cup buttermilk
1 teaspoon freshly grated lemon zest
⅓ cup fresh lemon juice
¼ cup olive oil
2 shallots, minced
1 tablespoon fresh thyme leaves
2 teaspoons salt
1½ teaspoons cayenne
a 3-pound chicken, cut into 8 pieces
¾ cup yellow cornmeal
½ cup fine dry bread crumbs
¼ cup freshly grated Parmesan
2 tablespoons minced fresh parsley leaves
½ teaspoon paprika
an egg wash made by beating 2 large eggs
    with 2 tablespoons cold water and
    1 tablespoon fresh lemon juice
3 tablespoons unsalted butter, melted

In a large bowl whisk together the buttermilk, the zest, the lemon juice, the oil, the shallots, the thyme, 1 teaspoon of the salt, and 1 teaspoon of the cayenne, add the chicken, stirring to coat it with the marinade, and let it marinate, covered and chilled, stirring occasionally, for 3 hours or overnight.

Preheat the oven to 425° F. In another large bowl combine the cornmeal, the bread crumbs, the Parmesan, the parsley, the remaining 1 teaspoon salt, the paprika, and the remaining ½ teaspoon cayenne. Remove the chicken from the marinade with a slotted spoon, letting the excess marinade drip off, dip it in the egg wash, and dredge it in the cornmeal mixture, shaking off the excess. Arrange the chicken in one layer on a rack and let it dry for 30 minutes. *The chicken may be prepared up to this point 6 hours in advance and kept covered loosely and chilled.* Arrange the chicken, skin side up, in one layer on a lightly oiled jelly-roll pan, drizzling the butter over it, and bake it in the middle of the oven for 35 minutes, or until it is crisp and golden. Transfer the chicken to paper towels to drain. Serve the chicken warm or at room temperature. Serves 4 to 6.

PHOTO ON PAGES 64 AND 65

Jerk Chicken
(Grilled Spicy Marinated Chicken)

For the marinade
2 cups finely chopped scallion
2 Scotch bonnet or *habañero* chilies, seeded
    and minced (wear rubber gloves), or
    1 tablespoon Scotch Bonnet Pepper Sauce*
    plus, if desired, additional Scotch bonnet
    chilies for garnish
2 tablespoons soy sauce
2 tablespoons fresh lime juice
5 teaspoons ground allspice
3 teaspoons English-style dry mustard
2 bay leaves, center ribs discarded and the
    leaves crumbled
2 garlic cloves, chopped
1 tablespoon salt
2 teaspoons sugar
1½ teaspoons dried thyme, crumbled
1 teaspoon cinnamon

5 pounds chicken parts, the wing tips
    discarded
vegetable oil for brushing the grill

*available by mail order from Mo Hotta–Mo Betta, P.O. Box 4136, San Luis Obispo, CA 93403, tel. (800) 462-3220

Make the marinade: In a food processor or blender purée the scallion, the chilies, the soy sauce, the lime juice, the allspice, the mustard, the bay leaves, the garlic, the salt, the sugar, the thyme, and the cinnamon.

Divide the chicken parts between 2 heavy-duty resealable plastic bags and spoon the marinade over them, coating them well. Seal the bags, pressing out the excess air, and let the chicken marinate, chilled, turning the bags over several times, for at least 24 hours and up to 2 days.

On an oiled rack set 4 to 6 inches over glowing coals grill the chicken, in batches if necessary and covered if possible, for 10 to 15 minutes on each side, or until it is cooked through. Transfer the chicken as it is cooked with tongs to a heated platter, keep it warm, covered loosely with foil, and garnish the platter with the additional chilies. Serves 10 as part of a buffet.

PHOTO ON PAGES 20 AND 21

per to taste until the mixture is smooth, transfer the mixture to a bowl, and stir in the remaining tomatoes, the cucumber, the bell pepper, the onion, and the coriander or parsley.

Brush the chicken with the additional oil, season it with salt and pepper to taste, and grill it on a rack set 5 to 6 inches over glowing coals, or in a hot well-seasoned ridged grill pan, covered, over moderately high heat, for 5 minutes on each side, or until it is cooked through. Cut the chicken on the diagonal into ¼-inch-thick slices and serve it with the *salsa*. Serves 2.

Braised Chicken with Mushrooms and
Sun-Dried Tomatoes

⅓ cup thinly sliced drained sun-dried
   tomatoes packed in oil, reserving
   1½ tablespoons of the oil
1 large whole chicken breast with skin and
   bones (about 1¼ pounds), halved
1 small onion, chopped fine
2 large garlic cloves, minced
½ teaspoon dried basil, crumbled
¼ teaspoon dried hot red pepper flakes,
   or to taste
½ pound mushrooms, sliced
½ cup dry red wine
½ cup chicken broth
2 tablespoons tomato paste
a *beurre manié* made by kneading together
   1½ teaspoons softened unsalted butter and
   1½ teaspoons all-purpose flour
3 tablespoons minced fresh parsley leaves
   (preferably flat-leafed)

In a heavy skillet heat the reserved tomato oil over moderately high heat until it is hot but not smoking, in it brown the chicken, patted dry and seasoned with salt and pepper, and transfer it to a plate. In the fat remaining in the skillet cook the onion, the garlic, the basil, and the red pepper flakes over moderately low heat, stirring, until the onion is softened. Add the mushrooms and salt and pepper to taste and cook the mixture over moderate heat, stirring, until the mushrooms are softened. Whisk in the wine, the broth, and the tomato paste, add the chicken to the skillet, and bring the liquid to a boil. Simmer the mixture, covered, for 15 to 20 minutes, or until the chicken is cooked through. Transfer the chicken to a platter and keep it warm, covered.

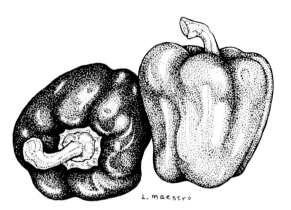

L. maestro

Grilled Chicken Breasts with Gazpacho Salsa

1 garlic clove, minced and mashed to a paste
   with ¼ teaspoon salt
1 tablespoon red-wine vinegar
2 tablespoons olive oil plus additional for
   brushing the chicken
2 tablespoons water
¼ teaspoon ground cumin, or to taste
Tabasco to taste
1 slice of homemade-type white bread, torn
   into pieces
2 plum tomatoes, seeded and chopped fine
½ cup finely chopped seeded peeled cucumber
⅓ cup finely chopped green bell pepper
¼ cup finely chopped red onion
2 tablespoons finely chopped fresh coriander
   or parsley leaves, or to taste
1 whole boneless chicken breast with skin
   (about 1 pound), halved

In a blender blend together the garlic paste, the vinegar, 2 tablespoons of the oil, the water, the cumin, the Tabasco, the bread, half the tomatoes, and salt and pep-

Whisk the *beurre manié* into the sauce, whisking until the sauce is smooth, add the sun-dried tomatoes, and simmer the sauce, whisking, for 2 to 3 minutes, or until it is thickened. Stir in the parsley and pour the sauce over the chicken. Serves 2.

Stir-Fried Chicken with Yellow Peppers and Snow Peas

1 tablespoon plus 1 teaspoon cornstarch
2 tablespoons plus 1½ teaspoons soy sauce
2 tablespoons plus 2 teaspoons rice vinegar*
1½ teaspoons Asian (toasted) sesame oil*
⅓ cup plus 1 tablespoon water
1 whole skinless boneless chicken
    breast (about ¾ pound), cut into
    ¾-inch-thick pieces
1½ teaspoons sugar
1½ teaspoons salt
⅓ cup chicken broth
½ cup vegetable oil
1 tablespoon minced scallion
2 teaspoons minced garlic
1½ teaspoons minced peeled fresh gingerroot
1 small yellow bell pepper, cut into thin strips
¼ pound snow peas, trimmed and
    halved crosswise
cooked rice as an accompaniment

*available at Asian markets and some
    specialty foods shops and supermarkets

In a bowl stir together 1 teaspoon of the cornstarch, 1½ teaspoons of the soy sauce, 2 teaspoons of the vinegar, ½ teaspoon of the sesame oil, and 1 tablespoon of the water until the cornstarch is dissolved, add the chicken, and let it marinate for 15 minutes. In a small bowl stir together the remaining 1 tablespoon cornstarch, 2 tablespoons soy sauce, 2 tablespoons vinegar, 1 teaspoon sesame oil, and ⅓ cup water with the sugar, the salt, and the broth until the cornstarch is dissolved and reserve the mixture. In a wok or large heavy skillet heat the vegetable oil over moderately high heat until it is hot but not smoking, in it stir-fry the chicken mixture until the chicken is opaque and just cooked through, and transfer the chicken with a slotted spoon to a sieve set over a bowl. Discard all but about 2 tablespoons of the oil remaining in the wok and in it stir-fry the scallion, the garlic, and the gingerroot for 10 seconds, or until the

mixture is fragrant. Add the bell pepper and the snow peas and stir-fry the mixture for 1 minute. Add the reserved broth mixture and the chicken and stir-fry the mixture for 1 minute, or until the chicken is heated through. Serve the chicken stir-fry over the rice. Serves 2.

Maple-Barbecued Chicken

½ cup white-wine vinegar
1 tablespoon salt
1 cup vegetable oil
5 whole chicken breasts (with skin and bone),
    halved
10 chicken thighs
10 chicken drumsticks
10 chicken wings
maple barbecue sauce (recipe follows) for
    basting and as an accompaniment

In a bowl whisk together the vinegar and the salt, add the oil in a stream, whisking, and whisk the marinade until it is emulsified. Divide the chicken pieces between 2 large bowls, pour the marinade over them, and let the chicken marinate, covered and chilled, overnight.

Grill the chicken on an oiled rack set about 4 inches over glowing coals for 10 minutes on each side, or until it is cooked through, baste it with some of the barbecue sauce, and grill it, turning it, for 2 minutes more. Serve the chicken with the remaining sauce. Serves 8 with leftovers.

Maple Barbecue Sauce

2 large onions, chopped fine
2½ tablespoons vegetable oil
2½ tablespoons Worcestershire sauce
1 tablespoon Dijon-style mustard
1¼ cups ketchup
2½ cups chicken broth
¾ cup cider vinegar
½ cup plus 2 tablespoons pure maple syrup

In a large heavy saucepan combine the onions, the oil, the Worcestershire sauce, the mustard, the ketchup, the broth, the vinegar, and the syrup, bring the mixture to a boil, and simmer it, stirring occasionally, for 50 minutes, or until it is reduced to about 3⅓ cups. *The sauce may be made 1 week in advance and kept covered and chilled*. Makes about 3⅓ cups.

Curried Chicken and Wild Rice Strudel

½ cup wild rice, rinsed
¾ stick (6 tablespoons) unsalted butter
3 teaspoons curry powder
1 whole skinless boneless chicken breast,
    halved and pounded between sheets of
    plastic wrap to a ½-inch thickness
2 tablespoons dry white wine, dry vermouth,
    or water
⅓ cup mayonnaise
2 tablespoons Major Grey's chutney, the
    solids chopped, plus additional chutney as
    an accompaniment
1 teaspoon fresh lemon juice, or to taste
¼ cup dry roasted cashews, chopped
¼ cup golden raisins, plumped in hot water to
    cover for 10 minutes and drained
six 18- by 14-inch sheets of *phyllo*, stacked
    between 2 sheets of wax paper and covered
    with a dampened kitchen towel
10 teaspoons fine dry bread crumbs

In a large saucepan cook the wild rice in 8 cups boiling salted water for 5 minutes, remove the pan from the heat, and let the rice stand for 1 hour. Drain the rice in a large sieve and in the pan cook it in 6 cups boiling salted water for 25 to 30 minutes, or until it is tender. Drain the rice in the sieve and let it cool in a large bowl.

In a small skillet melt 1 tablespoon of the butter with 1 teaspoon of the curry powder over moderately high heat until the foam subsides and in it sauté the chicken, patted dry and seasoned with salt and pepper, for 30 seconds on each side. Add the wine, vermouth, or water and cook the chicken, covered with a round of buttered wax paper and the lid, over moderately low heat for 5 minutes, or until it is just cooked through. Remove the skillet from the heat and let the chicken cool.

In a bowl whisk together the mayonnaise, 2 tablespoons of the chutney, 1 teaspoon of the remaining curry powder, the lemon juice, and the pan juices from the chicken. Cut the chicken into ½-inch dice, stir it well into the rice with the cashews, the raisins, the sauce, and salt and pepper to taste, and let the filling cool. *The filling may be made 1 day in advance and kept covered and chilled.*

Preheat the oven to 425° F. In a small saucepan melt the remaining 5 tablespoons butter with the remaining 1 teaspoon curry powder. On a work surface arrange two 20-inch-long sheets of wax paper with the long sides overlapping slightly and facing you. Put 1 sheet of the *phyllo* on the wax paper, brush it with some of the curry butter, and sprinkle it with 2 teaspoons of the bread crumbs. On this, layer, brush, and sprinkle 4 more sheets of the *phyllo* in the same manner and lay the sixth sheet of *phyllo* on top.

Spread the filling in a 3-inch-wide strip, mounding it on the *phyllo* 4 inches above the near long side, leaving a 2-inch border at each end. Using the wax paper as a guide, lift the bottom 4 inches of the pastry over the filling, fold in the ends, and roll up the strudel tightly. Transfer the strudel carefully, seam side down, to a lightly buttered baking sheet, brush it with the remaining curry butter, and bake it in the lower third of the oven for 25 minutes, or until it is golden. Let the strudel cool to warm on the baking sheet on a rack. *The strudel may be made 1 day in advance and kept covered loosely and chilled. Reheat the strudel in a preheated 400° F. oven for 15 minutes.* Serve the strudel warm, cut into 1-inch slices with a serrated knife, with the additional chutney. Serves 6.

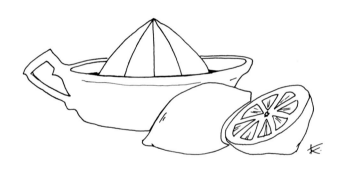

Cumin-Marinated Chicken Wings

2 pounds chicken wings (about 10)
⅔ cup buttermilk
2 garlic cloves, minced
4 tablespoons ground cumin
1 teaspoon salt
¼ cup fresh lemon juice

Cut off the wing tips, reserving them for another use such as stock if desired, and halve the wings at the joint. In a heavy-duty resealable plastic bag mix together the buttermilk, the garlic, 3 tablespoons of the cumin, and the salt. Add the wings, tossing them to coat them well, and let them marinate, chilled, for at least 6 hours or overnight.

Preheat the oven to 475° F. Drain the wings and bake them, skin side up, on the oiled rack of a broiler pan in the oven for 15 minutes. In a small bowl stir together the remaining 1 tablespoon cumin, the lemon juice, and salt to taste and brush the wings with the mixture. Bake the wings for 10 minutes more, or until they are golden. Serves 4 to 6.

Chicken Wings with Easy Mole Sauce

3 cups chopped onion
3 tablespoons vegetable oil
½ teaspoon coriander seeds
½ teaspoon aniseed
3 tablespoons chili powder
2 teaspoons sugar
¾ teaspoon cinnamon
⅛ teaspoon ground cloves
2 tablespoons unsweetened cocoa powder
2 tablespoons peanut butter
2 to 3 cups chicken broth
a 1-pound can tomatoes, drained and chopped
2 tablespoons raisins
3 garlic cloves, minced and mashed to a paste
    with ¾ teaspoon salt
2 pounds chicken wings (about 10)
cooked rice as an accompaniment
1 teaspoon sesame seeds

In a large heavy skillet sauté the onion in the oil over moderately high heat until it is golden brown. In a mortar with a pestle crush the coriander seeds and the aniseed, stir them into the onion mixture with the chili powder, the sugar, the cinnamon, and the cloves, and cook the mixture over moderate heat, stirring, for 1 minute. Stir in the cocoa powder, the peanut butter, 2 cups of the broth, the tomatoes, the raisins, the garlic paste, and salt to taste and simmer the sauce, uncovered, stirring occasionally, for 20 minutes.

While the sauce is cooking cut off the wing tips, reserving them for another use such as stock if desired, and halve the wings at the joint. Pat the wings dry, season them with salt and pepper, and on the oiled rack of a broiler pan broil them, skin side up, under a preheated broiler about 4 inches from the heat for 10 minutes, or until they are golden. Turn the wings and broil them for 10 minutes more, or until they are golden. In a blender or food processor purée the sauce in batches, adding the remaining broth as necessary to thin it to the desired

consistency. Transfer the sauce to the skillet, add the wings, and simmer the mixture, uncovered, for 30 minutes. Serve the wings with the mole sauce over the rice, sprinkled with the sesame seeds. Serves 4 to 6.

Red-Cooked Chicken Wings
(Chicken Wings Braised with Soy Sauce, Cinnamon, and Star Anise)

2 cups chicken broth
1 cup water
½ cup soy sauce
¼ cup medium-dry Sherry
¼ cup firmly packed dark brown sugar
1 tablespoon rice vinegar
two 3-inch cinnamon sticks
1 tablespoon star anise, crushed lightly with
    the flat side of a heavy knife
2 slices of fresh gingerroot, each about the
    size of a quarter, flattened with the flat side
    of a heavy knife
2 scallions, flattened with the flat side of a
    heavy knife, plus ¼ cup minced scallion
2 pounds chicken wings (about 10)
vegetable oil for deep-frying
1 teaspoon cornstarch dissolved in
    1 tablespoon water
cooked rice as an accompaniment

In a large saucepan combine the broth, the water, the soy sauce, the Sherry, the brown sugar, the vinegar, the cinnamon sticks, the star anise, the gingerroot, and the flattened scallions, bring the liquid to a boil, and simmer the mixture for 20 minutes. Cut off the wing tips, reserving them for another use such as stock if desired, halve the wings at the joint, and pat them dry. In a large deep-fryer or large deep kettle heat 2 inches of the oil to 375° F. on a deep-fat thermometer and in it fry the wings, 5 pieces at a time, for 5 to 8 minutes, or until they are golden and crisp. Transfer the wings with a slotted spoon as they are fried to paper towels to drain and make sure the oil returns to 375° F. before adding each new batch. Add the wings to the soy-sauce mixture and braise them, covered, over moderately low heat for 45 minutes. Stir the cornstarch mixture, stir it into the braising liquid, and simmer the mixture for 1 minute, or until it is thickened. Serve the chicken wings with the sauce over the rice, sprinkled with the minced scallion. Serves 4 to 6.

Sherried Chicken Wings with Mushrooms and Peas

2 pounds chicken wings (about 10)
all-purpose flour seasoned with salt and
    pepper for dredging the wings
2 tablespoons vegetable oil
2 tablespoons unsalted butter
1 large onion, halved lengthwise and sliced
    thin lengthwise
1 large garlic clove, minced
8 to 10 ounces mushrooms,
    sliced thin
½ teaspoon dried thyme, crumbled
½ cup medium-dry Sherry
1 cup chicken broth
1 teaspoon fresh lemon juice,
    or to taste
a 10-ounce package frozen peas
cooked noodles as an accompaniment

Cut off the wing tips, reserving them for another use such as stock if desired, and halve the wings at the joint. In a shallow bowl dredge the wings in the flour, shaking off the excess. In a heavy skillet large enough to hold the wings in one layer without crowding heat the oil and the butter over moderately high heat until the fat is hot but not smoking and in it brown the wings. With a slotted spoon transfer the wings to a plate. In the fat remaining in the skillet cook the onion and the garlic over moderate heat, stirring, until the onion is softened. Add the mushrooms and the thyme and cook the mixture, stirring, until the mushrooms are tender. Add the Sherry and boil the mixture until the liquid is reduced by half. Add the broth, the juice, and salt and pepper to taste, return the wings to the skillet, and simmer the mixture, covered partially, for 20 minutes. Stir in the peas and simmer the mixture, covered, for 5 minutes, or until the peas are tender. Serve the wings and the sauce with the noodles. Serves 4 to 6.

Thai-Style Broiled Chicken Wings with Hot-and-Sour Sauce

2 pounds chicken wings (about 10)
2 garlic cloves, minced and mashed to a paste
    with 1 teaspoon salt
1 tablespoon vegetable oil
1 teaspoon dried hot red pepper flakes
⅓ cup light corn syrup
½ cup distilled white vinegar

Cut off the wing tips, reserving them for another use such as stock if desired, and halve the wings at the joint. In a heavy-duty resealable plastic bag toss the wings with the garlic paste and the oil to coat them well and let them marinate, chilled, for at least 6 hours or overnight. Drain the wings and pat them dry. Preheat the broiler. Arrange the wings, skin side up, on the oiled rack of a broiler pan, sprinkle them with salt and pepper to taste, and broil them under the broiler about 4 inches from the heat for 8 to 10 minutes, or until they are golden brown. Turn the wings, sprinkle them with salt and pepper to taste, and broil them for 5 to 8 minutes more, or until they are golden. While the wings are broiling, in a saucepan stir together the red pepper flakes, the corn syrup, and the vinegar, bring the liquid to a boil, stirring, and transfer it to a bowl. Serve the wings with the sauce. Serves 4 to 6.

ASSORTED FOWL

Orange Duck Breasts on Braised Chicory

two 2-pound whole boneless duck breasts
    with skin*
1 teaspoon freshly grated orange zest
½ cup fresh orange juice
¼ cup soy sauce
¼ cup vegetable oil
2 tablespoons honey
1 tablespoon white-wine vinegar
1 teaspoon dried hot red pepper flakes
¼ teaspoon salt
2 large garlic cloves, sliced very thin
2 tablespoons unsalted butter
a 1½-pound head of chicory or curly
    endive, the leaves torn into large pieces
    and washed well
⅓ cup water

*available at many butcher shops and
    specialty foods shops and by mail order
    from D'Artagnan, tel. (800) 327-8246, or
    in New Jersey, (201) 792-0748

With a sharp knife halve the whole duck breasts and score the skin in a ¼-inch crosshatch pattern. Put the duck in a large resealable bag. In a bowl whisk together the zest, the orange juice, the soy sauce, the oil, the honey, the vinegar, the red pepper flakes, and the salt, pour the marinade over the duck, and seal the bag. Let the duck marinate, chilled, turning the bag occasionally, for 8 hours or overnight.

Remove the duck from the marinade, reserving the marinade, pat it dry between paper towels, and season it with salt and pepper. Heat 2 heavy skillets over moderately high heat until they are hot and in each skillet cook 2 duck breast halves, skin sides down, for 5 minutes. Pour off the fat, reduce the heat to moderate, and cook the duck, skin sides down, for 20 minutes more, adjusting the heat if necessary for the skin to turn dark brown but not burn. Pour off the fat, turn the duck breasts, and cook them, covered, over moderate heat for 8 to 10 minutes more, or until a meat thermometer registers 145° to 150° F. for medium meat.

While the duck is cooking, in a kettle sauté the garlic in the butter over moderately high heat, stirring, until it begins to turn golden, add the chicory with the water clinging to the leaves, and braise it, covered, stirring occasionally, for 8 to 10 minutes, or until it is just tender. Season the chicory with salt and pepper and keep it warm.

Transfer the duck to a cutting board and let it stand for 5 minutes. To one of the skillets add the water, deglaze the skillet over moderate heat, scraping up the brown bits, and add the deglazing liquid to the other skillet with the reserved marinade. Bring the liquid to a boil and deglaze the second skillet, scraping up the brown bits. Add any juices that have accumulated on the cutting board and simmer the sauce for 2 minutes, or until it is thickened slightly. Strain the sauce through a fine sieve into a small bowl. Cut the duck across the grain into thin slices, divide the chicory among 8 plates, and arrange the duck slices on it. Drizzle some of the sauce around each serving. Serves 8.

Roast Turkey with Chestnut Stuffing and Cider Gravy
    a 12- to 14-pound turkey, the neck and giblets
        (excluding the liver) reserved for making
        turkey giblet stock (page 154)
    1 recipe chestnut stuffing (page 154)
    1 stick (½ cup) unsalted butter,
        softened
    1 cup water
    1 cup turkey giblet stock or chicken broth

For the gravy
    1 cup apple cider
    2 tablespoons cider vinegar
    6 tablespoons all-purpose flour
    4 cups turkey giblet stock

sage, rosemary, and thyme sprigs for garnish

Preheat the oven to 425° F. Rinse the turkey, pat it dry, and season it inside and out with salt and pepper. Pack the neck cavity loosely with some of the stuffing, fold the neck skin under the body, and fasten it with a skewer. Pack the body cavity loosely with some of the remaining stuffing and truss the turkey. Transfer the remaining stuffing to a buttered 3-quart baking dish and reserve it, covered and chilled.

Spread the turkey with the butter and roast it on a rack in a roasting pan in the oven for 30 minutes. Reduce the temperature to 325° F., baste the turkey with the pan juices, and add the water to the pan. Roast the turkey, basting it every 20 minutes, for 2½ to 3 hours more, or until a meat thermometer inserted in the fleshy part of a thigh registers 180° F. and the juices run clear when the thigh is pierced. During the last 1½ hours of roasting, drizzle the reserved stuffing with the stock or broth, bake it, covered, in the 325° F. oven for 1 hour, and bake it, uncovered, for 30 minutes more. Transfer the turkey to a heated platter, reserving the juices in the roasting pan, discard the string, and keep the turkey warm, covered loosely with foil.

Make the gravy: Skim all the fat from the roasting pan juices, reserving ⅓ cup of the fat, and add the cider and the vinegar to the pan. Deglaze the pan over moderately high heat, scraping up the brown bits, and boil the mixture until it is reduced by half. In a saucepan combine the reserved fat and the flour and cook the *roux* over moderately low heat, whisking, for 3 minutes. Add the cider mixture and the stock in a stream, whisking, bring the mixture to a boil, whisking, and simmer the gravy, stirring occasionally, for 10 minutes. Season the gravy with salt and pepper and transfer it to a sauceboat.

Garnish the turkey with the herb sprigs and serve it with the gravy and the stuffing. Serves 8.

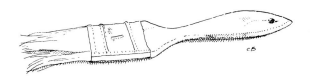

PHOTO ON PAGES 74 AND 75

Turkey Giblet Stock

the neck and giblets (excluding the liver) from
    a 12- to 14-pound turkey
5 cups chicken broth
5 cups water
1 rib of celery, chopped
1 carrot, chopped
1 onion, quartered
1 bay leaf
½ teaspoon dried thyme, crumbled
1 teaspoon black peppercorns

In a large saucepan combine the neck and giblets, the broth, the water, the celery, the carrot, and the onion and bring the liquid to a boil, skimming the froth. Add the bay leaf, the thyme, and the peppercorns, cook the mixture at a bare simmer for 2 hours, or until the liquid is reduced to about 5 cups, and strain the stock through a fine sieve into a bowl. *The stock may be made 2 days in advance, cooled, uncovered, and kept chilled or frozen in an airtight container.* Makes about 5 cups.

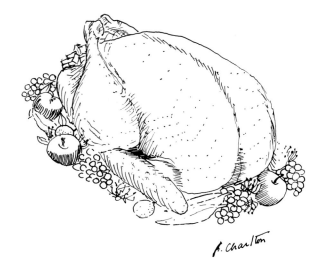

R. Charlton

Chestnut Stuffing

6 cups torn bite-size pieces of day-old
    homemade-style white bread
2 onions, chopped
4 ribs of celery, chopped
3 tablespoons minced fresh sage
    leaves or 1 tablespoon dried,
    crumbled
2 tablespoons minced fresh thyme
    leaves or 2 teaspoons dried,
    crumbled
1 tablespoon minced fresh rosemary
    leaves or 1½ teaspoons dried,
    crumbled
1 tablespoon minced fresh savory
    leaves or 1 teaspoon dried,
    crumbled
1 stick (½ cup) unsalted butter
1 pound fresh chestnuts, shelled and peeled
    (procedure follows), chopped coarse, or
    ¾ pound vacuum-packed whole chestnuts,
    chopped coarse (about 2 cups)
½ cup finely chopped fresh parsley leaves

Preheat the oven to 325° F. In a shallow baking pan arrange the bread pieces in one layer, bake them in the oven, stirring occasionally, for 10 to 15 minutes, or until they are golden, and transfer them to a large bowl. In a large skillet cook the onions, the celery, the sage, the thyme, the rosemary, and the savory in the butter over moderately low heat, stirring, until the vegetables are softened, add the chestnuts, and cook the mixture, stirring, for 1 minute. Add the vegetable mixture to the bread pieces, tossing the mixture well, stir in the parsley and salt and pepper to taste, and let the stuffing cool completely. *The stuffing may be made 1 day in advance and kept covered and chilled. (To prevent bacterial growth do not stuff the turkey cavities in advance.)* Makes about 10 cups, enough to stuff a 12- to 14-pound turkey with extra to bake on the side.

To Shell and Peel Chestnuts

With a sharp knife cut an X on the round side of each chestnut. Spread the chestnuts in one layer in a jelly-roll pan, add ¼ cup water, and bake the chestnuts in a preheated 450° F. oven for 10 minutes, or until the shells open. Remove the chestnuts, a handful at a time, and shell and peel them while they are still hot.

Sherried Turkey Cutlets with Green Peppercorns

½ pound turkey cutlets (each ½ inch thick)
all-purpose flour seasoned with salt and
    pepper for dredging the cutlets
1 tablespoon unsalted butter
1 tablespoon vegetable oil
⅓ cup medium-dry Sherry
1 teaspoon drained green peppercorns packed
    in brine, rinsed and crushed lightly
½ teaspoon honey or sugar
⅓ cup chicken broth

Dredge the cutlets in the flour, shaking off the excess. In a heavy skillet heat the butter and the oil over moderately high heat until the foam subsides, in the fat sauté the cutlets for 2 minutes on each side, or until they are just cooked through, and transfer them with a slotted spatula to a small platter. Deglaze the skillet with the Sherry over moderately high heat, stirring and scraping up the brown bits, add the peppercorns, and boil the sauce until the liquid is reduced to about 2 tablespoons. Stir in the honey and the broth and boil the sauce until it is reduced to about ¼ cup. Season the sauce with salt and pepper and spoon it over the cutlets. Serves 2.

Turkey Cutlets with Pan Salsa

four ⅜-inch-thick turkey cutlets
    (about ½ pound total)
⅓ cup all-purpose flour seasoned with
    salt and cayenne
1 tablespoon vegetable oil
⅓ cup low-salt chicken broth
2 tablespoons cider vinegar
½ teaspoon chili powder
cayenne to taste
2 plum tomatoes, peeled, seeded, and
    chopped fine
2 scallions, minced
1 fresh or pickled *jalapeño*,
    seeded and minced
    (wear rubber gloves)
1 tablespoon chopped dry-roasted peanuts
1 tablespoon minced fresh coriander

Dredge the cutlets in the flour mixture, shaking off the excess, in a heavy skillet (preferably cast-iron) heat the oil over moderately high heat until it is hot but not smoking, and in it sauté the cutlets for 1 to 2 minutes on each side, or until they are golden brown on the edges and cooked through. Transfer 2 cutlets to each of 2 plates and keep them warm. To the skillet add the broth, the vinegar, the chili powder, the cayenne, and salt to taste, deglaze the skillet over moderately high heat, scraping up the brown bits, and stir in the tomatoes, the scallions, and the *jalapeño*. Cook the sauce until it is thickened, pour it over the cutlets, and sprinkle the cutlets with the peanuts and the coriander. Serves 2.

EGGS, CHEESE, AND BREAKFAST ITEMS

EGGS AND CHEESE

Fried Eggs

1 tablespoon unsalted butter
8 large eggs

In an 11½- to 12-inch non-stick skillet heat the butter over low heat until it is melted and crack the eggs, 1 at a time, into a small bowl, adding them as they are cracked to the skillet. Cook the eggs, covered, for 3 minutes, remove the cover, and cook the eggs for 4 minutes more, or until the yolks are set. Serves 4.

PHOTO ON PAGES 40 AND 41

Asparagus, Gruyère, and Tarragon Souffléed Omelet

½ pound asparagus, trimmed
1 medium red onion, sliced thin
1½ tablespoons unsalted butter
a pinch of sugar
⅔ cup coarsely grated Gruyère
1 tablespoon minced fresh tarragon leaves,
  or to taste
4 large eggs, separated
2 tablespoons all-purpose flour

Preheat the oven to 375° F. In a 10-inch non-stick skillet simmer the asparagus in water to cover for 3 to 5 minutes, or until it is just tender. Drain the asparagus, rinse it under cold water, and pat it dry with paper towels. Cut the asparagus crosswise into ¼-inch pieces and transfer the pieces to a bowl. In the skillet cook the onion with salt and pepper to taste in 1 tablespoon of the butter over moderate heat, stirring frequently, for 5 minutes. Add the sugar, cook the mixture, stirring, for

3 to 5 minutes, or until the onion is golden, and transfer the mixture to the bowl. Stir in the Gruyère, the tarragon, and salt and pepper to taste.

In the skillet, cleaned, heat the remaining ½ tablespoon butter over moderate heat until it is melted, tilt the skillet to coat it, and remove it from the heat. In a bowl whisk the egg yolks with the flour and salt and pepper to taste until the mixture is thick and lemon-colored. In another bowl with an electric mixer beat the egg whites with a pinch of salt until they just hold stiff peaks, fold them into the yolk mixture gently but thoroughly, and pour the egg mixture into the skillet, spreading it evenly. (If the skillet handle is plastic, wrap it in a double thickness of foil.) Bake the omelet in the middle of the oven for 7 minutes, or until it is puffed and almost cooked through, spoon the filling down the middle of it, and with a spatula fold the omelet in half to enclose the filling. Bake the omelet in the middle of the oven for 1 minute more, or until the cheese is melted and the omelet is cooked through. Serves 2.

Cream Cheese and Chive Scrambled Eggs

16 large eggs
4 ounces cream cheese, cut into bits
  and softened
2 tablespoons minced fresh chives plus
  additional for garnish
2 tablespoons unsalted butter

In a bowl whisk together the eggs, the cream cheese, 2 tablespoons of the chives, and salt and pepper to taste. In a large heavy skillet melt the butter over moderate heat, add the egg mixture, and cook it, stirring, for 6 to 8 minutes, or until the eggs are cooked through. Serve the eggs sprinkled with the additional chives. Serves 8.

PHOTO ON PAGES 76 AND 77

Zucchini Frittata with Blossoms

12 large eggs
1 cup freshly grated Parmesan
2 medium zucchini, rinsed and cut into
   2-inch-long julienne strips (about 3 cups)
3 tablespoons olive oil
1 onion, chopped fine
1 red bell pepper, chopped fine
3 garlic cloves, minced
1½ tablespoons fresh thyme leaves or
   ½ teaspoon dried, crumbled
6 to 8 zucchini blossoms, pistils removed
   if desired

In a bowl whisk together the eggs, add ½ cup of the Parmesan and salt and pepper to taste, and whisk the mixture until it is combined well. In a 12-inch non-stick skillet sauté the zucchini in 2 tablespoons of the oil over moderately high heat, stirring, until it is softened and transfer it with a slotted spoon to a small bowl. Add the remaining 1 tablespoon oil to the skillet and in it cook the onion and the bell pepper with salt and pepper to taste over moderate heat, stirring, until the vegetables are softened. Add the garlic and the thyme and cook the mixture, stirring, for 1 minute. Stir in the zucchini, pour in the egg mixture, and arrange the zucchini blossoms decoratively on the surface.

Cook the *frittata* over moderate heat, without stirring, for 12 to 15 minutes, or until the edge is set but the center is still soft, and sprinkle the remaining ½ cup Parmesan over the top. (If the skillet handle is plastic, wrap it in a double thickness of foil.) Preheat the broiler. Broil the *frittata* under the broiler about 4 inches from the heat for 2 to 3 minutes, or until the cheese is bubbling and golden. Let the *frittata* cool in the skillet for 5 minutes, run a thin knife around the edge, and slide the *frittata* onto a serving plate. Cut the *frittata* into wedges and serve it warm or at room temperature. Serves 6.

Olive and Jarlsberg Salad Sandwich

an 8-inch round loaf of peasant bread
½ cup drained pimiento-stuffed green olives,
   chopped fine
½ cup drained Kalamata or other brine-cured
   black olives, pitted and chopped fine
2½ cups grated Jarlsberg cheese
   (about 6 ounces)
a 6-ounce jar marinated artichoke hearts,
   drained and chopped fine
1 cup drained bottled roasted red peppers,
   chopped fine
2 cups packed fresh parsley leaves, minced
1 tablespoon drained capers, chopped fine
¼ cup extra-virgin olive oil

Cut the top quarter off the loaf horizontally with a serrated knife and remove the soft crumb from the top and bottom sections, leaving two ½-inch-thick shells. In a bowl stir together the olives, the Jarlsberg, the artichoke hearts, the red peppers, the parsley, the capers, the oil, and salt and pepper to taste and spoon the mixture into the bottom bread shell, smoothing the surface. Fit the top bread shell on the filled bottom shell and press the sandwich together firmly, re-forming the loaf. Wrap the sandwich tightly in plastic wrap, chill it for 1 hour, and with the serrated knife cut it carefully into 4 wedges. *The sandwich may be made 1 day in advance and kept wrapped and chilled.* Serves 4.

PHOTO ON PAGE 59

BREAKFAST ITEMS

Stir-Fried Red Flannel Hash

1 tablespoon unsalted butter
1 tablespoon vegetable oil
3 cooked beets (about ¾ pound), peeled and
    cut into ½-inch cubes
3 cooked carrots, cut into ½-inch cubes
2 cooked boiling potatoes, cut into
    ½-inch cubes
a ¼-pound piece of corned beef, cut into
    ¼-inch cubes
1 bunch of scallions, sliced thin

In a heavy skillet heat the butter and the oil over moderately high heat until the foam subsides and in the fat stir-fry the beets, the carrots, the potatoes, the corned beef, and the scallions with salt and pepper to taste for 6 minutes, or until the hash is browned. Serves 4.

PHOTO ON PAGES 40 AND 41

Bacon and Chive Potato Pancakes

¾ pound (1 large) russet (baking) potato
2 slices of cooked lean bacon, crumbled fine
2 tablespoons finely chopped fresh chives or
    green part of scallion
2 tablespoons olive oil
sour cream as an accompaniment if desired

Peel the potato, grate it coarse, and press it between several thicknesses of paper towel to remove any excess moisture. In a bowl stir together the potato, the bacon, the chives, and salt and pepper to taste. In a large heavy skillet heat the oil over moderately high heat until it is hot but not smoking, form the potato mixture into 4 patties, and cook the patties, tamping them down with a spatula, for 5 to 7 minutes on each side, or until the pancakes are golden brown and cooked through. Serve the pancakes with the sour cream. Serves 2.

Shredded Potato Pancakes with Smoked Salmon

2 pounds russet (baking) potatoes
½ cup vegetable oil
1 pound thinly sliced smoked salmon
sour cream as an accompaniment

Peel half the potatoes, grate them coarse (preferably in a food processor), and press them between several thicknesses of paper towel to remove any excess moisture. In a large heavy skillet heat ¼ cup of the oil over moderately high heat until it is hot but not smoking. In a bowl toss the grated potatoes with salt and pepper to taste, form them into 4 patties, and in the skillet cook the patties, tamping them down with a spatula, for 5 minutes on each side, or until the pancakes are golden brown and cooked through. Transfer the pancakes to paper towels to drain and keep them warm in a 200° F. oven. Make 4 more pancakes in the same manner with the remaining potatoes and oil and serve the pancakes with the smoked salmon and the sour cream. Serves 8.

PHOTO ON PAGES 76 AND 77

Blueberry Buckwheat Pancakes

½ cup buckwheat flour (available at natural
    foods stores)
½ cup all-purpose flour
2 teaspoons double-acting baking powder
2 teaspoons sugar
1 teaspoon salt
½ stick (¼ cup) cold unsalted butter,
    cut into bits
2 large eggs
1 cup milk
1½ cups blueberries, preferably wild, picked
    over and, if large, halved
vegetable oil for brushing the griddle
pure maple syrup as an accompaniment

In a food processor blend together the flours, the baking powder, the sugar, and the salt, add the butter, and blend the mixture until it resembles fine meal. In a large bowl whisk together the eggs and the milk, add the flour mixture, and whisk the batter until it is combined well. Let the pancake batter stand for 5 minutes and stir in the blueberries.

Preheat the oven to 200° F. Heat a griddle over moderate heat until it is hot enough to make drops of water scatter over its surface and brush it with the oil. Spoon the batter onto the griddle to form 3-inch rounds and cook the pancakes for 1 to 2 minutes on each side, or until they are golden. Transfer the pancakes as they are cooked to a heatproof platter and keep them warm in the oven. Serve the pancakes with the syrup. Makes about twenty-four 3-inch pancakes.

Toasted Walnut Buttermilk Pancakes with
Cranberry Maple Syrup

½ cup pure maple syrup
½ cup cranberries,
   picked over
½ cup all-purpose flour
1 tablespoon sugar
¼ teaspoon baking soda
¼ teaspoon salt
¼ teaspoon cinnamon
½ cup walnuts, toasted lightly and
   chopped fine
½ cup plus 2 tablespoons buttermilk
1 large egg
1 tablespoon unsalted butter,
   melted, plus additional
   melted butter for brushing
   the griddle

In a small saucepan combine the syrup with the cranberries, simmer the mixture, covered, for 5 minutes, or until the cranberries have burst, and keep the syrup warm, covered. In a bowl stir together the flour, the sugar, the baking soda, the salt, the cinnamon, and the walnuts. In a small bowl stir together the buttermilk, the egg, and 1 tablespoon of the butter, add the buttermilk mixture to the flour mixture, and stir the batter until it is just combined.

Preheat the oven to 200° F. Heat a griddle over moderate heat until it is hot enough to make drops of water scatter over its surface and brush it with the additional butter. Spoon ¼-cup measures of the batter onto the griddle and cook the pancakes for 1 to 2 minutes on each side, or until they are golden. Transfer the pancakes as they are cooked to a heatproof plate and keep them warm in the oven. Serve the pancakes with the syrup. Makes about six 4-inch pancakes, serving 2.

PASTA AND GRAINS

PASTA

Bow-Ties with Bacon, Onion, and Tomato

4 slices of bacon, chopped fine
2 tablespoons olive oil
1 large onion, chopped
½ pound large *farfalle* (bow-tie pasta)
1 tomato (about ½ pound), chopped
¼ cup water
¼ teaspoon dried hot red pepper flakes,
    or to taste
⅓ cup finely chopped fresh parsley leaves
¼ cup freshly grated Parmesan

In a deep skillet cook the bacon over moderate heat, stirring, until it is crisp and transfer it with a slotted spoon to a bowl. Pour off all but 1 tablespoon of the fat from the skillet, add the oil, and in the fat cook the onion over moderate heat, stirring, until it is golden brown. In a kettle of salted boiling water cook the pasta until it is *al dente*. While the pasta is cooking, stir the tomato into the onion mixture with the ¼ cup water, the red pepper flakes, and salt to taste, simmer the sauce, stirring, for 5 minutes, and stir in the parsley and the bacon. Drain the pasta well, add it to the sauce, and toss it well. Add the Parmesan and toss the pasta well. Serves 2.

Fettuccine with Ham and Napa Cabbage

½ pound fettuccine
1 onion, chopped
2 cups chopped Napa cabbage
1 tablespoon vegetable oil
¼ pound cooked ham, chopped
½ teaspoon caraway seeds
⅓ cup heavy cream

In a large saucepan of salted boiling water cook the fettuccine until it is *al dente*, reserve ½ cup of the cook-

ing water, and drain the pasta well. While the pasta is cooking, in a heavy skillet cook the onion and the cabbage in the oil over moderate heat, stirring, until the vegetables are golden, stir in the ham and the caraway seeds, and cook the mixture, stirring occasionally, for 2 minutes, or until the cabbage is tender. Add the cream and simmer the mixture for 1 minute. In a large bowl toss together the fettuccine, the ham mixture, and salt and pepper to taste and add enough of the reserved cooking water to thin the sauce to the desired consistency. Serves 2.

Fettuccine with Red Pepper and Basil Sauce

2 large garlic cloves, minced
½ cup finely chopped onion
a pinch of dried hot red pepper flakes
¼ teaspoon dried thyme, crumbled
1 tablespoon olive oil
2 red bell peppers, sliced thin (about 2 cups)
⅔ cup chicken broth
1 tablespoon unsalted butter
2 tablespoons finely chopped
    fresh basil leaves
fresh lemon juice to taste
½ pound fettuccine
freshly grated Parmesan as an accompaniment

In a small skillet cook the garlic, the onion, the red pepper flakes, the thyme, and salt and pepper to taste in the oil over moderately low heat, stirring, until the onion is softened, add the bell peppers and the broth, and simmer the mixture, covered, for 10 minutes, or until the peppers are very soft. In a blender purée the mixture until it is smooth, return it to the skillet, and swirl in the butter. Stir in the basil, the lemon juice, and salt and pepper to taste and keep the sauce warm.

In a kettle of boiling salted water cook the fettuccine until it is *al dente*, drain it well, and transfer it to a serving bowl. Add the sauce, toss the pasta well, and serve it with the Parmesan. Serves 2.

Pasta with Shrimp, Tomato, and Arugula

2 tablespoons olive oil
½ pound shrimp (about 12), shelled and
    deveined
2 large garlic cloves, minced
¼ teaspoon dried hot red pepper flakes,
    or to taste
1 onion, chopped fine (about ¾ cup)
4 plum tomatoes, chopped (about 1 cup)
½ cup dry white wine
½ cup chicken broth
¼ cup heavy cream
1 bunch of *arugula*, the stems discarded
    and the leaves washed well, spun
    dry, and chopped
3 tablespoons minced fresh parsley leaves
    (preferably flat-leafed)
½ pound fettuccine or spaghetti

In a heavy skillet heat the oil over moderately high heat until it is hot but not smoking, in it sauté the shrimp, the garlic, and the pepper flakes, stirring, for 1 to 2 minutes, or until the shrimp are pink and almost cooked through, and transfer the shrimp with a slotted spoon to a bowl. To the skillet add the onion, the tomatoes, and salt and pepper to taste and cook the mixture over moderate heat, stirring, until the vegetables are softened. Add the wine and boil the mixture until the wine is reduced by half. Add the broth, boil the mixture until the liquid is reduced by half, and stir in the cream.

Simmer the sauce until it is thickened slightly, stir in the *arugula* and the shrimp, and simmer the sauce for 1 minute, or until the shrimp are cooked through. Stir in the parsley and salt and pepper to taste and keep the sauce warm, covered. In a kettle of boiling salted water cook the pasta until it is *al dente*, drain it well, and in a bowl toss it with the sauce. Serves 2.

Linguine with Brown-Butter Sauce

1 pound dried *linguine*
¾ stick (6 tablespoons) unsalted butter
¼ cup minced fresh parsley leaves
¼ cup freshly grated Parmesan
½ teaspoon dried orégano,
    crumbled
½ cup plain yogurt at room temperature

In a kettle of boiling salted water boil the *linguine* until it is *al dente*, reserve ½ cup of the cooking water, and drain the *linguine* well.

While the *linguine* is cooking, in a heavy skillet cook the butter over moderate heat, swirling the skillet occasionally, until it is nut-brown in color. In a large bowl whisk together the butter, the parsley, the Parmesan, and the orégano until the mixture is combined well and whisk in the yogurt and salt and pepper to taste. Add the *linguine*, toss the mixture well, and add enough of the reserved cooking water to thin the sauce to the desired consistency. Serves 4 to 6.

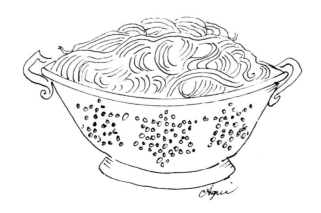

Linguine with Clams in Black Bean Sauce

1 cup water
30 small (about 2-inch) hard-shelled clams,
    scrubbed well
2 tablespoons cornstarch
3 tablespoons soy sauce
2 tablespoons Scotch
2 tablespoons rice vinegar
1 tablespoon sugar
3 tablespoons vegetable oil
3 tablespoons minced peeled fresh gingerroot
2½ tablespoons dried fermented black beans*,
    rinsed well, drained, and chopped
2 tablespoons minced garlic
¾ pound *linguine*
2 scallions, halved lengthwise and cut
    crosswise into 1-inch pieces

*available at Asian markets, some specialty
    foods shops, and by mail order from
    Adriana's Bazaar, tel. (212) 877-5757

In a kettle bring the water to a boil with the clams and
steam the clams, covered, checking them occasionally
and transferring them as they open with a slotted spoon
to a large bowl, for 3 to 8 minutes. Discard any unopened clams, strain the broth through a fine sieve into a
large glass measure, and if necessary add enough water
to measure a total of 1½ cups. Discard the shells, rinse
any clams that feel sandy, and chop the clams.

Stir the cornstarch into the clam broth and stir in the
soy sauce, the Scotch, the vinegar, and the sugar. In a
wok or large heavy skillet heat the oil over moderately
high heat until it just begins to smoke and in it stir-fry
the gingerroot, the black beans, and the garlic for 30
seconds, or until the mixture is fragrant. Stir the cornstarch mixture, add it to the wok, stirring, and bring the
sauce to a boil, stirring. Simmer the sauce, stirring, for
2 minutes and keep it warm.

In a kettle of salted boiling water cook the *linguine*
until it is *al dente*, drain it, and add it to the wok with the
clams and the scallions. Cook the mixture over moderate heat, tossing the *linguine*, until it is heated through
and the *linguine* is coated well with the sauce. Serves 4.

Linguine with Herbed Clam Sauce

½ cup chopped shallot
2 garlic cloves forced through a garlic press
2 tablespoons unsalted butter
2 tablespoons all-purpose flour
⅓ cup dry white wine
1 cup bottled clam juice
a 10-ounce can whole baby clams
    including the juice
¼ cup minced fresh parsley leaves
2 teaspoons minced fresh thyme leaves or
    ¾ teaspoon dried, crumbled
½ pound *linguine*

In a deep skillet cook the shallot and the garlic in the
butter over moderate heat, stirring, until they are pale
golden, add the flour, and cook the mixture, stirring, for
1 minute. Stir in the wine, the bottled clam juice, and
the clams with the juice and simmer the sauce, stirring,
for 5 minutes. Stir in the parsley, the thyme, and salt and
pepper to taste and keep the sauce warm. In a kettle of
salted boiling water boil the *linguine* until it is *al dente*,
drain it, and in the skillet toss it with the clam sauce.
Serves 2.

Linguine with Mussels and Arugula Cream Sauce

1 onion, chopped
2 tablespoons olive oil
½ cup dry white wine
½ cup bottled clam juice
½ cup water
36 mussels (preferably cultivated), scrubbed
    and the beards pulled off
½ cup heavy cream
2 small bunches of *arugula*, coarse stems
    discarded and the leaves washed well, spun
    dry, and chopped coarse (about 3 cups)
1 pound *linguine*

In a kettle cook the onion in the oil over moderately low heat, stirring, until it is softened, add the wine, the bottled clam juice, and the water, and bring the mixture to a boil. Add the mussels, steam them, covered, for 2 minutes, or until they are opened, transferring them with tongs as they open to a bowl, and discard any that are unopened. Let the mussels cool until they can be handled and remove them from their shells, discarding the shells.

Boil the liquid remaining in the kettle until it is reduced to about 1 cup, add the cream, and simmer the sauce, stirring occasionally, for 3 minutes, or until it is thickened. Stir in the *arugula*, the mussels with any liquid that has accumulated in the bowl, and salt and pepper to taste. In a kettle of boiling salted water boil the *linguine* until it is *al dente*, drain it well, and transfer it to a large bowl. Add the mussel mixture and toss the mixture well. Serves 4 to 6.

Herbed Orzo with Toasted Pine Nuts

¾ pound (about 2 cups) *orzo*
  (rice-shaped pasta)
3 tablespoons unsalted butter, cut into bits
⅓ cup pine nuts, toasted
fresh lemon juice to taste
3 tablespoons minced fresh coriander,
  or to taste
3 tablespoons minced fresh mint leaves,
  or to taste

In a kettle of boiling salted water boil the *orzo* until it is *al dente*, drain it well, and transfer it to a bowl. Stir in the butter, the pine nuts, the lemon juice, and salt and pepper to taste, add the coriander and the mint, and toss the mixture until it is combined well. Serves 6.

PHOTO ON PAGE 26

Penne with Stir-Fried Beef and Red Bell Pepper

2 tablespoons cornstarch
¼ cup soy sauce
1½ cups beef broth
2 tablespoons Scotch
1 tablespoon sugar
1 teaspoon Asian (toasted) sesame oil
  (available at Asian markets and some
    specialty foods shops and supermarkets)
3 tablespoons vegetable oil

1 pound boneless sirloin, cut into
  ¼-inch strips
2 red bell peppers, cut into julienne strips
2 large garlic cloves,
  minced
2 tablespoons minced peeled fresh gingerroot
6 scallions, sliced thin diagonally
1 teaspoon dried hot red pepper flakes
1 pound *penne* (quill-shaped pasta)

In a bowl whisk together the cornstarch, the soy sauce, the broth, the Scotch, the sugar, and the sesame oil. In a large heavy skillet or a wok heat 1 tablespoon of the vegetable oil over high heat until it just begins to smoke and in it stir-fry the beef, patted dry, in 2 batches, for 30 seconds, or until it is browned but still pink within, transferring it with a slotted spoon as it browns to a bowl. In the skillet heat 1 tablespoon of the remaining vegetable oil over moderately high heat until it is hot but not smoking, in it stir-fry the bell peppers for 2 minutes, or until they are crisp-tender, and transfer them to the bowl with the beef. In the remaining 1 tablespoon vegetable oil stir-fry the garlic and the gingerroot over moderately high heat for 30 seconds, stir the cornstarch mixture, and add it to the skillet. Cook the sauce, stirring, until it is thickened and stir in the beef mixture, the scallions, the red pepper flakes, and salt to taste. In a kettle of boiling salted water boil the *penne* until it is *al dente*, drain it well, and in a large bowl toss it with the beef mixture. Serves 4 to 6.

Penne with Sugar Snap Peas and Arugula Pesto

½ pound sugar snap peas,
  trimmed
¾ to 1 cup *arugula pesto* (page 164)
1 pound *penne rigate* (ridged, quill-shaped
  macaroni) or other tubular pasta

In a large saucepan of salted boiling water blanch the sugar snap peas for 45 seconds, or until they are crisp-tender, transfer them with a skimmer to a large serving bowl, and toss them with ½ cup of the *pesto*. In the boiling water cook the pasta until it is *al dente*, reserve ½ cup of the pasta-cooking water, and drain the pasta in a colander. In the bowl with the sugar snap peas toss the pasta with the reserved pasta-cooking water, ¼ cup of the remaining *pesto*, or to taste, and salt and pepper to taste. Serves 4 to 6.

Arugula Pesto

2 bunches of *arugula*, coarse stems discarded
    and the leaves washed well and spun dry
    (about 6 packed cups)
1½ cups walnuts
¾ cup freshly grated Parmesan or Sardo
1 teaspoon salt
1 large garlic clove
⅓ cup olive oil

In a food processor combine the *arugula*, the walnuts, the Parmesan or Sardo, the salt, and the garlic and pulse the motor until the walnuts are chopped fine. With the motor running add the oil in a stream and blend the *pesto* until it is smooth. Toss the *pesto* with hot cooked pasta, potatoes, or vegetables. The *pesto* keeps, chilled, its surface covered with plastic wrap, for 2 weeks. Makes about 2 cups.

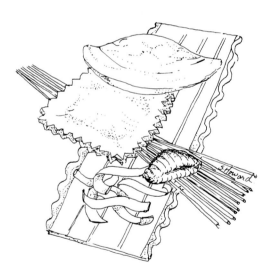

Eggplant Ravioli with Lemon Sage Oil and Fried Onions

For the lemon sage oil
⅔ cup chopped fresh sage leaves
the zest of 1 lemon, removed in strips with
    a vegetable peeler
2 large garlic cloves, chopped

½ teaspoon salt
1 teaspoon whole black peppercorns
¾ cup olive oil
For the ravioli
1 cup chopped onion
1 large garlic clove, minced
2 tablespoons olive oil
1 medium eggplant (about 1 pound), peeled
    and cut into ½-inch dice
1 cup chicken broth
2 tablespoons mayonnaise
⅓ cup freshly grated Parmesan
1 pound (about 60) won ton wrappers
    (available at Asian markets and many
    supermarkets), thawed if frozen

vegetable oil for frying the onions
3 small onions, halved lengthwise and cut
    crosswise into ¼-inch-thick slices
sage leaves for garnish

Make the lemon sage oil: In a small heatproof bowl combine the sage, the zest, the garlic, the salt, and the peppercorns. In a small saucepan heat the oil until it is hot but not smoking, pour it over the sage mixture, and let the mixture cool to warm. In a blender purée the oil mixture, return it to the bowl, and chill it, covered, for at least 12 hours and up to 4 days. Let the oil mixture come to room temperature and strain it through a fine sieve into a glass measure, pressing hard on the solids.

Make the ravioli: In a large heavy saucepan cook the onion and the garlic in the oil over moderate heat, stirring, until the vegetables are golden. Add the eggplant and cook the mixture, stirring, until the eggplant is just tender. Stir in the broth and simmer the mixture, stirring, until the excess liquid is evaporated. Transfer the mixture to a bowl, stir in the mayonnaise, the Parmesan, and salt and pepper to taste, and let the filling cool. *The filling may be made 1 day in advance and kept covered and chilled.* Put 1 won ton wrapper on a work surface, mound 1 tablespoon of the filling in the center of it, and brush the edges with water. Put a second wrapper over the first, pressing down around the filling to force out the air, seal the edges well, and trim the excess dough with a round cutter or sharp knife. Make more ravioli with the remaining wrappers and filling in the same manner, transferring the ravioli as they are formed to baking sheets or trays lined with wax paper. *The ravioli may be frozen in single layers on the lined sheets, transferred to freezer bags, and kept frozen for 1 month. If the ravioli have been frozen, do not thaw them before cooking.*

In a deep skillet heat ¼ inch of the vegetable oil over moderately high heat until it is hot but not smoking, in it fry the onions in batches until they are golden brown, transferring them with a slotted spoon to paper towels to drain, and season them with salt. In a kettle of salted, gently boiling water cook the ravioli in batches for 2 minutes, or until they are tender. (Do not let the water boil vigorously once the ravioli have been added.) Transfer the ravioli as they are cooked with a slotted spoon to a kitchen towel and keep them warm. Arrange 3 or 4 ravioli on each of 8 plates, drizzle them with some of the lemon sage oil, and sprinkle them with some of the fried onions. Garnish each serving with the sage leaves. Makes about 30 ravioli, serving 8 as a first course.

PHOTO ON PAGES 70 AND 71

Rotelle with Broccoli and Spicy Peanut Sauce

4½ tablespoons peanut butter
4 tablespoons hot water
1½ to 2 tablespoons soy sauce
1½ teaspoons Worcestershire sauce
1 teaspoon minced garlic
¾ teaspoon sugar
a scant ¼ teaspoon cayenne
½ pound *rotelle* or *fusilli*
½ pound broccoli, the flowerets cut into
    ¾-inch pieces and the stems peeled and cut
    crosswise into ¼-inch-thick slices
1 red bell pepper, chopped

In a large bowl whisk together the peanut butter, the water, the soy sauce, the Worcestershire sauce, the garlic, the sugar, the cayenne, and salt to taste until the sauce is smooth. In a saucepan of boiling salted water boil the pasta until it is barely *al dente*, add the broccoli and the bell pepper, and boil the mixture for 2 to 3 minutes, or until the pasta and the vegetables are *al dente*. Drain the mixture well, add it to the peanut sauce, and toss the mixture well. Serves 2.

Rotelle with Mushroom Sauce

1 onion, chopped fine
2 tablespoons unsalted butter
1½ pounds mushrooms, chopped fine
2 flat anchovy fillets, patted dry between
    paper towels and minced
2 teaspoons Worcestershire sauce
¼ cup heavy cream
1 tablespoon fresh lemon juice
1 pound *rotelle* (corkscrew-shaped pasta)
½ cup minced fresh parsley leaves

In a heavy skillet cook the onion in the butter over moderate heat, stirring, until it is softened, add the mushrooms, and cook the mixture, stirring occasionally, for 15 minutes, or until the liquid the mushrooms give off is evaporated and the mushrooms are browned lightly. Stir in the anchovies, the Worcestershire sauce, the cream, and the lemon juice, cook the mixture for 2 minutes, and season it with salt and pepper.

While the mushrooms are cooking, in a kettle of boiling salted water boil the *rotelle* until it is *al dente*, reserve ½ cup of the cooking water, and drain the *rotelle* well. Transfer the *rotelle* to a large bowl, add the mushroom mixture and the parsley, and toss the mixture well, adding enough of the reserved cooking water to thin the sauce to the desired consistency. Serves 4 to 6.

Rotelle with Summer Tomato and Herb Sauce

1 pound plum tomatoes, peeled, seeded,
    and chopped
⅓ cup minced red onion
⅓ cup Kalamata or other brine-cured black
    olives, pitted and sliced
¼ cup olive oil
3 tablespoons balsamic vinegar
1 pound *rotelle* or *fusilli*
2 tablespoons finely chopped fresh
    basil leaves
2 tablespoons finely chopped fresh
    mint leaves
2 tablespoons finely chopped fresh chives
yellow pear tomatoes, halved for garnish

In a large bowl stir together the plum tomatoes, the onion, the olives, the oil, the vinegar, and salt and pepper to taste and let the sauce stand for 30 minutes. In a saucepan of salted boiling water cook the pasta until it is *al dente*, drain it, and add the hot pasta to the sauce. Add the herbs, toss the mixture until it is combined well, and serve it warm, garnished with the pear tomato halves. Serves 6.

Rotelle with Roasted Zucchini and Italian Sausage

2½ pounds zucchini, scrubbed and sliced
    thin crosswise
2 tablespoons olive oil
1½ pounds fresh Italian sausage
¼ cup loosely packed fresh mint leaves,
    minced, or 2 teaspoons dried mint
    combined with ¼ cup minced fresh
    parsley leaves
⅔ cup plain yogurt at room temperature
½ pound *rotelle* (corkscrew-shaped pasta) or
    penne (quill-shaped pasta)

Preheat the oven to 450° F. Arrange the zucchini in a jelly-roll pan, drizzle it with the oil, and roast it in the middle of the oven, stirring occasionally, for 15 to 20 minutes, or until it is golden. While the zucchini is roasting, discard the casings from the sausage, in a heavy skillet cook the meat over moderate heat, stirring and breaking up the lumps, until it is no longer pink, and transfer it with a slotted spoon to paper towels to drain. In a large bowl stir together the zucchini, the sausage, the mint, the yogurt, and salt and pepper to taste. In a kettle of boiling salted water boil the *rotelle* until it is *al dente*, drain it well, and toss it with the zucchini mixture. Serves 4 to 6.

Spaghetti with Pork and Peanut Sauce

1 pound ground pork (not too lean)
1 tablespoon vegetable oil
4 teaspoons sugar
2 garlic cloves, minced
1 tablespoon minced peeled fresh gingerroot
4 tablespoons soy sauce
3 tablespoons fresh lemon juice
2 teaspoons Asian (toasted) sesame oil
    (available at Asian markets and some
    specialty foods shops and supermarkets)
⅔ cup smooth peanut butter
1 cup hot water
1 pound spaghetti or *penne*
    (quill-shaped pasta)
1 cup thinly sliced scallion greens

In a heavy skillet cook the pork in the oil over moderate heat, stirring and breaking up the lumps, until it is no longer pink, add 2 teaspoons of the sugar, the garlic, the gingerroot, and 1 tablespoon of the soy sauce, and sauté

the mixture over high heat until the pork is browned. In a blender blend together the remaining 3 tablespoons soy sauce, the lemon juice, the sesame oil, the remaining 2 teaspoons sugar, and the peanut butter and add enough of the hot water to thin the sauce to the desired consistency.

In a kettle of boiling salted water boil the spaghetti until it is *al dente*, drain it well, and in a large bowl toss it with the pork mixture, the peanut sauce, the scallion greens, and salt and pepper to taste. Serves 4 to 6.

Whole-Wheat Spaghetti with Goat Cheese and Arugula

3 red onions, sliced thin, plus additional red
    onion, diced fine, for garnish
6 garlic cloves, cut into thin slivers
3 tablespoons olive oil
½ pound whole-wheat spaghetti
¾ cup (about 6 ounces) soft mild goat cheese
    such as Montrachet
4 bunches of *arugula* (about 1 pound), the
    stems discarded and the leaves washed
    well, spun dry, and chopped (about 8 cups)
½ cup walnuts, toasted lightly and chopped
⅓ cup freshly grated Romano or Parmesan
½ cup finely shredded fresh basil
    or parsley leaves

In a large skillet cook the sliced onions, the garlic, and salt and pepper to taste in the oil over moderate heat, stirring, until the onions are golden around the edges, remove the skillet from the heat, and keep the mixture warm. In a kettle of boiling salted water cook the spaghetti until it is *al dente*, reserve ¼ cup of the cooking water, and drain the spaghetti well. In a serving bowl whisk the goat cheese with the reserved cooking water until it is melted and the mixture is smooth, add the spaghetti, the onion mixture, the *arugula*, the walnuts, the cheese, the basil or parsley, and salt and pepper to taste, and toss the mixture well. Garnish the pasta with the diced onion. Serves 4.

Paad Thai
(Stir-Fried Rice Noodles with Shrimp)

¾ pound dried flat rice noodles*
    (about ¼ to ½ inch wide)
3 tablespoons Asian fish sauce such as *naam pla**

3 tablespoons ketchup
2 tablespoons rice vinegar
1½ tablespoons firmly packed brown sugar
¼ teaspoon cayenne, or to taste
3 tablespoons vegetable oil
3 large eggs, beaten lightly
8 garlic cloves, minced
4 shallots, minced (about ½ cup)
¾ pound medium shrimp, peeled, deveined,
    and cut into ½-inch pieces
3 cups fresh bean sprouts, rinsed and spun dry
4 scallions, halved lengthwise and cut
    crosswise into 1-inch pieces
¾ cup water
For garnish
⅓ cup crushed roasted peanuts
¼ teaspoon dried hot red pepper flakes
small fresh red chilies if desired
fresh coriander sprigs if desired
lime wedges

*available at Asian markets, some specialty
    foods shops, and by mail order from:
    Adriana's Bazaar, tel. (212) 877-5757

In a large bowl soak the noodles in cold water to cover for 30 minutes, or until they are softened, and drain them well. In a bowl stir together the fish sauce, the ketchup, the vinegar, the brown sugar, and the cayenne.

In a wok or non-stick skillet heat 1 tablespoon of the oil over moderate heat until it is hot but not smoking, add the eggs, and cook them, stirring, until they are scrambled and just cooked through. Transfer the eggs to a bowl and break them into pieces with a spoon.

In the wok or a large heavy skillet heat the remaining 2 tablespoons oil over moderately high heat until it just begins to smoke and in it stir-fry the garlic and the shallots until the mixture is golden. Add the shrimp and stir-fry the mixture for 1 to 2 minutes, or until the shrimp are just cooked through. Add the ketchup mixture, the noodles, 2 cups of the bean sprouts, the scallions, and the water and cook the mixture, stirring, for 3 to 5 minutes, or until the noodles are tender and the excess liquid is evaporated. Add the egg, toss the mixture well, and mound it on a platter.

Sprinkle the noodle mixture with the peanuts and the red pepper flakes and arrange the remaining 1 cup bean sprouts around it. Garnish the dish with the chilies, the coriander sprigs, and the lime wedges. Serves 6.

Cold Sesame Noodles

2 tablespoons smooth peanut butter
2½ tablespoons Asian (toasted) sesame oil*
1½ tablespoons soy sauce
¼ cup water
2 teaspoons minced garlic
2 teaspoons minced peeled fresh gingerroot
2 teaspoons rice vinegar
1 teaspoon sugar
¼ teaspoon Asian chili paste* or
    dried hot red pepper flakes
¾ pound fresh** or dried* Asian egg
    noodles or spaghetti
3 tablespoons minced scallion

*available at Asian markets, some specialty
    foods shops and supermarkets, and by mail
    order from Adriana's Bazaar,
    2152 Broadway, New York, NY 10023,
    tel. (212) 877-5757
**available at some Asian markets

In a blender blend together the peanut butter, 2 tablespoons of the sesame oil, the soy sauce, the water, the garlic, the gingerroot, the vinegar, the sugar, the chili paste, and a pinch of salt. In a kettle of salted boiling water cook the noodles until they are *al dente*, drain them in a colander, and rinse them well under cold water. Drain the noodles well, in a bowl toss them with the remaining ½ tablespoon sesame oil, and mound them on a platter. Drizzle the noodles with the sesame mixture and sprinkle them with the scallion. Serves 4 as a main dish and 8 as a first course.

The following sauce makes an excellent accompaniment to the pasta of your choice.

Pine Nut and Parmesan Pasta Sauce

¾ cup pine nuts (about 4½ ounces),
    toasted lightly
¾ cup freshly grated Parmesan
½ cup chopped fresh parsley leaves
1 large garlic clove, chopped
2 tablespoons olive oil
½ cup milk

In a food processor or blender blend together ½ cup of the pine nuts, the Parmesan, the parsley, the garlic, and

the oil until the mixture forms a coarse paste, add the milk and salt and pepper to taste, and blend the sauce until it is combined well. Transfer the sauce to a bowl and stir in the remaining ¼ cup pine nuts. Toss the sauce with hot cooked pasta and enough of the pasta cooking water to reach the desired consistency. The sauce keeps in an airtight container, chilled, for 3 days. Makes about 1¼ cups, enough for 1½ pounds dried pasta.

GRAINS

Barley Torte

a ¼-ounce package dried mushrooms
    (available at most supermarkets)
2 cups warm water
2 small onions,
    diced
3 tablespoons unsalted butter
1 cup pearl barley
1 cup chicken broth
¾ teaspoon salt
¼ cup fine dry bread crumbs
½ cup coarsely grated Fontina
    (about ¼ pound)
1 large whole egg, beaten lightly
1 large egg yolk, beaten lightly

In a small bowl let the mushrooms soak in the warm water. In a heavy saucepan cook the onions in the butter over moderately low heat, stirring occasionally, for 15 minutes, or until they are soft. Strain the mushrooms through a fine sieve into a bowl, reserving the liquid, and chop them into ¼-inch pieces.

Preheat the oven to 400° F. Stir the barley into the onion mixture, coating it well, add the mushrooms, ½ cup of the reserved mushroom liquid, and ½ cup of the broth, and cook the mixture over moderate heat, stirring, for 5 minutes, or until almost all the liquid is absorbed. Add the remaining ½ cup broth and ½ cup of the remaining reserved mushroom liquid and cook the mixture, stirring, for 5 minutes, or until the liquid is absorbed. Stir in the remaining mushroom liquid and the salt and cook the mixture, adding up to ½ cup additional water if it is too dry, for 12 minutes, or until the barley is tender. Transfer the barley mixture to a jelly-roll pan and let it cool completely.

Butter an 8-inch round cake pan (2 inches deep) and coat it with the bread crumbs, knocking out any excess. In a bowl stir together the Fontina, the whole egg, the egg yolk and the barley mixture gently but thoroughly and spoon the mixture into the prepared pan, pressing it down and smoothing the top. Cover the pan tightly with foil, bake the torte in the oven for 40 minutes, or until it is set, and let it cool in the pan on a rack for 10 minutes. Invert the torte onto a serving plate and serve it warm, cut into wedges. Serves 6 as an accompaniment to meat or poultry.

Basil Couscous with Summer Squash

¾ cup water
1 tablespoon olive oil
¾ teaspoon salt
1 cup packed fresh basil leaves,
    cut into thin shreds
½ cup couscous
1 cup ¼-inch dice of zucchini
1 cup ¼-inch dice of yellow summer squash

In a small saucepan bring the water to a boil with the oil, stir in the salt and the basil, and simmer the mixture for 30 seconds, or until the basil is wilted. Stir in the couscous, remove the pan from the heat, and let the mixture stand, covered, for 5 minutes. While the couscous is standing, in a steamer set over boiling water steam the zucchini and the yellow squash, covered, for 3 minutes, or until the vegetables are just tender. Transfer the zucchini and the yellow squash to a bowl and stir in the couscous. Serves 4.

Herbed Couscous with Lemon

¾ cup water
¼ teaspoon freshly grated lemon zest
a rounded ¼ teaspoon dried thyme
½ cup couscous
¼ cup packed fresh parsley leaves, minced
1 tablespoon olive oil
fresh lemon juice to taste

In a small heavy saucepan bring the water to a boil, stir in the zest, the thyme, and the couscous, and remove the pan from the heat. Let the mixture stand, covered, for 5 minutes, fluff it, and stir in the parsley, the oil, the lemon juice, and salt and pepper to taste. Serves 2.

Kasha Paprikas

the white and pale green parts of 1 large leek,
    sliced thin, washed well, and drained
    (about 1 cup)
1 cup finely chopped celery including
    some of the leaves
1 garlic clove, minced
½ stick (¼ cup) unsalted butter
2 teaspoons paprika
    (preferably sweet Hungarian)
1 cup water
¾ cup beef broth
½ teaspoon salt
¼ teaspoon black pepper
1 cup coarse kasha (available at natural foods
    stores and most supermarkets)
2 tablespoons minced fresh parsley leaves
⅓ cup sour cream

In a heavy saucepan cook the leek, the celery, and the garlic in the butter with the paprika over moderate heat, stirring, until the vegetables are softened. Stir in the water, the broth, the salt, and the pepper, bring the liquid to a boil, and stir in the kasha. Cook the mixture, covered, for 12 minutes, or until the liquid is absorbed, remove the pan from the heat, and stir in the parsley. Let the mixture stand, covered, for 3 minutes and stir in the sour cream. Serves 4 to 6 as an accompaniment to meat or poultry.

Gorgonzola and Pear Millet Pilaf

1 tablespoon unsalted butter
1 cup millet (available at natural foods stores)
2 cups water
1 teaspoon salt
½ teaspoon paprika
2 pears (about ¾ pound)
1 tablespoon fresh lemon juice
½ cup crumbled Gorgonzola or Roquefort
½ cup sliced almonds, toasted

In a heavy saucepan melt the butter over moderately high heat, in it sauté the millet, stirring, until it turns golden brown, and stir in the water, the salt, and the paprika. Simmer the millet, covered, for 18 to 20 minutes, or until it is tender and the water is absorbed, transfer it to a bowl, and fluff it with a fork. In another bowl toss the pears, cut into ¼-inch dice, with the lemon juice. When the millet has cooled slightly add the pears, the Gorgonzola, the almonds, and pepper to taste and toss the pilaf gently. Serves 8.

Baked Polenta with Shiitake Ragout

For the mushroom ragout
1 large onion, chopped fine
4 garlic cloves, minced
1 teaspoon dried rosemary, crumbled
3 tablespoons olive oil
1 pound white mushrooms, sliced thin
1 pound fresh *shiitake* mushrooms, stems
   discarded and, if large, the caps quartered
1 tablespoon tomato paste
1 cup dry red wine
1 tablespoon cornstarch
1⅓ cups beef broth
2 teaspoons Worcestershire sauce

6 cups water
1 tablespoon olive oil
2 cups yellow cornmeal
2 tablespoons unsalted butter, cut into pieces
1 cup freshly grated Parmesan
⅓ cup minced fresh parsley leaves
¼ pound mozzarella, diced fine (about 1 cup)

Make the mushroom ragout: In a large deep skillet cook the onion, the garlic, and the rosemary in the oil over moderate heat, stirring, until the onion is softened,

add the mushrooms and salt to taste, and cook the mixture over moderately high heat, stirring, for 10 minutes, or until the liquid the mushrooms give off is evaporated. Stir in the tomato paste and the wine and boil the mushroom mixture until most of the liquid is evaporated. In a small bowl stir the cornstarch into the broth, add the mixture and the Worcestershire sauce to the mushroom mixture, and bring the ragout to a boil, stirring. Simmer the ragout for 2 minutes and season it with salt and pepper.

In a large heavy saucepan bring the water with the oil to a boil and add 1 cup of the cornmeal, a little at a time, stirring constantly. Reduce the heat to low, add the remaining 1 cup cornmeal in a slow stream, stirring constantly, and bring the mixture to a boil. Remove the pan from the heat and stir in the butter, ⅔ cup of the Parmesan, the parsley, and salt and pepper to taste.

Spread one third of the polenta evenly in a buttered 13- by 9-inch baking dish and chill the polenta sheet for 20 minutes, or until it is firm. While the polenta sheet is chilling, working quickly, spread half the remaining polenta in a buttered 3-quart shallow baking dish, top it with half the mushroom ragout, and top the ragout with the mozzarella. Spread the remaining polenta quickly over the mozzarella and top it with the remaining ragout.

Invert the polenta sheet onto a work surface and with 1 or more star-shaped cutters cut out as many stars as possible. Arrange the stars decoratively on the ragout and sprinkle them with the remaining ⅓ cup Parmesan. *The layered polenta may be prepared up to this point 2 days in advance and kept covered and chilled.* Preheat the oven to 400° F. Bake the layered polenta in the upper third of the oven for 30 to 40 minutes, or until the polenta stars are golden. Serves 6 to 8.

PHOTO ON PAGES 82 AND 83

Dried Apricot Pine Nut Pilaf

1 medium onion, chopped
2 tablespoons vegetable oil
1 cup converted rice
½ teaspoon salt
1 cup water
1 cup chicken broth
⅓ cup dried apricots, chopped fine
2 tablespoons pine nuts,
   toasted
1 tablespoon minced fresh parsley leaves

In a saucepan cook the onion in the oil over moderately low heat, stirring, until it is softened, add the rice, and cook the mixture over moderate heat, stirring, for 1 minute. Stir in the salt, the water, and the broth, bring the liquid to a boil, and cook the mixture, covered, over low heat for 18 to 20 minutes, or until the liquid is absorbed. Add the apricots, fluff the rice with a fork, and let the mixture stand, covered, off the heat for 5 minutes. Stir in the pine nuts, the parsley, and pepper to taste. Serves 4.

Celery Rice Pilaf with Caraway

2 ribs of celery, sliced thin
1 onion, chopped fine
1 tablespoon olive oil
½ cup long-grain rice
¼ teaspoon caraway seeds
1 cup water

In a small heavy saucepan cook the celery and the onion in the oil over moderately low heat, stirring, until the onion is softened, add the rice and the caraway seeds, and cook the mixture, stirring, for 1 minute. Stir in the water and salt and pepper to taste, bring the mixture to a boil, and simmer it, covered, for 15 minutes, or until the rice is tender and the liquid is absorbed. Let the pilaf stand, covered, for 5 minutes and fluff it with a fork. Serves 2.

Minted Rice with Peas

1 cup water
½ cup long-grain rice
1 tablespoon vegetable oil
¼ teaspoon salt
½ cup thawed frozen peas
1½ tablespoons finely chopped fresh mint leaves
¼ teaspoon fresh lemon zest

In a small heavy saucepan bring the water to a boil, stir in the rice, the oil, and the salt, and cook the mixture, covered, over low heat for 15 minutes. Remove the pan from the heat, stir in the peas, the mint, and the zest, and let the mixture stand, covered, for 5 minutes. Serves 2.

Yellow Rice

2 cups unconverted long-grain rice
2 tablespoons olive oil
3½ cups water
2 teaspoons salt
1 teaspoon turmeric

In a large bowl wash the rice in several changes of cold water until the water runs clear and drain it well in a large sieve. In a large heavy saucepan heat the oil over moderately high heat until it is hot but not smoking, add the rice, and sauté it, stirring, for 1 to 2 minutes, or until it begins to turn opaque and is coated well. Add the water, the salt, and the turmeric and boil the rice, uncovered and without stirring, until the surface of the rice is covered with steam holes and the grains on the top appear dry (about 8 to 10 minutes). Reduce the heat to as low as possible, cover the pan with a tight-fitting lid, and cook the rice for 15 minutes. Remove the pan from the heat and let the rice stand, covered, for 5 minutes. Fluff the rice with a fork and transfer it to a heated serving dish. Serves 10 as part of a buffet.

PHOTO ON PAGE 21

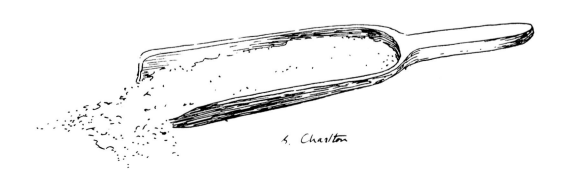

Brown- and Wild-Rice Pilaf with Porcini and Parsley

½ cup wild rice, rinsed in a sieve
1½ ounces dried *porcini* (available at specialty
    foods shops and some supermarkets)
1 cup hot water
1¾ cups cold water
1 cup long-grain brown rice (not converted)
1 teaspoon salt
1 cup chopped onion
3 tablespoons unsalted butter
1½ cups chopped fresh parsley leaves

To a small saucepan of boiling water add the wild rice, remove the pan from the heat, and let the rice soak for 30 minutes. In a small bowl combine the *porcini* and the hot water and let the mushrooms soak for 30 minutes. Strain the mixture through a rinsed and squeezed paper towel set over a measuring cup, reserving ¾ cup of the soaking liquid, wash the *porcini* under cold water to remove any grit, and chop them. In a large saucepan bring the cold water and the *porcini* soaking liquid to a boil, stir in the wild rice, drained well, the brown rice, and the salt, and simmer the mixture, covered, for 40 minutes, or until the liquid is absorbed and the rice is tender. While the rice is cooking, in a large skillet cook the onion in the butter over moderately low heat, stirring occasionally, until it is softened and stir in the *porcini*. Add the rice to the skillet with the parsley and salt and pepper to taste and combine the mixture well. Serves 6.

PHOTO ON PAGE 80

Wild Rice and Toasted Pecan Pilaf

1 cup pecan halves, chopped coarse
2 tablespoons unsalted butter, melted
¾ teaspoon dried thyme, crumbled
¼ teaspoon salt
1 large onion, halved lengthwise and
    sliced thin lengthwise
1 yellow bell pepper, cut into julienne strips
¼ cup olive oil
2½ cups wild rice (about 1 pound),
    rinsed well in several changes of
    water and drained
4½ cups chicken broth

Preheat the oven to 375° F. In a small baking pan toss the pecans with the butter, the thyme, and the salt until they are coated well and toast them in the middle of the oven for 10 minutes, or until they are crisp and fragrant.

In a flameproof casserole cook the onion and the bell pepper in the oil over moderately low heat, stirring, for 5 minutes, or until they are just softened, and with a slotted spoon transfer them to a bowl. Add the rice to the casserole and cook it, stirring constantly, for 1 minute. Stir in the broth, heated to boiling, and salt and pepper to taste and bring the mixture to a boil. Bake the mixture, covered, in the middle of the oven for 40 minutes. Stir in the onion mixture, bake the pilaf, covered, for 30 minutes more, or until the rice is tender and the broth has been absorbed, and stir in the pecans. Serves 8.

PHOTO ON PAGE 34

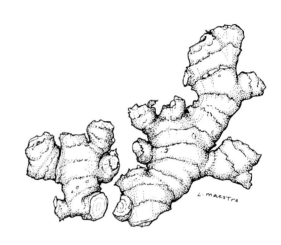

Spiced Basmati Rice

2 cups white *basmati* rice (available at
    specialty foods shops and East Indian
    markets), picked over
a 3-inch cinnamon stick
4 whole cloves
2⅔ cups water
¾ teaspoon salt
1 tablespoon vegetable oil

In a bowl wash the rice in several changes of cold water until the water runs clear, add enough cold water to cover the rice by 3 inches, and let the rice soak for 30 minutes. Drain the rice well and in a large heavy saucepan combine it with the cinnamon stick, the cloves, the water, the salt, and the oil. Bring the mixture to a boil and cook the rice, covered, over low heat for 15 minutes, or until the rice is tender and the liquid is absorbed. Fluff the rice with a fork. Serves 4 to 6.

Ginger and Garlic Triticale

1 cup triticale, wheat, rye, or spelt berries
  (available at natural foods stores)
3 tablespoons vegetable oil
2 scallions,
  chopped fine
2 teaspoons minced peeled fresh gingerroot
2 garlic cloves,
  minced
¼ teaspoon Asian (toasted) sesame oil,
  or to taste
3 tablespoons chopped salted
  dry-roasted peanuts

In a kettle of boiling water cook the triticale berries for 1 hour, or until they are tender. About 5 minutes before the triticale is done, in a large heavy skillet heat the vegetable oil over moderately high heat until it is hot but not smoking and in it sauté the scallions, the gingerroot, and the garlic, stirring frequently, for 2 to 3 minutes, or until the mixture is very fragrant.

Drain the triticale and add it to the scallion mixture. Stir in the sesame oil and salt to taste and cook the mixture for 1 minute. Stir in 2 tablespoons of the peanuts, transfer the mixture to a serving bowl, and sprinkle it with the remaining 1 tablespoon peanuts. Serves 4 as an accompaniment to meat or poultry.

VEGETABLES

Artichoke and Potato Purée

a ½-pound russet (baking) potato
a 9-ounce box frozen artichoke hearts, thawed
   and chopped
1½ tablespoons unsalted butter

In a small saucepan combine the potato, peeled and cut into ½-inch pieces, with enough cold water to cover it by 1 inch and simmer it, covered, for 10 to 15 minutes, or until it is very tender. While the potato is cooking, in a small skillet cook the artichoke hearts in the butter with salt and pepper to taste over moderate heat, stirring, until they are very tender. Drain the potato, return it to the pan, and cook it, covered, over moderate heat, shaking the pan, for 30 seconds, or until any excess liquid is evaporated. Force the artichoke mixture and the potato through a food mill fitted with the medium disk into a bowl, discarding the solids, and season the purée with salt and pepper. Makes about 2 cups, serving 2.

Asparagus with Scallion Butter

3 pounds thin asparagus (about 40),
   trimmed and peeled
½ stick (¼ cup) unsalted butter
½ cup minced white part of scallion
1 teaspoon freshly grated lemon zest
12 whole black peppercorns

In a kettle of boiling salted water cook the asparagus for 3 to 5 minutes, or until it is tender but not limp, and drain it well in a colander. In a small saucepan melt the butter, stir in the scallion, the zest, the peppercorns, and salt to taste, and simmer the mixture for 3 minutes. Strain the butter mixture through a fine sieve into the kettle, add the asparagus and salt and pepper to taste, and heat the asparagus over moderately high heat, tossing it gently, until it is heated through. Serves 8.

PHOTO ON PAGE 38

Black Beans

1 pound (about 2¼ cups) dried black beans,
   picked over and rinsed
2 teaspoons salt
1 onion, chopped fine
1 green bell pepper,
   chopped fine
1 red bell pepper,
   chopped fine
4 garlic cloves,
   minced
1 tablespoon ground cumin
⅓ cup olive oil
3 tablespoons tomato paste
2 tablespoons red-wine vinegar,
   or to taste
⅓ cup finely chopped scallion
⅓ cup chopped fresh coriander

In a large bowl let the beans soak in enough cold water to cover them by 2 inches for 1 hour and drain them. In a large heavy saucepan simmer the beans in enough cold water to cover them by 1 inch, uncovered, adding more water as necessary to keep the beans barely covered, for 1 to 2 hours, or until they are tender. Add the salt and simmer the beans for 5 minutes.

While the beans are cooking, in a heavy skillet cook the onion, the bell peppers, the garlic, and the cumin in the oil over moderately low heat, stirring, until the vegetables are softened, add the tomato paste, and cook the mixture, stirring, for 2 minutes. Stir the vegetable mixture into the beans, add the vinegar and salt and pepper to taste, and simmer the mixture, stirring occasionally, for 15 minutes, or until it is thickened to the desired consistency. *The beans may be prepared up to this point 2 days in advance, kept covered and chilled, and reheated, adding additional water if necessary.* Transfer the beans to a serving bowl and sprinkle them with the scallion and the coriander. Serves 10 as part of a buffet.

PHOTO ON PAGE 21

Green Beans with Red Onion and Olives

⅓ cup minced red onion
2 teaspoons balsamic or red-wine vinegar
¼ teaspoon salt, or to taste
1 tablespoon olive oil
½ pound green beans, trimmed and
   cut into thirds
5 Kalamata or other brine-cured black olives,
   pitted and sliced thin

In a bowl stir together the onion, the vinegar, the salt, and the oil and let the mixture stand. In a steamer set over boiling water steam the beans, covered, for 7 to 8 minutes, or until they are just tender, add them to the bowl while they are still hot, and toss them well with the olives. Serves 2.

Beets with Horseradish

2½ pounds beets without their greens
   (5½ pounds with greens), trimmed, leaving
   2 inches of the stem ends intact
½ cup finely grated peeled fresh horseradish
   or ⅓ cup drained bottled horseradish
2 tablespoons sugar
2 tablespoons wine vinegar
3 tablespoons water

In a kettle cover the beets by 2 inches with cold water, bring the water to a boil, and simmer the beets, covered, for 20 to 30 minutes, or until they are tender. Drain the beets and under cold water slip off and discard the skins and stems. Cut the beets into wedges, in a bowl combine them well with the horseradish, the sugar, the vinegar, the water, and salt and pepper to taste, and let them marinate, covered and chilled, for at least 8 hours and up to 3 days. Makes about 4 cups, serving 8.

PHOTO ON PAGE 33

Beets with Walnuts

6 beets (each 1½ to 2 inches in diameter),
   scrubbed and trimmed, leaving about 1 inch
   of the stems attached
¾ cup water
2 garlic cloves, unpeeled
1 tablespoon olive oil
1 tablespoon minced fresh coriander
1½ teaspoons red-wine vinegar, or to taste
1 teaspoon minced white part of scallion
5 walnut halves, toasted and chopped
   (about 2 teaspoons)

In a 2-quart microwave-safe round glass casserole with a lid microwave the beets with the water and the garlic, covered, on high power (100%), stirring every 2 minutes, for 6 to 9 minutes, or until they are tender when pierced with a fork, transferring them to a cutting board as they are cooked and reserving the garlic, and let them cool. Peel the beets, halve them, and slice them ¼ inch thick. Peel the reserved garlic, mash it to a paste with the flat side of a heavy knife, and in a serving bowl stir it together with the oil, the coriander, the vinegar, the scallion, and salt and pepper to taste. Stir in the sliced beets and sprinkle the mixture with the walnuts. Serves 2.

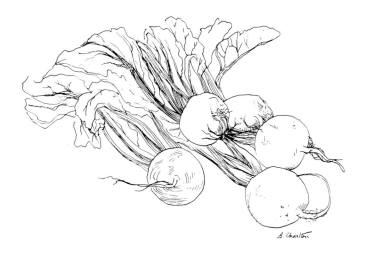

Deep-Fried Broccoli and Carrots in Scallion and Caper Beer Batter

1½ cups all-purpose flour
a 12-ounce bottle of beer (not dark)
6 scallions, chopped fine
2 tablespoons drained bottled capers,
    chopped fine
1½ teaspoons salt
vegetable oil for deep-frying
1 head of broccoli, cut into 1½-inch flowerets
3 carrots, cut into ½-inch-thick sticks

Preheat the oven to 325° F. In a bowl whisk together the flour, the beer, the scallions, the capers, and the salt. In a heavy kettle heat 1½ inches of the oil to 375° F. on a deep-fat thermometer, working in batches dip the broccoli in the batter, knocking off the excess batter, and fry it in the oil for 3 minutes, or until it is golden, transferring it as it is fried to paper towels to drain. Dip the carrots in the batter and fry them for 2 minutes in the same manner. Serves 4 to 6.

Broccoli with Cheddar Vinaigrette

1 tablespoon olive or vegetable oil
1½ teaspoons white-wine vinegar
1 tablespoon water
¼ teaspoon Tabasco
½ cup coarsely grated Cheddar
½ pound broccoli, cut into long flowerets

In a blender blend together the oil, the vinegar, the water, the Tabasco, the Cheddar, and salt and pepper to taste until the vinaigrette is smooth. In a small saucepan bring 1 inch of water to a boil and in it cook the broccoli, covered, over high heat for 4 to 5 minutes, or until it is crisp-tender. Drain the broccoli well and serve it topped with the vinaigrette. Serves 2.

Curried Carrots

½ pound carrots (about 4), sliced thin
    on the diagonal
1 tablespoon unsalted butter
½ teaspoon curry powder
fresh lemon juice to taste

In a large saucepan of boiling water boil the carrots for 3 minutes, or until they are crisp-tender, and drain them well. In a heavy skillet melt the butter over moderate heat, stir in the curry powder, and cook the mixture until it foams. Add the carrots, cook the mixture, stirring, for 1 minute, or until the carrots are tender, and stir in the lemon juice and salt and pepper to taste. Serves 2.

Pickled Carrots, Turnips, and Peppers

1 cup distilled white vinegar
1 cup rice vinegar (available at specialty
    foods shops, Asian markets, and many
    supermarkets)
2¾ cups water
⅔ cup sugar
8 slices of peeled fresh gingerroot, each
    the size of a quarter, crushed lightly
    with the flat side of a knife
2 garlic cloves, crushed lightly
1 tablespoon dill seeds
1 tablespoon celery seeds
1 tablespoon salt
1 teaspoon mustard seeds
1 teaspoon Dijon-style mustard
8 black peppercorns
4 carrots, cut into 3½- by ⅓-inch sticks
2 turnips (about ¾ pound), peeled and
    cut into 3½- by ⅓-inch sticks
2 red bell peppers, cut into 3½- by
    ⅓-inch strips

In a saucepan bring the vinegars and the water to a boil with the sugar, the gingerroot, the garlic, the dill seeds, the celery seeds, the salt, the mustard seeds, the mustard, and the peppercorns and simmer the mixture, stirring occasionally, for 3 minutes, or until the sugar is dissolved. Put the carrots, the turnips, and the bell peppers in a heatproof container, pour the vinegar mixture over them, covering them completely, and chill the vegetables, covered, overnight. The vegetables keep, covered and chilled, for 1 week. Makes about 5 cups.

PHOTO ON PAGE 23

Roasted Cauliflower with Rosemary

3 pounds cauliflower (about 1½ heads), cut
    into 1-inch flowerets
2 tablespoons olive oil
2 tablespoons fresh rosemary leaves or
    1 teaspoon dried, crumbled

Preheat the oven to 500° F. In a jelly-roll pan toss the cauliflower with the oil, the rosemary, and salt and pepper to taste until it is coated well and roast it in the middle of the oven for 12 to 15 minutes, or until it is browned in spots and tender. Serves 8.

Edgar Blakeney

Cauliflower with Shallot and Caraway

¼ cup finely chopped shallot
¼ teaspoon caraway seeds
1 tablespoon olive oil
1½ cups 1-inch cauliflower flowerets
1 tablespoon water

In a 2-quart microwave-safe baking dish stir together the shallot, the caraway seeds, and the oil and microwave the mixture, covered, at high power (100%) for 2 minutes, or until the shallot is softened. Stir in the cauliflower and the water, microwave the mixture, covered, at high power for 4 minutes, or until the cauliflower is tender, and season it with salt and pepper. Serves 2.

Sautéed Corn with Bacon and Scallions

1 tablespoon vegetable oil
1½ cups cooked fresh corn kernels
    (cut from about 3 ears)
2 scallions, chopped fine
2 slices of bacon, cooked and crumbled
a pinch of dried hot red pepper flakes

In a non-stick skillet heat the oil over moderately high heat until it is hot but not smoking and in it sauté the corn and the scallions, stirring, for 1 minute. Stir in the bacon and the red pepper flakes and sauté the mixture for 15 seconds. Serves 2.

Eggplant, Roasted Pepper, and Goat Cheese Terrine with Parsley Sauce

2 eggplants (about 2½ pounds total), cut
    lengthwise into ½-inch-thick slices
⅓ cup olive oil
¼ cup bottled black olive paste such as
    tapenade or *olivada* (available at specialty
    foods shops and some supermarkets)
3 red bell peppers, each roasted (procedure on
    page 114) and cut lengthwise into 3 sections
7 ounces soft mild goat cheese, such as
    Montrachet, sliced thin
parsley sauce (page 178) as an
    accompaniment
parsley sprigs for garnish if desired

Preheat the broiler. Arrange the eggplant slices in one layer on baking sheets, brush both sides of the eggplant with the oil, and sprinkle them with salt to taste. Broil the eggplant in batches about 4 inches from the heat for 4 to 5 minutes on each side, or until it is golden and tender, and transfer it with a metal spatula to paper towels to drain.

Line a loaf pan, 8½ by 4½ by 2½ inches, with plastic wrap, leaving a 3-inch overhang, and in it arrange the eggplant, the olive paste, the bell peppers, and the goat cheese in several layers, beginning and ending with the eggplant. Cover the eggplant with the plastic overhang, weight the terrine with a 3- to 4-pound weight (such as a loaf pan filled with canned goods), and chill it for 24 hours. *The terrine may be made 3 days in advance.*

Remove the weight, invert the terrine onto a cutting board, and discard the plastic wrap. Cut four ¾-inch-thick slices from the terrine, pour about 2 tablespoons of the parsley sauce onto the center of each of 4 plates, tilting the plates to spread the sauce, and arrange a slice of the terrine on each plate. Garnish each serving with a parsley sprig. Serves 4 with leftovers.

PHOTO ON PAGE 52

Parsley Sauce

½ cup chopped fresh parsley leaves,
    preferably flat-leafed
1 small garlic clove, sliced
4 teaspoons balsamic vinegar
2 tablespoons water
6 tablespoons extra-virgin olive oil

In a blender purée the parsley and the garlic with the vinegar, the water, the oil, and salt and pepper to taste until the sauce is smooth and strain it through a fine sieve set over a small bowl, pressing hard on the solids. Makes about ½ cup.

Kale with Garlic and Bacon

1 slice of bacon, chopped
1 garlic clove, minced
6 cups torn kale leaves, washed
1 cup water

In a large heavy skillet cook the bacon over moderate heat, stirring, until it is crisp and transfer it to paper towels to drain. In the fat remaining in the skillet cook the garlic, stirring, until it is golden, add the kale and the water, and simmer the mixture, covered, for 10 minutes, or until the kale is wilted and tender. Simmer the mixture, uncovered, until most of the liquid is evaporated and stir in the bacon and salt and pepper to taste. Serves 2.

Scalloped Onions, Leeks, and Shallots

3 pounds onions, cut into ¼-inch-thick slices
the white and pale green parts of 2 pounds
    (about 6) leeks, split lengthwise, washed
    well, and chopped
½ pound shallots, cut into ¼-inch-thick slices
½ stick (¼ cup) unsalted butter
¼ cup heavy cream
1 cup coarse fresh bread crumbs
1 cup grated extra-sharp Cheddar
    (about ¼ pound)
¼ teaspoon paprika

In a heavy kettle cook the onions, the leeks, and the shallots in the butter with salt and pepper to taste, covered, over moderate heat, stirring occasionally, for 10 minutes, reduce the heat to moderately low, and cook the vegetables, stirring occasionally, for 10 to 20 minutes more, or until they are soft. Remove the lid and cook the mixture over moderate heat, stirring, for 3 to 5 minutes more, or until the excess liquid is evaporated. *The onion mixture may be made 2 days in advance and kept covered and chilled.*

Preheat the oven to 375° F. Transfer the onion mixture to a 2-quart shallow baking dish and stir in the cream. In a small bowl toss together the bread crumbs and the Cheddar, sprinkle the mixture evenly onto the onion mixture, and dust it with the paprika. Bake the onion mixture in the middle of the oven for 20 to 30 minutes, or until the cheese is melted and the mixture is bubbly. Serves 8.

PHOTO ON PAGE 75

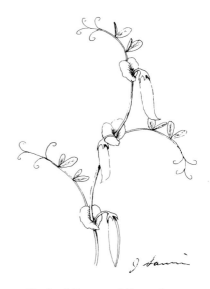

Herbed Buttered Parsnips

3 pounds parsnips, peeled and cut diagonally
    into ½-inch-thick slices
½ stick (¼ cup) unsalted butter, cut into pieces
    and softened
⅓ cup finely chopped fresh parsley leaves
1 tablespoon fresh thyme leaves, chopped
    fine, or 1 teaspoon dried, crumbled
1½ teaspoons fresh lemon juice, or to taste

In a steamer set over boiling water steam the parsnips, covered, for 8 minutes, or until they are tender. While the parsnips are steaming, put the butter, the parsley, and the thyme in a heatproof serving bowl. Add the hot parsnips and toss them with the butter mixture, the lemon juice, and salt and pepper to taste. Serves 8.

PHOTO ON PAGE 74

Parsnips and Carrots with Orange Butter

1 cup water
½ pound parsnips, peeled, halved lengthwise,
    and cut crosswise into ¼-inch-thick pieces
½ pound carrots, halved lengthwise and cut
    crosswise into ¼-inch-thick pieces
⅓ cup fresh orange juice
⅛ teaspoon freshly grated orange zest
1 tablespoon unsalted butter

In a skillet combine the water, the parsnips, the carrots, and salt to taste, simmer the vegetables for 15 minutes, or until they are just tender, and stir in the orange juice. Simmer the mixture for 5 minutes, or until the vegetables are tender, and transfer the vegetables with a slotted spoon to a bowl. Boil the liquid until it is reduced to about 2 tablespoons, remove the skillet from the heat, and stir in the zest and the butter, stirring until the butter is melted. Spoon the sauce over the vegetables. Serves 2.

Braised Peas and Scallions

1 tablespoon unsalted butter
½ teaspoon sugar
6 scallions, halved lengthwise and cut
    crosswise into 1-inch-thick pieces
1 cup shelled fresh peas
⅓ cup chicken broth

In a saucepan melt the butter over moderate heat, add the sugar, the scallions, the peas, and salt and pepper to taste, and cook the mixture, stirring, for 1 minute. Add the broth and simmer the mixture, covered partially, for 2 minutes, or until the peas are barely tender. Boil the mixture, uncovered, for 1 to 2 minutes, or until the peas are tender and the liquid is almost evaporated. Serves 2.

Buttered Snow Peas and Carrots

3 to 4 carrots, cut crosswise on the
    diagonal into ⅛-inch slices
    (about 1 cup)
¼ pound snow peas, trimmed, discarding the
    strings, and cut crosswise on the diagonal
    into ½-inch pieces (about 1 cup)
1 tablespoon unsalted butter

In a large saucepan of boiling water cook the carrots for 3 minutes, or until they are crisp-tender. Add the snow peas, cook the vegetables for 30 seconds, and drain them well. Return the vegetables to the pan, add the butter and salt and pepper to taste, and heat the vegetables over moderately low heat, stirring, until the butter is melted. Serves 4.

PHOTO ON PAGE 17

Minted Sugar Snap Peas

1½ pounds sugar snap peas, trimmed
2 tablespoons unsalted butter
2 tablespoons finely shredded fresh
    mint leaves

In a kettle of salted boiling water cook the snap peas for 1 to 3 minutes, or until they are crisp-tender, drain them, and plunge them into a bowl of ice and cold water to stop the cooking. Drain the peas well. In a large skillet melt the butter, add 1 tablespoon of the mint, the peas, and salt and pepper to taste, and heat the mixture over moderately low heat, stirring, until the peas are heated through. Sprinkle the peas with the remaining 1 tablespoon mint. Serves 4 to 6.

PHOTO ON PAGES 64 AND 65

Pommes Anna
(Sliced-Potato Cake)

1½ pounds russet (baking) potatoes
½ stick (¼ cup) unsalted butter, melted

Preheat the oven to 425° F. Peel the potatoes and, using a food processor fitted with the slicing blade or a mandoline, slice them very thin, transferring them as they are sliced to a large bowl of cold water. Drain the slices and pat them dry between paper towels. Generously brush the bottom and side of a 9-inch heavy ovenproof skillet, preferably non-stick, with some of the butter and in the skillet arrange the slices, overlapping them slightly, in layers, brushing each layer with some of the remaining butter and seasoning it with salt and pepper. Cover the layered potato slices with a buttered round of foil, tamp down the assembled potato cake firmly, and bake it in the middle of the oven for 30 minutes. Remove the foil and bake the potato cake for 25 to 30 minutes more, or until the slices are tender and golden. Invert the potato cake onto a cutting board and cut it into 8 wedges. Serves 4.

PHOTO ON PAGE 17

Crusty Garlic and Rosemary Potatoes

1 pound small red potatoes, quartered
3 large garlic cloves, sliced thin lengthwise
1 tablespoon olive oil
½ teaspoon dried rosemary, crumbled

In a steamer set over boiling water steam the potatoes, covered, for 8 to 10 minutes, or until they are just tender. In a non-stick skillet cook the garlic in the oil over moderate heat, stirring, until it is pale golden, add the potatoes, the rosemary, and salt and pepper to taste, and sauté the mixture over moderately high heat, stirring, for 5 minutes, or until the potatoes are golden. Serves 2.

Mashed Potatoes with Garlic and Shallots

12 shallots, unpeeled
1 large head of garlic, outer skin peeled
    leaving the head intact
4 tablespoons olive oil (preferably extra-virgin)
3½ pounds (about 6 large) russet (baking)
    potatoes
¾ stick (6 tablespoons) unsalted butter,
    softened

Preheat the oven to 425° F. In a bowl toss together the shallots, the head of garlic, 1 tablespoon of the oil, and salt and pepper to taste. Wrap the shallots and the garlic tightly in a foil package and roast them in the middle of the oven for 45 minutes. Unwrap the package carefully and let the shallots and the garlic cool until they can be handled. Peel the shallots and the garlic and purée them in a food processor.

In a kettle combine the potatoes, peeled and cut into ½-inch pieces, with enough cold water to cover them by 2 inches, bring the water to a boil, and add salt to taste. Simmer the potatoes for 15 minutes, or until they are very tender, drain them, reserving about 1 cup of the cooking water, and force them through a ricer or a food mill fitted with the coarse disk into a bowl. Beat in the garlic purée, the remaining 3 tablespoons oil, the butter, salt and pepper to taste, and enough of the reserved cooking water to reach the desired consistency. Serves 4 to 6.

PHOTO ON PAGES 64 AND 65

Goat Cheese Mashed-Potato Gratin

2 pounds yellow-fleshed potatoes or russet
    (baking) potatoes
6 garlic cloves
⅓ cup heavy cream
1 stick (½ cup) unsalted butter
⅓ cup mild goat cheese such as Montrachet
    (about 3½ ounces)
¼ cup minced scallion

In a large saucepan combine the potatoes, peeled and cut into 1½- to 2-inch pieces, and the garlic with enough salted cold water to cover the potatoes by ½ inch and simmer them, covered, for 15 to 25 minutes, or until they are tender but not falling apart. While the potatoes are cooking, in a small saucepan heat the cream with the butter, the goat cheese, and salt and pepper to taste over moderately low heat, stirring, until the butter and cheese are just melted and smooth and keep the mixture warm. Drain the potatoes and garlic and force them through a food mill fitted with the medium disk or a ricer into a bowl. With an electric mixer beat in the butter mixture, the scallion, and salt and pepper to taste, beating just until the potatoes are fluffy and smooth (do not over-beat), and transfer the mixture to a 1-quart shallow flameproof baking dish. *The potatoes may be prepared up to this point 2 days in advance and kept covered and chilled. Reheat the potatoes in a preheated 400° F. oven for 20 minutes, or until they are heated through, before broiling them.* Broil the potatoes under a preheated broiler about 4 inches from the heat for 3 to 5 minutes, or until the top is golden. Serves 4 to 6.

Goat Cheese Potato Cakes with Chives

two ½-pound russet (baking) potatoes
6 large shallots, sliced (about 1 cup)
2 garlic cloves, sliced
1 cup fine dry bread crumbs
a 3½-ounce log of soft mild goat cheese such
    as Montrachet, at room temperature

¼ cup minced fresh chives or scallion greens
½ stick (¼ cup) unsalted butter

In a saucepan combine the potatoes, peeled and cut into 1-inch pieces, the shallots, and the garlic with enough cold water to cover the mixture by 1 inch and simmer the mixture for 10 to 15 minutes, or until the potatoes are tender. Drain the potato mixture, return it to the pan, and steam it over moderate heat, shaking the pan, for 30 seconds, or until any excess liquid is evaporated. Force the potato mixture through a ricer or the medium disk of a food mill into a bowl and stir in ½ cup of the bread crumbs, the goat cheese, the chives or scallions, and salt and pepper to taste. Form ½-cup measures of the mixture into four ¾-inch-thick cakes, transferring the potato cakes as they are formed to a plate covered with the remaining ½ cup bread crumbs, and coat the potato cakes with the crumbs.

In a large heavy skillet heat the butter over moderately high heat until the foam subsides and in it sauté the potato cakes, turning them once, for 5 minutes on each side, or until they are crusty and golden brown. Makes 4 potato cakes.

Parchment-Baked Minted Potatoes

3 tablespoons unsalted butter, melted
1½ tablespoons finely shredded fresh
  mint leaves
1½ tablespoons minced shallot
a large pinch of freshly grated lemon zest
1 pound small new potatoes
4 pieces of parchment paper, each
  14 by 8 inches

Preheat the oven to 350° F. In a bowl stir together the butter, the mint, the shallot, the zest, and salt and pepper to taste until the mixture is combined well. Add the potatoes, trimmed and sliced as thin as possible, and toss the mixture gently to coat the potatoes well. Put the parchment paper on a work surface, fold each piece in half by bringing the short ends together, and with scissors trim the unfolded edges of each piece to form a half-heart shape. Unfold the papers, divide the potatoes among them, arranging the potatoes just to one side of the fold line, and fold the other halves of the papers over the potatoes. Beginning with a folded corner, twist and fold the edges of each paper together, forming half-heart-shaped packets, and seal the ends tightly by twist-ing them. Bake the packets on a baking sheet in the middle of the oven for 17 minutes. Serve the potatoes in the packets and slit the packets open at the table. Serves 4.

Potato, Spinach, and Feta Gratin

2 pounds russet (baking) potatoes
  (about 3 large)
2 pounds fresh spinach, washed well
  and the coarse stems discarded
½ pound Feta cheese
1½ cups half-and-half
3 large eggs
1½ teaspoons salt
¾ teaspoon black pepper

Preheat the oven to 350° F. Oil an 8-inch-square (2-quart) baking dish lightly, line it with wax paper, and oil the paper lightly. Peel the potatoes and in a food processor fitted with a 2-mm. slicing disk slice the potatoes crosswise. (Alternatively, the potatoes may be sliced thin with a hand-held slicing device.) In a kettle of salted boiling water boil the potatoes for 7 minutes, or until they are just tender, drain them in a colander, and rinse them briefly under cold water. In the kettle cook the spinach in the water clinging to the leaves, covered, over high heat, stirring occasionally, for 2 minutes, or until it is wilted, drain it, and refresh it under cold water. Squeeze the water from the spinach by wringing it by handfuls in a kitchen towel, transfer it to the food processor fitted with the metal blade, and add the Feta. In a bowl whisk together well the half-and-half, the eggs, the salt, and the pepper, add half the custard to the spinach mixture, and pulse the motor of the processor until the mixture is puréed coarse.

Transfer the potatoes to the prepared baking dish and spread them in an even layer. Pour the remaining custard over the potatoes, shaking the dish slightly to distribute the custard evenly, and top the potatoes with the spinach mixture, smoothing the top. Bake the gratin in the middle of the oven for 45 to 50 minutes, or until it is set in the middle, and let it cool on a rack for 30 minutes. Run a knife around the side of the dish, invert the gratin onto a flameproof plate, and peel off the wax paper. Preheat the broiler and broil the gratin about 4 inches from the heat for 10 to 15 minutes, or until the top is golden brown. Serve the gratin cut into squares. Serves 8.

PHOTO ON PAGE 33

Steamed New Potatoes with Mint and Parsley

¾ pound small red potatoes,
  quartered lengthwise
2 teaspoons minced fresh mint leaves
2 teaspoons minced fresh parsley leaves
1 tablespoon unsalted butter, softened
1 tablespoon sour cream

In a steamer set over boiling water steam the potatoes, covered, for 10 to 12 minutes, or until they are just tender. While the potatoes are steaming, in a bowl stir together the mint, the parsley, the butter, the sour cream, and salt and pepper to taste. Add the potatoes to the herb mixture and toss them well. Serves 2.

Spinach Gnocchi Gratin

¾ pound spinach (about 1 bunch),
  coarse stems discarded and the leaves
  washed well and drained
½ cup water
½ cup milk
½ stick (¼ cup) unsalted butter, cut into pieces
1 cup all-purpose flour
4 large eggs
1 teaspoon salt
½ teaspoon black pepper
¼ teaspoon freshly grated nutmeg, or to taste
⅓ cup heavy cream
½ cup freshly grated Parmesan

In a large heavy saucepan cook the spinach in the water clinging to the leaves, covered, over moderate heat, stirring once or twice, for 3 to 4 minutes, or until it is wilted, refresh it under cold water, and drain it well in a colander. Squeeze it dry by handfuls and chop it fine.

In a heavy saucepan bring the water and the milk just to a boil with the butter, stirring until the butter is melted, add the flour all at once, and stir the mixture briskly with a wooden spatula until it pulls away from the side of the pan and forms a ball. Cook the dough over moderate heat, stirring, for 1 minute. Transfer the dough to a bowl and with an electric mixer beat in the eggs, 1 at a time, beating well after each addition, the salt, the pepper, the nutmeg, and the spinach.

Preheat the oven to 425° F. Into a kettle of boiling salted water drop walnut-size spoonfuls of the paste, about 10 at a time, and simmer them, uncovered, for 5 minutes, or until they rise to the surface and are cooked

through. Transfer the *gnocchi* as they are cooked with a slotted spoon to a large colander and let them drain well. Arrange the *gnocchi* in one layer in a buttered 1½- to 2-quart shallow gratin dish or flameproof baking dish, drizzle the cream over them, and sprinkle them with the Parmesan and salt and pepper to taste. Bake the *gnocchi* in the middle of the oven for 10 minutes and broil them under a hot broiler about 4 inches from the heat for 1 minute, or until they are browned lightly. Serves 4 to 6.

Creamed Spinach with Croutons

For the croutons
2 slices of homemade-type white bread,
  cut into ¼-inch cubes
1½ tablespoons unsalted butter, melted
For the creamed spinach
2 pounds spinach (about 3 bunches),
  coarse stems discarded and the leaves
  washed well and drained
¼ cup minced shallot or onion
1½ tablespoons unsalted butter
1½ tablespoons all-purpose flour
1 cup milk
3 tablespoons sour cream
½ teaspoon freshly grated nutmeg
1 to 2 teaspoons fresh lemon juice

Make the croutons: Preheat the oven to 350° F. In a small bowl toss the bread cubes with the butter and salt to taste, spread them on a baking sheet, and bake them in the middle of the oven for 8 to 10 minutes, or until they are golden.

Make the creamed spinach: In a kettle cook the spinach in the water clinging to the leaves, covered, over moderate heat, stirring once or twice, for 5 to 6 minutes, or until it is wilted, refresh it under cold water, and drain it well in a colander. Squeeze out the excess water by handfuls and in a food processor purée the spinach.

In a heavy saucepan cook the shallot in the butter over moderately low heat, stirring, until it is softened, add the flour, and cook the *roux*, stirring, for 3 minutes. Add the milk, whisking, bring the mixture to a boil, whisking, and simmer it, whisking, for 3 minutes. Add the spinach purée, the sour cream, the nutmeg, the lemon juice, and salt and pepper to taste and heat the creamed spinach over moderately low heat, stirring, until it is heated through. Serve the creamed spinach topped with the croutons. Serves 4 to 6.

Stir-Fried Spinach in Garlic Sauce

⅓ cup chicken broth
1½ tablespoons soy sauce
1 tablespoon Scotch or medium-dry Sherry
1 tablespoon rice vinegar or white-wine
    vinegar
1 tablespoon cornstarch
1 teaspoon sugar
2 tablespoons vegetable oil
1½ tablespoons minced garlic
1 tablespoon minced peeled fresh gingerroot
1½ pounds spinach (about 2 bunches),
    coarse stems discarded and the leaves
    washed well and spun dry
cooked rice as an accompaniment if desired

In a glass measure stir together the broth, the soy sauce, the Scotch, the vinegar, the cornstarch, and the sugar until the cornstarch is dissolved. In a wok or large deep heavy skillet heat the oil over high heat until it is hot but not smoking, in it stir-fry the garlic and the gingerroot for 30 seconds, or until the garlic is golden, and add the spinach in batches, stir-frying until each batch is wilted slightly before adding each new one. Stir the cornstarch mixture, add it to the wok, and stir-fry the mixture for 1 to 2 minutes, or until the spinach is wilted evenly and the sauce is thickened. Serve the spinach with the rice. Serves 4.

Spinach and White Beans with Garlic

1 garlic clove, minced
1 tablespoon olive oil
½ pound spinach, coarse stems discarded
    and the leaves washed well, spun dry,
    and chopped coarse

a 15- to 16-ounce can white beans, rinsed
    and drained well
1 tablespoon balsamic vinegar

In a skillet cook the garlic in the oil over moderate heat, stirring, until it is pale golden, add the spinach, and cook it, stirring, until it is wilted. Add the beans, the vinegar, and salt and pepper to taste and simmer the mixture, stirring gently, for 2 minutes. Serves 2.

Butternut Squash Gratin

a 1½-pound butternut squash, peeled, seeded,
    and cut into ¾-inch pieces
1 tablespoon unsalted butter, softened
¼ cup walnuts, chopped fine
2 to 3 tablespoons freshly grated Parmesan

Preheat the oven to 400° F. In a steamer set over boiling water steam the squash, covered, for 15 minutes, or until it is tender. In a food processor purée the squash with the butter, season it with salt and pepper, and transfer it to a buttered 2- to 3-cup shallow baking dish, smoothing the top. Sprinkle the squash with the walnuts and the Parmesan and bake it in the upper third of the oven for 15 minutes, or until the cheese is melted and the walnuts are toasted. Serves 2.

Squash Purée with Olive Oil and Lime

3½ pounds *calabaza* (available at Hispanic
    markets) or butternut squash, peeled,
    seeded, and cut into 2-inch chunks
¼ cup olive oil (preferably extra-virgin)
2 to 3 tablespoons fresh lime juice, or to taste
freshly grated nutmeg to taste

In a steamer set over boiling water steam the squash, covered, for 15 to 20 minutes, or until it is very tender. Reserve the steaming liquid and force the squash through a ricer or food mill set over a large bowl. Stir in the oil, the lime juice, and enough of the reserved steaming liquid to reach the desired consistency and season the squash purée with the nutmeg and salt and pepper. *The squash purée may be made 3 days in advance, kept covered and chilled, and reheated, adding additional water as needed.* Makes about 6 cups, serving 10 as part of a buffet.

PHOTO ON PAGE 20

Maple Squash Purée

3½ pounds butternut squash, peeled, seeded,
    and cut into 1-inch chunks
2 tablespoons unsalted butter,
    cut into pieces
2 to 3 tablespoons pure maple syrup

In a steamer set over boiling water steam the squash, covered, for 15 minutes, or until it is very tender. Reserve the steaming liquid and in a food processor purée the squash with the butter, the maple syrup, and enough of the reserved steaming liquid to reach the desired consistency. Season the squash purée with salt and pepper. *The squash purée may be made 3 days in advance, kept covered and chilled, and reheated, adding additional water as needed.* Serves 8.

PHOTO ON PAGES 74 AND 75

Minted Cherry Tomatoes and Zucchini

1 small zucchini, quartered lengthwise
    and cut crosswise into
    1-inch pieces
1 tablespoon unsalted butter
1 cup cherry tomatoes
1 tablespoon minced fresh mint leaves,
    or to taste

In a skillet sauté the zucchini in the butter over moderately high heat, stirring occasionally, for 3 minutes, or until it is just tender. Add the tomatoes, cook the mixture, shaking the skillet, for 1 minute, or until the tomatoes are heated through, and stir in the mint and salt and pepper to taste. Serves 2.

Zucchini with Jalapeño Monterey Jack

1 medium zucchini, scrubbed and cut into
    ¼-inch-thick slices
½ cup coarsely grated *jalapeño* Monterey Jack
1 teaspoon all-purpose flour

Spread the zucchini in a microwave-safe dish. In a small bowl toss the *jalapeño* Monterey Jack with the flour, sprinkle the mixture over the zucchini, and microwave the zucchini mixture on high power (100%), uncovered, for 3 to 4 minutes, or until the zucchini is tender and the cheese is melted. Season the zucchini mixture with salt and pepper. Serves 2.

Caramelized Zucchini with Mint

2 tablespoons olive oil
1 pound zucchini, rinsed and cut into
    ⅓-inch-thick slices
3 tablespoons finely chopped fresh
    mint leaves
1 to 2 tablespoons balsamic vinegar

In a large heavy skillet heat the oil over moderately high heat until it is hot but not smoking, in it sauté the zucchini slices in batches with salt and pepper to taste for 2 minutes on each side, or until they are deep golden and tender, and stir in the mint and the vinegar to taste. Serves 4.

Purée of Three Root Vegetables

2 pounds russet (baking) potatoes
2 pounds celery root, peeled and cut into
    2-inch pieces, or Jerusalem artichokes
    (sunchokes), peeled and halved
2 whole carrots, peeled
¾ stick (6 tablespoons) unsalted butter

In a kettle combine the potatoes, peeled and halved, the celery root or Jerusalem artichokes, and the carrots with cold water to cover and simmer the vegetables, covered, for 25 to 30 minutes, or until they are tender. Reserve 1 cup of the cooking liquid and drain the vegetables in a colander. Force the potatoes through a ricer into a large bowl or mash them in the bowl with a potato masher. In a food processor purée the celery root or the Jerusalem artichokes with the butter until the mixture is smooth and stir the mixture into the potatoes. Using the coarse side of a grater shred the carrots into the bowl and combine the mixture well, adding salt and pepper to taste and enough of the reserved cooking liquid to achieve the desired consistency. *The purée may be made 1 day in advance and kept covered and chilled.* Serves 6.

PHOTO ON PAGE 80

Summer Vegetable Stew

1 onion, chopped fine
3 garlic cloves, minced
¼ cup olive oil
2 medium zucchini, rinsed and cut into
    ½-inch dice (about 3 cups)

1 medium yellow squash, rinsed and cut into
 ½-inch dice (about 1½ cups)
1 red bell pepper, chopped
1 cup fresh corn kernels
 (cut from about 2 ears)
2 tomatoes (about ¾ pound), cut into
 ½-inch dice
2 tablespoons minced fresh orégano leaves or
 ½ teaspoon dried, crumbled
½ cup packed fresh basil leaves,
 shredded

In a large deep skillet cook the onion and the garlic in the oil over moderately low heat, stirring, until the onion is softened, add the zucchini, the yellow squash, the bell pepper, and the corn, and cook the mixture over moderate heat, stirring, for 4 minutes. Add the tomatoes, the orégano, and salt and pepper to taste and simmer the stew, covered, stirring occasionally, for 10 minutes. Simmer the stew, uncovered, stirring occasionally, for 5 minutes more, or until the excess liquid is evaporated, sprinkle it with the basil, and serve it warm or at room temperature. Serves 4 to 6.

TAMALES

Tamales

Below are recipes for two doughs and three different fillings—all designed to be mixed and matched. (Plan on about three tamales per person.) For those who are pressed for time, we have included a recipe for tamale pie that can be made more quickly with the same doughs and fillings.

To Make and Steam Tamales

two ½-pound packages dried cornhusks
 (available at Hispanic markets and some
 specialty foods shops)
1 recipe plain tamale dough (page 186) or red
 chili tamale dough (page 186)
2 cups wild mushroom tamale filling (page
 186), bell pepper and cheese tamale filling
 (page 186), or pork and red chili tamale
 filling (page 187)

In a large bowl let the cornhusks soak in warm water, weighted to keep them submerged, for at least 3 hours or overnight. Drain the husks and pat them dry. Pick over the husks and select 21 of the most tender ones measuring about 8 by 5 inches. Tear 21 narrow strips (or 42 if using the alternate method) from the remaining husks to tie the tamales. Arrange 1 husk on a work surface, put 2 level tablespoons of the dough in the center of it, and pat the dough into a 3-inch square. Put a scant 1 tablespoon of the desired filling in a rounded log down the middle of the dough, bring the long sides of the husk together to seal the filling in the dough, and roll the dough loosely in the husk. To fold the tamales traditionally, fold about 2 inches of the tapered end over the filled husk, fold the remaining end over it, and tie the tamale securely but not too tightly with a strip of husk. (Alternatively, twist both ends and tie them with strips of husk.) Make more tamales in the same manner with the remaining husks, dough, and filling.

Stack the tamales in a large steamer, set the steamer over boiling water in a deep, heavy kettle, and top the tamales with a folded dish towel. (The towel absorbs condensation to prevent moisture from penetrating the tamales and making them soggy.) Steam the tamales, covered tightly, adding more boiling water to the kettle as necessary, for 1½ hours. *The tamales may be made 2 days in advance, kept covered and chilled, and steamed for 15 minutes, or until heated through.* Makes about 21 tamales.

PHOTO ON PAGE 68

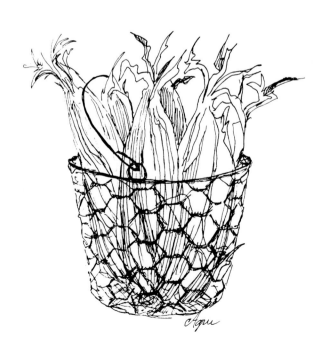

Plain Tamale Dough

½ cup softened lard, or ¼ cup softened
    vegetable shortening and ¼ cup softened
    unsalted butter
1 teaspoon salt
1 teaspoon double-acting baking powder
2½ cups Masa Harina* (corn tortilla flour mix)
1¼ cups chicken broth

*available at Hispanic markets, some
    specialty foods shops, or by mail order
    from The New Mexican Connection de
    Nuevo Mexico, 2833 Rhode Island NE,
    Albuquerque, NM 87110, tel. (505)
    292-5493

In the bowl of an electric mixer cream the lard with the salt and the baking powder, scraping down the side of the bowl several times with a rubber spatula, and beat the mixture on high speed for 3 minutes, or until it is light and fluffy and resembles frosting. Add the Masa Harina, about ½ cup at a time, scraping down the side of the bowl and beating well after each addition. (The mixture will resemble meal.) In a small saucepan heat the broth until it is lukewarm. (Do not let the broth get hot or it will melt the lard.) Beat the broth into the dough, about ½ cup at a time, and beat the dough until it is light and fluffy. (The dough should have the consistency of a soft cookie dough and a pinch of it should float briefly when laid gently on top of a glass of ice water. If the dough sinks, beat it longer.)

Red Chili Tamale Dough

½ cup softened lard, or ¼ cup softened
    vegetable shortening and ¼ cup softened
    unsalted butter
1 teaspoon salt
1 teaspoon double-acting baking powder
2½ cups Masa Harina* (corn tortilla flour mix)
1 cup plus 2 tablespoons chicken broth
2 tablespoons canned mild or hot
    enchilada sauce

*available at Hispanic markets, some
    specialty foods shops, or by mail order
    from The New Mexican Connection de
    Nuevo Mexico, 2833 Rhode Island NE,
    Albuquerque, NM 87110, tel. (505) 292-5493

In the bowl of an electric mixer cream the lard with the salt and the baking powder, scraping down the side of the bowl several times with a rubber spatula, and beat the mixture on high speed for 3 minutes, or until it is light and fluffy and resembles frosting. Add the Masa Harina, about ½ cup at a time, scraping down the side of the bowl and beating well after each addition. (The mixture will resemble meal.) In a small saucepan heat the broth until it is lukewarm (do not let the broth get hot or it will melt the lard) and stir in the enchilada sauce. Beat the broth mixture into the dough, about ½ cup at a time, and beat the dough until it is light and fluffy. (The dough should have the consistency of a soft cookie dough and a pinch of it should float briefly when laid gently on top of a glass of ice water. If the dough sinks, beat it longer.)

Wild Mushroom Tamale Filling

1 large onion, minced
2 garlic cloves, minced
¼ cup vegetable oil
¾ pound fresh *shiitake* mushrooms, stems
    discarded and the caps minced in a food
    processor (about 2½ cups)
¾ cup heavy cream
1 teaspoon *adobo* from canned *chipotle*
    chilies in *adobo* (available at Mexican
    and Hispanic markets and some
    specialty foods shops), or to taste
2 teaspoons fresh lemon juice, or to taste

In a large heavy skillet cook the onion and the garlic in the oil over moderate heat, stirring, until they are softened and golden, add the mushrooms, and cook the mixture, stirring occasionally, until the liquid the mushrooms give off is evaporated. Add the cream and salt and pepper to taste, simmer the mixture, stirring occasionally, for 5 minutes, or until it is thickened, and stir in the *adobo* and the lemon juice. Let the filling cool. *The filling may be made 2 days in advance and kept covered and chilled.* Makes about 2 cups.

Bell Pepper and Cheese Tamale Filling

3 pounds mixed red and yellow bell peppers,
    cut into thin 1-inch-long strips
    (about 6½ cups)
¼ cup vegetable oil
⅔ cup grated Monterey Jack (about 3 ounces)

In a large skillet cook the bell peppers with salt and pepper to taste in the oil over moderate heat, stirring occasionally, for 20 minutes, or until they are very soft. Let the peppers cool. *The filling may be prepared up to this point 2 days in advance and kept covered and chilled.* Before using the filling, stir in the Monterey Jack. Makes about 2 cups.

Pork and Red Chili Tamale Filling

1½ pounds meaty country-style pork
    spareribs, separated into ribs
two 10-ounce cans mild or hot enchilada sauce
½ cup water

In a large heavy saucepan simmer the ribs in boiling water to cover for 45 minutes and drain them. In the pan simmer the ribs in the enchilada sauce and the ½ cup water, covered, for 2 hours, or until the meat is very tender and falling off the bone. Drain the ribs in a colander set over a bowl, reserving the sauce, and let them cool until they can be handled. Shred the meat, discarding the fat and bones, and in a bowl combine it with ½ cup of the reserved sauce. *The filling may be made 2 days in advance and kept covered and chilled.* Makes about 2 cups.

Tamale Pie

1 recipe plain tamale dough (page 186) or red
    chili tamale dough (page 186)
2 cups wild mushroom tamale filling (page
    186), bell pepper and cheese tamale filling
    (page 186), or pork and red chili tamale
    filling (preceding recipe)

Preheat the oven to 350° F. With a rubber spatula spread two thirds of the dough evenly onto the bottom and up the side of a 10-inch glass pie plate and spread the filling in the shell. With the spatula fold the exposed dough over the filling. Pat out the remaining dough into a thin flat disk to cover the filling and pinch the top and sides together gently. Smooth the top gently and with the back of a fork make a decorative design lightly on the top. Bake the pie in the lower third of the oven for 40 minutes. Serves 8.

SALADS AND SALAD DRESSINGS

ENTRÉE SALADS

Herbed Beef and Rice-Noodle Salad
For marinating the beef
2 large garlic cloves, chopped
1 tablespoon Asian fish sauce such as
    *nuoc mam** or soy sauce
1 tablespoon Asian (toasted) sesame oil
2 teaspoons sugar
¼ teaspoon salt
1½ pounds flank steak
For the sauce
⅓ cup water
2 tablespoons minced garlic
⅓ cup Asian fish sauce such as *nuoc mam**
⅓ cup fresh lime juice
2 tablespoons sugar
½ teaspoon dried hot red pepper flakes,
    or to taste

1 pound dried rice-stick noodles*
    (rice vermicelli)
1 large seedless cucumber, quartered
    lengthwise, cored, and sliced into
    ¼-inch-thick pieces
4 cups shredded lettuce, rinsed and spun dry
½ cup chopped fresh mint leaves
½ cup chopped fresh coriander
½ cup chopped fresh basil leaves
½ cup crushed roasted peanuts
    (use a rolling pin)

*available at Asian markets, some specialty
    foods shops, and by mail order from
    Adriana's Bazaar, tel. (212) 877-5757

Marinate the beef: In a blender blend together the garlic, the fish sauce, the sesame oil, the sugar, and the

salt. In a shallow dish pour the marinade over the steak,
turning the steak to coat it well, and let the steak marinate, covered and chilled, for 4 hours or overnight.

Make the sauce: In the blender blend together the water, the garlic, the fish sauce, the lime juice, the sugar,
and the red pepper flakes.

In a large bowl soak the noodles in warm water to
cover for 5 minutes and drain them. In a kettle of salted
boiling water cook the noodles for 5 minutes and drain
them in a colander. Rinse the noodles well under cold
water and drain them well.

Grill the steak, discarding the marinade, on an oiled
rack set 4 to 5 inches over glowing coals or broil it under
a preheated broiler about 3 to 4 inches from the heat for
8 to 10 minutes on each side, or until it is springy to the
touch, for medium-rare meat. Transfer the steak to a
cutting board, let it stand for 10 minutes, and holding a
knife at a 45-degree angle slice it thin.

Divide the cucumber, the lettuce, and the herbs
among 8 large plates, mixing them, and mound the noodles over the mixture on each plate. Arrange the steak
decoratively over the noodles and sprinkle it with the
peanuts. Spoon some of the sauce over each plate and
serve the remaining sauce separately. Serves 8.

Curried Grilled Chicken Salad
For the dressing
1 large garlic clove, minced and mashed to a
    paste with ½ teaspoon salt
1½ tablespoons white wine vinegar, or to taste
2 teaspoons curry powder
½ cup mayonnaise
½ cup plain yogurt
1 tablespoon bottled mango chutney, any
    large pieces minced
3 tablespoons finely chopped fresh coriander
For the salad
2 whole boneless chicken breasts with the skin,
    halved

188

vegetable oil for brushing the chicken
¾ pound asparagus, trimmed and cut into
    1½-inch pieces
1 cup chopped orange or yellow bell pepper
½ pound (about 8 cups) *mesclun* (mixed baby
    greens), rinsed and spun dry

Make the dressing: In a bowl whisk together the gar-lic, the vinegar, the curry powder, the mayonnaise, the yogurt, the chutney, the coriander, and salt and pepper to taste. *The dressing may be made 1 day in advance and kept covered and chilled.*

Make the salad: Brush the chicken with the oil, sea-son it with salt and pepper, and grill it on a rack set 5 to 6 inches over glowing coals or in a hot well-seasoned ridged grill pan, covered, over moderately high heat, for 5 to 7 minutes on each side, or until it is cooked through. Transfer the breasts to a cutting board and let them cool for 15 minutes.

While the chicken is cooling in a saucepan of boiling salted water cook the asparagus for 3 to 4 minutes, or until it is just tender. Drain the asparagus in a colander, rinse it under cold water, and pat it dry between sheets of paper towel. In a large bowl toss together the pep-pers, the *mesclun*, and the asparagus and divide the mixture among 4 plates. Slice the chicken breasts diag-onally into ¼-inch pieces, fan 1 breast over each salad, and divide the dressing among the salads. Serves 4.

Grilled Chicken Salad with Mangoes and Greens
2 whole skinless boneless chicken
    breasts, halved
5 tablespoons olive oil
2 scallions, minced
2 teaspoons fresh thyme leaves
1 tablespoon balsamic vinegar
1 shallot, minced
4 cups shredded romaine, rinsed and spun dry
1 small bunch of watercress, coarse stems
    discarded and the leaves rinsed and
    spun dry
½ cup finely shredded red cabbage
1 large mango, peeled, pitted, and cut
    into 1-inch dice

On a large plate drizzle the chicken with 1 tablespoon of the oil, sprinkle it with the scallions, 1 teaspoon of the thyme, and salt and pepper to taste, turning it to coat it

well, and let it marinate at room temperature, turning it once, for 30 minutes.

In a small bowl whisk together the vinegar, the shal-lot, the remaining 1 teaspoon thyme, and salt and pep-per to taste, add the remaining 4 tablespoons oil in a stream, whisking, and whisk the vinaigrette until it is emulsified.

Grill the chicken on an oiled rack set 5 to 6 inches over glowing coals for 4 to 5 minutes on each side, or until it is cooked through. In a large bowl toss the ro-maine, the watercress, the cabbage, and the mango with just enough of the vinaigrette to coat the salad well, transfer the salad to a platter, and top it with the chicken. Serve the remaining vinaigrette separately. Serves 4.

Melon and Smoked Chicken Salad

2 shallots, minced
1 tablespoon white-wine vinegar
2 teaspoons minced fresh parsley leaves
1½ teaspoons minced fresh tarragon leaves
    plus tarragon sprigs for garnish
¼ cup vegetable oil
2 bunches of *arugula*, coarse stems discarded
    and the leaves washed well and spun dry
    (about 8 cups)
1 whole boneless smoked chicken breast
    (available at some butcher shops and
    specialty foods shops), skin and fat
    removed and the meat shredded
1 cup honeydew melon balls
1 cup cantaloupe balls

In a bowl whisk together the shallots, the vinegar, the parsley, the minced tarragon, and salt and pepper to taste, add the oil in a stream, whisking, and whisk the dressing until it is emulsified. Add the *arugula*, the chicken, and the melon balls, toss the salad until it is combined well, and garnish it with the tarragon sprigs. Serves 4.

Curried Tomato Chicken Salad

3 chicken breast halves with the skin and
    bones (about 1½ pounds)
1 small onion, chopped
2 tablespoons olive oil
½ cup tomato juice
2 tablespoons mango chutney
2½ teaspoons curry powder
1 teaspoon wine vinegar
¼ cup plain yogurt
2 tablespoons slivered or sliced almonds,
    if desired, toasted lightly

In a large saucepan combine the chicken with enough water to cover it by 1 inch, bring the water to a boil, and simmer the chicken for 20 minutes, or until it is cooked through. While the chicken is cooking, in a skillet cook the onion in the oil over moderate heat, stirring, until it is pale golden and add the tomato juice, the chutney, the curry powder, the vinegar, and salt and pepper to taste. Simmer the sauce, stirring, for 1 minute and transfer it to a bowl. Transfer the chicken to a cutting board and let it cool. Discard the skin and bones from the chicken, cut the meat into ½-inch pieces, and stir it into the sauce. Add the yogurt, toss the salad well, and sprinkle it with the almonds. Serves 2.

SALADS WITH GREENS

Arugula, Mushroom, and Radish Salad

2 large bunches of *arugula*, coarse stems
    discarded and the leaves washed well and
    spun dry (about 8 packed cups)
2 cups thinly sliced mushrooms
1 cup shredded radish
3 tablespoons olive oil
1½ tablespoons fresh lemon juice
Parmesan curls formed with a
    vegetable peeler

In a large bowl combine the *arugula*, the mushrooms, and the radish, drizzle the oil over the salad, and toss the salad gently. Sprinkle the salad with the lemon juice and salt and pepper to taste, toss it, and serve it topped with the Parmesan. Serves 4 to 6.

Arugula, Radicchio, and Endive Salad

3 bunches of *arugula*, cut crosswise into
    1½-inch pieces, washed well, and spun dry
    (about 12 cups)
1 medium head of *radicchio*,
    torn into bite-size pieces
    (about 3 cups)
4 Belgian endives, cut crosswise into
    1½-inch pieces and the leaves separated
    (about 4 cups)
1 carrot, shredded
¼ cup olive oil, or to taste
1 tablespoon fresh lemon juice,
    or to taste

In a salad bowl toss together the *arugula*, the *radicchio*, the endive, and the carrot. Drizzle the salad with the oil and toss it well. Drizzle the salad with the lemon juice, season it with salt and pepper, and toss it well. Serves 6 to 8.

PHOTO ON PAGE 82

Goat Cheese Salad

For the vinaigrette
1 tablespoon fresh lemon juice,
   or to taste
1 small shallot, minced
1 garlic clove, minced
1 teaspoon Dijon-style mustard, or to taste
1 tablespoon minced fresh parsley leaves
¼ cup walnut oil (available at specialty foods
   shops) or olive oil

a ½-pound log of soft mild goat cheese such
   as Montrachet, cut crosswise into 6 pieces
an egg wash made by beating 1 large egg with
   1 tablespoon water
1 cup fine dry bread crumbs
2 small heads of Boston lettuce, washed well,
   spun dry, and shredded fine
1 small head of *radicchio*, washed well, spun
   dry, and shredded fine

Make the vinaigrette: In a small bowl whisk together the lemon juice, the shallot, the garlic, the mustard, the parsley, and salt and pepper to taste, add the oil in a stream, whisking, and whisk the vinaigrette until it is emulsified.

Preheat the oven to 400° F. Dip the goat cheese pieces into the egg wash, dredge them in the bread crumbs, and transfer them to a lightly oiled baking sheet. Bake the goat cheese pieces in the middle of the oven for 6 minutes. While the goat cheese is baking, in a large bowl toss the lettuce and the *radicchio* with the vinaigrette and salt and pepper to taste.

Divide the salad among 6 plates, arrange 1 goat cheese piece on each plate, and serve the salads immediately. Serves 6.

Dandelion and Sorrel Salad with Paprika Stars

For the stars
4 slices of homemade-style white bread
2 tablespoons olive oil
⅛ teaspoon paprika
For the dressing
1 tablespoon raspberry vinegar
2 teaspoons water
¼ teaspoon sugar
3 tablespoons extra-virgin olive oil

5 cups lightly packed small tender dandelion
   greens, rinsed and spun dry
3 cups lightly packed sorrel leaves, rinsed
   and spun dry

Make the stars: Cut out as many stars as possible from the bread with a small star-shaped cutter, in a skillet cook them in the oil over moderately low heat, turning them, until they are golden, and in a small bowl toss them with the paprika and salt and pepper to taste.

Make the dressing: In a large bowl whisk together the vinegar, the water, the sugar, and salt and pepper to taste, add the oil in a stream, whisking, and whisk the dressing until it is emulsified.

Add the dandelion greens, the sorrel leaves, and the stars to the bowl and toss the salad well. Serves 8.

PHOTO ON PAGE 32

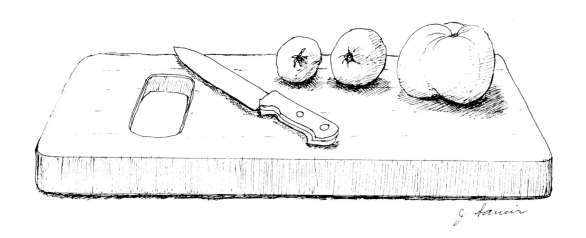

Escarole and Radicchio Salad

8 cups bite-size pieces of escarole,
   rinsed and spun dry
2 cups bite-size pieces of *radicchio*,
   rinsed and spun dry
1½ tablespoons white-wine vinegar
¼ teaspoon aniseed
¼ cup olive oil (preferably extra-virgin)

In a large bowl toss together the escarole and the *radicchio*. In a blender blend together the vinegar, the aniseed, and salt and pepper to taste, with the motor running add the oil in a stream, and blend the dressing until it is emulsified. Drizzle the dressing over the greens and toss the salad well. Serves 8.

PHOTO ON PAGES 28 AND 29

Herb Salad with Cassis Vinaigrette

1 tablespoon cassis (black-currant) vinegar or
   other fruit vinegar (available at specialty
   foods shops)
¼ cup vegetable oil
3 cups fresh flat-leafed parsley leaves
2 cups fresh curly parsley leaves
½ cup fresh mint leaves
½ cup fresh chervil leaves
½ cup fresh coriander leaves
½ cup small fresh basil leaves
the leaves from 2 fresh tarragon sprigs
edible flowers (available at specialty
   produce markets) for garnish

In a small bowl whisk together the vinegar and salt and pepper to taste, add the oil in a stream, whisking, and whisk the vinaigrette until it is emulsified. In a bowl toss the herbs with enough of the vinaigrette to just coat them until the salad is combined well, divide the salad among 8 chilled salad plates, and garnish it with the flowers. Serves 8.

Iceberg Lettuce Wedges with Stilton Dressing and Radishes

3 tablespoons crumbled Stilton or other
   fine-quality blue cheese
1 tablespoon vegetable oil
1 tablespoon sour cream or plain yogurt
1½ teaspoons water

1 teaspoon wine vinegar
four 1-inch-thick wedges of iceberg lettuce
3 radishes, diced fine

In a small bowl mash the Stilton with a fork and stir in the oil, the sour cream, the water, and the vinegar. Divide the lettuce wedges between 2 plates, spoon the dressing over them, and sprinkle the salads with the radishes. Serves 2.

Edgar Blakeney

Red-Leaf Lettuce, Curly Endive, and Cashew Salad

1½ teaspoons white-wine vinegar
2 teaspoons Dijon-style mustard
2 tablespoons olive oil
4 cups torn red-leaf lettuce,
   rinsed and spun dry
2 cups torn curly endive (chicory),
   rinsed and spun dry
2 tablespoons roasted cashews, chopped fine

In a bowl whisk together the vinegar, the mustard, and salt and pepper to taste and whisk in the oil, whisking until the dressing is emulsified. Add the red-leaf lettuce, the curly endive, and the cashews and toss the salad well. Serves 2.

Caesar Salad

For the croutons
2 tablespoons unsalted butter
2 tablespoons olive oil

2 garlic cloves, halved
3 cups ¾-inch cubes of Italian or French bread
For the dressing
2 flat anchovy fillets, or to taste,
    rinsed and drained
4 garlic cloves
2 teaspoons Sherry vinegar
2 teaspoons fresh lemon juice
1 teaspoon Worcestershire sauce
½ teaspoon dry mustard
½ cup olive oil

4 heads of romaine, the pale-green inner
    leaves washed, spun dry, and torn into
    bite-size pieces (about 12 cups) and the
    outer leaves reserved for another use
Parmesan curls formed with a
    vegetable peeler

Make the croutons: Preheat the oven to 350° F. In a small saucepan melt the butter with the oil, the garlic, and salt and pepper to taste over moderately low heat. Remove the mixture from the heat, let it stand for 10 minutes, and discard the garlic. In a bowl toss the bread cubes with the butter mixture, spread them on a baking sheet, and bake them in the middle of the oven for 12 to 15 minutes, or until they are golden. *The croutons may be made 1 day in advance and kept in an airtight container.*

Make the dressing: Mince and mash the anchovies with the garlic to form a paste and in a bowl whisk together the paste, the vinegar, the lemon juice, the Worcestershire sauce, and the mustard. Add the oil in a stream, whisking, and whisk the dressing until it is emulsified.

In a large bowl toss the romaine with the croutons and the dressing until the salad is combined well and sprinkle the salad with the Parmesan curls. Serves 4 to 6.

Romaine and Cucumber Salad with Garlic Vinaigrette

2 tablespoons white-wine vinegar
2 garlic cloves, minced and mashed
    to a paste with ½ teaspoon salt
⅓ cup olive oil
2 heads of romaine, torn into bite-size pieces,
    rinsed, and spun dry (about 14 cups)
2 cucumbers, peeled, halved lengthwise,
    seeded, and sliced crosswise

In a large bowl whisk together the vinegar, the garlic paste, and pepper to taste, add the oil in a stream, whisking, and whisk the vinaigrette until it is emulsified. Add the romaine and the cucumber and toss the salad well. Serves 8.

Hearts of Romaine with Creamy Lime Vinaigrette

1 large garlic clove, minced and mashed to a
    paste with ¼ teaspoon salt
½ teaspoon Dijon-style mustard
1½ tablespoons fresh lime juice, or to taste
2 tablespoons mayonnaise
¼ cup plus 2 tablespoons olive oil
1 to 2 tablespoons water
4 heads of romaine, the pale-green inner
    leaves washed, spun dry, and torn into
    bite-size pieces (about 12 cups) and the
    outer leaves reserved for another use

In a blender or small food processor blend the garlic paste, the mustard, the lime juice, the mayonnaise, and salt and pepper to taste until the mixture is smooth and with the motor running add the oil in a stream. Blend the mixture until it is emulsified, add enough of the water to thin the vinaigrette to the desired consistency, and blend the vinaigrette until it is combined well. In a large bowl toss the romaine with the vinaigrette. Serves 6.

Romaine and Mushroom Salad with
Garlic Caper Vinaigrette

1 garlic clove
1 teaspoon drained bottled capers
¼ teaspoon salt
1 tablespoon red-wine vinegar
¼ cup olive oil
14 romaine leaves, washed well,
    spun dry, the ribs discarded, and
    the leaves sliced thin (about 3 cups)
4 mushrooms, sliced thin

Mince the garlic and the capers and with the flat side of a knife mash the mixture with the salt to form a paste. In a bowl whisk together the garlic paste, the vinegar, and salt and pepper to taste, add the oil in a stream, whisking, and whisk the dressing until it is emulsified. Add the romaine and the mushrooms and toss the salad well. Serves 2.

Romaine and Red Onion Salad with Parmesan Balsamic Vinaigrette

enough Italian bread cut into ½-inch cubes to
    measure 1 cup
3 tablespoons olive oil
1 small garlic clove, minced
1 tablespoon balsamic vinegar
1 tablespoon water
3 tablespoons freshly grated Parmesan plus
    additional if desired
⅛ teaspoon dried orégano, or to taste,
    crumbled
1 small head of romaine, washed, spun dry,
    and torn into bite-size pieces
½ small red onion, sliced thin

Preheat the oven to 350° F. In a small bowl toss the bread cubes with 1 tablespoon of the oil and salt to taste and on a baking sheet toast them in the middle of the oven for 10 minutes, or until they are golden. Transfer the croutons to a salad bowl and let them cool. In a blender or small food processor blend together the garlic, the vinegar, the water, 3 tablespoons of the Parmesan, the orégano, the remaining 2 tablespoons oil, and salt and pepper to taste until the dressing is combined well. To the croutons add the romaine, the onion, and the dressing, toss the salad well, and sprinkle it with the additional Parmesan. Serves 2.

Spinach Salad with Goat Cheese Pita Croutons

For the croutons
a 7-inch *pita* pocket, halved crosswise and
    separated to form 4 semicircles
2½ ounces (about ⅓ cup) soft mild goat
    cheese such as Montrachet
¼ cup walnuts, minced

1 tablespoon white-wine vinegar
2 teaspoons Dijon-style mustard
6 tablespoons olive oil
    (preferably extra-virgin)
¾ pound spinach (about 1 bunch),
    coarse stems discarded and the
    leaves washed well and spun dry
1 pint cherry tomatoes, quartered

Make the croutons: Preheat the oven to 350° F. Spread the rough sides of the *pita* evenly with the goat cheese, season them with salt and pepper, and sprinkle the walnuts evenly over the cheese, pressing them in gently. Cut the *pita* into 1-inch pieces and bake the croutons on a baking sheet in the middle of the oven for 15 to 25 minutes, or until they are golden.

In a large salad bowl whisk together the vinegar, the mustard, and salt and pepper to taste, add the oil in a stream, whisking, and whisk the dressing until it is emulsified. Add the spinach, the tomatoes, and the croutons and toss the salad well. Serves 4.

Spinach and Mushroom Salad with Orange Vinaigrette

1 teaspoon freshly grated orange zest
2 tablespoons fresh orange juice
2 tablespoons fresh lemon juice
1 teaspoon Dijon-style mustard
¾ teaspoon salt, or to taste
⅔ cup olive oil
2 pounds fresh spinach, coarse stems discarded
    and the leaves washed well, spun dry,
    and torn into bite-size pieces
½ pound mushrooms, sliced

In a small bowl whisk together the zest, the juices, the mustard, and the salt, add the oil in a stream, whisking, and whisk the dressing until it is emulsified. In a large bowl toss the spinach and the mushrooms with the dressing. Serves 8.

PHOTO ON PAGE 34

Watercress Salad with Warm Vinaigrette

1½ tablespoons minced shallot
2 teaspoons Dijon-style mustard
1 teaspoon honey
1½ tablespoons red-wine vinegar
4 tablespoons olive oil
3 bunches of watercress, coarse stems discarded
    and the tender sprigs rinsed and spun dry

In a small saucepan whisk together the shallot, the mustard, the honey, the vinegar, and salt and pepper to taste, add the oil in a stream, whisking, and whisk the dressing until it is emulsified. Heat the dressing over moderately low heat, whisking occasionally, until it is hot and in a bowl toss it with the watercress. Serves 8.

PHOTO ON PAGE 77

In a large bowl whisk together the juices, the chili powder, and salt to taste, add the oil in a stream, whisking, and whisk the dressing until it is emulsified. Add the watercress, the *jícama*, and the pineapple and toss the salad well. Serves 8.

PHOTO ON PAGE 68

Watercress and Radish Salad

1 tablespoon red-wine vinegar
¼ cup olive oil
4 bunches of watercress, coarse stems
    discarded, rinsed and spun dry
    (about 14 cups)
1½ cups radishes, cut into
    julienne strips

In a large bowl whisk together the vinegar and salt and pepper to taste, add the oil in a stream, whisking, and whisk the dressing until it is emulsified. Add the watercress and the radishes and toss the salad well. Serves 8.

PHOTO ON PAGE 45

Mixed Greens with Honey Vinaigrette
and Gorgonzola

2 tablespoons Sherry vinegar (available at
    specialty foods shops and some
    supermarkets)
2 to 3 teaspoons honey
1 teaspoon Worcestershire sauce
1 small garlic clove, minced and mashed to a
    paste with ¼ teaspoon salt
½ teaspoon Dijon-style mustard
¼ cup olive oil
8 cups torn mixed lettuce leaves, rinsed
    and spun dry
about ¼ pound sweet Gorgonzola (available at
    specialty foods shops) or other fine-quality
    blue cheese, cut into 6 slices

In a large bowl whisk together the vinegar, the honey to taste, the Worcestershire sauce, the garlic paste, the mustard, and salt and pepper to taste, add the oil in a stream, whisking, and whisk the dressing until it is emulsified. Add the lettuce, toss the salad well, and divide it among 6 salad plates. Arrange 1 slice of the Gorgonzola at the edge of each plate. Serves 6.

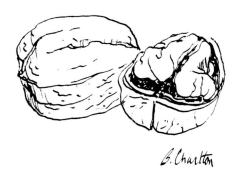

C. Charlton

Watercress and Boston Lettuce Salad with Walnuts

2 teaspoons fresh lemon juice
1 tablespoon olive oil
½ bunch of watercress, coarse stems
    discarded and the leaves washed well and
    spun dry (about 2 cups)
2 cups torn Boston lettuce, washed well
    and spun dry
3 radishes, cut into julienne strips
¼ cup walnuts, toasted lightly and chopped

In a large bowl whisk together the lemon juice, the oil, and salt and pepper to taste until the dressing is emulsified, add the watercress, the lettuce, the radishes, and the walnuts, and toss the salad well. Serves 2.

Jícama, Pineapple, and Watercress Salad with
Orange Chili Vinaigrette

2 tablespoons fresh orange juice
1 tablespoon fresh lemon juice
1 teaspoon chili powder, or to taste
⅓ cup vegetable oil
3 bunches of watercress, coarse stems
    discarded, and the sprigs rinsed well and
    spun dry (about 12 cups)
½ pound *jícama* (available at specialty
    produce markets and some supermarkets),
    peeled and cut into julienne strips
    (about 2 cups)
½ pineapple (about 1 pound), peeled, cored,
    and cut into 1- by ½-inch pieces
    (about 2½ cups)

Mixed Greens with Tarragon Vinaigrette

1½ teaspoons Dijon-style mustard
1 shallot, minced
4 teaspoons tarragon white-wine vinegar
2 tablespoons minced fresh tarragon
    leaves or 1 teaspoon dried,
    crumbled
⅓ cup extra-virgin olive oil
8 cups torn mixed baby greens such as
    red or green oak-leaf and Lollo rosso
    lettuces (available at specialty
    produce markets and some supermarkets),
    rinsed well and spun dry

In a large bowl whisk together the mustard, the shal-lot, the vinegar, the tarragon, and salt and pepper to taste, add the oil in a stream, whisking, and whisk the dressing until it is emulsified. Add the greens and toss the salad well. Serves 8.

VEGETABLE SALADS

Artichoke Heart, Fennel, and Parmesan Salad

2 teaspoons fresh lemon juice,
    or to taste
¼ teaspoon Dijon-style mustard
1 garlic clove, minced and mashed to
    a paste with ¼ teaspoon salt
a pinch of dried hot red pepper flakes
    if desired
2 tablespoons olive oil
a 14-ounce can artichoke hearts, rinsed,
    drained well, and sliced thin
1¼ cups thinly sliced fennel bulb
    (sometimes called anise) or celery
⅓ cup coarsely grated Parmesan
    (about 2 ounces)
¼ cup finely chopped fresh parsley leaves
    (preferably flat-leafed)

In a bowl whisk together well the lemon juice, the mustard, the garlic paste, the red pepper flakes, the oil, and salt and pepper to taste, stir in the artichoke hearts, the fennel, the Parmesan, and the parsley, and chill the salad, covered, for 20 minutes. Serves 2.

Warm Green Bean Salad with Dill

2 pounds green beans, trimmed and
    halved
2 tablespoons cider vinegar
⅓ cup olive oil
2 teaspoons dill seeds
¼ cup chopped fresh dill

In a steamer set over boiling water steam the beans, covered, for 6 to 8 minutes, or until they are just tender. While the beans are steaming, in a blender blend togeth-er the vinegar, the oil, the dill seeds, the chopped dill, and salt and pepper to taste. Transfer the beans to a serv-ing bowl and toss them with the dressing. Serves 8.

PHOTO ON PAGE 74

White Bean and Vegetable Salad

2 cups dried large lima beans, picked over,
    soaked in enough cold water to cover them
    by 2 inches overnight, and drained
1 onion, chopped fine
2 carrots, chopped fine
1 large garlic clove,
    minced
½ cup extra-virgin olive oil
½ cup minced red bell pepper
½ cup minced fresh flat-leafed parsley leaves
2 tablespoons fresh lemon juice
pita loaves, cut into wedges, as an
    accompaniment

In a large heavy saucepan combine the soaked beans with enough cold water to cover them by 1 inch and sim-mer them, uncovered, for 15 minutes, or until they are tender but not falling apart. While the beans are cook-ing, in a heavy skillet cook the onion, the carrots, and the garlic in 2 tablespoons of the oil over moderately low heat, stirring, until the carrots are softened and stir in the bell pepper. Reserve ½ cup of the cooking liquid, drain the beans, and in a bowl combine them with the vegetable mixture, the reserved cooking liquid, the re-maining 6 tablespoons oil, the parsley, the lemon juice, and salt and pepper to taste. Let the salad stand, covered and chilled, for 3 hours to allow the flavors to develop. *The salad may be made 1 day in advance and kept cov-ered and chilled.* Serve the salad at room temperature with the *pita* wedges. Serves 8 as a first course.

PHOTO ON PAGE 44

Sesame Carrot Salad

1 garlic clove, smashed
3 tablespoons vegetable oil
¼ cup sesame seeds
8 medium carrots, grated coarse
2 tablespoons fresh lemon juice

In a small heavy skillet cook the garlic in the oil over moderate heat, stirring, until it is golden and discard it. Add the sesame seeds, cook them, stirring, until they are golden, and in a bowl toss together the carrots, the sesame seed mixture, the lemon juice, and salt and pepper to taste. Serves 4 to 6.

Cumin and Coriander Spiced Chick-Pea Salad

For the dressing
2 tablespoons fresh lemon juice
2 tablespoons white-wine vinegar
2 garlic cloves, minced and mashed to a paste
  with ¼ teaspoon salt
1½ teaspoons grated peeled fresh gingerroot
1 teaspoon ground cumin, or to taste
¼ teaspoon cayenne or dried hot red pepper
  flakes, or to taste
½ cup olive oil

four 19-ounce cans chick-peas, rinsed
  and drained well
2 yellow bell peppers, chopped fine
1 small bunch of scallions, sliced thin
½ cup finely chopped fresh coriander, or to taste

Make the dressing: In a bowl whisk together the lemon juice, the vinegar, the garlic paste, the gingerroot, the cumin, the cayenne, and salt and pepper to taste, add the oil in a stream, whisking, and whisk the dressing until it is emulsified.

In a large bowl stir together the chick-peas, the bell peppers, the scallions, the coriander, and the dressing and chill the salad, covered, overnight. Serves 8.

PHOTO ON PAGE 63

Wilted Cucumber Salad

4 seedless cucumbers (about 3½ pounds), the
  skin scored lengthwise with a fork and the
  cucumbers sliced very thin
4 teaspoons salt
¼ cup fresh lime juice
a 4-inch-long fresh hot red or green chili,
  seeded and minced (wear rubber gloves)

In a large bowl toss the cucumbers with the salt and in a colander let them drain, covered with a plate and weighted with a 1-pound can, for 30 minutes. In the bowl toss the cucumbers with the lime juice, the chili, and salt to taste. *The salad may be prepared 4 hours in advance and kept covered and chilled.* Serve the salad chilled or at room temperature. Serves 10 as part of a buffet.

PHOTO ON PAGE 20

Dilled Cucumber Salad

¼ cup sour cream
2 tablespoons mayonnaise
2 tablespoons fresh lime juice
2 tablespoons minced fresh dill
two 1-pound unwaxed cucumbers

In a bowl whisk together the sour cream, the mayonnaise, the lime juice, the dill, and salt and pepper to taste. Score the cucumbers lengthwise with the tines of a fork, cut them crosswise into ⅛-inch-thick slices, and stir them into the dressing. Serves 6.

ZOE MAVRIDIS

197

Honeydew and Cucumber Salad with Sesame

1 tablespoon plus 2 teaspoons rice-wine
  vinegar (available at Asian markets and
  many supermarkets)
1 tablespoon minced peeled fresh gingerroot
2 teaspoons *tamari* (available at natural foods
  stores) or soy sauce
1½ teaspoons sugar
1 teaspoon Asian (toasted) sesame oil,
  or to taste
¼ teaspoon dried hot red pepper flakes,
  or to taste
¼ cup vegetable oil
1 seedless cucumber, halved lengthwise and
  sliced thin (about 2 cups)
2 cups 1-inch cubes of honeydew melon
2 scallions, minced
1 tablespoon sesame seeds, toasted
  lightly and cooled

In a bowl whisk together the vinegar, the gingerroot, the *tamari* or soy sauce, the sugar, the sesame oil, the red pepper flakes, and the vegetable oil until the dressing is combined well. Add the cucumber, the melon, and the scallions, toss the salad until it is combined well, and sprinkle it with the sesame seeds. Serves 4 to 6.

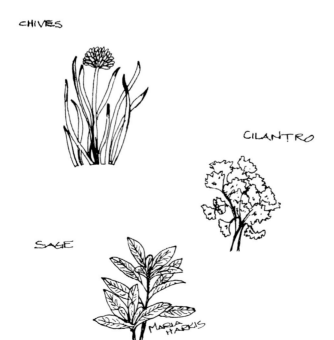

CHIVES

CILANTRO

SAGE

MARIA
HARRIS

Cucumber, Orange, and Aniseed Salad

¼ teaspoon aniseed
1 tablespoon white-wine vinegar
1 tablespoon olive oil
1 cucumber, peeled, quartered lengthwise,
  and cut crosswise into ¼-inch-thick pieces
1 navel orange, the peel and the pith
  cut away with a serrated knife and the
  sections cut free from the membranes
  and sliced thin crosswise
¼ red onion, sliced thin crosswise and
  rinsed in a sieve under cold water

In a bowl crush the aniseed lightly with the back of a spoon, add the vinegar, the oil, the cucumber, the orange, the onion, and salt and pepper to taste, and toss the salad well. Serves 2.

Potato, Corn, and Cherry Tomato Salad with Basil Dressing

2 tablespoons white-wine vinegar
½ cup olive oil
1 cup packed fresh basil leaves
2½ pounds small red potatoes
the kernels cut from 6 cooked ears of corn
½ pound cherry tomatoes, halved

In a blender or food processor blend together the vinegar, the oil, the basil, and salt and pepper to taste until the dressing is emulsified. In a large saucepan combine the potatoes with enough cold water to cover them by 2 inches, bring the water to a boil, and simmer the potatoes for 15 minutes, or until they are tender. Drain the potatoes, let them cool, and quarter them. In a large bowl combine the corn, the potatoes, the tomatoes, the dressing, and salt and pepper to taste and toss the salad gently. Serves 8.

Potato Salad with Smoked Trout and Fresh Herbs

2 pounds small new potatoes
⅓ cup dry vermouth
2 large shallots,
  minced
2 tablespoons white-wine vinegar
2 tablespoons fresh lemon juice
¼ cup olive oil
¼ pound smoked trout, flaked

2 tablespoons minced fresh parsley leaves
1 tablespoon minced fresh chervil
1 tablespoon minced fresh chives
1 tablespoon minced fresh tarragon leaves

In a steamer set over boiling water steam the potatoes, cut into ¾-inch pieces, covered, for 8 to 10 minutes, or until they are tender. While the potatoes are cooking, in a small bowl whisk together the vermouth, the shallots, the vinegar, and the lemon juice. Transfer the potatoes to a bowl, toss them with the vermouth mixture, and let them cool to room temperature. Add the oil, the smoked trout, the herbs, and salt and pepper to taste and toss the salad gently. Serves 6.

Panzanella
(Bread and Tomato Salad)

¾ pound day-old crusty peasant-style
  whole-grain bread, cut into 1-inch cubes
  (about 6 cups)
2 large tomatoes (about 1 pound), trimmed
  and each cut into 8 wedges
¾ cup sliced unwaxed cucumber
½ cup sliced red onion
½ cup extra-virgin olive oil
2 tablespoons red-wine vinegar
10 fresh basil leaves, shredded

In a serving bowl stir together the bread, the tomatoes, the cucumber, the onion, the oil, the vinegar, the basil, and salt and pepper to taste until the salad is combined well. Serves 4 to 6.

Tomato Salad with Red Onion and Herbs

1 tablespoon fresh lemon juice
1 tablespoon Sherry vinegar (available at
  specialty foods shops and some
  supermarkets)
1 teaspoon Dijon-style mustard
1 garlic clove, minced
½ teaspoon sugar
¼ cup olive oil (preferably extra-virgin)
2½ pounds (about 6 medium) tomatoes, cored
  and cut into ½-inch-thick slices
½ cup thinly sliced red onion,
  separated into rings
2 shallots, sliced thin

⅓ cup minced mixed fresh herbs such as
  basil, parsley, tarragon, and/or mint
  plus an herb sprig for garnish

In a small bowl whisk together the lemon juice, the vinegar, the mustard, the garlic, the sugar, and salt and pepper to taste, add the oil in a stream, whisking, and whisk the dressing until it is emulsified. Arrange the tomato slices on a deep platter, scatter the onion and the shallots over them, and pour the dressing over the salad. Chill the salad for 20 minutes, sprinkle it with the minced fresh herbs, and garnish it with the herb sprig. Serves 4 to 6.

Tomato, Potato, and Mustard Green Salad
For the dressing
¼ cup chopped shallot
1½ teaspoons Dijon-style mustard
4 tablespoons Sherry vinegar (available at
  specialty foods shops and some
  supermarkets)
¾ cup olive oil

2 pounds boiling potatoes
4 large tomatoes (about 1½ pounds)
½ pound mustard greens, stems and center
  ribs cut out and discarded and the leaves
  washed, spun dry, and shredded coarse
  (about 6 cups)
2 tablespoons minced fresh chives, or to taste

Make the dressing: In a blender blend together the shallot, the mustard, the vinegar, and salt and pepper to taste, with the motor running add the oil in a stream, and blend the dressing until it is emulsified. *The dressing may be made 2 days in advance and kept chilled in a tightly sealed jar.*

In a large saucepan combine the potatoes with enough water to cover them by 1 inch and simmer them for 20 minutes, or until they are tender. Drain the potatoes, peel them, and let them cool. *The potatoes may be prepared up to this point 1 day in advance and kept covered and chilled.* Slice the potatoes ¼ inch thick and arrange them decoratively on a platter with the tomatoes, cut into wedges, and the mustard greens. Pour the dressing over the salad and sprinkle the salad with the chives. Serves 8.

PHOTO ON PAGE 62

Yellow Tomato Salad with Lemongrass

½ cup vegetable oil
8 stalks of lemongrass (available at Asian
   markets and some specialty produce
   markets), the outer leaves discarded, ends
   trimmed, and 5 inches of the lower stalks
   minced
4 shallots, minced
2 tablespoons fresh lemon juice, or to taste
1 garlic clove, minced
¼ teaspoon finely grated fresh lemon zest
¼ teaspoon ground coriander seeds
cayenne to taste
6 medium yellow tomatoes (about 3 pounds),
   sliced crosswise
whole pear and currant tomatoes (available at
   specialty produce markets) and cherry
   tomatoes for garnish

In a small bowl whisk together the oil, the lemongrass, the shallots, the lemon juice, the garlic, the zest, the coriander, the cayenne, and salt to taste. Divide the tomato slices among 6 salad plates, spoon the dressing over them, and let the salad stand at room temperature for at least 30 minutes and up to 1 hour. Garnish each serving with some of the whole tomatoes. Serves 6.

SLAWS

Coleslaw with Golden Raisin Vinaigrette

2 tablespoons golden raisins
1 tablespoon white-wine vinegar
2 tablespoons vegetable oil
2 tablespoons water
1 tablespoon grated onion
1 teaspoon Dijon-style mustard
2 cups finely chopped cabbage
1 carrot, grated coarse

In a small saucepan combine the raisins, the vinegar, the oil, the water, the onion, the mustard, and salt and pepper to taste and boil the mixture, stirring, for 30 seconds. In a blender purée the vinaigrette until it is smooth and in a bowl toss it with the cabbage and the carrot. Serves 2.

Red Cabbage and Carrot Slaw

4 cups finely shredded carrot
4 cups finely shredded red cabbage
½ cup rice vinegar (available at Asian
   markets and some supermarkets)
1 tablespoon sugar,
   or to taste
1 teaspoon vegetable oil
½ teaspoon salt, or to taste

In a large bowl toss together the carrot and the cabbage. In a small bowl whisk together the vinegar, the sugar, the oil, and the salt. Just before serving add the dressing to the vegetables and toss the slaw well. Serves 6.

PHOTO ON PAGE 56

PASTA AND GRAIN SALADS

Pasta Salad with Tomatoes and Peas

⅓ cup white-wine vinegar
2 tablespoons water
2 teaspoons salt
½ teaspoon sugar
2 teaspoons minced fresh tarragon leaves
   or ½ teaspoon dried, crumbled
1 large garlic clove, minced and mashed
   to a paste with ¼ teaspoon salt
½ cup olive oil
1 pound medium pasta shells
½ pound shelled fresh or frozen peas (about
   1½ cups), boiled until tender and drained
2 pints red or yellow pear tomatoes or cherry
   tomatoes or a combination, halved
½ cup shredded fresh basil leaves

In a large bowl whisk together the vinegar, the water, the salt, the sugar, the tarragon, the garlic paste, and pepper to taste, add the oil in a stream, whisking, and whisk the dressing until it is emulsified. In a kettle of salted boiling water cook the pasta until it is tender, in a colander rinse it well, and drain it. In the bowl toss the pasta with the dressing, add the peas, the tomatoes, and the basil, and toss the salad well. Serves 10 to 12.

PHOTO ON PAGE 47

Green Goddess Pasta Salad with Cherry Tomatoes

3 drained flat anchovy fillets
1 garlic clove, chopped
2 tablespoons mayonnaise
2 tablespoons plain yogurt
2 scallions, minced
3 tablespoons minced fresh parsley leaves
1 tablespoon minced fresh dill
½ pound *rotelle* or *fusilli*
6 cherry tomatoes, quartered

Mince and mash the anchovies, the garlic, and a pinch of salt to a fine paste and in a large bowl whisk together the paste, the mayonnaise, the yogurt, the scallions, the parsley, and the dill. In a saucepan of boiling salted water boil the pasta until it is tender and drain it in a colander. Rinse the pasta under cold water and drain it well. Add the pasta to the dressing, tossing it to coat it well, and stir in the tomatoes gently. Serves 2.

Basil Tabbouleh
(Herbed Bulgur Salad with Tomatoes and Cucumbers)

¾ cup fine *bulgur* (such as Near East brand,
    available at many supermarkets)
¾ cup minced red onion
1 teaspoon salt
½ teaspoon ground allspice
1 cup finely chopped fresh basil leaves
1 cup minced fresh parsley leaves
⅓ cup minced fresh mint leaves
½ cup finely chopped scallion

¼ cup fresh lemon juice
¼ cup olive oil
1 cup finely diced seeded cucumber
1 cup finely diced seeded tomato

In a bowl wash the *bulgur* in several changes of cold water, letting it settle to the bottom before pouring off most of the water, until the water is clear and drain it in a large fine sieve. Return the *bulgur* to the bowl, add enough cold water to cover it by 1 inch, and let the *bulgur* soak for 1 hour.

While the *bulgur* is soaking, in a large bowl stir together the onion, the salt, and the allspice and let the mixture stand for 30 minutes. Drain the *bulgur* in the sieve, pressing hard to extract as much water as possible, add it to the onion mixture with the herbs, the scallion, the lemon juice, the oil, the cucumber, the tomato, and salt and pepper to taste, and toss the salad well. Serves 4.

Feta Wheat-Berry Salad

1 cup wheat, spelt, or rye berries
    (available at natural foods stores)
½ cup diced Feta (about 2 ounces)
½ cup thinly sliced red onion
½ cup julienne strips of seedless cucumber
5 tablespoons olive oil
¼ cup julienne strips of drained bottled
    roasted red pepper
¼ cup mixed minced fresh herbs
    such as parsley, mint, and dill
    plus herb sprigs for garnish
2 tablespoons fresh lemon juice, or to taste
1 tablespoon red-wine vinegar
1 tablespoon chopped pitted brine-cured
    black olives
1 teaspoon ground cumin
1 garlic clove, minced
dried hot red pepper flakes to taste

In a kettle of boiling salted water cook the wheat berries for 1 hour, or until they are tender, and drain them. In a large bowl stir together the wheat berries, the Feta, the onion, the cucumber, the oil, the roasted pepper, the minced herbs, the lemon juice, the vinegar, the olives, the cumin, the garlic, the red pepper flakes, and salt to taste and garnish the salad with the herb sprigs. Serves 4 to 6.

FRUIT SALADS

Spicy Orange Salad

1 small garlic clove, minced and
    mashed to a paste with
    ¼ teaspoon salt
1 tablespoon olive oil
⅛ teaspoon cayenne
⅛ teaspoon ground coriander
⅛ teaspoon ground cumin
2 navel oranges, peeled, the zest and
    pith cut away with a serrated knife,
    and each orange cut crosswise
    into 4 or 5 slices
1 teaspoon minced fresh coriander

In a small bowl stir together the garlic paste, the oil, the cayenne, the ground coriander, and the cumin. Arrange the orange slices on a serving dish or 2 plates, drizzle them with the dressing, and sprinkle the salad with the fresh coriander. Serves 2.

Southwestern-Style Watermelon Salad

½ teaspoon ground cumin
½ teaspoon salt,
    or to taste
¼ teaspoon chili powder
⅛ teaspoon cayenne, or to taste
2 pounds watermelon, seeds and rind
    discarded and the flesh cut into ¾-inch
    pieces (about 4 cups)
3 tablespoons fresh lime juice,
    or to taste
2 tablespoons shredded fresh coriander
    or basil leaves

In a small bowl stir together the cumin, the salt, the chili powder, and the cayenne. In a serving bowl toss the watermelon with the cumin mixture, the lime juice, and the coriander or basil until the salad is combined well and serve the salad immediately. Makes about 4 cups, serving 4 to 6.

SALAD DRESSINGS

Honey Mustard Dressing

2½ tablespoons honey mustard
    (available at specialty foods shops)
1 teaspoon grated peeled fresh gingerroot
2 tablespoons red-wine vinegar
1 teaspoon soy sauce
1 small garlic clove, minced and mashed
    to a paste with ¼ teaspoon salt
½ cup vegetable oil
1 tablespoon minced fresh chives

In a bowl whisk together the honey mustard, the gingerroot, the vinegar, the soy sauce, and the garlic paste, add the oil in a stream, whisking, and whisk the dressing until it is emulsified. Stir in the chives and salt and pepper to taste. Toss the dressing with salad greens. Makes about ¾ cup.

Herbed Pine Nut Salad Dressing

1½ tablespoons white-wine vinegar
1 teaspoon Dijon-style mustard
¼ teaspoon dried thyme, crumbled
⅛ teaspoon dried orégano, crumbled
3 tablespoons olive oil
2 tablespoons pine nuts, toasted and chopped fine

In a small bowl whisk together the vinegar, the mustard, the thyme, and the orégano, add the oil in a stream, whisking, and whisk the dressing until it is emulsified. Stir in the pine nuts and salt and pepper to taste. Makes about ⅓ cup.

SAUCES

SAVORY SAUCES

Savory Dried Cranberry Sauce

¼ cup firmly packed light brown sugar
1 tablespoon cornstarch
1 cup dry white wine
½ cup chicken broth
1 teaspoon balsamic vinegar
½ cup dried cranberries (available at
    specialty foods shops)
⅛ teaspoon dried tarragon, crumbled
2 teaspoons minced fresh parsley leaves plus
    sprigs for garnish

In a small saucepan whisk together the brown sugar and the cornstarch and add the wine and the broth, whisking until the mixture is smooth. Add the vinegar, the cranberries, the tarragon, and salt to taste and simmer the sauce, stirring occasionally, for 15 minutes. Stir in the minced parsley and simmer the sauce for 1 minute more. Serve the sauce hot, garnished with the parsley sprigs, with pork chops, ham, or poultry. Makes about 1¼ cups.

Mustard Aspic

1 envelope (about 1 tablespoon) of
    unflavored gelatin
1 cup cold water
¾ cup white-wine vinegar
¼ cup sugar
3 tablespoons English-style dry mustard
2 tablespoons mustard seeds
4 large eggs, beaten lightly
1 teaspoon sweet paprika

1 cup well-chilled heavy cream
⅓ cup minced fresh parsley leaves

In a small bowl sprinkle the gelatin over the water and let it stand. In a metal bowl set over a saucepan of barely simmering water whisk together the vinegar, the sugar, the mustard, the mustard seeds, and the eggs, cook the mixture, whisking constantly, until it registers 160° F. on a candy thermometer, and remove the bowl from the heat. Stir in the gelatin mixture, the paprika, and salt and pepper to taste, stirring until the gelatin is dissolved, transfer the bowl to a larger bowl of ice and cold water, and stir the mixture until it is cold. In a bowl beat the cream until it holds stiff peaks, fold it into the egg mixture with the parsley until the mixture is combined well, and pour the mixture into a lightly oiled 5- to 6-cup ring mold. Chill the aspic, covered, for 4 hours, or until it is set. Dip the ring mold in hot water, run a knife around the edges of the aspic, and invert the aspic onto a serving plate. Serve the aspic with cold poached salmon, shrimp, crab, or chicken. Serves 10 to 12.

Mustard Lemon Butter

1 stick (½ cup) unsalted butter, softened
1 tablespoon English-style dry mustard
1½ tablespoons fresh lemon juice
1 teaspoon Worcestershire sauce
⅛ teaspoon cayenne, or to taste

In a food processor or in a bowl with a whisk blend together the butter, the mustard, the lemon juice, the Worcestershire sauce, the cayenne, and salt to taste until the mixture is smooth. Transfer the butter to a bowl and chill it, covered, for 8 hours to let the flavors develop. Serve the mustard lemon butter on grilled fish or chicken. Makes about ½ cup.

Mustard Watercress Sauce

¼ cup minced shallot
2 tablespoons unsalted butter
¼ cup dry white wine
1 cup sour cream
3 tablespoons coarse-grained mustard
2 tablespoons Dijon-style mustard
1 cup finely chopped watercress
⅓ cup hot water

In a saucepan cook the shallot in the butter over moderately low heat, stirring, until it is softened, add the wine, and boil the mixture until the wine is almost evaporated. Remove the pan from the heat and whisk in the sour cream, the mustards, the watercress, the water, and salt and pepper to taste. Serve the sauce at room temperature with poached fish or steamed or grilled vegetables. Makes about 2 cups.

CONDIMENTS

Roasted Beet Relish with Apricots

1 pound beets, scrubbed and trimmed, leaving
   1 inch of the stems attached
6 ounces (about 1 cup packed) dried apricots,
   chopped fine
3 tablespoons pomegranate molasses (available
   at specialty foods shops and by mail order
   from Adriana's Bazaar, tel. (212) 877-5757)
¼ cup minced red onion
1 to 2 tablespoons olive oil

Preheat the oven to 350° F. Wrap the beets tightly in foil and roast them in the middle of the oven for 1½ to 2 hours, or until they are tender. Unwrap the beets carefully and let them cool. Peel the beets, grate them coarse into a bowl, and stir in the apricots, the molasses, the onion, the oil to taste, and salt to taste. Serve the relish with pot roast or pork. Makes about 2 cups.

Cranberry Fruit Relish

1 navel orange, peeled and chopped coarse
1 cup chopped fresh or drained canned pineapple
a 12-ounce bag of cranberries, picked over
1 Granny Smith apple, peeled and chopped coarse
½ cup sugar, or to taste

In a food processor grind together in batches if necessary the orange, the pineapple, the cranberries, and the apple until the mixture is chopped fine, transfer the mixture to a bowl, and stir in the sugar. Let the mixture stand, covered and chilled, for at least 2 hours. *The relish may be made 2 days in advance and kept covered and chilled.* Makes about 4 cups, serving 8.

PHOTO ON PAGE 75

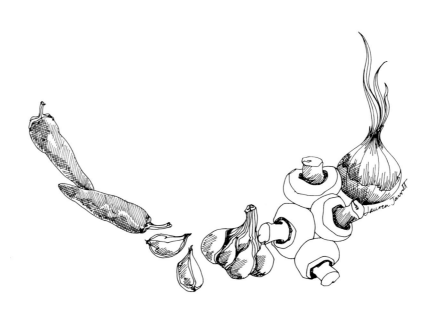

Green Olive and Coriander Relish

1 tablespoon coriander seeds
a 9½-ounce jar of green olives (about 2 cups),
    rinsed and pitted
3 tablespoons white-wine vinegar
3 tablespoons extra-virgin olive oil
pita loaves, cut into wedges,
    as an accompaniment

In a food processor grind coarse the coriander seeds, add the olives, the vinegar, and the oil, and blend the mixture until the olives are chopped fine. Let the relish stand, covered and chilled, overnight. *The relish may be made 3 days in advance and kept covered and chilled.* Serve the relish at room temperature with the *pita* wedges. Makes about 1½ cups.

Orange, Fig, and Pine Nut Relish

1 cup dried figs (about 6 ounces), stemmed
    and cut into ⅓-inch pieces
1 tablespoon freshly grated orange zest
½ cup water
2 navel oranges, the peel cut away with a
    serrated knife and the sections chopped
    (about 1 cup)
1 tablespoon honey
2 teaspoons minced shallot
1 teaspoon minced fresh rosemary leaves or
    ¼ teaspoon dried, crumbled, or to taste
½ teaspoon fresh lemon juice, or to taste
¼ cup pine nuts, toasted lightly

In a small saucepan simmer the figs and the zest in the water, covered partially, for 5 to 7 minutes, or until the figs are tender and most of the water is evaporated. Transfer the fig mixture to a bowl and let it cool. Stir in the orange, the honey, the shallot, the rosemary, and the lemon juice, let the mixture stand for at least 30 minutes and up to 2 days, and stir in the pine nuts. Serve the relish with duck, chicken, or pork. Makes about 1½ cups.

Fennel, Cucumber, and Tarragon Salsa

1 fennel bulb (sometimes called anise),
    chopped (about 2 cups)
1 unwaxed cucumber, chopped (about 2 cups)
1 tablespoon minced fresh tarragon leaves
1½ teaspoons freshly grated orange zest
⅓ cup plain yogurt
2 tablespoons fresh orange juice
1 teaspoon sugar

In a bowl stir together the fennel, the cucumber, the tarragon, the zest, the yogurt, the orange juice, the sugar, and salt to taste. Chill the *salsa*, covered, for at least 30 minutes and up to 1 hour. Serve the *salsa* with grilled seafood. Makes about 3½ cups.

Spicy Fruit Salsa

1 mango, peeled and cut into ½-inch dice
1 papaya, peeled, seeded, and cut into
    ½-inch dice
1 pint strawberries, hulled and quartered
2 tablespoons sugar
1 red *serrano* or *jalapeño* chili, seeded and
    minced (wear rubber gloves)
2 tablespoons minced fresh mint leaves

In a bowl stir together the mango, the papaya, the strawberries, the sugar, and the chili, let the mixture stand for 10 minutes, and stir in the mint. Serve the *salsa* with grilled chicken or fish. Makes about 2 cups.

Tomatillo Guacamole Salsa

¾ pound fresh tomatillos (available at
    specialty produce markets and some
    supermarkets), husked and rinsed
¼ to ⅓ cup packed fresh coriander
1 garlic clove
3 avocados (preferably California)

In a saucepan simmer the fresh tomatillos in salted boiling water to cover for 8 to 10 minutes, or until they are tender, transfer them with a slotted spoon to a bowl, and let them cool. (Alternatively, use a drained 11-ounce can tomatillos*.) In a food processor or blender purée the tomatillos with the coriander to taste, the garlic, and salt to taste and transfer the mixture to a bowl. Halve and pit the avocados, chop the flesh, and stir it into the tomatillo mixture. Serve the *salsa* with tortilla chips or with hamburgers, grilled meat, or fish. Makes about 2 cups.

*available at specialty foods shops and by mail order from Adriana's Bazaar, tel. (212) 877-5757

Scotch Bonnet Tomato Salsa

2 garlic cloves
1 lime, the peel cut away with a serrated knife
2 scallions, chopped coarse
½ Scotch bonnet chili (available at specialty
    produce markets) or 1 *serrano* chili, seeded
    (wear rubber gloves)
1 tablespoon fresh lime juice, or to taste
6 large plum tomatoes, seeded and chopped
3 tablespoons vegetable oil
2 tablespoons chopped fresh coriander

In a food processor chop fine the garlic, the lime, the scallions, and the chili, add the lime juice, the tomatoes, the oil, and the coriander, and purée the mixture. Serve the *salsa* with tortilla chips or with grilled meat or fish. Makes about 2 cups.

Alexandra Schultz

The following vinegars keep for several months once the steeping is completed. (Garnishes and other solids left in the jar, however, may become discolored or break down.)

Chili Vinegar

twenty 2-inch-long dried chilies
2 cups white-wine vinegar

In a very clean 1-quart glass jar combine the chilies and the vinegar and let the mixture steep, covered with the lid, in a cool dark place for at least 2 days and up to 2 weeks, depending on the strength desired. Strain the vinegar through a fine sieve into a glass pitcher, reserving 2 chilies for garnish and discarding the rest, and pour it into 2 clean ½-pint glass jars. Add the reserved chilies and seal the jars with the lids. Makes 2 cups.

Lemongrass Vinegar

3 stalks of lemongrass (available at Asian markets
    and some specialty produce markets)
2 cups rice vinegar (available at Asian
    markets and some supermarkets)

Slice thin the bottom 8 inches of the lemongrass stalks, put the sliced lemongrass in a very clean 1-quart glass jar, and bruise it with a wooden spoon. Add the vinegar and let the mixture steep, covered with the lid, in a cool dark place for at least 4 days and up to 2 weeks, depending on the strength desired. Strain the vinegar through a fine sieve into a glass pitcher, discarding the lemongrass slices, pour it into 2 very clean ½-pint glass jars, and seal the jars with the lids. Makes 2 cups.

Opal-Basil Cinnamon Vinegar

1 cup packed opal basil leaves including any
    blossoms (available at specialty produce
    markets) plus sprigs for garnish, rinsed and
    spun dry
a 3-inch cinnamon stick, broken in two
2 cups white-wine vinegar

Put the basil leaves and blossoms in a very clean 1-quart glass jar and bruise them with a wooden spoon. Add the cinnamon and the vinegar and let the mixture steep, covered with the lid, in a cool dark place for at least 4 days and up to 2 weeks, depending on the strength desired. Strain the vinegar through a fine sieve into a glass pitcher, discarding the solids, and pour it into 2 very clean ½-pint glass jars. Add the basil sprigs and seal the jars with the lids. Makes 2 cups.

Raspberry Mint Vinegar
1½ cups packed fresh mint leaves plus sprigs
    for garnish, rinsed and spun dry
3 cups raspberries, picked over
2 cups rice vinegar (available at Asian
    markets and some supermarkets)

Put the mint leaves in a very clean 1-quart glass jar and bruise them with a wooden spoon. Add the raspberries and mash them with the spoon. Add the vinegar and let the mixture steep, covered with the lid, in a cool dark place for at least 4 days and up to 2 weeks, depending on the strength desired. Strain the vinegar through a fine sieve into a glass pitcher, discarding the solids, and pour it into 2 very clean ½-pint glass jars. Add the mint sprigs and seal the jars with the lids. Makes 2 cups.

Rosemary Garlic Red-Wine Vinegar
1 cup fresh rosemary leaves plus long sprigs
    for garnish, rinsed and drained well
8 large garlic cloves, halved
2 cups red-wine vinegar

In a clean 1-quart glass jar combine the rosemary leaves, the garlic, and the vinegar and let the mixture steep, covered with the lid, in a cool dark place for at least 4 days and up to 2 weeks, depending on the strength desired. Strain the vinegar through a fine sieve into a glass pitcher, reserving the garlic and discarding the rosemary leaves, and pour it into 2 clean ½-pint glass jars. Add a rosemary sprig and some of the reserved garlic to each jar. Seal the jars with the lids. Makes 2 cups.

Sage Caraway Vinegar
1 cup packed fresh sage leaves plus sprigs for
    garnish, rinsed and spun dry
1½ teaspoons caraway seeds, bruised with a
    rolling pin
1¾ cups cider vinegar
¼ cup water

Put the sage leaves in a very clean 1-quart glass jar and bruise them with a wooden spoon. Add the caraway seeds, the vinegar, and the water and let the mixture steep, covered with the lid, in a cool dark place for at least 4 days and up to 2 weeks, depending on the strength desired. Strain the vinegar through a fine sieve into a glass pitcher, discarding the solids, and pour it into 2 very clean ½-pint glass jars. Add the sage sprigs and seal the jars with the lids. Makes 2 cups.

Tarragon Green-Peppercorn Vinegar
1 cup packed fresh tarragon leaves plus sprigs
    for garnish, rinsed and spun dry
1 tablespoon freeze-dried green peppercorns,
    cracked coarse, plus whole peppercorns
    for garnish
2 cups white-wine vinegar

Put the tarragon leaves in a very clean 1-quart glass jar and bruise them with a wooden spoon. Add the cracked peppercorns and the vinegar and let the mixture steep, covered with the lid, in a cool dark place for at least 4 days and up to 2 weeks, depending on the strength desired. Strain the vinegar through a fine sieve into a glass pitcher, discarding the solids, and pour it into 2 very clean ½-pint glass jars. Add the tarragon sprigs and the whole peppercorns and seal the jars with the lids. Makes 2 cups.

DESSERT SAUCES

Dark Chocolate Sauce
⅓ cup water or brewed coffee
½ cup firmly packed dark brown sugar
½ cup unsweetened Dutch-process cocoa powder
⅛ teaspoon salt
2 tablespoons unsalted butter, cut into pieces
½ teaspoon vanilla

In a heavy saucepan heat the water with the sugar over moderate heat, whisking until the sugar is dissolved, add the cocoa powder and the salt, and whisk the mixture until it is smooth. Add the butter and the vanilla and whisk the sauce until the butter is melted. Serve the sauce warm over ice cream. Makes ¾ cup.

Chocolate Caramel Sauce

½ cup sugar
¾ cup heavy cream
3 ounces fine-quality bittersweet chocolate
 (not unsweetened), chopped fine
⅛ teaspoon salt
½ teaspoon vanilla

In a dry heavy saucepan cook the sugar over moderate heat, undisturbed, until it begins to melt, cook it, stirring with a fork, until it is melted, and cook it, swirling the pan, until it is a deep golden caramel. Remove the pan from the heat, add the cream (the mixture will bubble up), and simmer the mixture, stirring, until the caramel is dissolved. Add the chocolate and the salt and cook the sauce over low heat, whisking, until the chocolate is melted and the sauce is smooth. Whisk in the vanilla and serve the sauce warm or at room temperature over ice cream. Makes about 1¼ cups.

Chocolate Coconut Sauce

½ cup well-stirred canned cream of coconut
½ cup heavy cream
½ cup semisweet chocolate chips
1 ounce unsweetened chocolate, chopped fine
¾ teaspoon coconut extract, or to taste
⅛ teaspoon salt
1 tablespoon Malibu or other coconut-
 flavored rum if desired

In a heavy saucepan whisk together the cream of coconut and the heavy cream, bring the mixture to a simmer, and whisk in the chocolates, whisking until they are melted and the sauce is smooth. Whisk in the coconut extract, the salt, and the Malibu and serve the sauce warm or at room temperature over ice cream. Makes about 1½ cups.

Milk Chocolate Peanut Butter Sauce

1 tablespoon unsalted butter
1 tablespoon firmly packed light brown sugar
1 tablespoon light corn syrup
¼ cup smooth peanut butter
½ cup half-and-half
4½ ounces milk chocolate, chopped
⅛ teaspoon salt
2 tablespoons water

In a heavy saucepan melt the butter with the brown sugar and the corn syrup over moderate heat, stirring, whisk in the peanut butter and the half-and-half, and bring the mixture to a simmer. Add the chocolate and the salt, whisk the sauce until it is smooth, and whisk in the water. Serve the sauce warm over ice cream. Makes about 1¼ cups.

Chocolate Raspberry Sauce

1 cup heavy cream
5 tablespoons raspberry jam
4½ ounces fine-quality bittersweet chocolate
 (not unsweetened), chopped fine
1 ounce unsweetened chocolate,
 chopped fine
1 to 2 tablespoons cassis,
 or to taste

In a heavy saucepan bring the cream to a simmer with the jam, whisking, remove the pan from the heat, and add the chocolates and a pinch of salt. Let the mixture stand for 3 minutes, whisk it until it is smooth, and whisk in the cassis. Strain the sauce through a fine sieve set over a bowl and serve it warm over ice cream. Makes about 1½ cups.

Old-Fashioned Hot Fudge Sauce

2 ounces unsweetened chocolate,
 chopped fine
2 tablespoons unsalted butter
2 tablespoons light corn syrup
¾ cup heavy cream
1 cup sugar
2 teaspoons vanilla
⅛ teaspoon salt

In a heavy saucepan melt the chocolate with the butter and the corn syrup over moderately low heat, stirring, add the cream and the sugar, and cook the mixture, stirring, until the sugar is dissolved. Bring the mixture to a boil over moderate heat and boil it, without stirring, for 8 minutes. Remove the pan from the heat and stir in the vanilla and the salt. Serve the sauce hot over ice cream. The sauce keeps, covered and chilled, for 1 month. (Let the sauce cool completely before covering it; condensation will make it grainy. Reheat the sauce, uncovered, in a double boiler.) Makes about 1⅓ cups.

Hot Fudge Peppermint Stick Sauce

⅔ cup heavy cream
2 tablespoons unsalted butter, cut into pieces
½ cup firmly packed light brown sugar
2 ounces unsweetened chocolate,
    chopped fine
⅛ teaspoon salt
½ cup coarsely crushed peppermint sticks or
    peppermint candies

In a heavy saucepan bring the cream to a boil with the butter, add the brown sugar, and simmer the mixture, stirring, until the brown sugar is dissolved. Add the chocolate and the salt and heat the mixture over low heat, whisking, until the chocolate is melted and the sauce is smooth. Stir in the peppermint candy and serve the sauce warm over ice cream. Makes about 1 cup.

Star Anise Kumquat Sauce

½ cup water
½ cup *sake* or dry vermouth
½ cup sugar
4 whole star anise (available at specialty foods
    shops and Asian markets)
1 pound kumquats (about 40), trimmed, sliced
    thin, and the seeds discarded

In a saucepan bring the water and the *sake* or vermouth to a boil with the sugar, the star anise, and a pinch of salt and boil the mixture for 5 minutes. Stir in the kumquats and simmer the mixture for 5 minutes, or until it is thickened. Discard the star anise, chill the sauce until it is cold, and serve it with ice cream, yogurt, or pound cake. *The sauce keeps, covered and chilled, for 1 week*. Makes about 1½ cups.

DESSERTS

CAKES

Rosewater Angel Food Cake

For the cake
1 cup cake flour (not self-rising)
1⅔ cups sugar
1¾ cups egg whites (about 13 large
   egg whites)
½ teaspoon salt
1 teaspoon cream of tartar
1 teaspoon rosewater (available at specialty
   foods shops) if desired
½ teaspoon vanilla
For the glaze
1 cup confectioners' sugar
2 tablespoons fresh lemon juice
⅛ teaspoon grenadine syrup

fresh raspberries for garnish
mint sprigs for garnish

Make the cake: Preheat the oven to 300° F. Sift the flour 3 times onto a sheet of wax paper. Sift together the sifted flour and ⅔ cup of the sugar onto another sheet of wax paper. In a large bowl with an electric mixer beat the egg whites until they are frothy, add the salt and the cream of tartar, and beat the mixture until it barely forms soft peaks. Beat in the remaining 1 cup sugar, a little at a time, the rosewater, and the vanilla and beat the mixture until it holds soft peaks. Sift one fourth of the flour mixture over the whites, fold it in gently but thoroughly, and sift and fold in the remaining flour mixture in the same manner. Spoon the batter into a very clean, ungreased tube pan, 10 by 8¼ by 4¼ inches, preferably with a removable bottom, smoothing the top, and rap the pan on a hard surface twice to remove any air bubbles. Bake the cake in the middle of the oven for 1 hour and 15 minutes, or until it is springy to the touch and a tester comes out clean. If the pan has feet invert it over a work surface; otherwise invert it over the neck of

a bottle. Let the cake cool for at least 2 hours or overnight. Run a thin knife in a sawing motion around the edge of the pan and the tube to loosen the cake from the pan and invert the cake onto a cake plate.

Make the glaze: In a small bowl stir together with a fork the confectioners' sugar, the lemon juice, and the grenadine syrup until the mixture is smooth.

Pour the glaze over the cake, let the cake stand for 10 minutes, or until the glaze is set, and garnish it with the raspberries and the mint.

PHOTO ON PAGE 39

Caramel Apple Shortcakes

For the shortcakes
1¾ cups all-purpose flour
3 tablespoons sugar plus additional for
   sprinkling the shortcakes
1 tablespoon double-acting baking powder
1½ teaspoons freshly grated lemon zest
1 cup well-chilled heavy cream plus
   additional cream or milk for brushing
   the shortcakes
1 teaspoon vanilla
For the caramel apples
½ cup plus 1 tablespoon sugar
¾ cup heavy cream, heated
5 tart cooking apples such as Granny Smith
   (about 2 pounds)
½ stick (¼ cup) unsalted butter

Make the shortcakes: Preheat the oven to 425° F. Into a bowl sift together the flour, 3 tablespoons of the sugar, the baking powder, and a pinch of salt and stir in the zest. In a bowl with an electric mixer beat 1 cup of the cream with the vanilla until it just holds soft peaks. Make a well in the center of the flour mixture, add the whipped cream, and with a fork combine the mixture until it just forms a dough. On a lightly floured surface knead the dough 6 times, or until it is just combined well, roll or pat it out ½ inch thick, and with a floured 4-inch cutter cut out a total of 6 rounds, gathering and rerolling the scraps. Brush the rounds with the additional cream or the milk and sprinkle them with the additional sugar. Bake the shortcakes on a greased baking sheet in the middle of the oven for 12 to 15 minutes, or until they are golden, transfer them with a spatula to a rack, and let them cool.

Make the caramel apples: In a dry heavy skillet cook ½ cup of the sugar over moderate heat, undisturbed, until it begins to melt and cook the sugar, stirring with a fork, until it is melted completely and turns a golden caramel. Remove the skillet from the heat and whisk in the cream carefully. Return the skillet to the heat and whisk the caramel sauce until it is smooth. In a large heavy skillet cook the apples, each peeled, cored, and cut into 8 slices, in the butter over moderately high heat, stirring, until they are browned lightly, add the remaining 1 tablespoon sugar, and cook the apples until they are soft and caramelized. Add the sauce to the apples and stir the mixture carefully.

Break each shortcake in half, arrange 2 halves on each of 6 dessert plates, and spoon the apples over them. Serves 6.

Apricot Financier
(Apricot Almond Cake)
½ stick (¼ cup) unsalted butter
1 teaspoon vanilla
¼ teaspoon almond extract
¾ cup sliced blanched almonds
⅔ cup plus 1 tablespoon superfine sugar
½ cup all-purpose flour
3 fresh apricots,
   sliced thin
4 large egg whites
¼ teaspoon salt
lightly sweetened whipped cream or vanilla
   ice cream as an accompaniment

Preheat the oven to 400° F. and butter an 8-inch round cake pan. In a small saucepan melt the butter over moderate heat, let it cool, and stir in the vanilla and the almond extract. In a food processor blend together the almonds, ⅔ cup of the sugar, and the flour until the almonds are ground fine. In a small bowl toss the apricots with the remaining 1 tablespoon sugar. In a bowl with an electric mixer beat the egg whites with the salt until they just hold stiff peaks, fold in the almond mixture gently but thoroughly, and fold in the butter mixture (the batter will deflate slightly). Spread the batter in the cake pan, arrange the apricot slices evenly over it, and bake the cake in the middle of the oven for 20 to 25 minutes, or until it is golden and a tester comes out clean. Turn the cake out onto a rack, let it cool, apricot side up, for 5 minutes, and serve it warm with the whipped cream or ice cream.

B. Charlton

Apricot Yogurt Cake with Orange Honey Syrup

two 8-ounce containers plain yogurt
2 cups all-purpose flour
1½ teaspoons double-acting baking powder
½ teaspoon baking soda
1 stick (½ cup) unsalted butter, softened
¾ cup sugar
2 large eggs
¾ cup dried apricots, chopped fine
1 cup walnuts, chopped fine
about ½ cup orange honey syrup
   (recipe follows)
mint sprigs for garnish

Let the yogurt drain in a fine sieve set over a bowl, covered and chilled, overnight, and measure out 1 cup of the drained yogurt, reserving the remaining yogurt for another use.

Preheat the oven to 350° F. and butter and flour a 10-inch springform pan. Into another bowl sift together the flour, the baking powder, the baking soda, and a pinch of salt. In the bowl of an electric mixer cream the butter with the sugar until the mixture is light and fluffy, beat in the eggs, 1 at a time, beating well after each addition, and beat in the 1 cup drained yogurt, beating until the mixture is just combined. Add the flour mixture, beat the batter until it is just combined, and stir in the apricots and the walnuts.

Spoon the batter into the prepared pan and bake the cake in the middle of the oven for 50 minutes, or until a tester comes out with a few crumbs adhering to it. Put the cake in the pan on a rack set over foil, pour the orange honey syrup over it, and let the cake absorb the syrup. *The cake may be made 2 days in advance and kept in the pan covered with plastic wrap and foil and chilled.* Remove the side of the pan and garnish the cake with the mint sprigs.

Orange Honey Syrup

1 cup honey
½ cup fresh orange juice
½ cup water
1¼ teaspoons minced fresh orange zest
2 tablespoons Manto (Greek orange herb-flavored liqueur, made by Metaxa)

In a heavy saucepan combine the honey, the orange juice, the water, and the zest and simmer the mixture, stirring occasionally, for 20 minutes, or until it is reduced to 1⅓ cups. (If the syrup is reduced too much, it becomes too thick and too sweet.) Stir in the Manto and let the syrup cool. *The syrup may be made 1 week in advance and kept, covered, at room temperature.* Makes about 1⅓ cups.

Red, White, and Blue Cheesecake
with Chocolate Cookie Crust

For the crust
28 chocolate wafers, ground fine in a blender
   or food processor (about 1½ cups crumbs)
1 stick (½ cup) unsalted butter, melted
For the filling
four 8-ounce packages cream cheese, softened
1½ cups sugar
2 tablespoons all-purpose flour
5 large eggs
½ cup sour cream
1 teaspoon freshly grated orange zest
1 teaspoon freshly grated lemon zest
½ teaspoon salt
1½ teaspoons vanilla

about 1½ cups raspberries
about 1½ cups blueberries

Make the crust: In a small bowl stir together the cookie crumbs and the butter until the mixture is combined well and pat the mixture onto the bottom and ½ inch up the side of a 9½-inch springform pan. Chill the crust for 30 minutes.

Make the filling: Preheat the oven to 325° F. In a bowl with an electric mixer beat the cream cheese until it is light and fluffy, add the sugar gradually, beating, and beat the mixture until it is combined well. Beat in the flour, add the eggs, 1 at a time, beating well after each addition, and beat in the sour cream, the orange and lemon zests, the salt, and the vanilla, beating the filling until it is combined well.

Pour the filling into the crust and bake the cheesecake in a foil-lined shallow baking pan in the middle of the oven for 1 hour and 10 minutes. (The cheesecake will not be completely set; it will set as it cools.) Turn the oven off and let the cheesecake stand in the oven with the oven door propped open about 6 inches until it is cooled completely. Chill the cheesecake, covered, overnight and remove the side of the pan.

Arrange the raspberries on top of the cheesecake in a star shape and arrange the blueberries around the star to cover the top of the cheesecake.

Warm Upside-Down Cheesecakes
with Pineapple Sauce

1 tablespoon unsalted butter
¼ cup graham cracker crumbs
6 ounces cream cheese, softened (¾ cup)
¼ cup plus 1 teaspoon sugar
¼ teaspoon freshly grated lemon zest
¼ teaspoon vanilla
1 large egg
1 teaspoon cornstarch
½ cup drained canned crushed pineapple in
   juice, reserving 1 tablespoon of the juice
½ cup water

Preheat the oven to 350° F. In a small saucepan melt the butter over moderate heat, stir in the graham cracker crumbs, and divide the mixture among 4 paper-lined ½-cup muffin tins, pressing it to form a crust. Bake the crusts in the middle of the oven for 5 minutes and let them cool on a rack for 5 minutes.

In a bowl with an electric mixer beat together the cream cheese, ¼ cup of the sugar, the zest, and the vanilla until the mixture is combined well, beat in the egg, beating until the mixture is combined well, and divide the batter among the tins. Bake the cheesecakes in the middle of the 350° F. oven for 20 minutes, or until they are set, and let them cool on a rack for 10 minutes.

While the cheesecakes are baking, in a small bowl dissolve the cornstarch in the reserved pineapple juice. In the small saucepan simmer the crushed pineapple with the water and the remaining 1 teaspoon sugar for 5

minutes, or until the liquid is reduced to about 2 tablespoons, stir the cornstarch mixture, and stir it into the pineapple mixture. Simmer the sauce, stirring, for 2 minutes, transfer it to a metal bowl set in a larger bowl of ice and cold water, and let it cool, stirring occasionally. Spoon the sauce onto 2 plates and invert the cheesecakes onto the sauce, discarding the paper. Serves 2.

Cherry Almond Cake

1 pound sour cherries (about 3 cups) plus
   additional for garnish if desired
¼ pound blanched whole almonds
1 cup plus 2 tablespoons all-purpose flour
1 teaspoon double-acting baking powder
¼ teaspoon salt
1½ sticks (¾ cup) unsalted butter, softened
¾ cup plus 1 tablespoon granulated sugar
3 large eggs, separated
1 teaspoon vanilla
¼ teaspoon almond extract
confectioners' sugar for dusting the cake

Preheat the oven to 375° F. Line the bottom of a buttered 9- by 2-inch round cake pan with a round of wax paper, butter the paper, and dust the pan with flour, knocking out the excess. Working over a bowl pit 1 pound of the cherries, reserving any juice.

In a food processor grind fine the almonds with the flour, the baking powder, and the salt. In a bowl with an electric mixer cream the butter with ¾ cup of the granulated sugar until the mixture is light and fluffy, add the egg yolks, 1 at a time, beating well after each addition, and stir in the flour mixture, the vanilla, the almond extract, and the reserved cherry juice.

In another bowl with the electric mixer, beaters cleaned, beat the egg whites until they just hold stiff peaks, stir one fourth of them into the batter to lighten it, and fold in the remaining whites gently but thoroughly. Turn the batter into the pan, smoothing the top, arrange the cherries evenly on it, pressing them into the batter slightly, and sprinkle them with the remaining 1 tablespoon granulated sugar. Bake the cake in the middle of the oven for 30 to 35 minutes, or until a tester comes out clean, and let it cool in the pan on a rack for 10 minutes. Invert the cake onto the rack, invert a cake plate over it, and invert the cake onto the plate. Dust the cake with the confectioners' sugar and garnish it with the additional cherries. Serve the cake warm or at room temperature.

Mexican Chocolate Torte
(Toasted Almond, Cinnamon, and Chocolate Torte)

1 cup (about 5 ounces) natural (with skins)
 whole almonds, toasted and cooled
 completely
⅓ cup firmly packed light brown sugar
1 tablespoon cinnamon
¾ teaspoon salt
5 ounces fine-quality bittersweet chocolate
 (not unsweetened), chopped
5 large eggs, separated
1 teaspoon vanilla
⅓ cup granulated sugar
For the glaze
4 ounces fine-quality bittersweet chocolate
 (not unsweetened), chopped
2 tablespoons unsalted butter
2 tablespoons heavy cream
1 tablespoon light corn syrup
For the icing
⅓ cup confectioners' sugar
1 to 1½ teaspoons milk

Preheat the oven to 325° F. Butter an 8½-inch spring-form pan and line it with a round of wax paper. Butter the paper and dust the pan with flour, knocking out the excess. In a food processor blend together the almonds, the brown sugar, the cinnamon, and the salt until the almonds are ground fine, add the chocolate, and blend the mixture until the chocolate is ground fine. Add the egg yolks and the vanilla, blend the mixture until it is combined well (it will be very thick), and transfer it to a bowl. In another bowl with an electric mixer beat the egg whites with a pinch of salt until they hold soft peaks, beat in the granulated sugar gradually, and beat the meringue until it just holds stiff peaks. Whisk about one third of the meringue into the chocolate mixture to lighten it and fold in the remaining meringue gently but thoroughly. Pour the batter into the pan, smoothing the top, and bake the torte in the middle of the oven for 45 to 55 minutes, or until a tester comes out clean. Let the torte cool in the pan on a rack for 5 minutes, run a thin knife around the edge, and remove the side of the pan. Invert the torte onto the rack, discarding the wax paper, and let it cool.

Make the glaze: In a metal bowl set over barely simmering water combine the chocolate, the butter, the cream, and the corn syrup, stir the mixture until it is smooth, and let the glaze cool until it is just lukewarm.

Set the torte on the rack over wax paper and pour the glaze over it, smoothing the glaze with a spatula and letting the excess drip down the side.

Make the icing: In a bowl whisk together the confectioners' sugar and 1 teaspoon of the milk and add enough of the remaining milk, drop by drop, to form a thick icing.

Transfer the icing to a small pastry bag fitted with a ⅛-inch plain tip and pipe it decoratively on the torte. Transfer the torte to a serving plate and let it stand for 2 hours, or until the glaze is set.

PHOTO ON PAGE 27

Maple Walnut Coffeecake

For the crumb mixture
1½ cups all-purpose flour
1 cup walnuts
⅔ cup firmly packed light brown sugar
¾ stick (6 tablespoons) unsalted butter,
 softened
1½ teaspoons cinnamon
¼ teaspoon salt
¼ cup pure maple syrup
For the batter
2 cups all-purpose flour
1¼ teaspoons double-acting baking powder
¾ teaspoon baking soda
1 teaspoon salt
1 stick (½ cup) unsalted butter, softened
⅔ cup firmly packed light brown sugar
¼ cup pure maple syrup
1½ teaspoons maple extract
½ teaspoon vanilla
2 large eggs
¾ cup sour cream

confectioners' sugar for sprinkling
 the coffeecake

Make the crumb mixture: In a food processor blend together the flour, the walnuts, the brown sugar, the butter, the cinnamon, and the salt until the nuts are ground and the mixture is crumbly, add the syrup, and pulse the motor until the mixture is combined well.

Preheat the oven to 350° F. and butter and flour lightly a 9-inch springform pan.

Make the batter: Into a bowl sift together the flour, the baking powder, the baking soda, and the salt. In another bowl with an electric mixer cream the butter with the brown sugar until the mixture is light and fluffy, beat in the maple syrup, the maple extract, and the vanilla, and beat in the eggs, 1 at a time, beating well after each addition. Add the flour mixture to the butter mixture alternately with the sour cream, beginning and ending with the flour mixture and beating the batter after each addition until it is just combined.

Spoon half the batter into the pan, spreading it evenly, sprinkle half the crumb mixture over it, and spread the remaining batter evenly over the crumb mixture. Sprinkle the remaining crumb mixture over the top and bake the cake in the middle of the oven for 50 to 60 minutes, or until a tester comes out clean. Let the cake cool in the pan on a rack for 5 minutes, remove the side of the pan, and transfer the cake, removing the bottom of the pan, to the rack. Let the cake cool completely and sprinkle the top with the confectioners' sugar. *The coffee-cake may be made 1 day in advance and kept wrapped in plastic wrap.*

PHOTO ON PAGE 76

Orange Caraway Seed Cakes

1½ cups cake flour (not self-rising)
¾ teaspoon double-acting baking powder
½ teaspoon salt
½ teaspoon baking soda
2 teaspoons caraway seeds, toasted lightly and cooled
1½ sticks (¾ cup) unsalted butter, softened
1 cup granulated sugar
2 large eggs
2 teaspoons freshly grated orange zest
1 teaspoon vanilla
⅔ cup sour cream
confectioners' sugar for dusting the cakes

Preheat the oven to 325° F. and butter and flour eighteen ⅓-cup brioche or muffin tins. Into a bowl sift together the flour, the baking powder, the salt, and the baking soda and stir in the caraway seeds. In another bowl with an electric mixer cream the butter with the granulated sugar until it is light and fluffy, beat in the eggs, 1 at a time, beating well after each addition, and beat in the orange zest and the vanilla. Add the flour mixture to the egg mixture alternately with the sour cream in batches, beginning and ending with the flour mixture and beating the batter after each addition. Di-

vide the batter among the tins, arrange the tins in a jelly-roll pan, and bake the cakes in the middle of the oven for 25 to 30 minutes, or until a tester comes out clean. Let the cakes cool in the tins for 3 minutes, turn them out onto a rack, and let them cool completely. *The cakes may be made 2 days in advance and kept in an airtight container.* Dust the cakes with the confectioners' sugar just before serving.

Peach Crumb Cake

For the topping
1 cup all-purpose flour
½ cup firmly packed brown sugar
¾ stick (6 tablespoons) unsalted butter, softened
¾ teaspoon cinnamon

1 stick (½ cup) unsalted butter, softened
⅔ cup granulated sugar
2 large eggs
1 cup all-purpose flour
¾ teaspoon double-acting baking powder
½ teaspoon salt
3 large peaches (about 1¼ pounds), sliced thin

Make the topping: In a food processor combine the flour, the brown sugar, the butter, and the cinnamon and pulse the motor until the topping is combined well and crumbly.

Preheat the oven to 350° F. and butter and flour an 8-inch round or square baking pan. In a bowl with an electric mixer cream together the butter and the granulated sugar until the mixture is light and fluffy, add the eggs, 1 at a time, beating well after each addition, and sift in the flour, the baking powder, and the salt. Beat the batter until it is just combined and spread it evenly in the pan. Arrange the peach slices in slightly overlapping rows over the batter, sprinkle the topping over them, and bake the cake in the middle of the oven for 50 minutes to 1 hour, or until a tester comes out clean. Serve the cake warm or at room temperature.

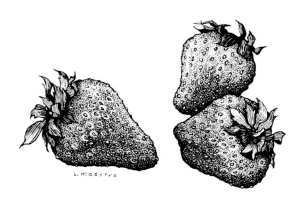

L. maestro

Stout Spice Cake with Lemon Glaze

3½ cups all-purpose flour
¾ teaspoon salt
1½ teaspoons baking soda
1½ teaspoons double-acting baking powder
1 tablespoon ground ginger
¾ teaspoon cinnamon
¼ teaspoon ground cloves
¾ teaspoon aniseed, ground in an electric
  spice grinder
¾ cup unsulfured molasses
1½ sticks (¾ cup) unsalted butter, melted and
  cooled slightly
¾ cup firmly packed dark brown sugar
a 12-ounce bottle of stout
2 large eggs, beaten lightly
¾ cup milk
2 cups chopped pecans, toasted lightly
1 cup confectioners' sugar
3½ tablespoons fresh lemon juice

Preheat the oven to 350° F. and butter a glass baking dish, 12 by 8 by 2 inches. Into a large bowl sift together the flour, the salt, the baking soda, the baking powder, and the spices. In a bowl whisk together the molasses, the butter, the brown sugar, the stout, the eggs, and the milk and add the mixture to the flour mixture. Whisk the batter until it is just combined and stir in the pecans. (The batter will be thin.) Pour the batter into the baking dish, bake the cake in the middle of the oven for 30 to 35 minutes, or until a tester comes out clean, and let it cool completely in the dish on a rack. Turn the cake out onto the rack.

In a small bowl whisk together the confectioners' sugar and the lemon juice, pour the glaze over the cake, and spread it with a metal spatula, letting it drip down the sides. Let the cake stand for 30 minutes, or until the glaze is set.

Strawberry Shortcake

3 pints strawberries, hulled and quartered
  lengthwise
⅓ cup granulated sugar, or to taste
1 cup well-chilled heavy cream
⅓ cup sour cream
1½ tablespoons confectioners' sugar,
  or to taste
1 teaspoon vanilla
8 cream or buttermilk biscuits (recipes follow)

In a large bowl combine the strawberries and the granulated sugar and with a potato masher mash the berries gently until they release their juices, being careful not to crush them to a pulp. Let the mixture stand at room temperature, stirring occasionally, for 1 hour.

In a bowl beat the heavy cream with the sour cream and the confectioners' sugar until it holds a soft shape and beat in the vanilla. Split the biscuits horizontally with a fork, arrange the bottom halves on 8 plates, and spoon the strawberry mixture over them. Top the strawberry mixture with some of the whipped cream and arrange the biscuit tops on the cream. Serve the remaining cream separately. Serves 8.

Cream Biscuits

2 cups White Lily* or all-purpose flour
1 tablespoon double-acting baking powder
½ teaspoon salt
1¼ cups heavy cream plus additional for
  brushing the biscuits

*available by mail order from The White Lily
  Foods Company, P.O. Box 871,
  Knoxville, TN 37901, tel. (615) 546-5511

Preheat the oven to 425° F. Into a bowl sift together the flour, the baking powder, and the salt and add 1¼ cups of the cream. Stir the mixture until it just forms a dough and gather the dough into a ball. On a lightly floured surface knead the dough gently 6 times and pat it out ½ inch thick. Cut out as many rounds as possible with a 3-inch round cutter dipped in flour and invert the rounds onto a lightly greased baking sheet. Gather the scraps, pat out the dough, and cut out more rounds in the same manner until there are 8 rounds. Brush the tops of the rounds with the additional cream, bake the biscuits in the middle of the oven for 12 to 15 minutes, or until they are pale golden, and transfer them to a rack. Serve the biscuits at room temperature. Makes 8 biscuits.

Buttermilk Biscuits

2 cups White Lily* or all-purpose flour
2 teaspoons double-acting baking powder
½ teaspoon baking soda
½ teaspoon salt
½ cup vegetable shortening
¾ cup buttermilk
milk for brushing the biscuits

*available by mail order from The White Lily
    Foods Company, P.O. Box 871,
    Knoxville, TN 37901, tel. (615) 546-5511

Preheat the oven to 425° F. Into a bowl sift together the flour, the baking powder, the baking soda, and the salt and blend in the shortening until the mixture resembles meal. Add the buttermilk, stir the mixture until it just forms a dough, and gather it into a ball. On a lightly floured surface knead the dough gently 6 times and pat it out ½ inch thick. Cut out as many rounds as possible with a 3-inch round cutter dipped in flour and invert the rounds onto a lightly greased baking sheet. Gather the scraps, pat out the dough, and cut out more rounds in the same manner until there are 8 rounds in all. Brush the tops of the rounds with the milk, bake the biscuits in the middle of the oven for 12 to 15 minutes, or until they are pale golden, and transfer them to a rack. Serve the biscuits at room temperature. Makes 8 biscuits.

COOKIES

Anise Pine-Nut Cookies

½ stick (¼ cup) unsalted butter, softened
¼ cup vegetable shortening
⅓ cup confectioners' sugar
¼ cup granulated sugar
1 teaspoon vanilla
1 cup plus 2 tablespoons all-purpose flour
½ teaspoon salt
¼ teaspoon double-acting baking powder
½ teaspoon aniseed
¾ cup pine nuts, toasted lightly and cooled

Preheat the oven to 325° F. In a bowl with an electric mixer cream together the butter, the shortening, and the sugars until the mixture is light and fluffy and beat in the vanilla. In another bowl whisk together the flour, the salt, and the baking powder and add the flour mixture to the butter mixture. In a food processor or blender grind fine the aniseed and ½ cup of the pine nuts, add the mixture to the dough, and blend the dough well.

Drop teaspoons of the dough 2 inches apart onto greased baking sheets, top each cookie with several of the remaining pine nuts, and bake the cookies in the oven, switching the positions of the baking sheets halfway through the cooking time, for 18 to 20 minutes, or until they are golden. Let the cookies cool on the baking sheets for 2 minutes, transfer them carefully (the cookies are very delicate) with a metal spatula to racks, and let them cool completely. The cookies keep in an airtight container for 4 days. Makes about 55 cookies.

PHOTO ON PAGE 15

Butterscotch Pecan Thins

1½ sticks (¾ cup) unsalted butter,
    softened
1 cup firmly packed light brown sugar
1 large egg
1½ teaspoons vanilla
1½ cups all-purpose flour
¾ teaspoon double-acting baking powder
½ teaspoon salt
about 48 pecan halves

In a bowl with an electric mixer cream the butter with the brown sugar until the mixture is light and fluffy and beat in the egg and the vanilla. Into the bowl sift together the flour, the baking powder, and the salt, beat the dough until it is combined well, and chill it for 1 hour, or until it is firm enough to handle. Halve the dough and on a piece of wax paper form each half into a 6-inch log, using the wax paper as a guide. Chill the logs, wrapped in the wax paper, for at least 4 hours or overnight.

Preheat the oven to 350° F. Cut the logs into ¼-inch-thick slices with a sharp knife, arrange the slices 3 inches apart on lightly buttered baking sheets, and press a pecan half onto each cookie. Bake the cookies in batches in the middle of the oven for 10 to 12 minutes, or until they are golden, and let them cool on the baking sheets for 1 minute. Transfer the cookies to racks and let them cool completely. Makes about 48 cookies.

Chocolate Chip Crunch Cookies

½ stick (¼ cup) unsalted butter, softened
⅓ cup firmly packed light brown sugar
1 large egg yolk plus 2 teaspoons water,
   or 1 large egg white
½ cup all-purpose flour
¼ teaspoon double-acting baking powder
¼ teaspoon salt
¼ teaspoon vanilla
1 cup semisweet chocolate chips
½ cup toasted rice cereal

Preheat the oven to 375° F. In a bowl with an electric mixer cream the butter with the brown sugar until the mixture is light and fluffy and beat in the egg yolk mixture or the egg white. Add the flour, the baking powder, the salt, and the vanilla, stirring until the dough is blended well, and stir in the chips and the cereal. Arrange level tablespoons of the dough 2 inches apart on a lightly greased baking sheet and bake the cookies in the middle of the oven for 8 to 10 minutes, or until they are golden. Transfer the cookies with a spatula to a rack and let them cool. Makes about 16 cookies.

Cornmeal Cookies

1¼ cups all-purpose flour
1 cup yellow cornmeal
1 teaspoon finely grated lemon zest
½ teaspoon ground ginger
2 sticks (1 cup) unsalted butter, softened
1 cup sugar
2 large egg yolks
½ teaspoon vanilla

In a bowl whisk together the flour, the cornmeal, the zest, the ginger, and a pinch of salt. In a large bowl with an electric mixer beat together the butter and the sugar until the mixture is light and fluffy, add the egg yolks and the vanilla, and stir the mixture until it is combined well. Add the flour mixture and stir the dough until it is combined well. Divide the dough in half, form each half into a 9½- by 1½-inch log, and chill the logs, wrapped in wax paper, for 3 hours, or until they are firm.

Preheat the oven to 400° F. Cut the logs into ¼-inch-thick rounds, arrange the rounds 2 inches apart on lightly buttered baking sheets, and bake them in batches in the middle of the oven for 10 minutes, or until the edges are golden. Transfer the cookies to racks and let them cool. Makes about 72 cookies.

Hazelnut Chocolate Stripes

2 sticks (1 cup) unsalted butter, softened
½ cup granulated sugar
¾ cup firmly packed light brown sugar
1 large egg
1½ teaspoons vanilla
2¼ cups all-purpose flour
1 teaspoon double-acting baking powder
¾ teaspoon salt
½ cup toasted and skinned hazelnuts
   (procedure follows), ground coarse
½ cup unsweetened cocoa powder

In a bowl with an electric mixer cream the butter with the sugars until the mixture is light and fluffy and beat in the egg and the vanilla. Into the bowl sift together 2 cups of the flour, the baking powder, and the salt, beat the

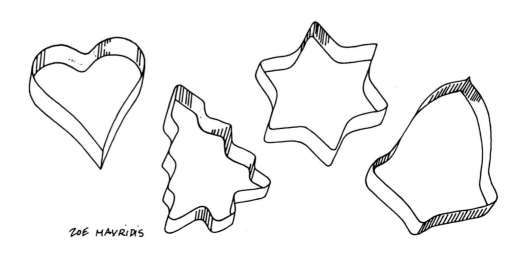

ZOE MAVRIDIS

dough until it is combined well, and transfer half the dough to another bowl. To half the dough beat in the hazelnuts and the remaining ¼ cup flour. Beat the cocoa powder into the remaining dough. On a sheet of wax paper form each dough into a 10- by 1½-inch squared-off log, using the wax paper as a guide, and chill the logs, wrapped in the wax paper, for 1 hour, or until they are firm. Cut each log carefully into 4 equal lengthwise slices with a sharp knife and reassemble the logs, alternating 2 slices from each dough to form a striped pattern. Chill the logs, wrapped in the wax paper, for at least 4 hours or overnight.

Preheat the oven to 350° F. Cut the logs into ⅜-inch-thick slices with a sharp knife and arrange the slices 2 inches apart on lightly buttered baking sheets. Bake the cookies in batches in the middle of the oven for 10 to 12 minutes, or until they are pale golden. Transfer the cookies to racks and let them cool completely. Makes about 54 cookies.

To Toast and Skin Hazelnuts

Preheat the oven to 350° F. Toast the hazelnuts in one layer in a baking pan in the oven for 10 to 15 minutes, or until they are colored lightly and the skins blister. Wrap the nuts in a kitchen towel and let them steam for 1 minute. Rub the nuts in the towel to remove as much of the skins as possible and let them cool.

Lemon Coconut Cookies

2 sticks (1 cup) unsalted butter, softened
½ cup sugar
1½ tablespoons freshly grated lemon zest
1 teaspoon vanilla
½ teaspoon lemon extract
2 cups all-purpose flour
¼ teaspoon salt
1 cup sweetened flaked coconut, toasted
  and cooled
confectioners' sugar for sprinkling the cookies

In a bowl with an electric mixer cream the butter with the sugar until the mixture is light and fluffy and beat in the zest, the vanilla, and the lemon extract. Add the flour and the salt, beat the mixture until it forms a dough, and stir in the coconut. Chill the dough for 1 hour, or until it is firm enough to handle. Halve the

dough and on a sheet of wax paper form each half into an 8-inch log, using the wax paper as a guide. Chill the logs, wrapped in the wax paper, for at least 4 hours or overnight.

Preheat the oven to 300° F. Cut the logs into ¼-inch-thick slices with a sharp knife and arrange the slices 2 inches apart on lightly buttered baking sheets. Bake the cookies in the middle of the oven for 25 to 30 minutes, or until they are pale golden, transfer them to racks, and sprinkle them generously with some of the confectioners' sugar. Let the cookies cool and dust them lightly with the remaining confectioners' sugar. Makes about 64 cookies.

Gingered Lemon Almond Squares

¼ cup unskinned almonds, toasted lightly and
  cooled completely
¼ cup confectioners' sugar plus additional for
  sifting over the squares
1 cup plus 2 tablespoons all-purpose flour
1 stick (½ cup) cold unsalted butter,
  cut into pieces
2 large eggs
¾ cup granulated sugar
¼ cup fresh lemon juice
½ teaspoon double-acting baking powder
1 teaspoon ground ginger

Preheat the oven to 350° F. In a food processor grind fine the toasted almonds with ¼ cup of the confectioners' sugar and 1 cup of the flour, add the butter, and blend the mixture until it just resembles meal. Pat the mixture into an 8-inch-square baking pan and bake the crust in the middle of the oven for 15 to 20 minutes, or until it is pale golden. Let the crust cool completely in the pan on a rack.

In the bowl of an electric mixer beat the eggs until they are thick and pale, beat in the granulated sugar and the lemon juice, and beat the mixture for 8 minutes. Sift in the remaining 2 tablespoons flour, the baking powder, the ginger, and a pinch of salt, stir the filling until it is combined well, and pour it over the crust. Bake the confection in the middle of the oven for 20 to 25 minutes, or until the filling is set and pale golden. Transfer the dessert in the pan to the rack, sift the additional confectioners' sugar over the top, and let the dessert cool completely. Cut the dessert into 2-inch squares. Makes 16 squares.

Mixed Dried Fruit Oatmeal Cookies

1 stick (½ cup) unsalted butter, softened
¾ cup firmly packed dark brown sugar
1 large egg, beaten lightly
½ teaspoon baking soda dissolved in
    1 tablespoon warm water
⅔ cup all-purpose flour
½ teaspoon salt
1 teaspoon vanilla
1½ cups old-fashioned rolled oats
½ cup chopped dried apricots
½ cup chopped pitted prunes
½ cup dried sour cherries or dried cranberries
    (available at specialty foods shops)

Preheat the oven to 375° F. In a bowl cream the butter with the brown sugar and beat in the egg, the baking soda mixture, the flour, the salt, and the vanilla. Stir in the oats, the apricots, the prunes, and the cherries and combine the dough well. Drop rounded tablespoons of the dough about 4 inches apart onto greased baking sheets and with a fork dipped in cold water flatten and spread each mound into a thin round, about 2½ inches in diameter. Bake the cookies in batches in the middle of the oven for 8 to 10 minutes, or until they are golden, transfer them with a spatula to racks, and let them cool. The cookies keep in an airtight container at room temperature for 5 days. Makes about 30 large cookies.

Pine Nut Cardamom Sand Cookies

½ stick (¼ cup) unsalted butter
¼ cup vegetable shortening
⅓ cup confectioners' sugar
2 tablespoons granulated sugar plus additional
    for flattening the cookies
1 teaspoon vanilla
1 cup all-purpose flour
½ teaspoon ground cardamom
¼ teaspoon double-acting baking powder
¾ teaspoon salt
½ cup pine nuts (about 3 ounces), toasted
    lightly and chopped fine, plus additional
    toasted whole pine nuts for garnish

Preheat the oven to 325° F. In a bowl with an electric mixer cream together the butter, the shortening, the confectioners' sugar, 2 tablespoons of the granulated sugar, and the vanilla until the mixture is combined well, add the flour, the cardamom, the baking powder, the salt, and the chopped pine nuts, and combine the dough well. Roll pieces of the dough into 1-inch balls, arrange the balls on a buttered large baking sheet, and with the bottom of a glass dipped in the additional granulated sugar flatten them into ¼-inch-thick rounds. Press several of the additional pine nuts into the top of each round and bake the cookies in the middle of the oven for 15 to 20 minutes, or until they are very pale golden. Transfer the cookies with a metal spatula to racks and let them cool. Makes about 24 cookies.

Classic Shortbread

1 stick (½ cup) unsalted butter
¼ cup confectioners' sugar
½ teaspoon vanilla
1 cup all-purpose flour or ¾ cup all-purpose
    flour and ¼ cup rice flour (available at
    specialty foods shops and natural foods stores)
⅛ teaspoon double-acting baking powder
⅛ teaspoon salt

Preheat the oven to 375° F. In a large bowl with an electric mixer cream the butter with the confectioners' sugar and add the vanilla. Into a bowl sift the flour (if using the rice flour, sift together the two flours) and stir it into the butter mixture with the baking powder and the salt.

On an ungreased cookie sheet pat the dough into an 8-inch circle (the dough will be soft and delicate) and score it into 6 wedges. Mark the edge of the shortbread with the tines of a fork and bake the shortbread in the middle of the oven for about 20 minutes, or until the edge is golden brown. Cut the shortbread into wedges while it is still warm.

Currant and Molasses Spice Cookies

1½ sticks (¾ cup) unsalted butter,
    softened
½ cup sugar
⅓ cup unsulfured molasses
2 cups all-purpose flour
½ teaspoon baking soda
½ teaspoon salt
1½ teaspoons ground ginger
¾ teaspoon cinnamon
¼ teaspoon ground cloves

½ cup dried currants, soaked in boiling
    water to cover for 5 minutes, drained,
    and patted dry

In a bowl with an electric mixer cream the butter with the sugar until the mixture is light and fluffy and beat in the molasses. Into the bowl sift together the flour, the baking soda, the salt, and the spices, beat the dough until it is combined well, and stir in the currants. Halve the dough and on a sheet of wax paper form each half into an 8-inch log, using the wax paper as a guide. Chill the logs, wrapped in the wax paper, for at least 4 hours or overnight.

Preheat the oven to 350° F. Cut the logs into ¼-inch-thick slices with a sharp knife and arrange the slices 2 inches apart on lightly buttered baking sheets. Bake the cookies in batches in the middle of the oven for 10 to 12 minutes, or until they are pale golden. Transfer the cookies to racks and let them cool. Makes about 64 cookies.

Sugar Crisps

about ¼ cup sugar
¼ pound frozen puff pastry, thawed

Preheat the oven to 375° F. Sprinkle a work surface with 1 tablespoon of the sugar, put the puff pastry on the sugared surface, and sprinkle it with 1 tablespoon of the remaining sugar. Roll the pastry into a 12- by 6-inch rectangle, adding more of the remaining 2 tablespoons sugar as necessary to keep the pastry coated well. Cut the rectangle crosswise, preferably with a fluted pastry wheel, into ¼-inch-thick strips. Twist the strips, arrange them on lightly greased baking sheets, pressing the ends gently onto the sheets to keep the strips twisted, and bake them in batches in the middle of the oven for 12 to 15 minutes, or until they are golden and crisp. Transfer the crisps as they are baked with a spatula to racks and let them cool. *The sugar crisps may be made 2 days in advance and kept in an airtight container at room temperature.* Makes about 48 crisps.

Dried Cherry Brownie Thins

½ cup dried sour cherries (available at
    specialty foods shops)
2 tablespoons kirsch
1 stick (½ cup) unsalted butter

2 ounces fine-quality bittersweet chocolate,
    chopped
½ cup firmly packed light brown sugar
1 teaspoon vanilla
1 large egg, beaten lightly
¼ cup all-purpose flour
½ teaspoon salt

Preheat the oven to 350° F. In a bowl toss the cherries with the kirsch and let the mixture stand for 30 minutes. In a metal bowl set over a saucepan of barely simmering water melt the butter and the chocolate, stirring until the mixture is smooth, and let the mixture cool. Whisk in the brown sugar, the vanilla, the egg, the flour, and the salt, whisking until the batter is combined well, and stir in the cherry mixture. Spread the batter in a buttered 8-inch-square baking pan and bake the brownies in the middle of the oven for 15 minutes, or until they pull away slightly from the sides of the pan. Let the brownies cool in the pan on a rack for 2 minutes, cut them into squares, and let them cool completely.

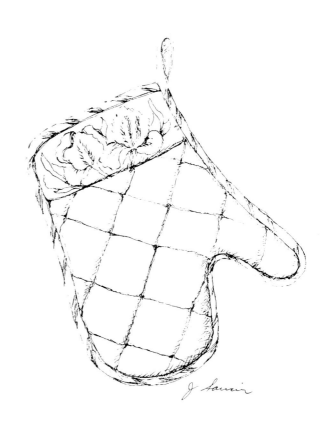

Chocolate Wafer and Graham Cracker Brownies

4 large eggs
½ cup granulated sugar
4 tablespoons water
½ teaspoon salt
¾ teaspoon vanilla
1 cup chocolate wafer crumbs (from about
    18 wafers)
½ cup semisweet chocolate chips
½ stick (¼ cup) unsalted butter, melted
    and cooled
½ cup firmly packed dark brown sugar
1 cup graham cracker crumbs
⅓ cup chopped pecans

Preheat the oven to 350° F. In a bowl whisk together 2 of the eggs, the granulated sugar, 2 tablespoons of the water, ¼ teaspoon of the salt, and ¼ teaspoon of the vanilla until the mixture is smooth and stir in the chocolate wafer crumbs, the chocolate chips, and half the butter. In another bowl whisk together the remaining 2 eggs, the brown sugar, the remaining 2 tablespoons water, the remaining ¼ teaspoon salt, and the remaining ½ teaspoon vanilla until the mixture is smooth and stir in the graham cracker crumbs, the pecans, and the remaining butter. Drop large spoonfuls of each mixture alternately into a greased 8-inch-square baking pan, run a knife blade through the mixtures to marble the batter, and smooth the top. Bake the brownies in the middle of the oven for 40 minutes, or until a tester comes out clean, and let them cool in the pan on a rack for 10 minutes. Cut the brownies into squares and let them cool completely.

PIES, TARTS, AND PASTRIES

Banana Coconut Cream Pie

For the shell
1 cup all-purpose flour
3 tablespoons sugar
¼ teaspoon double-acting baking powder
⅛ teaspoon salt
½ stick (¼ cup) cold unsalted butter,
    cut into bits
a 3½-ounce can (about 1⅓ cups) sweetened
    flaked coconut, toasted

1 large egg, beaten lightly
raw rice for weighting the shell
For the filling
⅓ cup sugar
3 tablespoons cornstarch
3 large eggs
2 cups milk, scalded
1 teaspoon coconut extract
1 teaspoon vanilla
2 tablespoons Malibu or other coconut-
    flavored rum

about 5 or 6 bananas
⅓ cup apple jelly
1 cup well-chilled heavy cream

Make the shell: Preheat the oven to 375° F. In a food processor or bowl combine well the flour, the sugar, the baking powder, and the salt, add the butter, and blend the mixture until it resembles fine meal. Stir in all but 1 tablespoon of the coconut, reserving the remaining 1 tablespoon for garnish, and the egg, stirring until the mixture forms a dough. Knead the dough lightly on a floured surface several times to blend it well and press it onto the bottom and up the side of an 11-inch fluted tart pan with a removable bottom. Chill the shell for 30 minutes, line it with foil, and fill the foil with the rice. Bake the shell in the lower third of the oven for 10 minutes, remove the rice and foil carefully, and bake the shell for 5 to 10 minutes more, or until it is golden. Let the shell cool completely in the pan on a rack.

Make the filling: In a heavy saucepan whisk together the sugar, the cornstarch, and the eggs, add the milk in a slow stream, whisking, and bring the mixture to a boil over moderate heat, whisking constantly. Simmer the pastry cream, whisking, for 2 minutes, transfer it to a bowl, and stir in the coconut extract, the vanilla, and the Malibu rum. Chill the pastry cream, its surface covered with plastic wrap, for 4 hours, or until it is cold. *The pastry cream may be made 1 day in advance and kept covered and chilled.*

Slice thin on the diagonal enough of the bananas (about 2½) to cover the bottom of the shell in one layer, arrange the slices in the shell, and cover them with the pastry cream, spreading it evenly. Slice thin on the diagonal the remaining bananas and arrange the slices decoratively over the pastry cream in solid layers, making each layer gradually smaller. In a small saucepan melt the apple jelly over moderate heat, while it is still warm brush it over the banana slices, coating them completely, and chill the tart for 1 hour. *The tart may be prepared up to this point 1 day in advance and kept covered loosely and chilled.*

Just before serving, in a chilled bowl beat the cream until it holds stiff peaks, transfer it to a pastry bag fitted with a medium star tip, and pipe it decoratively around the edge of the tart. Sprinkle the cream with the reserved 1 tablespoon coconut and remove the side of the pan.

Wild Blueberry Pie

2 recipes *pâte brisée* (recipe follows)
6 cups wild blueberries, picked over
¼ cup cornstarch
1 cup sugar plus additional for sprinkling
  the pie
2 tablespoons fresh lemon juice
½ teaspoon freshly grated nutmeg
½ teaspoon salt
1 tablespoon unsalted butter, cut into bits
2 tablespoons half-and-half or milk

Preheat the oven to 425° F. Roll out half the dough ⅛ inch thick on a lightly floured surface, fit it into a 9-inch (1-quart) pie plate, and trim the edge, leaving a ½-inch overhang. Chill the shell while making the filling. In a large bowl toss together well the blueberries, the cornstarch, 1 cup of the sugar, the lemon juice, the nutmeg, and the salt, mound the filling in the shell, and dot it with the butter.

Roll out the remaining dough into a 13- to 14-inch round on the lightly floured surface, cut out a 1½-inch star from the middle of the round, and drape the round over the filling. Trim the dough, leaving a 1-inch overhang, fold the overhang under the bottom crust, pressing the edge to seal it, and crimp the edge decoratively. Brush the crust with the half-and-half or milk, cut slits in the top crust around the star, and sprinkle the pie lightly with the additional sugar. Bake the pie in the bottom third of the oven for 20 minutes, reduce the temperature to 375° F., and bake the pie for 30 to 35 minutes more, or until the crust is golden and the filling is bubbling. Transfer the pie to a rack and let it cool.

Pâte Brisée

1¼ cups all-purpose flour
¾ stick (6 tablespoons) cold unsalted butter,
  cut into bits
2 tablespoons cold vegetable shortening
¼ teaspoon salt
2 tablespoons ice water plus additional
  if necessary

In a large bowl blend the flour, the butter, the vegetable shortening, and the salt until the mixture resembles meal. Add the 2 tablespoons ice water, toss the mixture until the water is incorporated, adding the additional ice water if necessary to form a dough, and form the dough into a ball. Dust the dough with flour and chill it, wrapped in wax paper, for 1 hour.

s. charlton

Boston Cream Pie

For the cake
1½ sticks (¾ cup) unsalted butter, softened
1¼ cups sugar
1 teaspoon vanilla
2 large eggs
2 cups cake flour (not self-rising)
2½ teaspoons double-acting baking powder
½ teaspoon salt
¾ cup milk
For the custard
3 tablespoons cornstarch
⅓ cup sugar
1 cup milk
3 large eggs
½ cup heavy cream
¼ teaspoon salt
1 vanilla bean, split lengthwise
3 tablespoons unsalted butter
For the glaze
6 ounces fine-quality bittersweet chocolate
   (not unsweetened), broken into pieces
3 tablespoons water
2 tablespoons unsalted butter
1½ tablespoons light corn syrup
¼ teaspoon salt

seasonal fruit or blossoms (non-toxic only)
   for garnish

Make the cake: Preheat the oven to 350° F. and butter and flour a 9½-inch springform pan. In a bowl with an electric mixer cream together the butter, the sugar, and the vanilla until the mixture is light and fluffy and beat in the eggs, 1 at a time, beating well after each addition. Into another bowl sift together the flour, the baking powder, and the salt and beat the mixture into the butter mixture in batches alternately with the milk, beginning and ending with the flour mixture. Pour the batter into the prepared springform pan and bake the cake in the middle of the oven for 50 to 55 minutes, or until a tester comes out clean. Let the cake cool in the pan on a rack.

Make the custard: In a saucepan whisk together the cornstarch, the sugar, and the milk, add the eggs, the heavy cream, and the salt, and whisk the mixture until it is smooth. Scrape the seeds from the vanilla bean, reserving the pod for another use, add them to the cream mixture, and bring the custard to a boil over moderate heat, whisking constantly. Boil the custard, whisking, for 2 minutes, remove the pan from the heat, and whisk in the butter. Let the custard cool completely, whisking occasionally.

Make the glaze: In a metal bowl set over a saucepan of barely simmering water melt the bittersweet chocolate with the water, the butter, the corn syrup, and the salt, stirring until the glaze is smooth, and remove the bowl from the pan.

Remove the cake from the pan, halve it horizontally with a long serrated knife, and arrange the bottom half, cut side up, on a plate. Top the bottom half with the custard, spreading the custard to the edge, put the remaining cake half, cut side down, on the custard, and pour the glaze on top of it, spreading the glaze to the edge and letting it drip down the side. *The Boston cream pie may be made 1 day in advance and kept covered loosely and chilled.* Garnish the pie with the fruit and the blossoms.

Ohio Shaker Lemon Pie

For the dough
1¾ cups all-purpose flour
9 tablespoons cold unsalted butter,
   cut into bits
3 tablespoons cold vegetable shortening
a scant ½ teaspoon salt
3 tablespoons ice water plus additional
   if necessary

2 lemons
1¾ cups sugar
4 large eggs
¼ teaspoon salt

Make the dough: In a large bowl blend the flour, the butter, the vegetable shortening, and the salt until the mixture resembles meal. Add the 3 tablespoons ice water, toss the mixture until the water is incorporated, adding the additional ice water if necessary to form a dough, and form the dough into a ball. Dust the dough with flour and chill it, wrapped in wax paper, for 1 hour.

In a large saucepan of boiling water blanch the lemons for 30 seconds, drain them, and rinse them under cold water. Trim the ends of the lemons, discarding them, and cut the lemons crosswise into paper-thin slices. In a bowl cover the lemon slices with the sugar and let the mixture stand, stirring once after 1 hour, for 8 hours or overnight.

Preheat the oven to 425° F. Roll out half the dough

⅛ inch thick on a lightly floured surface, fit it into a 9-inch (1-quart) pie plate, and trim the edge, leaving a ½-inch overhang. Remove the lemon slices from the sugar and arrange them in the shell. Add the eggs and salt to the sugar, whisk the mixture until it is combined well, and pour it over the lemon slices.

Roll out the remaining dough into a 12-inch round on a lightly floured surface, drape it over the filling, and trim it, leaving a 1-inch overhang. Fold the overhang under the bottom crust, pressing the edge to seal it, and crimp the edge decoratively. Cut slits in the crust with a sharp knife, forming steam vents, and bake the pie in the middle of the oven for 25 minutes. Reduce the temperature to 350° F. and bake the pie for 20 to 25 minutes more, or until the crust is golden. Let the pie cool on a rack and serve it warm or at room temperature.

Calvados Tarte Tatin
(Upside-Down Apple Tart with Apple Brandy)

For the dough
1½ cups all-purpose flour
7 tablespoons cold unsalted butter,
    cut into bits
2 tablespoons cold vegetable shortening,
    cut into bits
1 tablespoon sugar

¼ teaspoon salt
3 to 5 tablespoons ice water
For the filling
1 stick (½ cup) unsalted butter
1 cup sugar
¼ cup Calvados or applejack
four 3-inch strips of lemon zest removed with
    a vegetable peeler
three 3-inch cinnamon sticks, halved
7 large Golden Delicious apples
    (about 4 pounds)
2 tablespoons fresh lemon juice

crème fraîche as an accompaniment if desired

Make the dough: In a large bowl blend the flour, the butter, the shortening, the sugar, and the salt until the mixture resembles meal. Add 3 tablespoons of the ice water, toss the mixture until the water is incorporated, adding as much of the remaining water as is necessary to form a dough, and form the dough into a ball. Dust the dough with flour and chill it, wrapped in wax paper, for 1 hour.

Preheat the oven to 425° F.

Make the filling: In a large heavy skillet melt the butter over moderately high heat, stir in the sugar, the Calvados or applejack, the zest, and the cinnamon sticks, and boil the mixture for 1 minute. Stir in the apples, peeled, cored, and quartered, and cook the mixture, stirring frequently, for 30 minutes, or until the apples are glazed and the syrup is beginning to thicken. Discard the zest and the cinnamon sticks, add the lemon juice, and cook the mixture over high heat for 10 minutes, or until the syrup is almost completely evaporated and the apples are tender and a rich golden brown. Spoon the filling into an 11- by 2-inch (1½-quart capacity) glass pie plate, tamping the apples down with a metal spatula.

On a lightly floured surface roll out the dough into a round slightly larger than the pie plate and drape it over the filling. Tuck the dough down inside the edge of the pie plate and prick it in 4 places. Bake the tart in the middle of the oven for 20 minutes, or until the juices are bubbling and the crust is golden. Remove the tart from the oven and invert it immediately onto a heatproof serving plate. If any apples stick to the pie plate remove them with the metal spatula and rearrange them on the tart carefully. Serve the tart warm or at room temperature with the *crème fraîche.*

the mixture just forms a dough. Press the dough evenly onto the bottom and up the side of a 10-inch tart pan with a removable fluted rim and chill the shell for 1 hour. Brush the bottom of the shell with the jelly, prick it all over with a fork, and bake the shell in the lower third of the oven for 18 to 20 minutes, or until it is golden brown.

Reduce the oven temperature to 325° F. In a food processor blend together the farmer cheese, the sugar, the egg, the cornstarch, and the zest for 1 minute, or until the mixture is very smooth, add the cream, and blend the mixture until it is just combined. Arrange 1½ cups of the berries evenly in the shell, pour the cheese mixture slowly over them, and bake the tart in the middle of the oven for 25 to 30 minutes, or until the custard is just set. Let the tart cool completely in the pan on a rack and garnish it with the additional berries and the mint sprig.

Berry and Farmer Cheese Tart

For the shell
1 cup plus 2 tablespoons all-purpose flour
3 tablespoons sugar
¼ teaspoon salt
¼ teaspoon double-acting baking powder
¾ stick (6 tablespoons) cold unsalted butter,
  cut into bits
1 large egg
1 tablespoon fresh lemon juice
2 tablespoons berry jelly (any kind), melted

a 7½-ounce package farmer cheese
¼ cup sugar
1 large egg
1 teaspoon cornstarch
¼ teaspoon freshly grated lemon zest
½ cup heavy cream
1½ cups mixed red or black raspberries,
  blueberries, and blackberries plus
  additional berries for garnish
a mint sprig for garnish

Make the shell: Preheat the oven to 375° F. In a food processor blend together the flour, the sugar, the salt, and the baking powder, add the butter, and blend the mixture until it resembles meal. In a small bowl beat together lightly the egg and the lemon juice, add the egg mixture to the flour mixture, and pulse the motor until

Cranberry Raisin Tart

For the filling
¾ cup firmly packed light brown sugar
1 tablespoon cornstarch
1 teaspoon freshly grated orange zest
¼ cup fresh orange juice
2 cups cranberries, picked over
1 cup golden raisins, soaked in hot water for
  5 minutes and drained
¼ teaspoon salt
For the dough
1¼ cups all-purpose flour
3 tablespoons sugar
¼ teaspoon double-acting baking powder
⅛ teaspoon salt
¾ stick (6 tablespoons) cold unsalted butter,
  cut into bits
1 large egg
1 tablespoon water

an egg wash made by beating 1 egg with
  1 tablespoon water

Make the filling: In a saucepan stir together the brown sugar, the cornstarch, the zest, and the juice and add the cranberries, the raisins, and the salt. Bring the mixture to a boil, stirring, and simmer it, stirring, for 5 minutes, or until the berries have just burst. Transfer the filling to a bowl and chill it, covered, for 2 hours, or until it is cold. *The filling may be made 2 days in advance and kept covered and chilled.*

Make the dough: In a bowl stir together the flour, the sugar, the baking powder, and the salt, add the butter, and blend the mixture until it resembles meal. In a small bowl whisk together the egg and the water and add the mixture to the flour mixture, stirring with a fork until the mixture forms a dough. Dust the dough with flour and chill it, wrapped in wax paper, for 1 hour.

Preheat the oven to 425° F. Roll out the dough into a 12-inch round on a lightly floured surface and transfer it to a baking sheet. Spoon the filling onto the center of the dough, spreading it into an 8-inch circle, and fold the edges of the dough over it, leaving the center of the filling uncovered. Brush the dough with the egg wash and bake the tart in the middle of the oven, covering the exposed filling loosely with foil after 10 minutes, for 15 to 20 minutes, or until the pastry is golden. Let the tart cool completely on the baking sheet on a rack.

Individual Gingerbreads

7 tablespoons all-purpose flour
½ teaspoon ground ginger
¼ teaspoon cinnamon
¼ teaspoon baking soda
⅛ teaspoon freshly grated nutmeg
⅛ teaspoon ground allspice
3 tablespoons unsulfured molasses
2 tablespoons sour cream
2 tablespoons vegetable oil
¼ teaspoon vanilla
whipped cream or ice cream as an
    accompaniment if desired

Preheat the oven to 350° F. Grease two 4½-inch tart pans (¾ inch deep, without removable bottoms) and dust them with flour, knocking out the excess. In a small bowl whisk together the flour, the ginger, the cinnamon, the baking soda, the nutmeg, and the allspice until the mixture is combined well. In another small bowl whisk together the molasses, the sour cream, the oil, and the vanilla until the mixture is smooth. Make a well in the center of the flour mixture, pour in the molasses mixture, and whisk the batter until it is just combined.

Divide the batter between the prepared pans, bake the gingerbreads in the middle of the oven for 13 to 15 minutes, or until a tester inserted in the centers comes out clean, and let them cool in the pans on a rack. Turn the gingerbreads out and serve them with the whipped cream. Serves 2.

Chocolate Linzertorte

a 12-ounce jar (about 1 cup) seedless
    raspberry jam
1¾ sticks (14 tablespoons) unsalted butter,
    softened
½ cup granulated sugar
3 large egg yolks
1 teaspoon cinnamon
1 teaspoon freshly grated lemon zest
½ teaspoon salt
2 cups all-purpose flour
1½ cups hazelnuts, toasted and skinned
    (procedure on page 219) and ground fine
    in a food processor
3 ounces semisweet (not unsweetened)
    chocolate, ground fine in a
    food processor
confectioners' sugar for dusting
    the torte
whipped cream as an accompaniment

In a small saucepan boil the jam, stirring, for 3 minutes and let it cool. In a bowl with an electric mixer cream the butter with the granulated sugar until the mixture is light and fluffy, beat in the egg yolks, the cinnamon, the zest, and the salt, and beat the mixture until it is smooth. Add the flour and beat the dough until it is just combined. Beat in the hazelnuts and the chocolate.

Preheat the oven to 375° F. Press slightly more than half the dough onto the bottom and up the side of an 11-inch tart pan with a removable fluted rim. Roll out the remaining dough between 2 sheets of wax paper into a round slightly thicker than ⅛ inch and freeze the round in the paper on a baking sheet for 15 minutes. Spread the jam evenly on the tart shell to within ¼ inch of the edge. Remove the top sheet of wax paper from the round of dough, with a pastry wheel or sharp knife cut the round into ½-inch-wide strips, and, using a long metal spatula, arrange the strips in a lattice pattern over the jam. Trim the ends of the strips at the edge of the pan and with the remaining dough press a ¼-inch-thick rim over the ends of the strips. Bake the *Linzertorte* in the middle of the oven for 25 to 30 minutes, or until it is browned lightly, and let it cool in the pan on a rack. *The* Linzertorte *may be made 3 days in advance and kept covered loosely and chilled.* Remove the rim of the pan, dust the edge of the *Linzertorte* with the confectioners' sugar, and serve the *Linzertorte* with the whipped cream.

PHOTO ON PAGE 81

Black and White Chocolate Macaroon Tart with Raspberry Sauce

For the macaroon shell
2 cups sweetened flaked coconut
2 tablespoons all-purpose flour
½ teaspoon salt
2 large egg whites
⅓ cup sugar
For the filling
2 large egg yolks
⅔ cup heavy cream
6 ounces fine-quality bittersweet chocolate (not unsweetened), chopped
2 tablespoons rum
6 ounces fine-quality white chocolate, chopped
½ cup sour cream
For the raspberry sauce
a 10-ounce package frozen raspberries in light syrup, thawed

Make the macaroon shell: Preheat the oven to 375° F. Butter generously the bottom and sides of a 9-inch square or 10-inch round tart pan with a removable bottom, line the bottom with parchment paper, and butter the paper. In a bowl toss together the coconut, the flour, and the salt. In another bowl whisk together the egg whites and the sugar until the mixture is white and foamy, stir the sugar mixture into the coconut mixture, and with a rubber spatula spread the mixture evenly on the bottom and up the sides of the pan. Bake the shell in the middle of the oven for 20 to 25 minutes, or until it is

firm and golden, loosen it from the side of the pan with a small knife, and remove the sides of the pan. Let the shell cool completely on a rack, remove the bottom of the pan, peeling off the paper from the bottom of the shell, and put the shell on a platter.

Make the filling: In a small metal bowl whisk together the egg yolks and the heavy cream, set the bowl over a saucepan of simmering water, and cook the mixture, whisking constantly, until it is thickened and registers 160° F. on a candy thermometer. Remove the bowl from the pan, add the bittersweet chocolate, stirring until the chocolate is melted, and stir in the rum. In another small metal bowl set over the pan of barely simmering water melt the white chocolate, stirring, stir in the sour cream, and stir the mixture until it is just smooth. Remove the bowl from the pan and let the white and dark chocolate mixtures cool to warm, stirring frequently.

Spoon the chocolate mixtures into the macaroon shell, alternating them, shake the platter gently to settle the filling, and draw the back of a knife through the chocolate mixtures to swirl them together. Chill the tart, covered loosely, for 8 hours, or until it is set. *The tart may be made 1 day in advance and kept covered and chilled.*

Make the raspberry sauce: Force the raspberries through a fine sieve into a bowl, pressing hard on the solids, scrape the pulp from the underside of the sieve into the sauce, and whisk the sauce until it is combined well. *The sauce may be made 2 days in advance and kept covered and chilled.*

Arrange slices of the tart on dessert plates and pour some of the raspberry sauce around them. Serves 8.

PHOTO ON PAGE 70

Cream Cheese and Jam Turnovers

2 sheets frozen puff pastry, thawed
¾ cup (about 6 ounces) cream cheese
¾ cup jam, such as apricot or cherry
an egg wash made by beating together 1 large
   egg and 1 teaspoon water
about 1½ tablespoons sugar for sprinkling
   the turnovers

Preheat the oven to 425° F. On a lightly floured surface roll out each sheet of pastry into a 12-inch square and cut each square into four 6-inch squares. Put 1½ tablespoons of the cream cheese in the center of each square, top it with 1½ tablespoons of the jam, and brush the edges of each square with water. Fold the squares in half diagonally to form triangles, pressing the edges together firmly, and press the edges with the tines of a fork to seal them well. Arrange the turnovers on a dampened baking sheet, brush them with the egg wash, and with a sharp knife cut several slits (for steam vents) in the top of each turnover. Sprinkle the turnovers with the sugar, bake them in the upper third of the oven for 12 to 15 minutes, or until they are puffed and golden, and serve them warm. Makes 8 turnovers.

Louisiana Sweet-Dough Mincemeat Turnovers

1 cup plus 2 tablespoons all-purpose flour
½ teaspoon double-acting baking powder
¼ teaspoon salt
3 tablespoons unsalted butter, softened
3 tablespoons sugar
¼ teaspoon vanilla
1 tablespoon beaten egg
2 tablespoons milk
4 tablespoons bottled mincemeat

Preheat the oven to 375° F. In a bowl whisk together the flour, the baking powder, and the salt. In a bowl with an electric mixer cream together the butter and the sugar until the mixture is light and fluffy, beat in the vanilla and the egg, and beat in the flour mixture in batches alternately with the milk. Chill the dough, dusted with flour and wrapped in plastic wrap, in the freezer for 10 minutes.
Divide the dough into fourths and roll out 1 piece of the dough ⅛ inch thick on a well-floured surface, keeping the remaining pieces covered and chilled. Cut a 4-inch round from the dough, brush off any excess

flour, and brush the edges with water. Put 1 tablespoon of the mincemeat in the center of the round, fold the dough over to enclose the mincemeat, and pinch the edges together to seal them. Make 3 more turnovers in the same manner with the remaining dough and mincemeat. Bake the turnovers on a buttered baking sheet in the middle of the oven for 15 minutes, or until the edges are golden. Makes 4 turnovers.

PUDDINGS, MOUSSES, AND MERINGUES

Pinto Raisin Bread Pudding with Apples and Cheese

2½ cups water
1½ cups firmly packed light brown sugar
½ teaspoon cinnamon
5 slices of homemade-style white bread,
   toasted and the crusts discarded
5 slices of homemade-style raisin bread,
   toasted and the crusts discarded
½ stick (¼ cup) unsalted butter, softened
½ pound Longhorn (Colby) or mild Cheddar,
   grated
2 Granny Smith apples
1 cup apple jelly, melted
vanilla ice cream as an accompaniment

In a saucepan simmer the water with the brown sugar until the sugar is dissolved and stir in the cinnamon. Spread the 10 bread slices on one side with the butter and halve each slice diagonally. Arrange half the white bread and half the raisin bread, buttered sides down, decoratively in a buttered 13- by 9-inch baking dish and sprinkle half the Longhorn over the bread. Peel the apples, grate them coarse, and sprinkle them over the cheese. Top the apples with the remaining cheese and arrange the remaining bread, buttered sides down, decoratively on top, trimming the bread as necessary to fit in one layer. Pour the brown sugar syrup evenly over the bread pudding, pressing down on the top slightly with a spatula, and let the pudding stand, covered, for 1 hour.
Preheat the oven to 350° F. Bake the pudding in the middle of the oven for 30 minutes, spread the jelly over the top, and let the pudding stand for 5 minutes. Serve the pudding warm with the ice cream. Serves 8.

Almond Pear Clafouti
(Baked Almond Pear Pudding)

4 firm-ripe pears, peeled, cored, and sliced
2 tablespoons fresh lemon juice
¾ cup sliced blanched almonds
¾ cup milk
1 stick unsalted butter, melted and cooled
3 large eggs, beaten lightly
½ teaspoon vanilla
½ teaspoon almond extract (preferably pure)*
¾ cup self-rising cake flour
½ cup plus 2 tablespoons sugar

*Pure almond extract is available at specialty
 foods shops and by mail order from Maison
 Glass, tel. (212) 755-3316

Preheat the oven to 400° F. and butter a 10- by 2-inch round (1-quart capacity) baking dish. In the dish toss the pears gently with the lemon juice and spread them evenly in the dish.

In a blender grind fine ½ cup of the almonds, add the milk, 6 tablespoons of the butter, the eggs, the vanilla, and the almond extract, and blend the mixture until it is smooth. In a bowl whisk together the flour, ½ cup of the sugar, and a pinch of salt and stir in the milk mixture, stirring until the batter is combined well. Pour the batter over the pears, drizzle it with the remaining 2 tablespoons butter, and sprinkle it with the remaining 2 tablespoons sugar and the remaining ¼ cup almonds. Bake the *clafouti* in the middle of the oven for 40 minutes, or until it is golden brown, and let it cool on a rack for 15 minutes. Serve the *clafouti* warm. Serves 6 to 8.

Bing Cherry Clafouti
(Baked Sweet Cherry Pudding)

⅓ cup plus 1 tablespoon sugar
2 tablespoons all-purpose flour
2 large eggs
⅔ cup milk
1½ teaspoons vanilla
½ teaspoon orange zest
¼ teaspoon almond extract
¼ teaspoon salt
1 cup Bing cherries, halved and pitted
½ tablespoon unsalted butter, cut into bits
vanilla ice cream as an accompaniment
 if desired

Preheat the oven to 400° F. In a blender blend together ⅓ cup of the sugar, the flour, the eggs, the milk, the vanilla, the zest, the almond extract, and the salt until the custard is just smooth. Arrange the cherries in one layer in a buttered 3-cup gratin dish or flameproof shallow baking dish, pour the custard over them, and bake the *clafouti* in the middle of the oven for 20 to 25 minutes, or until the top is puffed and springy to the touch. Sprinkle the top with the remaining 1 tablespoon sugar, dot it with the butter, and broil the *clafouti* under a preheated broiler about 3 inches from the heat for 1 minute, or until it is browned. Serve the *clafouti* with the ice cream. Serves 2.

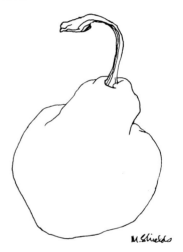

M. Shields

Dark Chocolate Mint Velvets
(Bittersweet Chocolate Spearmint Puddings)

1¼ cups milk
½ cup packed fresh mint leaves, preferably
 spearmint, chopped fine, plus mint sprigs
 for garnish
2 teaspoons sugar
⅛ teaspoon salt
¼ cup heavy cream
1 tablespoon cornstarch
6 ounces fine-quality bittersweet chocolate
 (not unsweetened), chopped fine

In a heavy saucepan scald the milk, stir in the chopped mint, and let the mixture steep, covered, for 1 hour. Strain the mixture through a fine sieve set over a bowl, pressing hard on the solids, return the liquid to the pan, and add the sugar and the salt. In a small bowl stir together the cream and the cornstarch. Bring the milk mixture to a simmer, stir the cornstarch mixture, and stir it into the milk mixture. Simmer the mixture, whisking, for 2 minutes, remove the pan from the heat, and stir in the chocolate, stirring until it is melted and the mixture is smooth. Divide the mixture among four ½-cup bowls or ramekins and chill the desserts, covered, for 2 hours, or until they are cold. *The desserts may be made 1 day in advance and kept covered and chilled.* Garnish the desserts with the mint sprigs. Serves 4.

Cranberry Winter Pudding

a 12-ounce bag of fresh cranberries,
    picked over
1 firm-ripe pear, peeled, cored,
    and chopped fine
¾ cup firmly packed light brown sugar
½ cup dried sour cherries (available at
    specialty foods shops) or golden raisins
⅓ cup finely chopped dried apricots
two 2-inch strips of lemon zest removed with
    a vegetable peeler
a 3-inch cinnamon stick
2 cups cranberry juice cocktail
¼ teaspoon vanilla
about 10 slices of homemade-type white
    bread, crusts removed
lightly sweetened whipped cream as
    an accompaniment

In a saucepan combine the cranberries, the pear, the brown sugar, the dried fruit, the zest, the cinnamon stick, the cranberry juice cocktail, the vanilla, and a pinch of salt and simmer the mixture for 10 minutes. Strain the mixture through a sieve into a bowl, reserving the solids, and transfer the cranberry liquid to a shallow dish. Line a 1½-quart soufflé dish with plastic wrap and trim enough of the bread slices to cover the bottom and the side of the dish. Soak the trimmed slices in the cranberry liquid and line the bottom and the side of the soufflé dish with them.

Discard the zest and the cinnamon stick from the reserved cranberry solids and add the solids to the soufflé dish. Trim enough of the remaining bread slices to cover the cranberry solids, soak the trimmed slices in the cranberry liquid, and top the cranberry solids with them. Cover the pudding with plastic wrap, put a plate on top of the plastic wrap, and weight the pudding with three 1-pound cans. Chill the pudding, weighted, for at least 12 hours and up to 1 day. Invert the pudding onto a serv-

ing plate, discarding the plastic wrap, and serve it, cut into wedges, with the whipped cream. Serves 6 to 8.

Honey Vanilla Rice-Pudding Crème Brûlée

⅔ cup water
⅓ cup long-grain rice
2 cups milk
½ cup heavy cream
1 vanilla bean, split lengthwise
2 large whole eggs
3 large egg yolks
½ cup honey
¼ teaspoon salt
⅓ cup firmly packed light brown sugar
orange sections as an accompaniment

In a small saucepan bring the water to a boil, add the rice with a pinch of salt, and simmer it gently, covered, for 15 to 20 minutes, or until all the water is absorbed and the rice is tender. Transfer the rice to a small bowl and let it cool.

Preheat the oven to 300° F. and butter a 9-inch (1-quart capacity) flameproof shallow baking dish. In the pan bring the milk and the cream just to a boil with the vanilla bean and remove the pan from the heat. Scrape the seeds from the vanilla bean into the milk mixture and discard the pod (or reserve it for another use). In a bowl whisk together the whole eggs, the egg yolks, the honey, and the salt, whisk in the rice, and whisk the mixture until it is combined well. Add the milk mixture in a stream, whisking, and pour the custard into the baking dish. Transfer the baking dish to a baking pan, add enough hot water to the pan to reach halfway up the side of the dish, and bake the custard in the middle of the oven for 1 hour to 1 hour and 10 minutes, or until it is set completely. Transfer the custard to a rack, let it cool, and chill it, covered, for at least 6 hours or overnight.

Just before serving, preheat the broiler, blot the top of the custard dry with a paper towel, and force the brown sugar through a coarse sieve onto the top of it, covering it evenly. Put the baking dish in a baking pan filled with ice and broil the custard about 2 inches from the heat for 2 to 3 minutes, or until the brown sugar is melted and crisp (be careful not to let the brown sugar burn). Let the *crème brûlée* cool in the pan of ice for 3 minutes and serve it, cut into wedges, with the orange sections. Serves 8 to 10.

Iced Coffee Mousse

½ teaspoon unflavored gelatin
2 tablespoons water
½ cup sweetened condensed milk
  (not evaporated)
1½ teaspoons instant espresso powder
½ teaspoon vanilla
½ cup well-chilled heavy cream

In a small saucepan sprinkle the gelatin over the water and let it soften for 2 minutes. Add the milk and the espresso powder and heat the mixture over moderate heat, whisking constantly, until the espresso powder is dissolved. Remove the pan from the heat, stir in the vanilla, and set the pan in a bowl of ice and cold water, stirring the mixture every few minutes until it is thick and cold. In a small bowl beat the cream until it just holds stiff peaks and fold the coffee mixture into it gently but thoroughly. Spoon the mousse into 2 chilled long-stemmed glasses and chill it until ready to serve. Serves 2.

Mexican Floating Island with Kahlúa Custard Sauce and Sesame Pumpkin-Seed Brittle

1¾ cups sugar
6 large egg whites
¼ teaspoon salt
¼ teaspoon cream of tartar
Kahlúa custard sauce and sesame pumpkin-seed
  brittle (recipes follow) as accompaniments

In a dry heavy skillet cook 1 cup of the sugar over moderate heat until it begins to melt and continue cooking, stirring with a fork, until it is melted completely and is a golden caramel. Pour the caramel into a 1½-quart ring mold. Using potholders to hold the mold tilt and rotate the mold to coat the bottom and let the caramel cool.

Preheat the oven to 350° F. In a bowl with an electric mixer beat the egg whites with the salt until they are foamy, add the cream of tartar, and beat the whites until they just hold stiff peaks. Beat in the remaining ¾ cup sugar, a little at a time, and beat the meringue until it holds stiff glossy peaks. Spoon the meringue into the ring mold, rapping the mold sharply on a hard surface to expel any air bubbles, and smooth the top. (The meringue will fill the mold completely.) Transfer the mold to a deep baking pan, add enough hot water to the pan to reach 1 inch up the side of the mold, and bake the me-

ringue in the middle of the oven for 1 hour. (The meringue will rise completely and will deflate as it cools.) Turn off the oven and let the meringue stand in the oven for 15 minutes. Transfer the mold to a rack and let it cool completely. *The meringue may be made 1 day in advance and kept covered and chilled.* Invert the meringue onto a deep serving plate, letting the melted caramel drip over the top and down the sides. Some of the caramel will remain, hardened, in the bottom of the mold. Put the mold in a skillet of simmering water and heat the caramel, stirring occasionally, until it has melted. Spoon the Kahlúa custard sauce around the meringue, drizzle the meringue decoratively with the melted caramel, and crumble some of the sesame pumpkin-seed brittle over it. Serve the remaining custard sauce separately.

PHOTO ON PAGE 69

Kahlúa Custard Sauce

2 cups half-and-half
1 vanilla bean, split lengthwise
6 large egg yolks
½ cup sugar
3 tablespoons Kahlúa, or to taste

In a small heavy saucepan bring the half-and-half just to a boil with the vanilla bean and remove the pan from the heat. In a bowl whisk together the egg yolks and the sugar until the mixture is combined well and add the half-and-half mixture in a slow stream, whisking. Transfer the mixture to a heavy saucepan and cook it over moderate heat, stirring constantly with a wooden spoon, until it thickens slightly and registers 175° F. on a candy thermometer. (The sauce will thicken as it cools.) Strain the custard sauce through a fine sieve into a metal bowl set in a larger bowl of ice and cold water, let it cool, stirring, and stir in the Kahlúa. Chill the sauce, covered, for at least 2 hours, or until it is very cold. *The sauce may be made 2 days in advance and kept covered and chilled.* Makes about 2 cups.

Sesame Pumpkin-Seed Brittle

1 cup sugar
3 tablespoons *pepitas* (hulled green pumpkin
  seeds, available at natural foods stores and
  some Hispanic markets), chopped
1½ teaspoons sesame seeds

In a dry heavy skillet cook the sugar over moderate heat until it begins to melt and continue cooking it, stirring with a fork, until it is melted completely and is a golden caramel. Remove the skillet from the heat, stir in the *pepitas* and the sesame seeds, and, working quickly, pour the mixture onto a sheet of foil. Let the brittle cool and break it into small pieces. *The brittle may be made 1 week in advance and kept in an airtight container.* Makes about ½ pound.

FROZEN DESSERTS

Butterscotch Rum Raisin Banana Splits

2 tablespoons raisins
¼ cup water
⅓ cup sugar
½ tablespoon unsalted butter
⅛ teaspoon salt
2 tablespoons rum
2 to 4 scoops of vanilla ice cream
1 banana

In a small bowl let the raisins soak in the water. In a dry small heavy skillet heat the sugar over moderate heat, undisturbed, until it begins to melt, cook it, swirling the skillet occasionally, until it is a golden caramel, and remove the skillet from the heat. Add the raisins with the water, the butter, and the salt, stir in the rum, and cook the mixture over moderately low heat, stirring, until the caramel is dissolved. Divide the ice cream between 2 dishes, halve the banana lengthwise and crosswise, and arrange 2 banana pieces in each dish. Spoon the butterscotch sauce over the ice cream and banana. Serves 2.

Cantaloupe Sherbet

½ cup water
½ cup sugar
2 tablespoons Pernod
two 3-inch strips of lemon zest
1 tablespoon fresh lemon juice
1 cantaloupe (about 2½ pounds), seeds and
    rind discarded and the flesh chopped
    (about 3½ cups)
¼ cup heavy cream

In a saucepan stir together the water, the sugar, the Pernod, and the zest, boil the mixture, stirring, until the sugar is dissolved, and simmer it for 5 minutes. Stir in the lemon juice, transfer the syrup to a bowl, and chill it, covered, until it is cold. In a blender or food processor purée the cantaloupe, scraping down the sides with a rubber spatula, until it is smooth, blend in the cream and the syrup, and force the mixture through a coarse sieve set over a bowl, pressing hard on the solids. Freeze the mixture in an ice-cream freezer according to the manufacturer's instructions. Makes about 3 cups.

Chocolate Profiteroles with Caramel Coffee Ice Cream and Bittersweet Chocolate Sauce

For the profiteroles
½ cup all-purpose flour
2 tablespoons unsweetened cocoa powder
   (preferably Dutch-process)
3 tablespoons unsalted butter, cut into bits
¼ cup plus 2 tablespoons water
1 tablespoon granulated sugar
2 large eggs

caramel coffee ice cream (recipe follows)
   or other coffee ice cream
confectioners' sugar for sprinkling the
   profiteroles if desired
bittersweet chocolate sauce (page 235)

Make the profiteroles: Preheat the oven to 400° F. Into a bowl sift together the flour and the cocoa powder. In a small heavy saucepan combine the butter, the water, the granulated sugar, and a pinch of salt and bring the mixture to a boil over high heat, stirring until the

butter is melted. Reduce the heat to moderate, add the flour mixture, and cook the mixture, beating it with a wooden spoon, until it pulls away from the side of the pan, forming a ball. Transfer the mixture to a bowl and with an electric mixer at high speed beat in the eggs, 1 at a time, beating well after each addition. Drop the mixture by rounded tablespoons onto a buttered baking sheet, forming 12 mounds, bake the profiteroles in the middle of the oven for 20 to 25 minutes, or until they are puffed and crisp, and let them cool on a rack. *The profiteroles may be made 1 day in advance and kept in an airtight container. Reheat the profiteroles on a baking sheet in a preheated 375° F. oven for 5 minutes, or until they are crisp, and let them cool on the rack.*

With a serrated knife cut each profiterole in half crosswise, discard any uncooked dough from the centers, and sandwich a small scoop (about 1½ inches in diameter) of the ice cream between the top and bottom of each profiterole. Sprinkle the profiteroles with the confectioners' sugar, pour about ¼ cup of the sauce onto each of 4 dessert plates, and arrange 3 profiteroles on each plate. Makes 12 profiteroles, serving 4.

Caramel Coffee Ice Cream
¼ cup coffee beans, crushed lightly
1 vanilla bean, split lengthwise
1½ cups milk
1½ cups heavy cream
⅔ cup plus 3 tablespoons sugar
3 tablespoons water
5 large egg yolks

In a saucepan combine the coffee beans, the vanilla bean, the milk, and 1 cup of the cream, bring the liquid just to a boil, and remove the pan from the heat. Let the mixture stand, covered, for 30 minutes.

While the coffee mixture is steeping, in a small heavy saucepan combine ⅔ cup of the sugar with the water, bring the mixture to a boil, stirring and washing down any sugar crystals clinging to the side of the pan with a brush dipped in cold water until the sugar is dissolved, and boil the mixture, undisturbed, until it is a deep golden caramel. Remove the pan from the heat and set it in the sink. To the caramel add the remaining ½ cup cream (the mixture will bubble up), whisk the mixture until it is smooth, and let it cool. In a bowl whisk together the yolks, the remaining 3 tablespoons sugar, and a pinch of salt, add the coffee mixture in a stream, whisking, and transfer the mixture to the heavy saucepan. Cook the custard over moderately low heat, stirring, until it registers 170° F. on a candy thermometer, remove it from the heat, and whisk in the caramel mixture. Pour the custard through a fine sieve set over a bowl, let it cool, and freeze it in an ice-cream maker according to the manufacturer's instructions. Makes about 1 quart.

Bittersweet Chocolate Sauce

6 ounces fine-quality bittersweet chocolate, chopped
3 tablespoons water
¼ cup heavy cream
2 tablespoons Kahlúa or other coffee-flavored liqueur, or to taste

In a heatproof bowl set over a saucepan of simmering water melt the chocolate with the water and the cream, stirring until the mixture is smooth, and stir in the Kahlúa. *The sauce may be made 1 week in advance, kept covered and chilled, and reheated.* Makes about 1 cup.

Cranberry Swirl Ice-Cream Cake

28 chocolate wafers, ground fine in a food processor or blender (about 1½ cups crumbs)
½ stick (¼ cup) unsalted butter, melted, plus 1 tablespoon unmelted butter
1½ cups cranberries, picked over
½ cup light corn syrup
⅓ cup granulated sugar
⅓ cup water
1½ pints vanilla ice cream
½ cup shelled natural pistachio nuts, chopped fine
¼ teaspoon salt
1 cup well-chilled heavy cream
3 tablespoons confectioners' sugar
1 teaspoon vanilla
chocolate curls (procedure follows) or grated bittersweet chocolate for garnish if desired

In a bowl with a fork stir together the wafer crumbs and the melted butter until the mixture is combined well, pat the mixture onto the bottom and 1 inch up the side of a lightly oiled 8-inch springform pan (2½ inches deep), and freeze the crust for 30 minutes, or until firm.

In a saucepan simmer the cranberries, the corn syrup, the granulated sugar, and the water, covered, for 10 minutes, or until the cranberries are soft, and in a food processor or blender purée the mixture. In a small bowl chill the purée, covered, for 1 hour, or until it is cold and stir it until it is smooth.

Spread half the ice cream, softened, over the crust, drizzle it with all but ⅓ cup of the cranberry purée, and spread the remaining ice cream, softened, over it. Draw a knife through the ice-cream mixture in loops to marble it, smooth the top, and freeze the mixture for 30 minutes, or until it is firm. Spread the remaining ⅓ cup cranberry purée evenly over the top and freeze the cake for 15 minutes, or until the purée is firm.

In a small skillet cook the pistachios in the remaining 1 tablespoon butter with the salt over moderate heat, stirring, for 1 minute and let them cool. In a bowl with an electric mixer beat the heavy cream until it holds soft peaks, add the confectioners' sugar and the vanilla, and beat the mixture until it holds stiff peaks. Fold in the pistachios, spread the mixture over the cake, and freeze the cake for 30 minutes, or until the top is firm. Freeze the cake, covered with plastic wrap and foil, for 4 hours more. *The cake may be made 5 days in advance and kept covered tightly and frozen.*

Just before serving, wrap a warm, dampened kitchen towel around the side of the pan, remove the side of the pan, and transfer the cake to a serving plate. Garnish the cake with the chocolate curls or grated chocolate and serve it cut into wedges with a knife dipped in hot water.

To Make Chocolate Curls

3 ounces fine-quality bittersweet chocolate (not unsweetened), chopped

In a small metal bowl set over a saucepan of barely simmering water melt the chocolate and on a flat marble surface or kitchen counter (not wood) spread it with a metal spatula as thinly and evenly as possible. Let the chocolate cool until it is firm to the touch but not hard. (If your kitchen is hot, a fan can be helpful.) With a pastry scraper or metal spatula held at an angle scrape the chocolate from the marble, letting it gather and curl. Transfer the curls carefully as they are made to a baking sheet lined with wax paper. *The chocolate curls may be made 8 hours in advance and kept at room temperature.* Makes enough chocolate curls to garnish an 8-inch cake.

Coconut Mango Sorbet

¾ cup water
¼ cup sugar
1 large mango, peeled, pitted, and chopped
¾ cup unsweetened pineapple juice
¼ cup well-stirred canned cream of coconut
2 tablespoons fresh lime juice, or to taste
a pinch of freshly grated lime zest

In a small saucepan boil the water with the sugar, stirring, until the sugar is dissolved, simmer the mixture for 5 minutes, and remove the pan from the heat. Let the syrup cool to room temperature and chill it, covered, until it is cold. In a blender purée the mango with the pineapple juice, the cream of coconut, the lime juice, the zest, and the syrup until the mixture is smooth. Freeze the mixture in an ice-cream freezer according to the manufacturer's instructions. Makes about 1 pint.

Gingersnap and Lemon Ice Cream Sandwiches
For the gingersnaps
1 stick (½ cup) unsalted butter, softened
½ cup granulated sugar plus additional for
    coating the cookies
½ cup firmly packed light brown sugar
⅓ cup unsulfured molasses
1 large egg
2 cups all-purpose flour
2½ teaspoons ground ginger
½ teaspoon cinnamon
¼ teaspoon ground allspice
1 teaspoon baking soda
¾ teaspoon salt

lemon ice cream (recipe follows)
1 cup shelled natural pistachio nuts, the loose
    skins rubbed off and the nuts chopped

Make the gingersnaps: Preheat the oven to 350° F. In a bowl with an electric mixer cream together the butter, ½ cup of the granulated sugar, and the brown sugar until the mixture is light and fluffy, add the molasses, and beat the mixture until it is smooth. Add the egg and beat the mixture until it is smooth. In another bowl whisk together the flour, the ginger, the cinnamon, the allspice, the baking soda, and the salt, add the flour mixture to the butter mixture, and stir the mixture until it forms a soft dough. Form the dough into 24 balls (each about

1½ inches in diameter), roll the balls in the additional granulated sugar, coating them, and arrange them 2 inches apart on buttered baking sheets. Bake the gingersnaps in batches in the middle of the oven for 13 to 15 minutes, or until they are crisp and cracked but still soft inside, and let them cool on the sheets for 5 minutes. Transfer the gingersnaps with a metal spatula to racks and let them cool completely.

Sandwich a scoop of the ice cream between 2 of the gingersnaps, pressing the cookies together, form 11 more sandwiches in the same manner, and roll the edges in the pistachios. Freeze the sandwiches on a tray, covered, until they are hard. *The sandwiches may be made 2 days in advance and kept covered and frozen.* Makes 12 ice-cream sandwiches.

Lemon Ice Cream

1 tablespoon freshly grated lemon zest
½ cup fresh lemon juice
1 cup sugar
3 large eggs
2 cups half-and-half
½ teaspoon vanilla

In a saucepan whisk together the zest, the lemon juice, the sugar, and the eggs, whisk in 1 cup of the half-and-half and the vanilla, and cook the mixture over moderately high heat, whisking constantly, until it just comes to a simmer. Strain the custard through a fine sieve into a bowl, pressing hard on the zest, and chill it, covered with plastic wrap, until it is cold. Whisk in the remaining 1 cup half-and-half and freeze the mixture in an ice-cream freezer according to the manufacturer's instructions. Makes about 1 quart.

Halvah Vanilla Ice Cream

3 large egg yolks
½ cup sugar
1 tablespoon cornstarch
1½ cups milk, scalded
1 teaspoon vanilla
1½ cups well-chilled heavy cream
¼ pound halvah (a ground sesame-seed and
    honey candy, available at Middle Eastern
    groceries), cut into bits
½ cup orange honey syrup (page 212)
    as an accompaniment

In a bowl whisk together the egg yolks, the sugar, the cornstarch, and a pinch of salt and add the milk in a slow stream, stirring. In a heavy saucepan cook the custard over moderate heat, stirring constantly with a wooden spoon, until it comes to a boil, boil it, stirring constantly, for 2 minutes, and strain it through a fine sieve into a metal bowl set in a larger bowl of ice and cold water. Stir in the vanilla, let the custard cool, stirring, and chill it, covered, until it is cold. Stir in the cream, freeze the custard in an ice-cream freezer according to the manufacturer's instructions, and stir in the halvah. (Alternatively, the halvah may be stirred into a quart of softened premium vanilla ice cream.) Transfer the ice cream to a metal bowl, freeze it until it is frozen solid, and scoop it into glasses. Spoon the orange honey syrup over the ice cream. Makes about 1 quart.

Nectarine Ice Cream

3 large nectarines
¾ cup sugar
1 tablespoon fresh lemon juice
1 cup half-and-half
½ cup heavy cream
a 2-inch piece of vanilla bean
¼ teaspoon finely grated fresh lemon zest

Peel the nectarines, reserving the peelings, and slice them, reserving the pits. In a food processor combine the nectarine slices, ½ cup of the sugar, and the lemon juice and pulse the motor until the nectarine slices are chopped coarse. Transfer the mixture to a bowl and chill it, covered. In a saucepan heat the half-and-half, the cream, the reserved nectarine peelings and pits, the remaining ¼ cup sugar, the vanilla bean, the zest, and a

pinch of salt over moderate heat until the mixture is very hot but not boiling. Remove the pan from the heat, let the mixture cool to room temperature, and chill it, covered, for 1 hour, or until it is very cold.

Strain the cream mixture through a fine sieve into the bowl with the chopped nectarines, stir the mixture until it is combined well, and freeze it in an ice-cream freezer according to the manufacturer's instructions. Makes about 1 quart.

Ice Cream with Raspberry Sauce and Praline Bits

½ cup sugar
⅓ cup sliced almonds,
    toasted lightly
a 10½-ounce package frozen raspberries
    in syrup
chocolate or vanilla ice cream

Line a baking sheet with foil. In a heavy skillet cook the sugar over moderate heat, stirring with a fork, until it is melted, and cook the sugar, swirling the skillet occasionally, until it is a golden caramel. Working quickly, stir in the almonds with the fork, stirring until they are coated completely, pour the mixture onto the foil, and pat it out thin with the fork. Let the praline cool completely and break enough of it into bits to make about ⅔ cup, reserving the remaining praline for another use.

In a heavy saucepan cook the raspberries with the syrup over moderate heat until the mixture is reduced to about ¾ cup and force the mixture through a fine sieve into a bowl, pressing hard on the solids. Scoop the ice cream into bowls, spoon the raspberry sauce around it, and sprinkle the praline bits over the top. Serves 2.

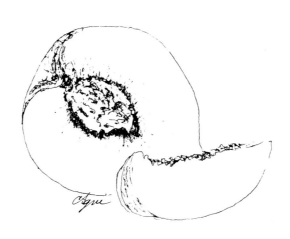

Ricotta Gelato with Blackberry Sauce

For the gelato
1¼ cups half-and-half
1¼ cups milk
a 15- or 16-ounce container whole-milk ricotta
½ cup sugar
a 3-inch cinnamon stick
a 2-inch strip of lemon zest
2 tablespoons light corn syrup
¼ teaspoon vanilla
For the blackberry sauce
1 cup sugar
¼ cup water
2 cups blackberries
1 tablespoon fresh lemon juice
1 teaspoon *crème de cassis*

1 mango, pitted, peeled, and cut in
    ½-inch dice for garnish
blackberries for garnish

Make the *gelato*: In a saucepan whisk together the half-and-half, the milk, the ricotta, and the sugar, add the cinnamon, and bring the mixture just to a boil, stirring. Remove the pan from the heat, add the lemon zest, and let the mixture stand, covered, for 10 minutes. Force the mixture through a fine sieve set over a bowl and stir in the corn syrup and the vanilla. Chill the mixture, covered, until it is cold and freeze it in an ice-cream freezer according to the manufacturer's instructions. Pack the *gelato* tightly into six ½-cup molds, cover each mold with plastic wrap, and freeze the *gelato* for 30 minutes, or until it is ready to be served.

Make the blackberry sauce: In a heavy saucepan melt the sugar over moderate heat, stirring with a fork, and cook the syrup, swirling the pan occasionally, until it is a golden caramel. Working carefully and quickly, stir in the water, the blackberries, the lemon juice, and the *crème de cassis* (the mixture will bubble up), stirring until the mixture is combined well, and cook the mixture over moderately low heat until the caramel is dissolved. Strain the mixture through a fine sieve set over a bowl, pressing hard on the solids, and chill the sauce, covered, until it is cold.

Divide the sauce among 6 dessert plates, unmold the *gelato*, and arrange it in the center of the plates. Garnish each serving with some of the mango and the blackberries. Serves 6.

PHOTO ON PAGE 57

b.charlton

Watermelon Granita

1 cup water
⅓ cup sugar
2 tablespoons *crème de cassis*
2 pounds watermelon, seeds and rind
    discarded and the flesh chopped
1 tablespoon fresh lime juice
1 teaspoon Angostura bitters

In a small saucepan stir together the water, the sugar, and the *crème de cassis*, boil the mixture, stirring, until the sugar is dissolved, and simmer it for 5 minutes. Transfer the syrup to a bowl and chill it, covered, until it is cold. In a blender purée the watermelon in batches, forcing it as it is puréed through a coarse sieve set over a large bowl, pressing hard on the solids. Stir into the watermelon purée the syrup, the lime juice, and the bitters and transfer the mixture to an 8-inch-square metal pan. Freeze the mixture, stirring and crushing the lumps with a fork every 30 minutes, for 2 to 3 hours, or until the granita is firm but not frozen solid. Scrape the granita with a fork to lighten the texture and serve it immediately. Makes about 1 quart.

FRUIT FINALES

Sliced Baked Apples

4 McIntosh apples
3 tablespoons fresh lemon juice
¼ cup firmly packed light brown sugar
½ stick (¼ cup) unsalted butter, cut into bits
2 tablespoons light rum
four 3-inch cinnamon sticks
apple or mint leaves for garnish if desired

Preheat the oven to 450° F. Peel and core the apples, leaving them whole. Slice the apples horizontally into even ¼-inch-thick slices, reassemble the slices to form whole apple shapes, and brush the apples with the lemon juice. Put the apples in a pie plate, fill the cavities with some of the brown sugar, butter, and rum, and sprinkle the apples with the remaining brown sugar, butter, and rum. Bake the apples in the middle of the oven, basting frequently, for 25 minutes. Reduce the temperature to 350° F., insert the cinnamon sticks in the cavities of the apples, and bake the apples, basting frequently, for 20 minutes more, or until they are tender and browned well and the juices are thick and syrupy. Divide the apples among 4 plates, spoon the syrup over them, and garnish the apples with the apple or mint leaves. Serves 4.

Dried Apple and Cheddar Strudel

¾ pound dried apples (available at natural foods stores and some supermarkets)
3 cups apple cider
1½ cups grated Cheddar (about 6 ounces)
¼ cup dried cranberries (available at specialty foods shops and some supermarkets) or raisins

4 tablespoons sugar
2½ teaspoons cinnamon
¼ teaspoon allspice
10 teaspoons fine dry bread crumbs
5 tablespoons unsalted butter, melted
six 18- by 14-inch sheets of *phyllo*, stacked between 2 sheets of wax paper and covered with a dampened kitchen towel

In a large saucepan combine the dried apples with the apple cider and simmer them, stirring occasionally, for 15 to 25 minutes, or until they are softened but not mushy. Drain the apples and let them cool. In a large bowl toss the apples with the Cheddar, the cranberries or raisins, 3 tablespoons of the sugar, ½ teaspoon of the cinnamon, and the allspice and combine the filling well. *The filling may be made 1 day in advance and kept covered and chilled.*

In a small bowl stir together the bread crumbs and 1 teaspoon of the remaining cinnamon and reserve the mixture. In another small bowl stir together the remaining tablespoon sugar and the remaining teaspoon cinnamon and reserve the cinnamon sugar.

Preheat the oven to 425° F. On a work surface arrange two 20-inch-long sheets of wax paper with the long sides overlapping slightly and facing you. Put a sheet of the *phyllo* on the wax paper, brush it with some of the butter, and sprinkle it with about 2 teaspoons of the reserved bread crumb mixture. On this, layer, brush, and sprinkle 4 more sheets of the *phyllo* in the same manner and lay the sixth sheet of *phyllo* on top.

Spread the filling in a 3-inch-wide strip, mounding it on the *phyllo* 4 inches above the near long side, leaving a 2-inch border at each end. Using the wax paper as a guide, lift the bottom 4 inches of the pastry over the filling, fold in the ends, and roll up the strudel tightly. Transfer the strudel carefully, seam side down, to a lightly buttered baking sheet and brush it with the remaining butter. Arrange ½-inch-wide strips of wax paper ½ inch apart diagonally across the strudel. Transfer the reserved cinnamon sugar to a small sieve, shake it evenly over the strudel, and remove the wax paper strips carefully. Bake the strudel in the lower third of the oven for 20 to 25 minutes, or until it is golden, and let it cool to warm on the baking sheet on a rack. *The strudel may be made 1 day in advance and kept covered loosely and chilled. Reheat the strudel in a preheated 400° F. oven for 20 minutes.* Serve the strudel warm, cut into 1-inch slices with a serrated knife. Serves 8 to 10.

Cranberry Applesauce

4 apples (about 2 pounds), peeled, cored,
    and chopped
1 cup fresh cranberries,
    picked over
½ cup sugar
¼ cup apple juice or water
a 3-inch cinnamon stick
a 3-inch strip of lemon zest
    removed with a
    vegetable peeler
2 tablespoons unsalted butter

In a heavy saucepan cook the apples, the cranberries, the sugar, the apple juice or water, the cinnamon stick, and the zest over moderate heat, stirring, for 15 minutes, or until the apples are very soft. Discard the cinnamon stick and the zest, force the apple mixture through the medium disk of a food mill into a bowl, and stir in the butter. Serve the applesauce warm or chilled. *The applesauce keeps, covered and chilled, for 1 week.* Makes about 3 cups.

Dried Cranberry and Apple Crisp

1 cup dried cranberries (available at specialty
    foods shops)
1 cinnamon stick
1 cup water
⅔ cup all-purpose flour
⅔ cup firmly packed light brown sugar
¼ teaspoon salt
¾ stick (6 tablespoons) unsalted butter,
    cut into bits
9 McIntosh apples
    (about 3 pounds)

Preheat the oven to 400° F. In a small saucepan simmer the dried cranberries, the cinnamon stick, and the water for 10 minutes. Drain the cranberries and remove the cinnamon stick. In a small bowl blend the all-purpose flour, the brown sugar, the salt, and the butter until the mixture resembles coarse meal and toss the mixture well. Peel, core, and slice the McIntosh apples thin and in a buttered 13- by 9-inch glass dish toss them with the cranberries. Sprinkle the brown sugar mixture over the apples and the cranberries and bake the crisp in the oven for 25 minutes, or until the apples are tender and the topping is golden. Serves 6.

Cranberry Apricot Pecan Strudel

1 stick (½ cup) unsalted butter
2 Golden Delicious apples
¾ pound fresh cranberries,
    picked over
¾ cup plus 2 tablespoons sugar
¼ pound dried apricots, chopped
    (about ½ cup)
½ cup pecans, toasted lightly and chopped
1¼ teaspoons cinnamon
six 18- by 14-inch sheets of *phyllo*, stacked
    between 2 sheets of wax paper and covered
    with a dampened kitchen towel
10 teaspoons fine dry bread crumbs
vanilla ice cream as an accompaniment

In a large heavy skillet melt 2 tablespoons of the butter over moderately high heat until the foam subsides and in it sauté the apples, peeled and grated coarse, stirring, for 5 minutes. Stir in the cranberries and the sugar and cook the mixture over moderate heat, stirring, for 5 minutes, or until the cranberries burst. Stir in the apricots, the pecans, and the cinnamon and let the filling cool. *The filling may be made 1 day in advance and kept covered and chilled.*

Preheat the oven to 425° F. In a small saucepan melt the remaining 6 tablespoons butter. On a work surface arrange two 20-inch-long sheets of wax paper with the long sides overlapping slightly and facing you. Put 1 sheet of the *phyllo* on the wax paper, brush it with some of the butter, and sprinkle it with 2 teaspoons of the bread crumbs. On this, layer, brush, and sprinkle 4 more sheets of the *phyllo* in the same manner and lay the sixth sheet of *phyllo* on top.

Spread the filling in a 3-inch-wide strip, mounding it on the *phyllo* 4 inches above the near long side, leaving a 2-inch border at each end. Using the wax paper as a guide, lift the bottom 4 inches of the pastry over the filling, fold in the ends, and roll up the strudel tightly. Transfer the strudel carefully, seam side down, to a lightly buttered baking sheet, brush it with the remaining butter, and bake it in the lower third of the oven for 25 minutes, or until it is golden. Let the strudel cool to warm on the baking sheet on a rack. *The strudel may be made 1 day in advance and kept covered loosely and chilled. Reheat the strudel in a preheated 400° F. oven for 15 minutes.* Serve the strudel warm, cut into 1-inch slices with a serrated knife, with the vanilla ice cream. Serves 8.

In a saucepan bring the wine and the apple juice to a boil with the honey, the thyme, and the vanilla and simmer the mixture for 3 minutes. Add the figs and simmer the mixture, covered partially, for 5 minutes, or until the figs are very soft. Serve the figs warm with the syrup in stemmed glasses topped with the *mascarpone* and the zest. Serves 4.

Honeydew in Rosemary Syrup

½ cup water
½ cup white wine
½ cup sugar
a 3-inch strip of orange zest
1 tablespoon chopped fresh rosemary leaves
    plus rosemary sprigs for garnish
1 teaspoon whole black peppercorns
¼ cup fresh orange juice
4 cups melon balls cut from a honeydew
    melon, cantaloupe, Persian melon,
    or casaba, chilled

In a small saucepan stir together the water, the wine, the sugar, the zest, the chopped rosemary, and the peppercorns, boil the mixture, stirring, until the sugar is dissolved, and simmer it for 4 minutes. Strain the syrup through a fine sieve set over a bowl, pressing hard on the solids, and chill it, covered, until it is cold. Stir the orange juice into the syrup, in a serving bowl toss the melon balls with the syrup, and garnish the dessert with the rosemary sprigs. Serves 4.

Melon with Coconut Milk

a 3½-ounce can (about 1 cup) sweetened
    flaked coconut
1 cup boiling water
¼ teaspoon freshly grated lime zest
4 cups julienne strips of honeydew melon,
    cantaloupe, Persian melon, or casaba,
    or a combination, chilled

In a blender purée the coconut with the water and the zest at high speed for 1 minute, let the mixture stand for 10 minutes, and force it through a fine sieve set over a bowl, pressing hard on the solids. Chill the coconut milk, covered, until it is very cold. Put the melon in a serving bowl, pour the coconut milk over it, and serve the dessert immediately. Serves 4.

Honey-and-Thyme-Poached Figs

1 cup Sauternes or other dessert wine
½ cup apple juice
1 tablespoon honey, or to taste
½ teaspoon fresh thyme leaves
¼ teaspoon vanilla
½ pound dried Calimyrna figs, stemmed,
    halved, and each half cut into 5 thin strips
mascarpone (Italian-style cream cheese,
    available at cheese shops and some
    specialty foods shops), *crème fraîche*, or
    sour cream as an accompaniment
1 tablespoon julienne strips of lemon zest

Melon with Green-Peppercorn Raspberry Sauce

1 cup raspberries
2 small peaches, peeled, pitted, and chopped
1 tablespoon sugar, or to taste
1 tablespoon extra-virgin olive oil
⅛ teaspoon coarsely crushed freeze-dried
    green peppercorns plus additional for
    sprinkling the melon
16 thin wedges of seeded and peeled
    honeydew melon, cantaloupe, or Persian
    melon, or a combination, chilled
2 fresh basil leaves, sliced very thin,
    for sprinkling the melon plus 8 basil sprigs
    for garnish

In a food processor or blender purée the raspberries, the peaches, the sugar, the oil, and ⅛ teaspoon of the crushed peppercorns, force the mixture through a fine sieve set over a bowl, pressing hard on the solids, and chill the sauce, covered, until it is very cold. Divide the melon wedges among 4 chilled dessert plates and pour some of the sauce over each serving. Sprinkle each serving with some of the sliced basil and some of the additional crushed peppercorns and garnish the plates with the basil sprigs. Serves 4.

Nectarine Blueberry Cobbler

8 small nectarines, pitted and sliced thin
    (about 4½ cups)
2 cups blueberries, picked over
½ cup water
½ cup sugar, or to taste
1 tablespoon plus 1 teaspoon cornstarch
1 tablespoon fresh lemon juice
For the biscuits
1¾ cups all-purpose flour
3 tablespoons sugar
1 tablespoon double-acting baking powder
a pinch of salt
1 cup heavy cream

heavy cream or milk for brushing the biscuits
sugar for sprinkling the biscuits
vanilla ice cream as an accompaniment
    if desired

Preheat the oven to 450° F. In a saucepan combine the nectarines, the blueberries, the water, the sugar, the cornstarch, and the lemon juice, bring the mixture to a boil, stirring constantly, and simmer it for 5 minutes, or until the fruit is softened. Transfer the fruit mixture to a shallow 1½-quart baking dish.

Make the biscuits: Sift the flour onto a sheet of wax paper, into a bowl sift together the flour, the sugar, the baking powder, and the salt, and make a well in the center. In a bowl beat the cream until it holds soft peaks, spoon it into the well in the flour mixture, and combine the mixture with a fork until it just forms a dough. On a lightly floured surface knead the dough until it is combined well, roll or pat it out about ¾ inch thick, and with a 2½-inch round cutter cut out 6 biscuits.

Arrange the biscuits on top of the fruit mixture, brush them with the cream or milk, and sprinkle them with the sugar. Bake the cobbler in the middle of the oven for 15 to 17 minutes, or until the biscuits are browned and the fruit is bubbling. Let the cobbler cool slightly and serve it with the ice cream. Serves 4 to 6.

Roasted Nectarines with Caramel Sauce and Hazelnut Praline

5 nectarines (about 2 pounds), halved
    and pitted
1¼ cups sugar
½ cup heavy cream
1 teaspoon fresh lemon juice
¼ cup toasted and skinned hazelnuts
    (procedure on page 219), chopped
raspberries for garnish
fresh mint sprigs for garnish

Preheat the oven to 375° F. Put 8 of the nectarine halves, cut sides down, in a glass baking dish just large enough to hold them in one layer and roast them in the oven for 20 minutes, or until they are softened. While the nectarines are roasting, chop the remaining 2 nectarine halves, in a non-stick skillet cook them over moderate heat, stirring frequently, for 5 minutes, or until they are very soft, and in a blender purée them.

In a heavy saucepan melt ¾ cup of the sugar over moderate heat, stirring with a fork, and cook the syrup, swirling the pan occasionally, until it is a golden caramel. Working carefully and quickly, stir in the cream, the nectarine purée, and the lemon juice, stirring until the caramel sauce is combined well. Keep it warm.

Line an 8-inch cake pan with foil and in it spread the hazelnuts in one layer. In another heavy saucepan melt the remaining ½ cup sugar over moderate heat, stirring with a fork, and cook the syrup, swirling the pan occasionally, until it is a golden caramel. Working quickly, pour the caramel over the hazelnuts. Let the hazelnut praline cool completely and chop it into small pieces.

Put 2 roasted nectarine halves, cut sides up, in each of 4 compotes and top each serving with about 2 tablespoons of the caramel sauce and 1 tablespoon of the praline. Garnish each serving with some of the raspberries and some of the mint sprigs and serve the remaining caramel sauce and praline separately. Serves 4.

Spiced Caramel Oranges

½ cup sugar
1 cup water
two 3-inch cinnamon sticks
¾ teaspoon whole allspice berries
3 tablespoons dark rum
6 navel oranges, the peel and the pith cut
    away with a serrated knife and the sections
    cut free from the membranes

In a heavy saucepan melt the sugar over moderate heat, stirring with a fork, and cook the syrup, swirling the pan occasionally, until it is a golden caramel. Remove the pan from the heat, pour the water carefully down the side of the pan, and add the cinnamon and the allspice. Return the pan to the heat and simmer the syrup until the caramel is dissolved. Remove the pan from the heat, add the rum carefully, and simmer the syrup for 5 minutes. Arrange the orange slices in a large bowl, pour the syrup over them, and let the oranges macerate, covered and chilled, for at least 2 hours or overnight. Serve them at room temperature. Serves 10 as part of a buffet.

Port and Honey Poached Pears with Lemon Curd Mousse

1 cup dry red wine
⅔ cup Ruby Port
1½ cups water
½ cup sugar
½ cup honey
five 3-inch strips of orange zest, removed
    with a vegetable peeler
4 cloves
8 firm-ripe pears, preferably Anjou or Bartlett
    (about 3 pounds)

lemon curd mousse as an accompaniment
  (page 244)

In a large heavy saucepan simmer the wine, the Port, and the water with the sugar, the honey, the zest, and the cloves, stirring, until the sugar is dissolved and add the pears, peeled, halved, and cored. Simmer the pears, covered, turning them occasionally, for 10 to 15 minutes, or until they are tender, transfer them and the zest with a slotted spoon to a shallow bowl or serving dish, and boil the poaching liquid until it is reduced to about 1½ cups. Let the poaching liquid cool, pour it over the pears, and chill the mixture, covered, until it is cold. *The poached pears may be made 2 days in advance and kept covered and chilled.* Serve the poached pears with the lemon curd mousse. Serves 8.

Lemon Curd Mousse

10 large egg yolks
1¼ cups sugar
¾ cup fresh lemon juice
1 stick (½ cup) unsalted butter, cut into
    pieces and softened
1 tablespoon freshly grated lemon zest
1¼ cups heavy cream

In a heavy saucepan whisk together the egg yolks and the sugar, whisk in the lemon juice and the butter, and cook the mixture over moderately low heat, whisking constantly, for 5 to 7 minutes, or until it just reaches the boiling point. (Do not let the mixture boil.) Strain the curd through a fine sieve set over a bowl, stir in the zest, and let the mixture cool, its surface covered with plastic wrap. Chill the curd, covered, for at least 4 hours or overnight.

In a bowl with an electric mixer beat the cream until it holds stiff peaks, whisk one fourth of it into the curd to lighten it, and fold in the remaining cream gently but thoroughly. Transfer the mousse to a serving bowl and chill it, covered, overnight. Serve the mousse as an accompaniment to the poached pears. Serves 8.

Orange Flans with Candied Zest

the zest of 5 navel oranges, removed in strips
    with a vegetable peeler
½ cup water
½ cup Grand Marnier
2 cups sugar
4 cups milk
8 large egg yolks
4 large whole eggs
1 teaspoon orange-flower water (available at
    specialty foods shops and some
    supermarkets) or 1 teaspoon vanilla
    if desired
½ teaspoon salt
orange sections, the rind and pith cut
    away with a serrated knife,
    for garnish

Cut the zest of 2 of the oranges into long, very thin shreds with a sharp knife, in a saucepan of boiling water blanch it for 1 minute, and drain it. In a small heavy saucepan boil the water and the Grand Marnier with the blanched zest and 1 cup of the sugar, stirring and wash-

ing down any sugar crystals clinging to the side of the pan with a brush dipped in cold water, for 5 minutes. Transfer the candied zest with a slotted spoon to a plate lined with wax paper and let it stand, uncovered, for 2 hours, or until it is dry. Cook the syrup over moderate heat, undisturbed, until it is a deep caramel and divide the caramel among eight ¾-cup ramekins, coating the bottoms evenly. *The candied zest and the caramel may be made and the ramekins coated 1 day in advance and the caramel and the zest kept separately, covered, at room temperature.*

Preheat the oven to 325° F. In a saucepan simmer the milk with the remaining 1 cup sugar and the remaining zest for 5 minutes. In a bowl whisk together gently the egg yolks, the whole eggs, the orange-flower water, and the salt until the mixture is just combined. Discard the zest and add the milk mixture to the egg mixture in a stream, stirring. Strain the custard through a fine sieve into a large measuring cup or heatproof pitcher and divide it evenly among the ramekins. Put the ramekins in a baking pan, add enough hot water to the pan to reach halfway up the sides of the ramekins, and bake the flans, covered with a baking sheet, in the middle of the oven for 1 hour to 1 hour and 10 minutes, or until they are just set but still tremble slightly. (The flans will continue to set as they cool.) Remove the ramekins from the pan, let the flans cool, uncovered, to room temperature, and chill them, covered, for 2 hours. *The flans may be prepared up to this point 1 day in advance and kept covered and chilled.* Run a thin knife around the edge of each flan, invert a dessert plate over each ramekin, and invert the flans onto the plates.

Garnish the flans with the candied zest and the orange sections. Serves 8.

PHOTO ON PAGE 15

Baked Rhubarb with Raspberries

1⅓ cups raspberries
    (about 6 ounces)
¾ cup firmly packed light brown sugar
¼ cup very hot water
2 tablespoons unsalted butter,
    cut into bits
¼ teaspoon vanilla
1 pound rhubarb, trimmed and cut into
    ½-inch pieces (about 4 cups)
vanilla ice cream or whipped cream
    as an accompaniment

Preheat the oven to 350° F. In a blender purée the raspberries with the brown sugar and the water, strain the purée through a sieve into a bowl, pressing hard on the solids, and stir in the butter, the vanilla, and the rhubarb. Transfer the mixture to an 11- by 7-inch baking dish and bake the dessert in the middle of the oven, stirring very gently after 15 minutes, for 30 minutes, or until the rhubarb is soft. Let the dessert cool for 10 minutes and serve it with the ice cream or whipped cream. Serves 4.

CONFECTIONS

Pine Nut and Honey Brittle

½ cup pine nuts (about 3 ounces)
¼ cup honey
½ teaspoon salt

In a small heavy saucepan cook the pine nuts, the honey, and the salt over moderate heat, stirring, for 5 minutes, or until the pine nuts are golden and the honey is a deep caramel color. Pour the mixture onto a piece of foil, let it cool completely, and break it into pieces. The brittle keeps in an airtight container, chilled, for 2 weeks. The brittle can be eaten as is or sprinkled over ice cream. Makes about 1 cup.

Goat Cheese Chocolate Truffles

6 ounces fine-quality bittersweet chocolate (not unsweetened), chopped
6 ounces (about ¾ cup) fresh goat cheese (also known as goat *fromage blanc*, available in bulk at specialty foods shops)
2 tablespoons confectioners' sugar
½ teaspoon vanilla
⅛ teaspoon pure lemon extract
¼ cup unsweetened cocoa powder, sifted, for coating the truffles

In a metal bowl set over a pan of barely simmering water melt the chocolate, stirring until it is smooth, remove the bowl from the pan, and let the chocolate cool slightly. In a bowl whisk together the goat cheese, the confectioners' sugar, the vanilla, and the lemon extract until the mixture is light and fluffy, whisk in the chocolate until the mixture is combined well, and chill the mixture, covered, for 1 hour, or until it is firm. Form heaping teaspoons of the mixture into balls and roll the balls in the cocoa powder. Chill the truffles on a baking sheet lined with wax paper for 30 minutes, or until they are firm. *The truffles keep in an airtight container, chilled, for 3 days.* Makes about 25 truffles.

BEVERAGES

ALCOHOLIC BEVERAGES

Cranberry Champagne Cocktails

2 well-chilled 750-ml. bottles Champagne or
    sparkling cider
1 cup well-chilled cranberry juice cocktail,
    or to taste
3 tablespoons Grand Marnier or other orange-
    flavored liqueur, or to taste, if desired

In a large pitcher stir together well the Champagne,
the cranberry juice cocktail, and the Grand Marnier.
Makes about 7 cups, serving 8.

PHOTO ON PAGE 77

Gimlet

2 ounces (¼ cup) gin
½ ounce (1 tablespoon) Rose's lime juice,
    or to taste
1 lime slice

In a cocktail glass filled with ice combine the gin and
the lime juice, stir the drink well, and garnish it with the
lime. Makes 1 drink.

PHOTO ON PAGES 60 AND 61

Pimm's Cup

1½ ounces (3 tablespoons) Pimm's No. 1 Cup
1 cucumber slice
1 orange slice
a 2- to 3-inch strip of lemon zest
chilled ginger ale or club soda
1 mint sprig

In a tall glass filled with ice cubes combine the
Pimm's, the cucumber, the orange, and the zest, pour in
enough ginger ale or club soda to fill the glass, and stir
the drink well. Garnish the drink with the mint. Makes
1 drink.

PHOTO ON PAGES 60 AND 61

Jamaican Sorrel Rum Punch

2 ounces (about 1½ cups) dried sorrel calyxes
    (also called jamaica or hibiscus)*
two 1-inch cubes of peeled fresh gingerroot,
    chopped fine
3 whole cloves
5¾ cups water
¾ cup sugar
1½ cups amber rum
2 cups ice cubes, or to taste
lime and orange slices for garnish

*available at some health foods stores and
    by mail order from Adriana's Bazaar,
    2152 Broadway, New York, NY 10023,
    tel. (212) 877-5757

In a heatproof bowl combine the sorrel, the gingerroot, and the cloves. In a saucepan bring 5 cups of the
water to a boil, pour it over the sorrel mixture, and let
the mixture steep for 4 hours or overnight. While the
mixture is steeping, in a small saucepan bring the remaining ¾ cup water and the sugar to a boil, stirring until the sugar is dissolved, and let the syrup cool. Strain
the sorrel liquid into a pitcher, discarding the solids, stir
in the sugar syrup, the rum, and the ice cubes, and garnish the punch with the lime and orange slices. Makes
about 8 cups.

PHOTO ON PAGE 19

Piña Colada Punch

8 ounces (1 cup) well-stirred canned cream
of coconut
2½ cups unsweetened pineapple juice
1½ cups light rum
2 cups ice cubes, or to taste
a wedge of fresh pineapple with its leaves for
garnish plus additional small, thin wedges
for garnishing the drinks

In a blender blend together, in batches if necessary,
the cream of coconut, the pineapple juice, and the rum
and transfer the punch to a large pitcher. Stir in the ice
cubes and garnish the punch with the pineapple wedge.
Garnish each drink with a pineapple wedge. Makes
about 6½ cups.

PHOTO ON PAGE 19

Rusty Nail Milk Punch

3 tablespoons honey,
or to taste
3 cups milk
½ teaspoon ground ginger
½ teaspoon freshly grated nutmeg plus
additional for garnish
½ cup Scotch, or to taste
¼ cup Drambuie,
or to taste

In a saucepan stir together the honey, the milk, the
ginger, and ½ teaspoon of the nutmeg and heat the mixture over moderately low heat, stirring, until it is hot.
Stir in the Scotch and the Drambuie, divide the milk
punch among heated mugs, and sprinkle each drink
with some of the additional nutmeg. Makes about 4
cups, serving 4 to 6.

Tropical Sparkling Sangría

2 limes, sliced thin
2 small carambolas (star fruit, available
at specialty produce markets), sliced thin
crosswise
1 chilled 750-ml. bottle dry white wine
1 chilled 12-ounce can mango nectar
1 mango, cut into ½-inch cubes
1 chilled 12-ounce can ginger ale
1 chilled 750-ml. bottle Champagne

Reserve some of the lime and carambola slices for
garnish. In a large pitcher stir together the white wine,
the mango nectar, the mango, and the remaining lime
and carambola slices. *The sangría may be prepared up
to this point 1 day in advance and kept covered and
chilled.* Just before serving, stir in the ginger ale, the
Champagne, and ice cubes and serve the sangría garnished with the reserved lime and carambola slices.
Makes about 2½ quarts.

Hot Apricot Buttered Rum

¼ cup firmly packed dark brown sugar
2½ cups water
½ stick (¼ cup) unsalted butter, cut into bits
½ teaspoon cinnamon
¼ teaspoon freshly grated nutmeg, or to taste
3 whole cloves
½ cup dark rum, or to taste
¼ cup apricot-flavored brandy, or to taste
fresh lemon juice to taste
4 cinnamon sticks for garnish if desired

In a saucepan stir together the brown sugar, the water, the butter, the cinnamon, the nutmeg, and the
cloves and simmer the mixture, stirring occasionally,
for 5 minutes. Stir in the rum, the brandy, and the lemon
juice, divide the mixture among 4 heated mugs, and
garnish each drink with a cinnamon stick. Makes about
3 cups, serving 4.

Warm Beaujolais Kir

a bottle of Beaujolais
¾ cup *crème de cassis*, or to taste
two 3-inch strips of lemon or orange zest
    removed with a vegetable peeler plus, if
    desired, lemon or orange slices for garnish

In a saucepan stir together the Beaujolais, the *crème de cassis*, and the zest and simmer the mixture, covered, for 5 minutes. Discard the zest, divide the mixture among wineglasses, and garnish each drink with a lemon or orange slice. Makes about 4 cups, serving 4 to 6.

Warm Bourbon Lemonade

1½ cups fresh lemon juice plus, if desired,
    lemon slices for garnish
1 cup sugar
2 cups water
¾ cup bourbon, or to taste

In a saucepan stir together the lemon juice, the sugar, and the water and simmer the mixture, stirring, until the sugar is dissolved. Stir in the bourbon, divide the lemonade among heated mugs, and garnish each drink with a lemon slice. Makes about 4 cups, serving 4 to 6.

Mulled Cider with Calvados

3 cups apple cider
2 tablespoons firmly packed light brown sugar
3 whole allspice berries
¼ teaspoon freshly grated nutmeg
4 whole cloves
two 3-inch cinnamon sticks, broken
    into pieces
½ Granny Smith or other tart apple,
    cored and sliced thin
½ cup Calvados, or to taste

In a saucepan stir together the cider, the brown sugar, the allspice, the nutmeg, the cloves, the cinnamon pieces, and the apple, simmer the mixture, covered, for 10 minutes, and stir in the Calvados. Heat the mixture over moderate heat until it is hot and discard the allspice, the cloves, and the cinnamon. Divide the mulled cider among heated mugs and garnish each drink with a few of the apple slices. Makes 4 cups, serving 4 to 6.

Spiced Cranberry Rum Tea

4 cranberry herb tea bags such as Celestial
    Seasonings brand
1½ cups boiling water
⅓ cup sugar
½ cup cranberry juice
4 to 6 whole star anise (available at specialty
    foods shops and Asian markets)
two 3-inch strips of orange zest removed
    with a vegetable peeler
two 3-inch strips of lemon zest removed
    with a vegetable peeler plus lemon
    slices for garnish
1 cup strained fresh orange juice
1 cup amber rum,
    or to taste

In a saucepan submerge the tea bags in the boiling water and remove the pan from the heat. Let the tea bags steep for 5 minutes and discard them. To the tea add the sugar, the cranberry juice, the star anise, and the zests and simmer the mixture, covered, stirring occasionally, for 10 minutes. Stir in the orange juice and the rum and heat the mixture over moderate heat until it is hot. Discard the zests, divide the tea among heated mugs, and garnish each drink with 1 of the star anise and a lemon slice. Makes about 4½ cups, serving 4 to 6.

Hot White Russian

2½ cups freshly brewed coffee
½ cup heavy cream
½ cup Kahlúa or other coffee-flavored
    liqueur, or to taste
¼ cup vodka, or to taste
whipped heavy cream for garnish if desired

In a saucepan stir together the coffee, the ½ cup cream, the Kahlúa, and the vodka and heat the mixture over moderate heat until it is hot. Divide the mixture among heated mugs and garnish each drink with some of the whipped cream. Makes 4 cups, serving 4 to 6.

NON-ALCOHOLIC BEVERAGES

Iced Turkish Café au Lait

½ cup milk
½ cup half-and-half
1 tablespoon sugar
6 whole cardamom pods, crushed
1 cup strong brewed coffee, chilled

In a small saucepan stir together the milk, the half-and-half, the sugar, and the cardamom pods, bring the mixture to a boil, stirring until the sugar is dissolved, and let it cool. Strain the mixture through a fine sieve set over a small pitcher, stir in the coffee, and chill the mixture, covered, for 20 minutes, or until it is cold. Divide the iced café au lait between 2 stemmed glasses filled with ice cubes. Makes about 1¾ cups, serving 2.

Nectarine Basil Lemonade

3½ cups water
1 cup fresh basil leaves plus additional
    for garnish
2 nectarines
¾ cup sugar, or to taste
1 cup fresh lemon juice

In a small saucepan stir together 2 cups of the water, 1 cup of the basil, 1 of the nectarines, chopped coarse, and the sugar, bring the mixture to a boil, stirring until the sugar is dissolved, and simmer it for 5 minutes. Let the mixture cool and strain it through a fine sieve set over a pitcher, pressing hard on the solids. Stir in the remaining 1½ cups water, the remaining nectarine, sliced thin, and the lemon juice. Divide the lemonade among tall glasses filled with ice cubes and garnish each drink with some of the additional basil. Makes about 6 cups, serving 4 to 6.

Strawberry Rhubarb Lemonade

3½ cups water
½ pound rhubarb, trimmed and cut into
    1-inch pieces (about 2 cups)
¾ cup sugar, or to taste
two 3-inch strips of lemon zest removed
    with a vegetable peeler plus additional
    for garnish
½ teaspoon vanilla
2 cups sliced strawberries
1 cup fresh lemon juice

In a saucepan stir together the water, the rhubarb, the sugar, 2 strips of the zest, and the vanilla, bring the mixture to a boil, stirring until the sugar is dissolved, and simmer it, covered, for 8 minutes. Stir in 1 cup of the strawberries and boil the mixture, covered, for 2 minutes. Let the mixture cool and strain it through a coarse sieve set over a pitcher, pressing hard on the solids. Stir in the remaining 1 cup strawberries and the lemon juice, divide the lemonade among stemmed glasses filled with ice cubes, and garnish each glass with some of the additional zest. Makes about 7 cups, serving 6.

Ginger Limeade

3½ cups water
¾ cup sugar, or to taste
2 tablespoons minced fresh gingerroot
1 cup fresh lime juice
thin lime slices for garnish

In a small saucepan stir together 2 cups of the water, the sugar, and the gingerroot, bring the mixture to a boil, stirring until the sugar is dissolved, and simmer it for 3 minutes. Strain the syrup through a fine sieve set over a bowl and let it cool. In a pitcher combine the cooled syrup, the remaining 1½ cups water, and the lime juice and stir the limeade well. Divide the limeade among tall glasses filled with ice cubes and garnish each drink with a lime slice. Makes about 5 cups, serving 4.

Raspberry Limeade

2 cups raspberries
3½ cups water
¾ cup sugar, or to taste
1 cup fresh lime juice
mint sprigs for garnish

In a blender or food processor purée 1 cup of the raspberries with 1 cup of the water and force the purée through a fine sieve set over a pitcher, pressing hard on the solids. Add the remaining 1 cup raspberries, the remaining 2½ cups water, the sugar, and the lime juice and stir the mixture until the sugar is dissolved. Divide the limeade among tall glasses filled with ice cubes and garnish each drink with some of the mint sprigs. Makes about 5 cups, serving 4.

Tamarind Cooler

2½ cups boiling water
¼ cup firmly packed light brown sugar
2 tablespoons minced crystallized ginger
1 tablespoon tamarind paste (the soft
    pliable variety, available at Thai,
    East Indian, and other Asian markets),
    or to taste
1 tablespoon fresh lemon juice,
    or to taste
thin lemon slices for garnish

In a bowl whisk together the boiling water, the brown sugar, the ginger, and the tamarind paste until the mixture is combined well, let the mixture cool, and strain it through a fine sieve set over a pitcher. Stir in the lemon juice and chill the mixture for at least 1 hour, or until it is very cold. Divide the cooler among tall glasses filled with ice cubes and garnish each drink with a lemon slice. Makes about 4 cups, serving 4.

Lemon Fennel Iced Tea

4 cups water
½ cup honey, or to taste
1 tablespoon fennel seeds
4 orange pekoe tea bags
three 3-inch strips of lemon zest removed
    with a vegetable peeler plus additional
    for garnish
6 tablespoons fresh lemon juice, or to taste

In a saucepan stir together the water, the honey, and the fennel seeds and bring the mixture to a boil. Remove the pan from the heat, add the tea bags and 3 strips of the zest, and let the tea steep for 5 minutes. Strain the tea through a fine sieve set over a heatproof pitcher, let it cool, and add the lemon juice. Chill the tea, covered, for 1 hour, or until it is very cold. Divide the iced tea among tall glasses filled with ice cubes and garnish each glass with some of the additional zest. Makes about 4 cups, serving 4.

Peach and Raspberry Milk Shakes

1 cup picked-over raspberries plus additional
    for garnish
½ cup milk
1 pint vanilla ice cream, softened slightly
1 pound (about 6 small) peaches, peeled,
    pitted, and chopped
2 tablespoons sugar, or to taste

In a blender purée 1 cup of the raspberries with the milk, strain the purée through a coarse sieve into a glass measure, pressing hard on the solids, and return it to the blender, cleaned. Add the ice cream, the peaches, and the sugar, blend the mixture until it is smooth but still thick, and serve the milk shakes garnished with the additional raspberries. Makes about 4 cups, serving 2 to 4.

PART THREE

CUISINES OF THE WORLD

THE FLAVORS OF

China

The misty serenity of stone mountains rising from the lakes of Guilin at sunset; the winding flow of the powerful Jinsha Jiang (Yangtze) River; the massive, meandering Great Wall . . . these are images of China that remain long after a visit to this faraway land. But perhaps the most impressive image is that of the Chinese people themselves. Their faces reveal lifetimes of hard work, and yet their smiles are warm and welcoming.

Food, and the enjoyment of it, is one of the most important aspects of life in China. Hours are spent searching out the finest goods in the marketplace, snacks are enjoyed throughout the day, and almost all workers spend their two-hour lunch break at home eating with the family. Several generations often live under one roof, and kitchens are usually rudimentary, but this does not deter the cooking of delicious, nutritious dishes. No doubt, the finest meals in China are to be found in private homes, where the average urban family spends more than half of its budget on food!

To truly understand the role that food plays in this ancient culture, one must know a little about the customs and beliefs of the people. The Chinese are dedicated to their many gods and ancestors and pay homage to them at the family table during banquets, birthdays, and feast days in exchange for protection and favors. They believe in the balance of nature, harmony in all things, the duality of existence, and the blending of contrasts, and this *yin* and *yang* philosophy is as prevalant in a Chinese kitchen as it is in a Chinese temple. Food is divided into two major categories: *fan*, including rice and other grains, breads, and noodles; and *cai*, which includes poultry, seafood, meat, and vegetables. Whether a meal is simple or elaborate, you will always find components from both groups. Also, flavors are consciously juxtaposed and contrasted in a balanced way. Common-

ly used flavorings are sweet (honey or sugar), sour (vinegar), salty (salt or soy), bitter (green onions or leeks), spicy (chilies), fragrant (garlic and ginger), and nutty (sesame seeds or oil). *Yin* foods are cold, soft, dark, and feminine, while *yang* foods are hot, hard, bright, and masculine. Seafood *(yin)*, for example, is naturally complemented by ginger *(yang)*.

Despite the frugal nature of the Chinese people, throughout the ages there have been periods when food was scarce. Wars, overpopulation, and natural disasters forced millions to emigrate, and rationing of basic foodstuffs was necessary. Today, however, with government controls on family planning and food production, the food supply is ample. In fact, after government quotas are met, farmers are allowed to grow and sell whatever they want, and this accounts for the wide variety of delicious vegetables appearing in the marketplace. And, now that the Cultural Revolution has passed, many fine restaurants have opened and there is a renewed pride in cooking.

This vast country is filled with raw ingredients, but goods are unevenly distributed and transportation is poor. For the most part, regional foods are eaten exclusively in the particular area where they are grown, resulting in remarkable differences in various cuisines throughout the country. For example, the cabbage, turnips, and grains of the chilly north dictate a bland cuisine; the mighty Yangtze Delta region near Shanghai offers a gourmet diet rich in vegetables, fish, and rice; the fertile crops from Sichuan, along with the Indian spices introduced by the Buddhists centuries ago, account for fiery vegetarian dishes; and the mild southern coastal region of Guangdong (Canton) looks to the South China Sea for dishes of plentiful seafood.

The following pages offer a simple overview of the basics of Chinese cooking. First we introduce some commonly used ingredients (page 255), including rice,

Terraced Fields, Yunnan Province
Photograph: Shao Zi Bai/China Tourism Photo Library

noodles, vegetables, mushrooms, seasonings and spices, and condiments. Then we give instructional advice on how to use standard Chinese kitchen equipment (page 259), which includes the wok, the bamboo steamer, and the cleaver, as well as the various traditional cooking methods—stir-frying, deep-frying, steaming, and braising. Finally, we discuss the importance of *dim sum* and snacks in China (page 263) and give you tips on making some of these treats.

Three menus follow and put all our basic information to use. While our recipes include traditional Chinese ingredients and techniques, we have bent the rules when necessary for accessibility or when a Western ingredient adds an exciting dimension (as Chinese chefs outside of their native country often do). If you are feeling overwhelmed by the number of dishes included in a single menu, we suggest that you choose just one or two that are particularly tempting. Many, such as our Chicken Broth with Chard (page 280), can serve as a lovely luncheon entrée on their own; while others, such as our Mushroom Turnovers (page 288), make delicious hors d'oeuvres for a non-Chinese menu.

We offer A Lunar New Year's Buffet to observe the most important Chinese public holiday of the year, which begins on the first day of the first month of the lunar calendar (sometime between January 21 and February 19). This three-day holiday marks the start of the agricultural year. It is a time of new beginnings—homes are swept clean of bad spirits, debts are paid, presents are exchanged, and gods and ancestors are given homage. Most important, all generations of a family are gathered and special symbolic foods are prepared. Our menu is an ambitious one that is mindful of tradition, yet filled with creativity. We begin with Candied Walnuts, a sweet snack typically enjoyed during the festivities, and Pork and Shrimp Spring Rolls made with bean sprouts, Napa cabbage, and shiitake mushrooms—all Chinese favorites. Our entrée dishes follow and include: beef, a treat often saved for special occasions by non-Buddhists, accompanied by long noodles (symbolic of long life), and Steamed Red Snapper in Black Bean Sauce and a distinctive Soy-Braised Chicken and Black Mushrooms (both are served whole to represent whole life). Desserts rarely appear in China, but exceptions are made during New Year's and on

special occasions. Our Almond Cookies and Poached Tangerines in Spiced Ginger Syrup (tangerines are a fruit of good fortune) add a sweet, light end to the meal.

Later in the year, in mid-autumn, the Chinese celebrate the harvest and pay homage to the moon with an Autumn Moon Festival. This feast gives thanks for the bounty that will be stored and used during the long winter months. Ideally, the celebration takes place out of doors under a full, luminous moon. The family is gathered, poetry is read, and a feast is enjoyed with plenty of wine. Our *nouvelle*-style Harvest Moon Dinner is filled with lots of fresh produce—chard, fennel, butternut squash, shallots, garlic, scallions, and watercress, to name a few. Our spicy Stir-Fried Chili Shrimp and a succulent Braised Pork with Anise, Orange Flavor, and Fennel serve as entrée dishes. Then we offer a sweet and delicious moon cake. A traditional delicacy since ancient times, Chinese moon cakes are small, usually round, thickly crusted cakes filled with either savory salty duck egg or a sweet purée of lotus seeds, candied fruits, and nuts. Our tart is bigger than the traditional treats, and it is filled with dried fruit and walnuts and topped with sweetened ginger whipped cream.

We also present a *dim sum* menu, a brunch or lunchtime meal that highlights the small snacks so loved by the Chinese. Our menu offers a variety of dishes, including traditional Pot Stickers (ground pork-, chive-, and water chestnut-filled dumplings), crisp Shrimp Toast Rolls, hot Curry Chicken Wings, and our unique Turkey Won Tons and Chinese Broccoli with Spicy Peanut Sauce (made with ground turkey instead of pork). Here, as in China, *dim sum* dishes are time-consuming to prepare; to make the menu more manageable, our recipes indicate which dishes can be made ahead and refrigerated or frozen.

Let The Flavors of China open up a whole new world for you. Begin by perusing this entire section at your leisure. Stop to enjoy each of our intriguing photographs, which will transport you halfway around the world to an amazing culture that is totally different from our own. Then allow our informational section, our menus, and our tempting food photography to unlock some of the secrets of this glorious cuisine. You will be rewarded with a whole new way of balancing and blending ingredients that you will savor for a lifetime.

Essentials of Chinese Cuisine

BASIC INGREDIENTS

Chinese dishes, with their unfamiliar vegetables, sauces, and condiments, can look *very* exotic. Where will you find those thin rice noodles, that sweet bean paste, the spicy chili oil? If you are lucky enough to live near an Asian market, you need look no further. There you will find a visual feast—fresh, clear-eyed fish displayed on ice; crisp glazed ducks hanging on hooks; barrels of dried shrimp, scallops, and black mushrooms; shelves packed with colorful jars and cans of sauces and condiments; and strange-looking fruits and vegetables of every description. We assure you, however, that while developing our three menus we chose only those Chinese ingredients that are readily available and more familiar to you. *Most of the foods you will need can be purchased in your supermarket; others can be found in*

Asian markets. If you do not have access to an Asian market, you can order most items by mail from Kam Man Food Products, Inc., 200 Canal Street, New York, N.Y., phone (212) 571-0330; fax (212) 766-9085.

With one billion people to feed (that's four times the population of the United States), the Chinese look to their oceans, rivers, lakes, and land, and utilize all to the fullest. Ample water sources provide plentiful fish and seafood, and fish farming assures that the supply of fish is secure. Likewise, every inch of arable land is put to use. Since more people can be fed by using the land to grow rice and vegetables than to raise livestock, the land is primarily used to produce these goods. Consequently, there is little beef in Chinese cuisine. Instead, pork is the preferred meat, chicken is an everyday ingredient, and duck is reserved for days of celebration.

Rice is by far the most important and abundant food in China, and it is not surprising that the Sichuan basin that produces three bountiful harvests a year is one of the most heavily populated areas. The old Chinese saying "A meal without rice is like a beautiful girl with one eye" reveals the true feelings of the people of southern China who eat rice three times a day. Long-grain white rice is the preferred variety, although many different types are grown. One of our menus calls for steamed rice, and for this any long-grain rice (not Converted) found in your grocery store will do. In southern China, noodles made from rice are also enjoyed; these come in various shapes and are sold in both fresh and dried form. Our Stir-Fried Vegetables with Crisp Rice Noodles (page 290) uses thin, dried rice stick, a white noodle that puffs up and crisps as it is fried.

North of the Jinsha Jiang (Yangtze) River the climate is cooler and more suitable for growing wheat, which supplies flour for savory pancakes, buns, and noodles. These food items often replace rice and appear in myriad guises at northern meals. Wheat noodles are made from soft or hard wheat flour and water; if egg is added, the noodles are called egg noodles. Both types of noodles are available in various sizes, and they are either flat or round. Chinese egg noodles accompany our Beef and Bell Peppers with Oyster Sauce and Noodles (page 272). Wheat flour is also used to make various wrappers for *dim sum*: won ton wrappers (squares), spring roll wrappers (large squares), and round dumpling skins.

Throughout China vegetables are a fundamental part of every meal, and the Chinese insist on buying only the freshest produce available. In fact, meal planning usually takes place at the market once the best vegetables are found. Unfortunately, however, food transportation does not always exist between provinces, and selections are limited to local harvests. And, since only 10 percent of the population own refrigerators, two or three trips to the market are required a day! Despite these difficulties, the Chinese love their vegetables and use them in many creative ways with various sauces. Below is a list of produce used in our menus that, although available in Asian markets and some supermarkets, may be unfamiliar to you:

- *bean curd (tofu)*—A high-protein food made from puréed soybeans pressed into square cakes. Its spongy texture and bland taste allow it to readily absorb the flavor of other ingredients. Bean curd is available "soft," "firm," or "extra-firm."

- *mung bean sprouts*—Thin, delicate sprouts of the green mung bean that require little or no cooking. They should not be confused with the fatter, less delicate soy bean sprouts. Avoid canned sprouts, which tend to be mushy. Fresh sprouts can be stored briefly in plastic bags in the refrigerator.

- *Chinese broccoli*—This green vegetable has long stems, white flowers, and large leaves and is cooked like broccoli, although it is slightly more bitter. Broccoli stems can be substituted for a sweeter taste, while broccoli rabe will offer a more bitter flavor.

- *Napa cabbage*—Also known as Peking cabbage, this mild-tasting cabbage is common throughout China. When raw, it is sweet and crunchy. It has various shapes, from long, compact, and bullet-shaped to fat and squat.

- *snow peas*—These are edible peapods. Young snow peas are flat with small bulges where the immature peas are located inside. Choose pods that are soft and thin. They should be juicy, crisp, and sweet. Avoid older snow peas with thick pods and large peas.

- *water chestnuts*—These are not nuts at all but rather the walnut-sized bulbs of a root vegetable. They have brown skins and white interiors that are sweet, juicy, and crunchy. In China, they are enjoyed as snacks. The fresh variety can be found in Asian markets but requires peeling; the canned variety, in water, is peeled and is less sweet.

- *shiitake mushrooms*—The dried form of these mushrooms, known as black mushrooms to the Chinese, are revered throughout Asia for their robust, smoky flavor that permeate sauces. The best have a savory fragrance and thick caps, preferably 1 to 2 inches in diameter, that are brown in color with white cracks. Our menus call for both fresh and dried shiitakes.

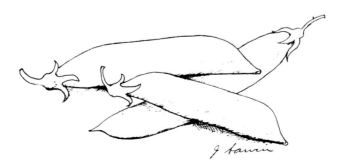

It is impossible to imagine the cuisine of China without the distinctive flavors of its condiments. Moderation, however, is always upheld, and although particular flavors are clearly tasted in each dish, they are never overpowering. Ginger, scallions, and garlic are referred to as the trinity of Chinese seasonings, and, as you will see, they are used in a wide variety of dishes. A host of other flavorings, however, also appear throughout the cuisine. Condiments are sold in bottles or cans. Bottles, once opened, should be refrigerated. Canned items should be transferred to glass jars with tight-fitting screw-tops before being refrigerated. Below is a list of Chinese condiments found in our recipes:

- *salted black beans*—Sold in cans and plastic bags, these fermented black soybeans are preserved in ginger, garlic, salt, and spices. Before cooking they are strong and pungent; after cooking they are milder and greatly enhance other foods. Rinse them before using.

- *sweet bean sauce*—A salty-sweet paste made from a fermentation of puréed beans, salt, flour, and water and used in various ways—in sauces, as a condiment, and in marinades.

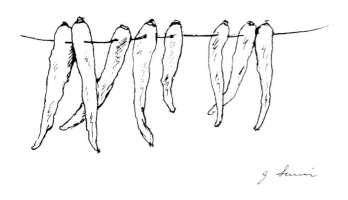

- *chili paste*—A thick hot sauce made from mashed chili peppers, vinegar, and seasonings that offers fiery taste and lends a vibrant red color to dishes.

- *chili peppers*—The elongated cousin of bell peppers; spicy varieties are used in sauces, particularly hot Sichuan sauces.

- *hot chili oil*—A spicy oil made with the flesh and seeds of dried red chilies.

- *garlic chives*—These chives, with their flowers often intact, have flat leaves. They are stronger in flavor than common chives and have a garlicky taste. Both buds and blades are used.

- *coriander*—A flat-leafed, fresh herb also known as cilantro and Chinese parsley, with a distinctive aroma and strong taste.

- *curry powder*—A strong, pungent spice mixture from India that made its way to China.

- *duck (or plum) sauce*—A bottled or canned chutney-like sweet-and-sour sauce made from plums, ginger, apricots, chilies, vinegar, sugar, and water. It is traditionally used as a dipping sauce.

- *five-spice powder*—A spice mixture made from cinnamon, star anise, fennel seed, ground pepper, and ground cloves, for a very strong anise flavor.

- *garlic*—The most pungent bulb in the ''onion'' family in both flavor and aroma.

- *gingerroot*—Also known as fresh ginger, this knobby rhizome has a brown or buff-colored covering and pale yellow flesh. Quite pungent on its own, it is used to mask odors as well as to add aromatic sweetness. For maximum flavor, choose smooth, plump gingerroot; old, wrinkled specimens are dry and may be fibrous. Spring ginger, the newest growth, has a fresh flavor and crisp texture. Do not substitute powdered ginger.

- *Chinese mustard sauce*—A widely used table condiment in Chinese cuisine, this is a hot sauce made with Asian mustard flour and mustard seed.

- *oyster sauce*—A thick caramel-colored, salty, pungent sauce used to flavor meat and poultry, or used as a table condiment. The best grade is not too thick; it should pour freely.

- *peanut oil*—The preferred mild, pleasant-flavored cold-pressed oil that is ideal for stir-frying, with its high smoking temperature.

- *rice vinegar*—Milder and sweeter than Western vinegars, this condiment is made from glutinous rice. There are three types: white rice vinegar (the most common form used in our recipes) is clear and mild, and ideal for sauces and dressings; black rice vinegar is dark with a rich, mild taste, and is used with noodles, braised dishes, and sauces; and red rice vinegar is sweet and spicy, the perfect dipping sauce for seafood.

- *rice wine*—A Chinese wine used for both drinking and cooking made from glutinous rice, yeast, and spring water.

- *sesame seeds*—Either black seeds, roasted or not, used in sweet fillings or decorations; or white seeds, roasted, used as fillings or garnishes.

- *sesame oil*—The golden brown or dark-colored oil with a nutlike smell that is made from roasted sesame seeds. Seldom used as a cooking oil, it is primarily used as a flavoring in many dishes. Do not substitute with sesame oil from natural food stores, made from cold-pressed sesame seeds.

- *scallions*—Very young bulb onions that have a mild onion flavor. The Chinese use the white bulb as a flavoring and the green leaves as a garnish.

- *soy sauce*—A mixture of soybeans, flour, and water that is aged for months and then distilled. There are three varieties: light (not to be confused with ''lite'' soy sauce) is light in color, and usually used for seafood, chicken, and vegetable sauces; medium-grade soy sauce is darker and thicker, and is the general all-purpose choice for cooking; and thick, heavy, or dark soy sauce is a black sauce (colored with molasses) that is best in stews. Beware of some supermarket brands of soy sauce that are strong and salty. Kikkoman is a good choice. Do not substitute with Tamari.

- *star anise*—A star-shaped seed-pod from a Chinese evergreen tree (member of the Magnolia family) with a stronger licorice flavor than common anise.

- *dried tangerine peel or orange peel*—Offers a pungent flavoring for stir-fried and braised dishes. To make your own, air-dry tangerine or clementine peel for several days. It keeps indefinitely when kept in a cool, dry place.

As you can see, the tastes of China are distinctive but incredibly varied. Trying out new spices and learning how to combine different flavors can take a lifetime to master, but it will take no time at all to enjoy the simple pleasures of this glorious cuisine.

EQUIPMENT AND TECHNIQUES

Crisp stir-fried snow peas, tender steamed red snapper, juicy braised chicken and pork . . . these are just some of the distinctive tastes of China. Knowing how to capture the true flavors and textures of this cuisine is as important as having a good recipe, and here we offer a primer of cooking methods and utensils that will help bring the authentic flavors of China to your kitchen.

The average Chinese household kitchen would astonish any Western visitor. In this mainly agricultural country, stone houses with brick walls and stone floors are the norm, and basic kitchens are often not equipped with any of the modern conveniences we are so accustomed to. In the rural areas ''stoves'' usually consist of two or three braziers in which wood or charcoal is burned to produce the high heat that is necessary for Chinese cooking, and a large wok sits in each brazier.

Large, flat wooden surfaces serve as work areas for the extensive chopping, shredding, and mincing that is required. Dwellings with refrigerators and ovens are the exception, not the rule, so food storage and preparation are vastly different. Fish is caught or bought live from the market and prepared in the same afternoon, vegetables are freshly picked from the garden or purchased shortly before the meal, and dried and preserved foods are widely utilized because of the lack of refrigeration.

In the cities, living quarters are very crowded and most apartment dwellers must share a single kitchen with other families. Even in apartments with private kitchens, space is tight and equipment is minimal—here one generally finds only two gas burners and occasionally a small refrigerator. Such limitations mean that every part of the meal must be specially planned, and often food must be made in advance. Fortunately, you do not need to replicate a Chinese kitchen in order to cook authentic Chinese food. The essential cooking techniques highlighted below are easily adapted to a Western kitchen. Chinese cooking equipment, while not mandatory, will facilitate your work. These items are all inexpensive and can be found in Asian markets or specialty kitchenware shops.

The *wok* is the most important piece of equipment in Chinese cooking. Stir-frying, deep-frying, even steaming can be done in this one versatile instrument! The wok is made of thin metal, and it has a rounded bottom and very high sides. The open U-shape of the wok allows high heat to spread evenly over its surface, thus enabling the rapid cooking that is so much a part of Chinese cuisine. In China, woks are traditionally quite large to hold huge amounts of food, and they have rounded bottoms that fit into the braziers. For a Western type of stove a medium-sized wok is best (about 12 to 14 inches in diameter). You can get a wok with a flat bottom that can sit securely on the stove-top burner, or a wok with a rounded bottom and a wok stand, a metal collar that will keep the wok steady on the burner. Select a wok with deep sides so food can be tossed and stir-fried quickly without falling out of the pot. Heavier, carbon-steel woks are preferable to the lighter stainless-steel or aluminum varieties, which tend to scorch more easily.

Woks should always be seasoned before they are used for the first time. This process cleans the pan and enhances the flavor of the food cooked in it. (For this reason avoid nonstick woks, as they cannot be seasoned.) *To season your wok:* Scrub the wok well with kitchen cleanser and water to remove the machine oil that has been applied by the manufacturer to protect it in transit. Dry the wok and place it over low heat. With a paper towel, lightly coat the entire surface of the wok with 2 tablespoons of cooking oil. Heat the wok for 10 to 15 minutes more and wipe it clean with a paper towel. The wok will darken with use once it has been seasoned. To clean a seasoned wok, scrub it with a light brush in water and a mild detergent, thoroughly dry it over low heat to prevent rusting, and wipe the surface with an oiled paper towel. If the wok should rust, scrub it with kitchen cleanser and repeat the seasoning process.

As you will notice, there are many ingredients in Chinese recipes, and they must be prepared and measured before you begin to cook. Good chopping implements are necessary in any kitchen, but they are crucial for Chinese chefs. Most use various *cleavers* (instead of knives) for everything from fine shredding to chopping bones. One medium-sized, carbon and stainless-steel cleaver is all you will need. It is important to grip the cleaver correctly for the most efficient cutting: Grasp the handle firmly, rest your index finger on one side of the blade, and press your thumb against the other side of the blade. This grip will give you the best control while chopping, slicing, or shredding. A broad-bladed chef's knife will also do. To chop foods properly you will also need a large, steady hardwood or white acrylic *chopping board;* they are strong and easy to clean, and last for years. For health reasons, keep a separate board for cutting raw meat and poultry, and always clean your boards well with soap and hot water after each use.

Assorted *stainless-steel bowls* are the best containers for chopped ingredients, since they are light and easy to handle when you are cooking quickly at a wok. It would also be helpful to have a *Chinese spatula* on hand. These wide spatulas are shaped like small, rounded-edged shovels and are very useful for tossing and turning foods in the wok (see illustration on this page). Any metal long-handled spoon or spatula could be used in place of a Chinese spatula if necessary. You will also find that a *skimmer* is very worthwhile. This long-handled, rounded spoon with holes is perfect for draining and removing foods that have been stir-fried or deep-fried (see illustration on this page).

The wok is ideal for *stir-frying,* the rapid cooking method that is the most popular Chinese cooking technique. Bite-sized ingredients are vigorously tossed and cooked in small amounts of hot oil, thus retaining much of the food's natural flavor, texture, and color. Stir-frying is a wonderful way to cook fresh vegetables (see our Stir-Fried Mixed Vegetables with Crisp Rice Noodles, page 290) as well as meat, poultry, and seafood (see our Stir-Fried Chili Shrimp, page 280). One of the best ways to prepare vegetables for stir-frying is roll-cutting. This method produces irregularly shaped, bite-sized pieces of food that are perfect for tossing in the wok. The many sides of each roll-cut piece allow the food to jump off the sides of the wok without sticking. *To roll-cut*: On a cutting board, hold the food down firmly with one hand, hold the cleaver at a 45° angle, and push it away from you, cutting on the diagonal. Roll the food a quarter turn and slice it again on the diagonal.

With the food preparation out of the way, your dish will be ready in no time. Stir-frying rarely takes more than 3 to 5 minutes, and it is as easy as it is fast. These simple steps will help you secure authentic Chinese texture and taste. Heat the wok until it is hot but not smoking. Carefully pour in the oil and spread it around evenly using a spatula and tipping the wok. Heat the oil until it is very hot but not smoking and immediately begin to add the ingredients. With the Chinese spatula, toss the ingredients in the wok, mixing constantly and gently, yet swiftly, bringing the food from all directions to the center so it will be evenly cooked and blended. If a wok is not available, a large, heavy skillet may be substituted.

Deep-frying, another popular cooking technique in China, totally immerses food in hot oil to seal the surfaces of the food and lock in flavor. Meat, poultry, fish, vegetables, and spring rolls can all be crisped to perfection using this method (see our delicious Pork and Shrimp Spring Rolls, page 270). To ensure deep-frying success: Fill a wok (or a deep skillet) halfway with oil and heat the oil until it reaches 375° F. on a deep-fat thermometer. Obtaining the correct temperature is the most vital part of deep-frying. If you do not have a deep-fat thermometer, you can estimate the temperature by waiting for the oil to be just ''moving'' but not smoking, or you can drop a bread cube in the oil—if it browns in about 60 seconds, the oil is hot enough to start frying. While the oil is heating, dry the food thoroughly to prevent splattering. Then, with a spatula, strainer, tongs, or chopsticks, carefully lower the food into the oil. When the food is cooked, remove it with a skimmer or slotted spoon and drain it on paper towels. If you are deep-frying in batches, be sure the oil temperature returns to 375° F. before adding a new batch.

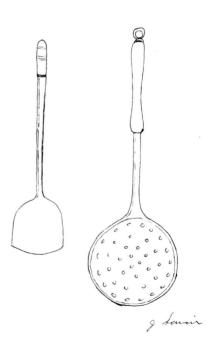

Of course not all Chinese foods are cooked in oil. *Steaming* requires no oil at all, and this process retains the inherent flavors of fresh food better than any other by simply suspending foods over boiling water in a container with a tight-fitting lid. Centuries ago, steaming was developed as an efficient way to preserve scarce fuel by cooking multiple dishes simultaneously. This was made possible with the creation of the hand-woven *bamboo steamer,* a utensil consisting of a bottom steamer tray with a rim and several round interlocking trays that stack up on top of it to hold many layers of food at the same time. There are several different steamer sizes to choose from, and it is crucial for the steamer to fit properly in the pan it will sit in (the steamer should be about 2 inches smaller than the pan). *Before using a bamboo steamer for the first time, soak it in cold water to cover and turn it occasionally for about an hour.* When ready for use, the steamer trays should be lined with oiled parchment paper or wax paper and filled with food. *It is very important that the bottom rim of the steamer sit in boiling water in a wok or pot and the steamer tray be at least ½ inch above the boiling water.* Alternatively, we recommend a collapsible steamer rack, an inexpensive kind of wire basket that adjusts to fit into any pot, or you can even use a colander set over simmering water instead.

Braising is a slow-cooking process that infuses dishes with strong aromas and intense flavors while tenderizing them. Since most kitchens in China do not have ovens, braising takes place on the stove top in *sandy or clay pots.* These pots are made from a mixture of sand and clay and have glazed interiors to help conduct heat and hold in moisture. They come in various shapes and sizes with tight-fitting lids. Cast-iron kettles or enamelware casseroles are good substitutes and most appropriate for a Western kitchen, where braising can be done in the oven, as in our succulent Braised Pork with Anise, Orange Flavor, and Fennel (page 280).

Finally, when it's time to eat your delectable Chinese dishes, *chopsticks* are the most authentic utensils to use. Wooden chopsticks are common in China, but plastic is often used for hygienic purposes. And, of course, bright, beautiful dinnerware from this fascinating country will surely lift the spirit and set the stage for the memorable meal to come.

DIM SUM AND SNACKS

*E*veryone gets a craving for a little snack now and then—a quick bite that will tide you over in between meals, or just enough food to satisfy a yearning without filling you up. But in China, snacking is not just a passing fancy, it is a way of life. Whether it's a soft *biaozi* (a meat-filled bread bun) to nibble on while shopping, a bowl of fresh rice noodles in steaming broth for a quick warm-up before the big midday meal, or a full *dim sum* meal of assorted bite-sized foods, *xiao chi* (small eats) have been a major component in the Chinese diet for thousands of years. Most people in China eat two main meals a day (at midday and in the evening) and three smaller snacks (before the midday meal, during the afternoon, and late at night). *Xiao chi* are sometimes prepared at home, but very often they are purchased from street vendors or at roadside food carts.

As far back as A.D. 960, during the Northern Song Dynasty, there are accounts of street vendors selling teas and snacks at all hours to people going to and from work. Some food outlets were located in permanent buildings, but most were movable thatched shacks. The popularity of these vendors continued throughout the centuries, but when the People's Republic of China was established in 1949, private food stalls were banned. Fortunately, policy reforms in the last decade have allowed a reemergence of these businesses, and food stalls are becoming a common sight again in the villages and towns.

On a stroll through any market district in China you will be greeted with the aromas of foods ready to eat on the spot or to take away. In a hectic carnival atmosphere with jostled customers, rows of vendors offer baked or steamed dumplings filled with pork, garlic, and scallions, plump bread buns stuffed with meats and vegetables, fresh, thick noodles in rich soup, or light rice noodle pastries—all freshly made and waiting to be served. The inexpensive foods prepared at these stalls are considered by some to be better than restaurant cuisine, and they are certainly more accessible to the everyday laborer working long hours. Night markets that stay open very late have become widespread, and there is never a shortage of eager patrons.

The best and most famous snacks come from the southern region of China known as Guangdong (Canton). It is here that *dim sum* (literally "heart's delight) snacks originated and the first teahouses appeared. The warm climate of the Canton region and the tight living quarters in this highly populated area encourage activities outside the home. Families and friends happily escape to the informal, social atmosphere of the teahouses, where from midmorning to midafternoon they can enjoy leisurely conversation, delicious food, and good company. Some of these teahouses accommodate hundreds, even thousands of people at a time. In a typical teahouse, women workers wheel around carts filled with various *dim sum* delicacies and call out the contents of their trolleys. As they make their way through the maze of large round tables in the noisy, crowded room, diners get the server's attention by pointing to their choice of food. Each serving contains three or four dumplings, just enough to have a taste but still leave room for some of the many other specialties available. As each dish is chosen, the server is handed the bill by the diner so she can keep a tally of the number of dishes ordered. At the end of the meal a male waiter is summoned to add up the total.

An abundance of snacks is available, including dozens of different types of steamed, fried, or baked dumplings and various other *dim sum* treats: shrimp dumplings made with translucent rice noodles, deep-fried bean curd filled with pork and shrimp, flattened chive dumplings made with thick pastry, shark-fin soup with shrimp won tons and crab, marinated beef and squash kebabs, crescent-shaped pork dumplings seasoned with green onions and ginger—the list goes on and on. One Canton teahouse offers over two thousand *dim sum* dishes on a rotation basis.

Tea, of course, is the beverage of choice with *dim sum*, but choosing exactly *which* tea is no small matter. Lu Yu, an ancient Chinese writer, claimed that tea was a drink for the mind as well as the body—a mental stimulant and perhaps a drink that would pave the way to im-

mortality. The Chinese still prize their tea, as their large variety attests. Here are just a few: Dragon Well (*Lung Ching*), a green tea grown in the Canton region and sold for twelve dollars an ounce, considered the epitome of great teas; Jasmine, a clean tasting, fragrant tea that cleanses the palate; and two *dim sum* favorites, Iron Goddess of Mercy (*Tiht Koon Yum*), a tea from Fukien Province that tastes slightly bitter, and *Bo Lei*, a Cantonese tea that is thought to be a digestive aid.

There are also teahouses that serve nothing but tea and sweets. These establishments are more like men's social clubs, where elderly male patrons gather, especially on Sundays and holidays, to drink tea, smoke, play cards, and relax. It is very common for the men to bring along their caged pet birds and sit for hours engaging in conversation and drinking tea with friends.

In Canton, families usually go out to a teahouse for *dim sum*, but in the colder, northern regions, where people tend to stay indoors, these "small eats" are usually prepared at home on holidays or feast days only, when every member of the family can lend a hand in preparing the time-consuming dishes. In this section we offer an innovative and ambitious Dim Sum menu (page 285) for you to try on your own. We suggest you do as the Chinese do, and gather friends to share in the preparation. Or, simply ask everyone to bring one dish.

Of course, with a bit of organization and some advanced preparation, you *can* make the entire meal by yourself. Start off by reviewing the recipes and deciding the order in which you will work on the menu. We offer plenty of make-ahead and freezing instructions to help you prepare the various dumplings and fillings weeks in advance. For example, the filling for our Mushroom

Turnovers can be made up to one week ahead of time, or if you'd prefer, you could stuff the turnovers and freeze them for up to two weeks. Our savory pork-filled Pot Stickers and contemporary turkey won tons can also be frozen for two weeks and be ready to cook and serve the day of the meal. Next, organize the ingredients that you will need. Get as much chopping done as possible beforehand so when it is time to prepare the various fillings all the makings will be ready. Also, you will need assorted wrappers for the different dumplings, such as dumpling skins for the pot stickers and won ton wrappers for the purse-like turkey won tons, and you will need to make a pastry dough for the crescent-shaped turnovers. Our recipes include step-by-step instructions that clearly explain how to create the variety of fanciful dumpling shapes, and our photographs on pages 286 and 287 will also help you visualize the delightful treats. To make the usually light *dim sum* meal a bit more substantial, we've added a stir-fry vegetable dish with noodles. And remember, these dishes can also be served on their own, some as unique hors d'oeuvres and others, like the Curry Chicken Wings, as a light luncheon entrée.

We also encourage you to go out for *dim sum* if it is available in your area. With the increase of Asian immigrants to the United States over the past two decades, authentic Chinese cuisine is becoming more popular than ever before. Some of our favorites across the country are New York City's 98 Mott Street (name and address of the restaurant are the same), Triple Eight Palace, 88 East Broadway, and Chiam, 160 East 48th Street; San Francisco's Ton Kiang, 5821 Geary Boulevard, and Wu Kong, 101 Spear Street, Ricon Center; and Los Angeles' Ocean Star, 145 North Atlantic Avenue, and Harbor Village Restaurant, 111 North Atlantic Avenue, both in Monterey Park.

A LUNAR NEW YEAR'S BUFFET

農曆新年自助餐

Candied Walnuts

Pork and Shrimp Spring Rolls

———————

Steamed Red Snapper in Black Bean Sauce

Beef and Bell Peppers with Oyster Sauce and Noodles

Soy-Braised Chicken and Black Mushrooms

Stir-Fried Lettuce and Snow Peas with Sesame Seeds

Pickled Cucumber

Columbia Winery's Washington State Cabernet Franc 1991

———————

Poached Tangerines in Spiced Ginger Syrup

Almond Cookies

Summer Palace, Beijing
Photograph: Charles Offerman

Soy-Braised Chicken and Black Mushrooms; Pickled Cucumber;
Steamed Red Snapper in Black Bean Sauce; Beef and Bell Peppers
with Oyster Sauce and Noodles; Stir-Fried Lettuce and Snow Peas
with Sesame Seeds

Candied Walnuts

4 cups walnuts (about 1 pound)
1½ cups sugar
4 cups vegetable oil

In a large saucepan of simmering water simmer the walnuts for 5 minutes, drain them well in a large sieve, and in a large bowl toss them with the sugar. In the sieve shake the walnuts to remove the excess sugar and arrange them on baking sheets to dry for 1 hour, turning them occasionally.

In a wok or deep skillet heat the oil over high heat until a deep-fat thermometer registers 350° F., fry the walnuts in 3 batches, turning them, for 1 minute, or until the sugar caramelizes and the walnuts turn golden, and transfer the walnuts with a slotted spoon to the sieve to drain for 1 minute. Arrange the walnuts on brown-paper-lined baking sheets to drain and cool completely. (Do not use paper towels to drain. The walnuts will stick to them.) Fry the remaining walnuts in the same manner, making sure the oil returns to 350° F. before adding each new batch. *The walnuts may be made 1 week in advance and kept in an airtight container.* Makes about 4 cups candied walnuts, serving 6 as part of a buffet.

Pork and Shrimp Spring Rolls

For the pork mixture
¾ pound boneless center-cut pork loin, trimmed of all fat, sliced thin crosswise, and the slices cut into matchstick-size pieces
2 teaspoons soy sauce
2 teaspoons rice wine* or dry Sherry or Scotch
½ teaspoon Asian (toasted) sesame oil**
½ teaspoon cornstarch
½ teaspoon water
For the shrimp mixture
¼ pound medium shrimp (about 6), peeled, deveined, and chopped fine
2 teaspoons rice wine* or dry Sherry or Scotch
¼ teaspoon salt
⅛ teaspoon Asian (toasted) sesame oil**
For the sauce
2 teaspoons soy sauce
2 teaspoons rice wine* or dry Sherry or Scotch
¼ teaspoon salt
½ teaspoon cornstarch
For the paste
¼ cup all-purpose flour
¼ cup water
1 large egg, beaten lightly
For the vegetable mixture
2 tablespoons vegetable oil
3 cups shredded Napa cabbage
1½ cups coarsely grated carrot
2 cups 1-inch pieces scallion greens
1 cup fresh mung bean sprouts**

3 tablespoons vegetable oil plus 4 cups vegetable oil for deep-frying the spring rolls
15 spring-roll wrappers**
Chinese duck sauce** and Chinese mustard** as accompaniments

*available at Asian markets and some liquor stores
**available at Asian markets and some specialty foods shops and supermarkets

Make the pork mixture: In a bowl combine well the pork, the soy sauce, the rice wine, the sesame oil, the cornstarch, and the water and let the mixture marinate, covered, for 15 minutes.

Make the shrimp mixture: In a bowl combine well the shrimp, the rice wine, the salt, and the sesame oil and let the mixture marinate, covered, for 15 minutes.

Make the sauce: In a small bowl stir together the soy sauce, the rice wine, the salt, and the cornstarch and reserve the mixture.

Make the paste: In a small bowl whisk together the flour, the water, and the egg and reserve the mixture.

Make the vegetable mixture: Heat a wok over high heat until it is hot, add the oil, and heat it until it is hot but not smoking. Add the cabbage and the carrot and stir-fry the mixture for 1½ minutes, or until the cabbage is wilted. Add the scallions and the bean sprouts, stir-fry the mixture for 1 minute, and transfer the mixture to a jelly-roll pan to cool it completely.

Heat the wok over high heat until it is hot, add 2 tablespoons of the oil, and heat it until it is hot but not smoking. Add the pork mixture, stir-fry it for 1 minute, and transfer the pork with a skimmer to paper towels to drain. Heat the wok in the same manner, adding 1 tablespoon of the remaining oil, add the shrimp mixture, and stir-fry it for 30 seconds. Add the pork and the sauce mixture, stir-fry the mixture for 30 seconds, and transfer it to another jelly-roll pan to cool completely.

In a bowl combine well the vegetable mixture and the pork mixture. On a work surface arrange 1 spring-roll wrapper with a corner facing you and keep the remaining wrappers covered with plastic wrap. Squeeze ⅓ cup of the filling to remove the excess liquid, arrange it horizontally across the center of the wrapper from the left corner to the right corner, leaving 2 inches at each end, and fold the corner closest to you tightly over the filling. Brush the unfolded edges with some of the paste, fold the left and right corners over the filling, and, rolling away from you, roll up the filling tightly in the wrapper. Make more spring rolls with the remaining wrappers, filling, and paste in the same manner, transferring them as they are made to a wax-paper-lined baking sheet and keeping them covered with plastic wrap.

In a wok or deep skillet heat the remaining 4 cups vegetable oil until a deep-fat thermometer registers 375° F. and in it fry the spring rolls, 3 at a time, turning them, for 2 minutes, or until they are golden, transferring them with tongs as they are fried to paper towels to drain. Fry the remaining spring rolls in the same manner, making sure the oil returns to 375° F. before adding each new batch. *The spring rolls may be made 2 days in advance, cooled completely, wrapped in plastic wrap, and chilled. To reheat the rolls place them on a rack set in a jelly-roll pan in a preheated 450° F. oven, turning them once, for 10 minutes, or until they are crisp.* Serve the spring rolls with the Chinese duck sauce and the Chinese mustard. Makes 15 spring rolls, serving 6 as part of a buffet.

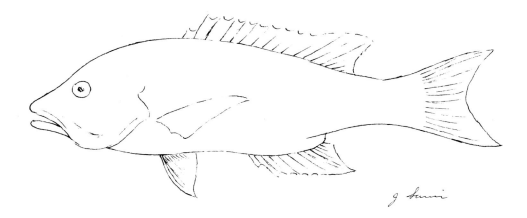

Steamed Red Snapper in Black Bean Sauce

1 tablespoon soy sauce
1 tablespoon rice wine (available at Asian
    markets and some liquor stores) or dry
    Sherry or Scotch
½ teaspoon sugar
⅓ cup chicken broth
2 tablespoons vegetable oil
1 tablespoon salted dried black beans
    (available at Asian markets and some
    specialty foods stores and supermarkets),
    rinsed, drained well, and minced
1 tablespoon minced garlic
1 tablespoon minced peeled fresh gingerroot
a 2-pound whole red snapper or sea bass,
    cleaned, leaving the head and tail intact,
    rinsed well, and patted dry
6 Napa cabbage leaves

In a small bowl stir together the soy sauce, the rice wine, the sugar, and the broth until the sugar is dissolved and reserve the mixture. Heat a wok over high heat until it is hot, add the oil, and heat it until it is hot. Add the black beans, the garlic, and the gingerroot and stir-fry the mixture for 10 seconds, or until it is fragrant. Add the reserved soy mixture and boil the mixture, stirring, for 2 minutes.

With a sharp knife score the fish lightly ¼ inch deep at ½-inch intervals on both sides, arrange it in a large heatproof dish, and pour the soy mixture over it, rubbing the mixture on the inside and all over the outside of the fish. Arrange the cabbage leaves over the top of the fish to cover it completely. Put a large steamer rack in a large kettle, add enough water to reach just below the bottom of the rack, and bring the water to a boil, covered. (We used an 11½-inch steamer rack and a kettle measuring 13 inches across. The fish tail curved slightly.) Set the heatproof dish on the rack and steam the fish, covered, adding more boiling water if necessary, for 25 minutes, or until it just flakes. Remove the cabbage leaves just before serving. Serves 6 as part of a buffet.

Beef and Bell Peppers with Oyster Sauce and Noodles
For the marinade
2 tablespoons cornstarch
⅓ cup water
⅓ cup soy sauce
3 tablespoons rice wine* or dry Sherry or Scotch
1 tablespoon sugar
1 tablespoon Asian (toasted) sesame oil**
1 tablespoon minced garlic

2 pounds eye of round or top sirloin roast,
    sliced thin crosswise and the slices
    cut into ¼-inch strips

For the beef mixture

1¾ cups vegetable oil

2 large red bell peppers, cut into ¼-inch strips

¼ cup minced peeled fresh gingerroot

¼ cup minced scallion

4 cups chicken broth

½ cup oyster sauce**

⅓ cup soy sauce

3 tablespoons rice wine* or dry Sherry
  or Scotch

2 teaspoons sugar

2 teaspoons Asian (toasted) sesame oil**

3 tablespoons cornstarch dissolved in
  ¼ cup water

1 pound Chinese egg noodles** or spaghetti

2 teaspoons Asian (toasted) sesame oil**

1 cup thinly sliced scallion greens

*available at Asian markets and some
  liquor stores

**available at Asian markets and some
  specialty foods shops and supermarkets

Make the marinade: In a large bowl stir together the cornstarch, the water, the soy sauce, the rice wine, the sugar, the sesame oil, and the garlic until the cornstarch is dissolved.

Stir the beef into the marinade and let it marinate, covered and chilled, for at least 3 hours or overnight. Drain the beef and pat it between paper towels to remove the excess marinade.

Make the beef mixture: Heat a wok over high heat until it is hot, add the oil, and heat it until a deep-fat thermometer registers 400° F. Fry the beef in the oil in 4 batches, stirring, for 1 minute, or until the strips separate and change color, and transfer it with a skimmer to paper towels to drain. Return the oil to 400° F. before adding each new batch. Pour off all but 2 tablespoons of the oil, heat the oil remaining in the wok over high heat until it is hot, and in it stir-fry the peppers for 1½ minutes, or until they are crisp-tender. Add the gingerroot and the scallion and stir-fry the mixture for 10 seconds. Add the chicken broth, the oyster sauce, the soy sauce, the rice wine, the sugar, and the sesame oil and bring the mixture to a boil, stirring. Stir the cornstarch mixture, stir it into the oyster sauce mixture, and simmer the sauce, stirring constantly, for 1 minute, or until it is thickened. Stir in the beef. *The beef mixture may be made 1 day in advance, cooled completely, and kept*

covered and chilled. Reheat the beef mixture in a large saucepan over moderate heat, stirring occasionally.

In a kettle of boiling salted water boil the noodles until they are *al dente*, drain them well, and in a large bowl toss them with the sesame oil. Add the beef mixture and the scallion greens and toss the mixture well. Serves 6 as part of a buffet.

Soy-Braised Chicken and Black Mushrooms

a 3½- to 4-pound chicken

6 cups cold water

1 cup soy sauce

¼ cup rice wine (available at Asian
  markets and some liquor stores)
  or dry Sherry or Scotch

3 slices of fresh gingerroot, each the size of a
  quarter, flattened with the side of a cleaver

2 star anise* or ¼ teaspoon aniseed

1 cinnamon stick

¼ cup sugar

6 small dried *shiitake* mushrooms*

2 teaspoons Asian (toasted) sesame oil*

*available at Asian markets and some
  specialty foods shops and supermarkets

In a kettle just large enough to fit the chicken simmer the water, the soy sauce, the rice wine, the gingerroot, the star anise, the cinnamon, and the sugar, uncovered, for 30 minutes. Add the chicken, breast side down, and braise it at a simmer, covered and turning it twice, for 35 minutes.

While the chicken is braising, in a bowl let the mushrooms soak in hot water to cover, stirring occasionally, for 20 minutes, or until they are soft and spongy. Drain the mushrooms, cut away and discard the stems, and pat the mushrooms dry.

Stir the mushrooms into the chicken mixture and braise the mixture for 10 minutes. Remove the kettle from the heat and let the chicken and mushrooms stand, covered, in the cooking liquid for 15 minutes. *The chicken and mushrooms in the cooking liquid may be made up to this point 1 day in advance, cooled completely, and kept covered and chilled. Reheat the chicken and mushrooms in the cooking liquid over moderate heat, covered.* Cut the chicken into serving pieces, brush it with the sesame oil, and arrange it on a platter with the mushrooms. Serves 6 as part of a buffet.

Stir-Fried Lettuce and Snow Peas with Sesame Seeds

2 tablespoons vegetable oil
½ pound snow peas, strings discarded and the
  snow peas cut diagonally into ½-inch pieces
1 teaspoon sugar
½ teaspoon salt
3 tablespoons raw sesame seeds*
1 pound lettuce, such as Boston or romaine,
  washed well, spun dry, and cut into
  1-inch-wide shreds
1 teaspoon rice vinegar*

*available at Asian markets and some
  specialty foods shops and supermarkets

Heat a wok over high heat until it is hot, add 1 table-spoon of the oil, and heat it until it is just smoking. Add the snow peas, ½ teaspoon of the sugar, and ¼ teaspoon of the salt and stir-fry the mixture for 1 minute, or until the snow peas are crisp-tender. Transfer the snow peas to a bowl. Heat the remaining 1 tablespoon oil in the wok until it is just smoking, add the sesame seeds, and stir-fry them for 5 seconds. Add the lettuce, the remaining ½ teaspoon sugar, and the remaining ¼ teaspoon salt and stir-fry the mixture for 1 minute, or until the lettuce is wilted. Add the snow peas and the vinegar and toss the mixture until the vegetables are hot. Serves 6 as part of a buffet.

Pickled Cucumber

1 large seedless cucumber, halved crosswise
1 teaspoon salt
1½ tablespoons sugar
2 tablespoons rice vinegar (available at Asian
  markets and some specialty foods shops
  and supermarkets)

Halve each cucumber piece lengthwise, cut each half into 3 spears, and discard the seeds. Roll-cut the spears into 1-inch pieces (procedure on page 261), in a bowl toss the cucumber with the salt, and let the mixture stand for 1 hour. Drain the cucumber in a sieve, rinse it under cold water, and pat it dry. In a bowl dissolve the sugar in the vinegar, add the cucumber, and toss it to coat it with the mixture. Let the mixture marinate, covered and chilled, for at least 3 hours or overnight. *The pickled cucumber may be made 4 days in advance and kept covered and chilled.* Serves 6 as part of a buffet.

Poached Tangerines in Spiced Ginger Syrup

6 tangerines, peeled and the strings discarded,
  or 6 small navel oranges, the peel and pith
  cut away with a serrated knife
6 cups water
1½ cups sugar
a 2-inch dried hot red chili, seeds discarded
  and the pepper cut into thin strips
  (wear rubber gloves)
2 cinnamon sticks
6 slices of fresh gingerroot, each the size of a
  quarter, flattened with the side of a cleaver
2 teaspoons rice vinegar (available at Asian
  markets and some specialty foods shops
  and supermarkets)

In a heavy saucepan just large enough to fit the tangerines simmer the water, the sugar, the chili, the cinnamon, and the gingerroot, uncovered, stirring until the sugar dissolves, for 30 minutes. Add the tangerines and poach them at a simmer, covered, turning them once, for 10 minutes. Transfer the tangerines with a slotted spoon to a bowl, boil the syrup until it is reduced to about 2 cups, and stir in the vinegar. Pour the syrup over the tangerines and let the mixture cool completely. Chill the poached tangerines, covered, overnight. *The tangerines may be made 2 days in advance and kept covered and chilled.* Serves 6 as part of a buffet.

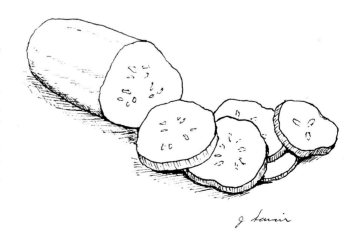

Almond Cookies

1½ cups all-purpose flour
1 teaspoon baking soda
½ teaspoon salt
1 stick (½ cup) unsalted butter, softened
¾ cup sugar
2 large eggs
1 teaspoon almond extract
½ cup almonds, toasted lightly, cooled,
　　and chopped fine
30 blanched whole almonds, halved
　　lengthwise

Into a bowl sift together the flour, the baking soda, and the salt. In the bowl of an electric mixer cream the butter with the sugar until the mixture is light and fluffy, beat in 1 of the eggs and the almond extract, and beat in the flour mixture and the chopped almonds, beating until the dough is combined well. Halve the dough and on a piece of wax paper form each half into a log 1½ inches in diameter, using the wax paper as a guide. Chill the logs, wrapped in the wax paper, for at least 4 hours or overnight.

Preheat the oven to 350° F. In a small bowl beat the remaining egg lightly. Cut the logs into ¼-inch-thick slices with a sharp knife and arrange the slices 1 inch apart on ungreased baking sheets. Brush the slices with the egg, press an almond half lightly in the center of each slice, and bake the cookies in the middle of the oven for 10 to 12 minutes, or until they are golden. Transfer the cookies to racks and let them cool. *The cookies may be made 5 days in advance and kept in an airtight container.* Makes about 60 cookies as part of a buffet.

HARVEST MOON DINNER

中秋宴會

Chicken Broth with Swiss Chard

———

Stir-Fried Chili Shrimp

*Braised Pork with Anise,
Orange Flavor, and Fennel*

Steamed Rice

*Baked Butternut Squash
with Chinese Mustard and Duck Sauce*

Watercress and Kumquat Salad

Duckhorn Napa Valley Sauvignon Blanc

———

*Dried Fruit and Walnut Moon Cake
with Ginger Whipped Cream*

Chengdu, Sichuan Province
Photograph: United Nations Photo Library

277

Dried Fruit and Walnut Moon Cake with Ginger Whipped Cream

Braised Pork with Anise, Orange Flavor, and Fennel;
Steamed Rice; Stir-Fried Chili Shrimp; Baked Butternut Squash
with Chinese Mustard and Duck Sauce

Chicken Broth with Swiss Chard

a 3- to 3½-pound chicken or 3 pounds
    chicken wings and backs
3 pieces of fresh gingerroot, each the size of a
    quarter, flattened with the side of a cleaver
1 small onion, halved
½ cup rice wine (available at Asian
    markets and some liquor stores)
    or dry Sherry or Scotch
1 teaspoon salt
13 cups cold water
¼ pound Swiss chard, the stems sliced thin
    and the leaves shredded
1 teaspoon Asian (toasted) sesame oil
    (available at Asian markets and some
    specialty foods shops and supermarkets)

Cut the chicken into large pieces with a cleaver or heavy chef's knife and discard the loose fat. In a kettle of boiling water blanch the chicken for 1 minute, drain it in a large colander, and rinse it under cold water. Rinse out the kettle, return the chicken to it, and add the gingerroot, the onion, the rice wine, the salt, and the water. Bring the liquid to a boil, skimming the froth, and simmer the mixture, skimming the froth, for 2 hours. Strain the broth through a large sieve lined with a triple thickness of rinsed and squeezed cheesecloth into a large bowl. Let the broth cool completely, uncovered, chill it, and remove the fat. *The broth may be made 3 days in advance and kept covered and chilled, or it may be frozen.*

In a large saucepan bring 8 cups of the broth to a boil, reserving the remaining broth for another use, add the chard stems, and simmer the soup for 2 minutes. Stir in the chard leaves, simmer the soup for 2 minutes more, or until the stems are tender, and stir in the sesame oil and salt to taste. *The soup may be made 1 day in advance and kept covered and chilled.* Makes about 8 cups, serving 8.

Stir-Fried Chili Shrimp

5 shallots, chopped fine
3 large garlic cloves, chopped fine
a 1½-inch piece of fresh gingerroot, peeled
    and chopped fine
1 tablespoon bottled Chinese chili paste
    (available at Asian markets and some
    specialty foods shops)

½ teaspoon turmeric
2 tablespoons plus 1 teaspoon vegetable oil
1½ pounds jumbo shrimp (about 40), shelled,
    leaving the last segment and tail intact,
    deveined, rinsed, and patted dry
1 teaspoon cornstarch dissolved in
    2 teaspoons cold water
2 tablespoons rice wine (available at Asian
    markets and some liquor stores) or dry
    Sherry or Scotch
¾ cup chicken broth
steamed rice (recipe follows) as an
    accompaniment

In a food processor blend to a coarse paste the shallots, the garlic, the gingerroot, the chili paste, the turmeric, and 2 tablespoons of the oil. *The paste may be made 3 days in advance and kept covered and chilled.*

Heat a wok over high heat until it is hot, add the remaining 1 teaspoon oil, and heat it until it is hot but not smoking. Add the paste and stir-fry it for 1 minute. Add the shrimp and stir-fry the mixture for 3 minutes. Stir the cornstarch mixture, add it with the wine and the broth to the shrimp, and cook the mixture for 1 minute, or until the shrimp are just cooked through. Serve the shrimp with the rice. Serves 8.

Steamed Rice

5 quarts water
1 tablespoon salt
3 cups long-grain rice

In a large saucepan bring the water to a boil with the salt. Sprinkle in the rice, stirring until the water returns to a boil, and boil it for 10 minutes. Drain the rice in a large colander and rinse it. Set the colander over a large saucepan of boiling water and steam the rice, covered with a kitchen towel and the lid, for 15 minutes, or until it is fluffy and dry. Makes about 9 cups.

Braised Pork with Anise, Orange Flavor, and Fennel

4 pork tenderloins (each about ¾ pound), cut
    ½ inch thick on the diagonal, and the pieces
    halved lengthwise to form strips
¼ cup all-purpose flour
½ cup vegetable oil
1 large onion, chopped

4 garlic cloves, smashed

2 whole cloves

2 whole star anise (available at Asian markets
    and some specialty foods shops and
    supermarkets), crushed lightly with the side
    of a cleaver, or ½ teaspoon aniseed

2 large slices of fresh gingerroot, each
    about ⅛ inch thick, flattened with
    the side of a cleaver

two 2-inch pieces of Chinese dried tangerine
    or orange peel (available at Asian markets)
    or ½ teaspoon chopped dried orange peel

1 tablespoon sugar

½ cup soy sauce

½ cup rice wine (available at Asian
    markets and some liquor stores)
    or dry Sherry or Scotch

2 cups chicken broth

½ cup water

3 fennel bulbs (sometimes called anise,
    available at most supermarkets) or
    8 celery ribs, sliced thin

⅓ cup minced fresh coriander

steamed rice (page 280) as an accompaniment

Preheat the oven to 350° F. In a bowl toss the pork with the flour. In a heavy, oven-proof kettle heat 1 tablespoon of the oil over moderately high heat until it is hot but not smoking, in it brown the pork in batches, adding 6 tablespoons of the remaining oil as necessary, and transfer the pork with a slotted spoon to paper towels to drain. Add 1 tablespoon oil to the kettle and cook the onion, the garlic, and the cloves in it over moderate heat, stirring, until the vegetables are golden. Add the star anise, the gingerroot, the tangerine peel, and the sugar and cook the mixture, stirring, for 1 minute. Stir in the soy sauce, the rice wine, the broth, the water, and

the pork, braise the mixture, covered, in the oven for 1 hour, or until the pork is tender, and season it with salt to taste. *The pork may prepared up to this point 2 days in advance and kept covered and chilled.*

In a kettle of boiling salted water cook the fennel for 5 minutes, or until it is crisp-tender, and drain it. Arrange the fennel around the edge of a platter, spoon the braised pork in the center, and sprinkle the pork with the coriander. Serve the braised pork and the fennel over the rice. Serves 8.

*Baked Butternut Squash with Chinese Mustard
and Duck Sauce*

¼ cup bottled Chinese duck sauce*

1 tablespoon bottled Chinese mustard*

¾ cup water

⅓ cup chopped white part of scallion

2½ pounds butternut squash, quartered,
    seeded, peeled, and cut into ¾-inch pieces
    (about 6 cups)

½ cup thinly sliced scallion greens

*available at Asian markets and some
    specialty foods shops and supermarkets

Preheat the oven to 350° F. In a large bowl whisk together the duck sauce, the mustard, salt to taste, and the water, add the white part of scallion and the butternut squash, and combine the mixture well. Turn the mixture into a 3-quart buttered baking dish and bake it, uncovered, in the middle of the oven, stirring occasionally, for 40 minutes, or until it is tender. *The squash mixture may be made up to this point 1 day in advance and kept covered and chilled. Reheat the mixture in a 350° F. oven until it is hot.* Toss the mixture with the scallion greens. Serves 8.

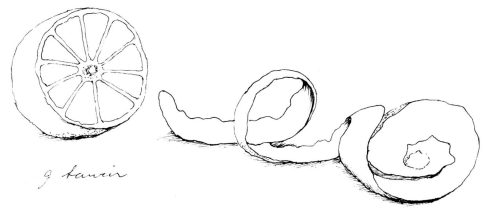

Watercress and Kumquat Salad

1 tablespoon fresh lemon juice
2 tablespoons rice vinegar (available at Asian
    markets and some specialty foods shops
    and supermarkets)
½ cup peanut oil
3 bunches watercress, coarse stems discarded,
    rinsed well and spun dry (about 16 cups)
1 cup kumquats (about ¼ pound), sliced thin
    lengthwise and the seeds discarded
    (available seasonally at specialty foods
    shops and some supermarkets)

In a large bowl whisk together the lemon juice, the
vinegar, and salt and pepper to taste, add the oil in a
stream, whisking, and whisk the dressing until it is
emulsified. Add the watercress and the kumquats and
toss the salad well. Serves 8.

Dried Fruit and Walnut Moon Cake with
Ginger Whipped Cream

2 recipes sweet pastry dough (recipe follows)
1½ cups mixed dried fruit such as apples,
    apricots, pears, and prunes
1 cup pitted dates
¼ teaspoon salt
½ to ¾ teaspoon five-spice powder, or to taste
¼ cup plus 1 tablespoon sugar
2 cups water
1 tablespoon cornstarch dissolved in
    2 tablespoons cold water
¾ cup walnut pieces, chopped and
    toasted lightly
an egg wash made by beating 1 large egg with
    1 tablespoon water
1 cup well-chilled heavy cream
3 tablespoons chopped fine bottled
    candied ginger

Roll out half the dough ⅛ inch thick between sheets of
plastic wrap, using the plastic wrap as an aid, fit the
dough into a non-stick 9- x 2-inch round cake pan, and
trim the edge, leaving a ½-inch overhang. Reserve the
dough scraps and chill the shell for 30 minutes.

In a food processor chop fine the mixed dried fruit
and the dates with the salt, the five-spice powder, and
¼ cup of the sugar. In a heavy saucepan combine the
dried fruit mixture and the water and simmer the mixture, stirring occasionally, for 10 minutes, or until
the fruit is tender (the mixture will be very thick). Stir
the cornstarch mixture, stir it into the dried fruit mixture, and simmer the mixture, stirring frequently, for
2 minutes. Let the fruit filling cool completely and stir
in the walnuts. Spoon the fruit filling into the shell,
spreading it evenly.

Preheat the oven to 375° F. Roll out the remaining
dough ⅛ inch thick between the plastic wrap, using the
plastic wrap as an aid, drape the dough over the filling,
and trim it, leaving a ½-inch overhang. Fold the overhang under the bottom crust, pressing the edge to seal it,
and score the edge decoratively with the back of a knife.
Roll out the reserved dough scraps on a floured surface
¼ inch thick and cut out the Chinese character for
''moon'' as seen in our photograph on page 278. Brush
the top crust with some of the egg wash, arrange the
pastry cut-out on the crust, and brush the cut-out with
some of the egg wash. Bake the moon cake in the middle
of the oven for 30 minutes, or until the pastry is golden,

transfer it to a rack to cool completely, and invert it carefully onto the rack. Reinvert the cake carefully onto a platter. *The cake may be made 1 day in advance and kept, covered with plastic wrap and foil, in a cool place.*

In a large bowl beat the cream until it holds soft peaks, beat in the remaining 1 tablespoon sugar, and beat the cream until it just holds stiff peaks. Fold in the chopped ginger and serve the cake cut into wedges with the ginger whipped cream. Serves 8.

Sweet Pastry Dough

1½ cups all-purpose flour
¼ teaspoon salt
¼ cup sugar
1 teaspoon double-acting baking powder
½ stick (¼ cup) cold unsalted butter,
    cut into bits
¼ cup cold shortening,
    cut into bits
1 large egg, beaten lightly
¼ teaspoon vanilla
1 to 2 tablespoons ice water

In a bowl whisk together the flour, the salt, the sugar, and the baking powder and blend in the butter and the shortening until the mixture resembles meal. Add the egg, the vanilla, and 1 tablespoon of the ice water, toss the mixture until the liquid is incorporated, adding the additional ice water if necessary to form a dough, and form the dough into a ball. Dust the dough with flour and chill it, wrapped in wax paper, for 1 hour.

DIM SUM

Turkey Won Tons and Chinese Broccoli with
Spicy Peanut Sauce

Mushroom Turnovers

Shrimp Toast Rolls

Stir-Fried Vegetables with Crisp Rice Noodles

Pot Stickers

Curry Chicken Wings

Simi Mendocino County Chenin Blanc 1991

———————

Assorted Fruits

Guangzhou (Canton)
Photograph: Ray Cranbourne/Black Star

Mushroom Turnovers;
Curry Chicken Wings;
Turkey Won Tons and
Chinese Broccoli with
Spicy Peanut Sauce

Stir-Fried Vegetables with Crisp Rice Noodles

Pot Stickers; Shrimp Toast Rolls

286

*Turkey Won Tons and Chinese Broccoli
with Spicy Peanut Sauce*

For the sauce
⅓ cup peanut butter
3 tablespoons soy sauce
2 tablespoons vegetable oil
2 tablespoons Asian (toasted) sesame oil*
2 tablespoons rice vinegar*
1 garlic clove, crushed
1½ teaspoons sugar
1 teaspoon Chinese chili paste*
½ teaspoon salt
⅓ cup water
For the won tons
½ pound ground turkey
1½ teaspoons soy sauce
1½ teaspoons rice wine (available at Asian
    markets and some liquor stores) or dry
    Sherry or Scotch
¼ teaspoon salt
1 teaspoon Asian (toasted) sesame oil*
1 teaspoon minced peeled fresh gingerroot
1½ teaspoons cornstarch
⅓ cup coarsely grated carrot
2 tablespoons minced red bell pepper
36 won ton wrappers
¾ pound Chinese broccoli*, large leaves
    discarded, or broccoli stems

*available at Asian markets and some
    specialty foods stores and supermarkets

Make the sauce: In a blender combine the peanut butter, the soy sauce, the oils, the vinegar, the garlic, the sugar, the chili paste, the salt, and the water and blend the mixture until it is smooth. *The sauce may be made 1 week in advance and kept covered and chilled. Return the sauce to room temperature before proceeding.*

Make the won tons: In a bowl stir together well the turkey, the soy sauce, the rice wine, the salt, the sesame oil, the gingerroot, the cornstarch, the carrot, and the bell pepper, throwing the mixture lightly against the inside of the bowl to combine and compact it. Put a level teaspoon of the turkey mixture in the center of 1 of the wrappers, bring the corners of the wrapper together, and squeeze the wrapper around the filling to enclose it. (The won tons will have a draw-string purse shape, see photo on page 287.) Make won tons with the remaining wrappers and filling in the same manner, placing them,

as they are formed, ½ inch apart in a shallow baking dish sprinkled with flour or cornstarch. *The won tons may be made 2 weeks in advance, frozen, uncovered, for 1 hour, or until they are frozen hard, and kept frozen in a resealable plastic bag.*

Trim and discard any yellow or coarse leaves and the tough stem ends from the Chinese broccoli. Cut off the flowerets, reserving them, and cut the stems and the leaves diagonally into ⅛-inch slices. In a kettle of boiling salted water boil the won tons, the broccoli flowerets, and the stems and the leaves for 3 to 5 minutes, (5 to 7 minutes if the won tons are frozen), or until the won tons rise to the surface and the broccoli is tender. Drain the won tons and the broccoli and in a large shallow bowl toss them gently with the peanut sauce. Serves 8.

Mushroom Turnovers

For the filling
6 ounces fresh *shiitake* mushrooms, rinsed
    and stems discarded
1 tablespoon vegetable oil
1 large garlic clove, minced
3 scallions, including the green,
    minced
¼ cup drained canned sliced water chestnuts*,
    blanched in boiling water to cover for
    30 seconds, drained well, and minced
1½ teaspoons cornstarch
½ teaspoon hot chili oil*
For the dough
2 cups all-purpose flour
¾ teaspoon salt
¾ cup cold lard or vegetable shortening
¼ to ⅓ cup ice water
an egg wash made by whisking 1 large egg
    together with 1 teaspoon water

*available at Asian markets and some
    specialty foods shops and supermarkets

Make the filling: In a food processor chop the mushrooms fine. In a wok or a small heavy skillet heat the vegetable oil over moderately high heat until it is hot but not smoking and in it stir-fry the mushrooms with the garlic, stirring, until the liquid the mushrooms give off is evaporated. Stir in the scallions, the water chestnuts, and salt and pepper to taste, stir-fry the mixture for 1 minute, and stir in the cornstarch and the chili oil.

Transfer the filling to a bowl and chill it for 1 hour, or until it is cold. *The filling may be made 1 week in advance and kept covered and chilled.*

Make the dough: In a bowl stir together the flour and the salt, add the lard, cut into bits, and blend the mixture until it resembles meal. Add ¼ cup of the ice water, toss the mixture until the water is incorporated, adding more ice water if necessary to form a dough, and form the dough into a ball. Chill the dough, wrapped in plastic wrap, for 1 hour.

Preheat the oven to 400° F. Roll out half the dough 1/16 inch thick on a floured surface and with a floured 3-inch cutter cut out rounds. Put a teaspoon of the filling in the center of each round and fold the dough over the filling to form a half moon. Crimp the edges with the tines of a fork or scallop and pinch them sealed in a decorative manner. Continue to make turnovers with the remaining dough and filling in the same manner. *The turnovers may be made 2 weeks in advance, arranged ½ inch apart in a shallow baking pan, frozen for 1 hour, or until they are frozen hard, and kept frozen in a resealable plastic bag.* Arrange the turnovers ½ inch apart on a greased baking sheet, brush them with the egg wash, and bake them in the lower third of the oven for 20 minutes, or until they are golden. Makes about 35 turnovers.

Shrimp Toast Rolls

36 medium shrimp (about 1½ pounds), shelled
vegetable oil for the skewers and for deep-frying the rolls
1 large egg white, beaten lightly
5 slices peeled fresh gingerroot, each the size of a quarter
2 scallions, cut into 1-inch pieces
1½ tablespoons rice wine (available at Asian markets and some liquor stores) or dry Sherry or Scotch
2 tablespoons cornstarch
1 tablespoon lard or vegetable shortening
¾ teaspoon salt
16 slices homemade-type white bread, crusts removed
Chinese mustard and duck sauce (available at Asian markets and some specialty foods shops and supermarkets) as accompaniments

Reserve 16 shrimp, covered and chilled. In a shallow dish soak sixteen 6-inch bamboo skewers in the oil for 10 minutes. In a food processor mince the remaining shrimp to a paste, add the egg white, the gingerroot, the scallions, the rice wine, the cornstarch, the lard, and the salt, and blend the mixture, pulsing the motor, until it is a smooth paste. Thread each of the reserved shrimp from head to tail lengthwise on a skewer so that the shrimp is straightened. With a rolling pin roll each slice of bread very thin and spread each slice with about 1½ tablespoons of the shrimp paste, leaving a ¼-inch border around the edges of the bread. Arrange each shrimp skewer on the shrimp paste at one edge of the bread and roll up the bread jelly-roll fashion, enclosing the shrimp in the shrimp paste and the bread. (The skewers will protrude from one end.) *The shrimp rolls may be made 12 hours in advance and kept covered and chilled.*

In a wok or a large deep skillet heat 2 inches of the oil until a deep-fat thermometer registers 375° F. and in it fry the shrimp rolls, 4 at a time, for 4 minutes, transferring them as they are cooked to paper towels to drain. Gently push, do not pull, the skewers through the shrimp rolls, cut each roll crosswise into thirds, and serve the rolls with the Chinese mustard and the duck sauce. Makes 48 rolls.

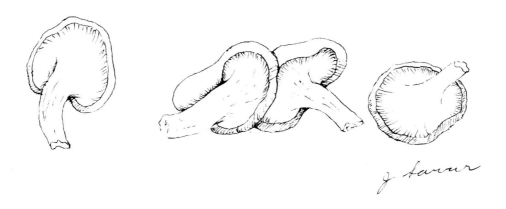

Stir-Fried Vegetables with Crisp Rice Noodles

a 1-pound cake firm bean curd

3 cups vegetable oil

¼ pound dried rice-stick noodles
  (rice vermicelli)*

For the sauce

3 tablespoons sweet bean paste*

3 tablespoons soy sauce

3 tablespoons rice wine (available at Asian
  markets and some liquor stores) or dry
  Sherry or Scotch

1 tablespoon sugar

1 cup chicken broth

1 pound broccoli, cut into flowerets and the
  stems reserved for another use

6 carrots, peeled

1 teaspoon minced garlic

2 teaspoons minced peeled fresh gingerroot

2 tablespoons minced scallion

2 teaspoons Chinese chili paste*

2 red bell peppers, cut into bite-size pieces

6 medium mushrooms, stems discarded and
  the caps cut into sixths

a 16-ounce can baby corn, drained, blanched
  in boiling water for 15 seconds, and halved

6 ounces snow peas, trimmed

2 tablespoons cornstarch dissolved in
  ½ cup water

¼ cup peanuts, chopped

*available at Asian markets and some
  specialty foods shops and supermarkets

Put the bean curd in a shallow bowl lined with a triple layer of paper towels, cover it with another layer of paper towels and an inverted plate, and weight the plate with a 1-pound can for 1 hour to compress the bean curd. Cut the bean curd into ½-inch cubes.

In a large wok or deep fryer heat the oil until it registers 375° F. on a deep-fat thermometer and in it fry half the noodles for 5 to 10 seconds, or until they are puffed and pale golden. Turn the noodles, fry them for 3 seconds longer, and transfer them with a skimmer to paper towels to drain. Fry and drain the remaining noodles in the same manner and, when they are cool enough to handle, gently break them into 2-inch pieces. Pour off all but ¼ cup of the oil from the wok. Arrange the noodles on a large, deep platter and form a well in the center.

Make the sauce: In a small bowl stir together the sweet bean paste, the soy sauce, the rice wine, the sugar, and the broth.

In a saucepan of boiling salted water blanch the broccoli for 3 minutes, or until it is just tender, and transfer it with a skimmer to a plate. In the pan cook the carrots for 5 minutes, or until they are just tender. Drain the carrots and roll-cut them (procedure on page 261) into ¾-inch pieces. Heat the oil remaining in the wok over moderately high heat until it is hot but not smoking and in it stir-fry the garlic, the gingerroot, and the scallion for 30 seconds. Add the chili paste and stir-fry the mixture for 10 seconds. Add the bell peppers and the mushrooms, stir-fry the mixture for 1 minute, and stir in the bean curd, the broccoli, the carrots, the corn, and the snow peas. Stir-fry the mixture for 1 minute, add the sauce, and bring the liquid to a boil. Stir the cornstarch mixture, add it to the pan, and simmer the mixture for 1 minute, or until it is thickened. Spoon the vegetable mixture into the well of the rice stick noodles and sprinkle the top with the peanuts. Serves 8.

Pot Stickers

For the pot stickers

¾ cup minced Napa cabbage

½ teaspoon salt

6 ounces ground pork

½ cup minced garlic chives or chives

1 tablespoon Asian (toasted) sesame oil*

1 tablespoon soy sauce

1½ teaspoons rice wine (available at Asian
  markets) or dry Sherry or Scotch

1 teaspoon cornstarch

¾ teaspoon minced peeled fresh gingerroot

½ to ¾ teaspoon minced garlic

a 12-ounce package round dumpling skins or
  gyoza wrappers (about 45 wrappers)*
  or won tons cut with a 3-inch round cutter

For the sauce

½ cup soy sauce

¼ cup rice vinegar, or to taste*

2 tablespoons hot chili oil*

6 tablespoons vegetable oil

1½ cups cold water

* available at Asian markets and some
  specialty foods shops and supermarkets

Make the pot stickers: In a colander stir together the cabbage and the salt, let the mixture stand for 20 minutes, and squeeze out the excess moisture. In a large bowl stir together the cabbage, the pork, the garlic chives, the sesame oil, the soy sauce, the rice wine, the cornstarch, the gingerroot, and ½ teaspoon of the garlic if using garlic chives (use ¾ teaspoon garlic if using regular chives), throwing the mixture lightly against the inside of the bowl to combine and compact it. Put a teaspoon of the mixture in the center of 1 of the dumpling skins and fold the dumpling skin over the filling to form an open half moon shape. With a wet finger create a moistened border along the inner edge of the dumpling skin that is furthest from you. Using the thumb and forefinger of one hand form 10 to 12 tiny pleats along the unmoistened edge of the dumpling skin that is closest to you, pressing the pleats as they are formed against the moistened border to enclose the filling. The moistened border will stay smooth and will automatically curve in a semi-circle (see photo on page 286). Put the pot stickers as they are made ½ inch apart in a shallow baking pan sprinkled with flour or cornstarch. *The pot stickers may be made 2 weeks in advance, frozen for 1 hour,* *or until they are frozen hard, and kept frozen in a resealable plastic bag.*

Make the sauce: In a small bowl stir together the soy sauce, the vinegar, and the chili oil.

Heat a non-stick skillet measuring 8 to 9 inches across the bottom over moderately high heat until it is very hot, add 2 tablespoons of the vegetable oil, and heat it until it is hot but not smoking. Arrange half the dumplings, pleated edge up, in the skillet, and fry them for 1 to 2 minutes, or until they are golden. Add ¾ cup of the water, cover the skillet, and reduce the heat to moderate. Cook the dumplings, covered, for 7 to 10 minutes, or until most of the liquid has evaporated and pour off any excess liquid. Drizzle 1 tablespoon of the vegetable oil around the edge of the pan and cook the dumplings, uncovered, for 1 to 2 minutes more, or until they are crisp on the bottom. Loosen the dumplings, if necessary, with a spatula, invert a heated serving plate over the skillet, and invert the dumplings onto the plate. Keep the dumplings warm and cook the remaining dumplings in the same manner with the remaining 3 tablespoons oil and the remaining ¾ cup water. Serve the dumplings with the sauce. Makes about 40 pot stickers.

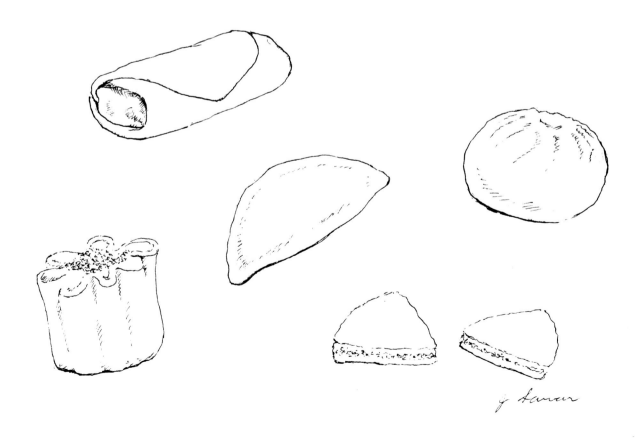

Curry Chicken Wings

2 pounds chicken wings (about 10)

For the marinade

2 tablespoons soy sauce

1 tablespoon rice wine (available at Asian markets and some liquor stores) or dry Sherry or Scotch

1½ teaspoons curry powder

1 teaspoon Asian (toasted) sesame oil*

2 slices of fresh gingerroot, each the size of a quarter, flattened with the side of a cleaver

1 scallion, flattened with the side of a cleaver

For the sauce

1½ cups chicken broth

½ cup water

3 tablespoons rice wine

2 tablespoons soy sauce

1 tablespoon rice vinegar*

2 teaspoons curry powder

1 teaspoon sugar

vegetable oil for deep-frying the chicken wings

2 teaspoons cornstarch dissolved in 2 tablespoons water

1 tablespoon minced fresh coriander or scallion

*available at Asian markets and some specialty foods shops and supermarkets

Cut off the wing tips, reserving them for another use such as Chinese chicken broth if desired, and halve the wings at the joint.

Make the marinade: In a resealable plastic bag combine the soy sauce, the rice wine, the curry powder, the sesame oil, the gingerroot, and the scallion, add the chicken wings, and marinate them, chilled, for at least 30 minutes or overnight.

Make the sauce: In a large saucepan combine the broth, the water, the rice wine, the soy sauce, the rice vinegar, the curry powder, and the sugar and simmer the mixture for 5 minutes.

Drain the chicken wings and pat them dry. In a wok or large deep fryer heat 2 inches of the vegetable oil until a deep-fat thermometer registers 375° F., in it fry the wings, 5 pieces at a time, for 5 to 8 minutes, or until they are golden and crisp, and transfer them to paper towels to drain. Return the oil to 375° F. before adding each new batch of wings.

Add the chicken wings to the broth mixture and simmer them, covered, for 45 minutes, or until they are tender. Stir the cornstarch mixture, stir it into the broth mixture, and simmer the sauce for 1 minute, or until it is thickened. Transfer the chicken wings and the sauce to a deep platter and sprinkle them with the minced fresh coriander. Serves 8.

PART FOUR

A GOURMET ADDENDUM

COOKING FROM
A BASIC PANTRY

Vicky

Whether you have only a few cupboards or you are lucky enough to have an entire room in which to store your staples and condiments, there is nothing quite like a well-stocked pantry. Good chefs depend on their plentiful larders for immediate access to a palate of flavors; busy everyday cooks rely on them when they need to prepare an entire meal without shopping. This addendum offers a comprehensive grocery list of essential pantry items (see our chart on page 296), as well as 24 delicious recipes for breakfasts, lunches, dinners, desserts, and snacks that demonstrate how easy it is to cook when you have the right ingredients on hand.

You can tell a lot about people by what they have in their pantry. In fact, historians have been able to tell how entire civilizations lived by the goods that they stored. We know, for example, that the Greeks and Romans had sophisticated pantries filled with dried figs, olives, honeyed wine, and various spices from conquered lands. Centuries later, after the discovery of America, New World foods such as coffee, chocolate, potatoes, paprika, and tomatoes were introduced to European homes, and American settlers began bringing European and Asian goods—such as oils, rice, tea, and a host of spices—to theirs. Happily, today's modern commerce continues the exchange of foods from around the world.

Our basic pantry is not as complete as a professional chef's might be, but it contains all that a good cook really needs. You will notice that we have included refrigerated and frozen goods. After all, fruits, vegetables, greens, and fresh herbs should be an essential part of our daily diet. We suggest that you begin with this starter pantry and add to it as you travel through life and discover your own favorite foods. With our chart in hand, examine your cupboards, shelves, refrigerator, and freezer, take note of the items that are missing or those past their peak of freshness, and over the next several weeks try to purchase these items.

Once you have assembled your pantry goods you will want to store them properly to maximize their shelf life. If you have a separate room for these items you have plenty of storage options; if you are dealing with a small kitchen, you will need to choose your shelves and cabinets carefully. *All pantry items should be kept in a cool, dry place, out of direct sunlight, and away from heat sources. All dry goods should be stored in tightly sealed containers to avoid insect problems.* Many cooks prefer to display their goods proudly on open shelves, and this also allows quick access to them. Just remember that foods kept behind closed doors and away from heat stay cooler, and consequently their storage life is longer. Also, dried herbs and spices, grains, and root vegetables should always be stored in a cool, dark place to maximize freshness. If you choose to display a braid of garlic bulbs or a bunch of dried herbs from your wall or ceiling beams, just remember that their flavor will diminish quickly. If they do pass their prime for cooking, you can, however, still enjoy their beauty.

Many people feel that all pantry items keep indefinitely, but this is not true. Correctly packaging and storing your goods will help to prolong storage life, but with the exception of vinegar, which lasts for years, all items in your pantry will have to be replaced periodically.

Once the ideal locations have been chosen for your pantry goods, you will need to decide how to organize them so that you will not forget what you have or where you put a particular item. Of course, organization is completely up to the cook, but you may want to arrange your shelves according to our chart: dried goods together (grouped into baking goods, pasta and grains, and others); canned and bottled staples in another space (keep cooking oils in front for easy access); and condiments (flavoring foods) stored in another area.

There is quite a bit of confusion about which pantry goods should or should not be refrigerated, and our chart indicates where items are best stored. Olive oil, for example, once opened should be stored on your shelf; any unopened bottles may be stored in your re-

Shelf Life of Pantry Goods

PANTRY ITEM	KEEPS FOR UP TO:
flour, salt, and sugar	2 years
canned or bottled meats, vegetables, or legumes	18 months
virgin olive oil	6 months
pure olive oil	2 years
canned fish	1 year
dried herbs	1 year
dried pasta	2 years
dried whole-wheat pasta and dried flavored pasta	6 months
whole grains	5 months
refrigerated	1 year
processed grains	1 year
nuts and seeds, unshelled	6 weeks
shelled, refrigerated	2 months
shelled, frozen	1 year
dried fruits	6 months
vacuum-packed bacon, refrigerated	2 weeks
smoked ham, refrigerated	1 week
canned ham	6 months

frigerator (bring the oil to room temperature before using.) Other canned goods, however, once opened, always should be decanted and refrigerated to avoid health hazards. Certain goods are often stored on shelves when they could benefit from refrigeration or freezing. Baking powder, for example, keeps longer if refrigerated, while active dry yeast and fresh bread crumbs are ideally stored frozen. Also, both unshelled nuts and seeds will last much longer if chilled (up to 2 months if refrigerated or up to 1 year if frozen). Whole grains also will last for about 1 year if refrigerated.

Now that you have a well-stocked pantry, you will be able to make any of the recipes that follow. Enjoy sweet Puffed Apple Pancake with your weekend guests, comforting Macaroni and Cheese when you arrive home late from work, elegant and delicious Dried Mushroom Risotto when you want to impress. . . Twenty-four delicious ideas and endless possibilities are now at your fingertips.

THE BASIC PANTRY

DRY GOODS

all-purpose flour
sugars—granulated sugar,
    brown sugar,
    confectioners' sugar
baking soda
vanilla
salt
semisweet chocolate
whole nuts—pecans, walnuts

pasta—spaghetti, elbow
    macaroni, Asian egg
    noodles
rice—Arborio or long grain
    white rice
old-fashioned rolled oats
oat bran
wheat germ
yellow cornmeal
hominy grits
dried bread crumbs

dried fruit—apples, apricots,
    prunes, pears, raisins
pitted dates
dried mushrooms—shiitake,
    porcini, cèpes
dried black beans
tortilla chips
dried herbs and spices—bay
    leaf, cayenne, cinnamon,
    chili powder, cloves,
    cumin, ginger, nutmeg,
    orégano, sweet paprika,
    black peppercorns,
    crushed red pepper
    flakes, thyme

CANNED AND BOTTLED GOODS

cooking oils—vegetable oil,
    canola oil, olive oil
anchovies
canned tuna
canned beans—black beans,
    white beans
canned baby corn
canned bean sprouts
canned whole tomatoes
canned chicken broth
canned beef broth
bottled marinara sauce
peanut butter
coffee and tea

CONDIMENTS

Asian (toasted) sesame oil
Asian chili oil
rice vinegar
Worcestershire sauce
soy sauce
white wine or dry vermouth
medium dry or dry Sherry
Tabasco
Kalamata olives
sun-dried tomatoes
    (packed in oil)
canned green chilies
jarred roasted red peppers
chutney
pickles
jams and jellies
maple syrup
honey
molasses
Dijon-style mustard
mayonnaise
ketchup

FRESH GOODS

breads—white or whole-grain
fruit—oranges, apples, lemons
potatoes—baking, red
onions
garlic cloves

REFRIGERATED GOODS

milk
orange juice
apple cider or apple juice
half-and-half
whipping cream
butter
yogurt or sour cream
cheese—Cheddar, mozzarella,
    Parmesan, Monterey Jack
eggs
vegetables for crudités
carrots
celery
salad greens
shallots
smoked ham
bacon
shelled nuts
sunflower seeds
fresh herbs and spices—basil,
    coriander, gingerroot,
    orégano, parsley, sage,
    rosemary, thyme
baking powder

FROZEN GOODS

whole-kernel corn
leaf spinach
puff pastry
ice cream or frozen yogurt
fresh bread crumbs
active dry yeast

BREAKFAST DISHES

Vicky

Puffed Apple Pancake

2 McIntosh or Granny Smith apples, peeled,
  cored, and sliced ¼ inch thick
1 tablespoon fresh lemon juice
3 tablespoons firmly packed light brown sugar
3 tablespoons granulated sugar
½ teaspoon cinnamon
⅛ teaspoon ground cloves
2 tablespoons unsalted butter
For the pancake
1 cup milk
5 large eggs
½ cup all-purpose flour
2 tablespoons granulated sugar
1 teaspoon vanilla
2 tablespoons unsalted butter

sifted confectioners' sugar for sprinkling the
  pancake

In a bowl combine the apples, the lemon juice, the sugars, the cinnamon, and the cloves. In a skillet set over moderate heat melt the butter, add the apple mixture, and cook it, stirring occasionally, for 5 to 7 minutes, or until the apples are just tender. Transfer the mixture to a bowl and let it cool.

Make the pancake: Preheat the oven to 425° F. Heat a heavy 10-inch skillet, preferably cast iron, in the oven for 5 minutes. In a blender combine the milk, the eggs, the flour, the sugar, the vanilla, and a pinch of salt and blend the mixture until it is smooth. Remove the skillet from the oven and set it over moderately high heat. Add the butter to the skillet, let it melt, and pour the batter into the skillet. Spoon the apple mixture evenly on top of the batter. Return the skillet to the oven and bake the pancake for 15 to 20 minutes, or until it is puffed, golden, and a tester comes out clean.

Sprinkle the top of the apple pancake with the confectioners' sugar. Serves 4 to 6.

Corn Fritters with Maple Syrup

½ cup all-purpose flour
½ teaspoon double-acting baking powder
freshly grated nutmeg to taste
2 large eggs
⅔ cup milk
one 10-ounce package frozen whole-kernel
   corn, thawed and drained
vegetable oil for deep frying the fritters
maple syrup as an accompaniment

Into a bowl sift the flour, the baking powder, the nutmeg, and salt to taste. In another bowl whisk together the eggs and the milk. Add the egg mixture to the flour mixture, whisking until the batter is smooth, and stir in the corn.

In a deep fat fryer heat 2 inches of the oil to 375° F. Add the batter, in batches, by scant ¼ cups to the oil and fry the fritters for 1 to 2 minutes on each side, or until they are golden brown. Transfer the fritters to a tray lined with paper towels and serve them with the maple syrup. Serves 6.

Cinnamon-Flavored Granola with Dried Fruits and Almonds

4 cups old-fashioned rolled oats
1 cup oat bran (available at natural foods
   stores)
½ cup wheat germ
½ cup raw sunflower seeds
½ cup sliced blanched almonds
1 teaspoon cinnamon, or to taste
¼ teaspoon freshly grated nutmeg
½ cup honey
⅓ cup canola oil
⅓ cup apple cider or apple juice
½ cup diced dried apples
½ cup diced dried apricots
½ cup raisins

Preheat the oven to 350° F. In a large shallow baking pan combine the oats, the oat bran, the wheat germ, the sunflower seeds, the almonds, the cinnamon, and the nutmeg. In a small saucepan set over moderate heat whisk together the honey, the oil, and the apple cider until the mixture is smooth. Add the honey mixture to the granola mixture and stir the mixture until it is combined well.

Bake the granola in the oven, stirring occasionally, for 20 minutes, or until it is golden. Stir in the apples, the apricots, and the raisins, let the granola cool, and transfer it to an airtight container. Makes about 8 cups.

Vicky

Grits and Cheddar Casserole

6 cups water
1 teaspoon salt
1 cup hominy grits (not quick-cooking)
2 tablespoons unsalted butter
3 large eggs, separated
2¼ cups grated sharp Cheddar
¼ teaspoon cayenne, or to taste

Preheat the oven to 350° F. In a large heavy saucepan bring the water to a boil, add the salt, and stir in the grits slowly. Simmer the mixture, covered, stirring occasionally, for 15 to 20 minutes, or until it is thickened. Remove the pan from the heat, beat in the butter, and beat in the egg yolks, one at a time. Add 2 cups of the Cheddar and the cayenne and stir the mixture to combine it.

In a bowl with an electric mixer beat the egg whites until they just form stiff peaks, stir one fourth of the whites into the grits mixture to lighten it, and fold in the remaining whites.

Pour the grits mixture into a buttered 2-quart soufflé dish or baking dish, smooth the top, and sprinkle it with the remaining ¼ cup cheese.

Bake the grits, covered with foil, in the oven for 30 minutes. Uncover the casserole and continue to bake the grits for 10 minutes more, or until bubbles form around the edge of the casserole. Serves 6 to 8.

Omelette Parmentier
(Potato Omelet)

2 boiling potatoes (about ¾ pound), peeled
    and cut into ½-inch dice (2 cups)
2 tablespoons vegetable oil
3 tablespoons minced fresh parsley leaves
    plus additional for garnishing the omelets
8 large eggs
8 teaspoons water
4 tablespoons unsalted butter

Pat the potatoes dry and sprinkle them with salt and pepper to taste. In a skillet heat the oil over moderately high heat until it is hot but not smoking, add the potatoes, and sauté them, stirring occasionally, for 10 to 15 minutes, or until they are golden brown and tender. Transfer the potatoes to a bowl and sprinkle them with the parsley.

Make each omelet separately: In a bowl whisk together 2 of the eggs, 2 teaspoons of the water, and salt and pepper to taste. In an 8-inch skillet, preferably nonstick, heat 1 tablespoon of the butter over moderately high heat until the foam subsides. Pour in the egg mixture, tilting the skillet to spread the mixture evenly over the bottom, and cook it for 1 minute, or until it is almost set. Arrange one fourth of the potatoes on half of the omelet and cook the omelet for 1 minute, or until it is set. With a spatula fold the omelet over the potatoes, shaping the omelet into a half circle. Invert the omelet onto a plate, sprinkle it with the additional parsley if desired, and keep it warm. Make 3 more omelets in the same manner with the remaining ingredients. Serves 4.

Orange Date-Nut Muffins

1 navel orange
⅔ cup orange juice
1 large egg
6 tablespoons unsalted butter, melted and cooled
2 cups all-purpose flour
½ cup chopped pitted dates
½ cup sugar
1 teaspoon double-acting baking powder
1 teaspoon baking soda
½ teaspoon salt
½ cup chopped walnuts

Preheat the oven to 400° F. Grate the zest from the orange and reserve it. Remove the pith from the orange and cut the flesh into fine dice. In a bowl stir together the grated orange zest, the orange flesh, the juice, the egg, and the melted butter. In another bowl stir together the flour, the dates, the sugar, the baking powder, the baking soda, and the salt.

Add the orange mixture and the walnuts to the flour mixture and stir the batter until it is just combined. Divide the batter among 12 buttered ½-cup muffin tins and bake the muffins in the middle of the oven for 15 to 20 minutes, or until a tester comes out clean. Transfer the muffins to a rack and let them cool. Makes 12 muffins.

LUNCH DISHES

Vicky

Asian Soup with Noodles, Black Mushrooms, and Spinach

1 ounce dried *shiitake* mushrooms
  (about 8 large)
1 cup hot water
1 cup minced onion
2 garlic cloves, minced
1 tablespoon minced peeled fresh gingerroot
1 tablespoon vegetable oil
7 cups chicken broth
½ cup diagonally sliced carrot
half of a ten-ounce package frozen leaf
  spinach, thawed, drained,
  and squeezed dry
4 ounces Asian egg noodles (available
  at Asian markets and some
  supermarkets)

1 to 2 tablespoons soy sauce
1 tablespoon dry Sherry, if desired

In a bowl cover the mushrooms with the water, let them soak for 15 minutes, and drain them, reserving the soaking liquid. Discard the tough stems, slice the caps thin, and strain the cooking liquid through a fine sieve into a bowl.

In a large saucepan cook the onion, the garlic, and the gingerroot in the oil over moderate heat, stirring, for 5 minutes. Add the reserved mushroom liquid, the broth, and salt to taste and simmer the soup for 10 minutes. Add the carrot and the spinach and simmer the soup for 5 minutes or until the carrot is crisp-tender. Add the noodles and simmer the soup, stirring occasionally, for 3 to 5 minutes, or until the noodles are just tender. Stir in the soy sauce and the Sherry. Makes 8 cups, serving 6.

Sun-Dried Tomato, Onion, and Black Olive Pizza
For the pizza dough
a ¼-ounce package (2½ teaspoons) active
  dry yeast
¼ teaspoon sugar
¾ cup lukewarm water
2 to 2¼ cups all-purpose flour
1 teaspoon salt
2 tablespoons olive oil

3 tablespoons olive oil
1 large onion, sliced thin
1 tablespoon minced garlic
¾ to 1 cup bottled marinara sauce, or to taste
10 large sun-dried tomatoes (packed in oil),
  drained well and cut into thin strips
½ cup Kalamata or other brine-cured olives,
  pitted and sliced
1 cup grated mozzarella if desired
3 tablespoons freshly grated Parmesan

Make the dough: In a large bowl proof the yeast with
the sugar in ½ cup of the water for 5 minutes, or until the
mixture is foamy. In a food processor combine 2 cups of
the flour and the salt. With the motor running add the
yeast mixture, the olive oil, and the remaining ¼ cup
water in a stream and process the mixture until it forms a
ball. Add the additional flour, as necessary, 1 tablespoon at a time, to form a firm dough and knead the
dough by processing it for 20 seconds more. Put the
dough in an oiled bowl and turn it to coat it with the oil.
Let the dough rise in a warm place, covered with plastic
wrap and a kitchen towel, for 1 to 1½ hours, or until it is
doubled in bulk.

Preheat the oven to 500° F. In a skillet heat 2 tablespoons of the olive oil over moderate heat until it is hot,
add the onion and salt and pepper to taste, and cook the
onion, stirring occasionally, for 5 to 7 minutes, or until
it is lightly golden. Add the garlic and cook the mixture,
stirring, for 1 minute more.

Roll out the dough on a lightly floured surface into a
14-inch round and fit it into a 14-inch pizza pan or baking sheet (preferably black steel for a crisper crust).
Spoon the marinara sauce over the dough, leaving a
1-inch border, and top it with the onion mixture, the
sun-dried tomatoes, the olives, and salt and pepper to
taste. Sprinkle the pizza with the mozzarella and the
Parmesan and drizzle it with the remaining 1 tablespoon
olive oil. Bake the pizza on the bottom rack of an elec-

tric oven or on the floor of a gas oven for 12 to 15 minutes, or until the crust is golden brown. Transfer the
pizza with spatulas to a cutting board and cut it into
wedges. Serves 4 to 6.

Open-Faced Peanut Butter, Chutney,
and Bacon Sandwiches

4 slices of lean bacon
⅔ cup smooth peanut butter
¼ cup chopped chutney
4 slices homemade-type whole grain or
  white bread

In a saucepan of boiling water blanch the bacon for 5
minutes, drain it, and pat it dry. Cut the bacon slices in
half. In a bowl combine the peanut butter and the chutney and spread the mixture on each slice of bread. Top
the peanut butter mixture with the bacon and broil the
sandwiches under a preheated broiler about 4 inches
from the heat for 3 to 5 minutes, or until the bacon is
crisp. Serves 4.

Sage Focaccia with Sliced Potatoes, Roasted Red Peppers, and Shallots

For the dough

a ¼-ounce package (2½ teaspoons) active
   dry yeast
1 cup lukewarm water
4 tablespoons olive oil
1 teaspoon salt
2¾ to 3 cups all-purpose flour
1 tablespoon minced fresh sage leaves or
   1½ teaspoons dried, crumbled

For the topping

½ cup minced shallot
3 tablespoons olive oil
a 3-ounce jar roasted red peppers, drained,
   diced, and patted dry
2 garlic cloves, minced fine
3 small new potatoes or red potatoes
¼ cup freshly grated Parmesan

Make the dough: In a bowl proof the yeast with ¼ cup of the water for 10 minutes, or until it is foamy. In another bowl combine the remaining ¾ cup water with 2 tablespoons of the olive oil and the salt. In a food processor combine 2¾ cups of the flour and the sage leaves. With the motor running add the oil mixture in a stream, add the yeast mixture in a stream, and process the mixture until it is combined well. Slowly add the additional ¼ cup flour, as necessary, 1 tablespoon at a time, until the mixture forms a ball and knead the dough by processing it for 20 seconds more. Put the dough in a large oiled bowl and turn it to coat it with the oil. Cover the bowl with plastic wrap and a kitchen towel and let the dough rise in a warm place for 1 hour, or until it is doubled in bulk.

Punch down the dough and transfer it to a lightly floured surface. Roll the dough into a rectangle ¼-inch thick. Transfer the rectangle to an oiled heavy baking sheet or pizza pan and brush it with the remaining 2 tablespoons oil. Using your fingertips, make impressions in the dough about 1 inch apart. Let the dough rise for 20 minutes.

Make the topping: Preheat the oven to 450° F. In a skillet set over moderate heat cook the shallot, seasoned with salt and pepper, in 2 tablespoons of the oil, stirring occasionally, for 3 minutes, or until it is softened. Add the roasted red peppers and the garlic and cook the mixture, stirring, for 2 minutes more. Remove the mixture from the heat and let it cool. Cut the potatoes into paper-thin slices and arrange the slices, overlapping them slightly, on the dough. Sprinkle the potatoes with the shallot and the red pepper mixture, the Parmesan, and the remaining 1 tablespoon oil.

Bake the *focaccia* in the lower third of the oven for 20 to 25 minutes, or until the crust is golden brown and the potatoes are tender. Serves 4 to 6.

Cheddar Bread Pudding with Roasted Red Peppers and Chilies

6 slices homemade-type white bread
½ stick (¼ cup) unsalted butter, softened
a 4-ounce can chopped green chilies, drained
   and patted dry
a 7-ounce jar roasted red peppers,
   drained and chopped

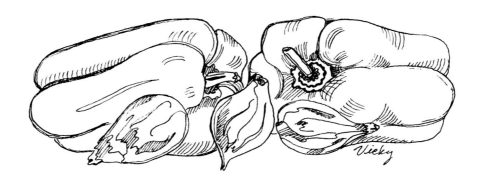

1 pound sharp Cheddar, grated
2 cups milk
4 large eggs, beaten lightly
2 teaspoons Dijon-style mustard
¼ teaspoon cayenne, or to taste

Preheat the oven to 375° F. Spread the bread with the butter and cut the slices into 1-inch cubes. In a buttered 2½-quart baking dish arrange half the bread cubes and top them with half the green chilies, half the peppers, and half the Cheddar. Arrange another layer with the remaining bread cubes, chilies, peppers, and Cheddar.

In a bowl combine the milk, the eggs, the mustard, the cayenne, and salt to taste, pour the mixture over the bread and cheese mixture, and chill the casserole, covered, for at least 3 hours or overnight. Put the casserole in a baking pan, add enough hot water to the pan to come halfway up the sides of the casserole, and bake the casserole in the oven for 1 hour, or until it is golden and the pudding is set. Serves 8.

Sesame Noodle Salad

For the sauce
½ cup peanut butter
½ cup chicken broth
2 garlic cloves, minced
2 tablespoons Asian (toasted) sesame oil*
3 tablespoons soy sauce
1 tablespoon minced peeled fresh gingerroot
1 tablespoon rice vinegar*

¼ teaspoon Asian chili oil*
1 teaspoon sugar

an 8-ounce package Asian egg noodles*
1 tablespoon Asian (toasted) sesame oil*
an 8-ounce can baby corn, blanched in boiling water for 15 seconds, drained, refreshed under cold water, and patted dry
2 carrots, sliced thin
a 14-ounce can bean sprouts*, blanched in boiling water for 15 seconds, drained, refreshed under cold water, and patted dry
minced fresh coriander for garnish

*available at Asian markets and some specialty foods shops and supermarkets

Make the sauce: In a blender or food processor combine all the sauce ingredients, add salt to taste, and process the sauce until it is smooth. Transfer the sauce to a serving dish.

In a large saucepan of salted boiling water cook the noodles for 3 to 5 minutes, or until they are *al dente*. Drain the noodles in a colander and refresh them under cold water, draining them well. Toss the noodles with the sesame oil and some of the sauce and transfer them to a platter. Arrange the corn, the carrots, and the bean sprouts around the noodles, sprinkle the salad with the coriander, and serve it with the remaining sauce. Serves 4 to 6.

DINNER DISHES

Vicky

Vegetarian Chili

1½ cups minced onion
⅔ cup minced carrot
⅔ cup minced celery
1½ tablespoons minced garlic
2 tablespoons vegetable oil
1 tablespoon ground cumin, or to taste
1 tablespoon chili powder, or to taste
1 teaspoon dried orégano, crumbled
¼ teaspoon cayenne, or to taste
a 28-ounce can crushed tomatoes in purée
1 cup beef broth
2 cups canned black beans, drained
  and rinsed

2 tablespoons minced fresh coriander
yogurt or sour cream as an accompaniment,
  if desired

In a saucepan cook the onion, the carrot, the celery, and the garlic in the oil, covered, over moderate heat, stirring occasionally, for 5 minutes. Add the cumin, the chili powder, the orégano, and the cayenne and cook the mixture, stirring, for 1 minute. Add the tomatoes and the broth and simmer the mixture, stirring occasionally, for 20 minutes. Add the beans and salt to taste and simmer the chili for 10 minutes more, or until it is heated through. Garnish the chili with the coriander and serve it with the yogurt. Serves 4 to 6.

Dried Mushroom Risotto

1 ounce dried mushrooms, such as *porcini*, *shiitake*, or *cèpes*

2½ cups chicken broth diluted with ½ cup water

1 tablespoon olive oil

½ cup minced shallot or onion

1 cup Arborio rice (available at specialty foods shops and some supermarkets) or long-grain white rice

½ cup dry white wine or dry vermouth

¼ cup freshly grated Parmesan

2 tablespoons unsalted butter, softened

In a bowl combine the mushrooms with 1 cup of the broth, heated, and let the mushrooms soak for 15 minutes, or until they are softened. Drain the mushrooms in a sieve lined with dampened cheesecloth over a bowl, reserving the liquid, remove and discard the tough stems, and slice the mushroom caps thin.

In a saucepan combine the reserved mushroom liquid and the remaining 2 cups of broth, bring the mixture to a simmer, and keep the broth warm over very low heat.

In a heavy saucepan heat the oil over moderate heat until it is hot, add the shallot, and cook it, stirring, for 2 minutes. Add the mushrooms and salt and pepper to taste and cook the mixture, stirring, for 2 minutes more. Add the rice and cook it, stirring, until it is coated with the oil. Add the wine and cook the mixture, stirring, for 3 minutes, or until the wine has been absorbed. Add ½ cup of the broth to the pan and cook the mixture, stirring, for 2 to 3 minutes, or until almost all the liquid has been absorbed. Continue adding the broth to the skillet, ½ cup at a time, keeping the liquid at a simmer and stirring until the rice is tender and creamy and most of the liquid has been absorbed. Stir in the Parmesan and the butter. Serves 4 as a first course.

Spaghetti Carbonara

¼ pound bacon, cut into 1-inch pieces

1 cup minced onion

2 tablespoons unsalted butter

⅔ cup half-and-half

2 large eggs

¼ cup minced fresh parsley leaves

1 pound spaghetti

freshly grated Parmesan to taste

In a skillet cook the bacon over moderate heat, stirring, until it is crisp. Drain the bacon on paper towels. In a saucepan cook the onion in the butter over moderate heat, stirring occasionally, for 5 to 7 minutes, or until it is golden. In a bowl whisk together the half-and-half and the eggs, add the mixture to the pan, and cook the mixture over moderately low heat, stirring constantly, until it is slightly thickened. Do not let it boil. Remove the pan from the heat and stir in the bacon pieces and the parsley.

In a large saucepan of boiling salted water cook the spaghetti until it is *al dente*, drain it, and transfer it to a large bowl. Toss the spaghetti with the sauce and serve it with the Parmesan. Serves 4.

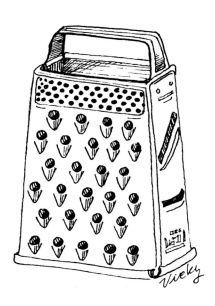

mixture to a buttered 2-quart shallow flameproof baking dish, sprinkle the top with the bread crumbs, and dot the crumbs with the remaining 2 tablespoons butter. Bake the gratin in the oven for 25 to 30 minutes, or until it is bubbling. Put the dish under a preheated broiler about 4 inches from the heat and broil the macaroni and cheese until the top is golden. Serves 6.

Black Bean Soup

1½ cups dried black beans, rinsed and
    picked over
4 cups chicken broth diluted with 2 cups
    water, plus additional broth, if necessary
¼ pound bacon, cut into dice
1 large onion, chopped
1 carrot, diced
1 celery stalk, diced
3 garlic cloves, minced
1 bay leaf
1 tablespoon minced fresh orégano leaves or
    1 teaspoon dried, crumbled
1½ teaspoons fresh thyme or ½ teaspoon
    dried, crumbled
¼ teaspoon red pepper flakes, if desired
2 tablespoons dry Sherry, or to taste
3 tablespoons minced fresh coriander or
    parsley

In a bowl soak the beans, uncovered, in enough water to cover them by 2 inches overnight. Alternatively, quick-soak the beans: In a saucepan combine the beans with enough water to cover them by 2 inches, bring the water to a boil, and simmer the beans, uncovered, for 5 minutes. Remove the pan from the heat and let the beans soak for 1 hour, uncovered. Drain the beans.

In a large saucepan combine the beans with the broth, the bacon, the onion, the carrot, the celery, the garlic, the bay leaf, the orégano, the thyme, and the red pepper flakes, bring the liquid to a boil, and simmer the beans, uncovered, for 2 to 2½ hours, or until they are tender, adding more broth if necessary. Remove the bay leaf and discard it.

Transfer two cups of the mixture to a blender or food processor and process the mixture until it is smooth. Return the purée to the saucepan, stir in the Sherry, and add salt to taste. Bring the soup to a simmer, heat it until it is heated through, and garnish it with the coriander. Makes about 7 cups, serving 6.

Macaroni and Cheese

½ pound elbow macaroni
1 onion, minced
¾ stick (6 tablespoons) unsalted butter
¼ cup all-purpose flour
2½ cups milk, scalded
3 cups grated sharp Cheddar
1 tablespoon Dijon-style mustard, or to taste
2 teaspoons Worcestershire sauce, or to taste
¼ teaspoon cayenne, or to taste
1 cup diced smoked ham, if desired
⅓ cup fresh bread crumbs

Preheat the oven to 350° F. In a large saucepan of boiling salted water cook the macaroni for 7 to 8 minutes, or until it is *al dente*, and drain it.

In a large saucepan set over moderate heat cook the onion in 4 tablespoons of the butter for 3 minutes, stirring occasionally, until it is softened. Add the flour and cook the mixture over moderately low heat, stirring, for 3 minutes. Add the milk, bring the liquid to a boil, whisking, and simmer the sauce, stirring occasionally, for 10 minutes. Remove the pan from the heat and stir in the cheese, in batches, until the mixture is smooth. Add the mustard, the Worcestershire sauce, the cayenne, and salt to taste.

Add the macaroni and the ham to the sauce and gently stir the mixture to combine it. Transfer the macaroni

Layered Polenta Casserole

1½ cups minced onion
2 garlic cloves, minced
3 tablespoons olive oil
a 28-ounce can tomatoes, drained and
    chopped
1½ teaspoons fresh thyme leaves or
    ½ teaspoon dried, crumbled
1½ teaspoons fresh orégano leaves or
    ½ teaspoon dried, crumbled
a 10-ounce package frozen spinach,
    thawed, squeezed dry,
    and chopped
1¾ cups yellow cornmeal
5 cups water
1 teaspoon salt
6 tablespoons freshly grated Parmesan
minced fresh basil leaves
    for garnish

Preheat the oven to 400° F. In a skillet cook the onion, the garlic, and salt and pepper to taste in 2 tablespoons of the olive oil over moderate heat, stirring occasionally, for 5 minutes. Add the tomatoes, the thyme, and the orégano and simmer the mixture, stirring occasionally, for 5 to 7 minutes, or until it is dry.

In another skillet cook the spinach and salt and pepper to taste in the remaining 1 tablespoon oil over moderately low heat, stirring occasionally, for 5 minutes.

In a bowl whisk together the cornmeal and 2½ cups of the water until the mixture is smooth. In a large saucepan bring the remaining 2½ cups water to a boil with the salt and add the cornmeal mixture in a stream, whisking constantly to prevent any lumps from forming. Simmer the mixture over moderately low heat, stirring constantly with a long-handled wooden spoon, for 10 to 15 minutes, or until it is very thick.

Spread one third of the polenta in a buttered 2½-quart casserole or soufflé dish. Top the polenta layer with half the tomato mixture and sprinkle it with 2 tablespoons of the Parmesan. Top the tomato layer with half the remaining polenta, smooth the spinach over the polenta, and sprinkle it with 2 tablespoons of the remaining Parmesan. Add the remaining polenta to the dish, smooth it into an even layer, and top it with the remaining tomato. Sprinkle the top with the remaining Parmesan.

Bake the polenta in the oven for 30 minutes, or until it is heated through. Serves 6 to 8.

SNACKS AND DESSERTS

Mexican-Style White Bean Dip

3 slices of bacon

1½ cups minced onion

2 large garlic cloves, minced fine

1 tablespoon ground cumin, or
  to taste

1 tablespoon chili powder, or to taste

two 19-ounce cans white beans, such as
  cannellini or navy, drained and rinsed

¼ pound (about 1 cup) grated Monterey Jack

cayenne pepper to taste

¼ cup sour cream or plain yogurt

3 tablespoons minced fresh coriander, or
  to taste

tortilla chips or *crudités* as an accompaniment

In a skillet cook the bacon over moderate heat, turning it, until it is crisp and transfer it to paper towels to drain. Pour off all but 2 tablespoons of fat from the skillet and add the onion and the garlic. Cook the vegetables over moderate heat, stirring occasionally, until the onion is golden, add the cumin and the chili powder, and cook the mixture, stirring, for 1 minute. Add the beans and salt and pepper to taste and cook the mixture, stirring occasionally, for 5 minutes, or until it is dry.

In a food processor or in batches in a blender combine the bean mixture with the cheese and the cayenne and purée the mixture until it is smooth. Transfer the bean dip to a bowl, fold in the bacon, crumbled, the sour cream, and the coriander, and serve the dip with the tortilla chips. Makes about 4 cups.

Puff Pastry Cheese Straws

½ pound puff pastry, thawed if frozen
an egg wash made by beating 1 large egg with
    1 teaspoon water
1 cup freshly grated Parmesan
sweet paprika for sprinkling the pastry

Roll out the dough on a lightly floured surface into a rectangle about ¼ inch thick. Brush the dough lightly with some of the egg wash, sprinkle it with half the Parmesan, and dust it with the paprika. Roll a rolling pin gently over the dough to press the cheese mixture into the dough. Turn the dough over, brush it with some of the remaining egg wash, and sprinkle it with the remaining Parmesan and paprika. Roll the rolling pin gently over the dough again to press the cheese mixture into the dough, transfer the dough to a baking sheet lined with parchment paper, and chill it for at least 30 minutes.

Preheat the oven to 425° F. Line another baking sheet with a piece of parchment paper, leaving 1 inch borders uncovered on each long side. With a pastry wheel or sharp knife cut the dough lengthwise into ½-inch strips. Twist the strips corkscrew fashion and arrange them, ½ inch apart, on the baking sheet, pressing the ends of the strips onto the uncovered portion of the baking sheet to hold the dough stretched and in place.

Bake the cheese straws in the oven for 10 to 15 minutes, or until they are puffed and golden. While the straws are still hot, cut them crosswise into 4-inch lengths and let them cool on racks. *The cheese straws may be made up to 2 days in advance and kept in airtight containers in a cool, dry place. Before serving, heat the straws in a preheated 425° F. oven for 5 to 7 minutes, or until they are crisp.* Makes about 75 cheese straws.

Apple Brown Betty

1½ cups dry bread crumbs
⅓ cup unsalted butter, melted
4 cups thinly sliced apples such as McIntosh
½ cup firmly packed light brown sugar
¼ cup granulated sugar
2 tablespoons fresh lemon juice
1 teaspoon freshly grated lemon zest
½ teaspoon cinnamon
½ teaspoon freshly grated nutmeg
¼ teaspoon ground ginger
½ cup hot water
ice cream or whipped cream as an accompaniment

Preheat the oven to 350° F. In a bowl toss together the bread crumbs and the butter. In another bowl toss together the apple slices, the sugars, the lemon juice, the lemon zest, the cinnamon, the nutmeg, and the ginger.

In a buttered 1½-quart casserole layer the bread crumb mixture with the apple mixture, beginning and ending with the bread crumb mixture. Pour the water over the top of the casserole and bake the Brown Betty, covered with foil, in the oven for 20 minutes. Uncover the casserole and bake it for 20 to 25 minutes more, or until it is lightly browned. Cool the dessert slightly and serve it warm with the ice cream. Serves 6.

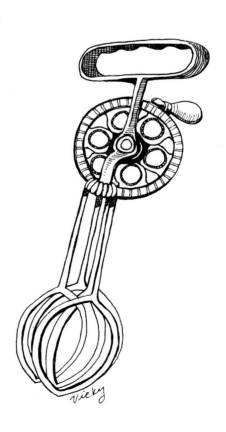

Dried Fruit Turnovers

6 ounces (1½ cups) chopped dried fruit such
    as raisins, apples, apricots, prunes, pears,
    or a combination
2 tablespoons unsalted butter
⅓ cup water
3 tablespoons maple syrup
1 tablespoon fresh lemon juice
1 teaspoon freshly grated orange zest
½ teaspoon freshly grated lemon zest
½ teaspoon cinnamon
¼ teaspoon freshly grated nutmeg
⅛ teaspoon ground ginger
1 pound puff pastry, thawed if frozen
an egg wash made by beating 1 large egg with
    1 teaspoon water

Preheat the oven to 425° F. In a saucepan cook the fruit in the butter over moderate heat, stirring occasionally, for 5 minutes. Add the water, the maple syrup, the lemon juice, the orange zest, the lemon zest, the cinnamon, the nutmeg, and the ginger and cook the mixture, stirring occasionally, for 15 minutes, or until the mixture is thick and almost dry.

Roll the dough into a rectangle ⅛ inch thick on a lightly floured surface and with a 4-inch round cutter cut out rounds. Brush the rounds lightly with water and put 1 tablespoon of the fruit mixture in the center of each round. Fold the rounds in half and press the edges together gently to seal in the filling. Invert the turnovers onto a dampened baking sheet and chill them for 30 minutes.

Brush the turnovers with some of the egg wash and bake them in the oven for 10 to 12 minutes, or until they are puffed and golden. Transfer the turnovers to racks to cool. Makes 6 to 8 turnovers.

Pecan Chocolate Chunk Cookies

2 sticks (1 cup) unsalted butter,
    softened
¾ cup firmly packed light brown sugar
¾ cup granulated sugar
1 teaspoon vanilla
2 large eggs, beaten lightly
2 cups all-purpose flour
½ teaspoon salt
1 teaspoon baking soda
¼ teaspoon cinnamon
8 ounces semisweet chocolate, chopped into
    ½-inch chunks
1 cup chopped toasted pecans

Preheat the oven to 375° F. In a large bowl with an electric mixer cream the butter, add the brown sugar and the granulated sugar, a little at a time, beating, and beat the batter until it is light and fluffy. Beat in the vanilla and the eggs, a little at a time, and beat the mixture until it is combined well.

Into another bowl sift together the flour, the salt, the baking soda, and the cinnamon. Add the flour mixture to the butter mixture and stir in the chocolate chunks and the pecans.

Drop rounded teaspoons of the dough 2 inches apart onto buttered baking sheets and bake the cookies, in batches, in the oven for 8 to 10 minutes, or until the edges are golden. Transfer the cookies to racks and let them cool completely. Makes about 48 cookies.

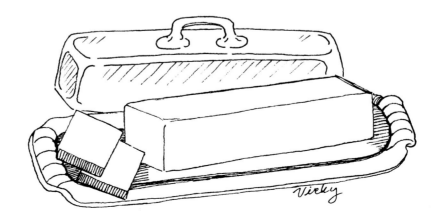

Indian Pudding

½ cup yellow cornmeal
4 cups milk
½ cup unsulphured molasses
¼ cup firmly packed light brown sugar
¼ cup granulated sugar
4 tablespoons unsalted butter, softened
½ teaspoon salt
½ teaspoon cinnamon
¼ teaspoon ground ginger
⅛ teaspoon ground cloves
ice cream or whipped cream as an accompaniment

Preheat the oven to 325° F. In a bowl combine the cornmeal with 1 cup of the milk and whisk the mixture until it is smooth.

In the top of a double boiler set over simmering water heat 2 cups of the milk until it is hot. Add the cornmeal mixture, stirring, and simmer the mixture, stirring occasionally, for 15 to 20 minutes, or until it is lightly thickened. Add the unsulphured molasses, the sugars, the butter, the salt, the cinnamon, the ginger, and the cloves and simmer the mixture, stirring occasionally, for 5 minutes more.

Pour the pudding into a buttered 1½-quart shallow baking dish, pour the remaining 1 cup milk on top of the pudding but do not stir it in, and put the baking dish in a shallow baking pan. Add enough hot water to the baking pan to reach halfway up the sides of the baking dish and cook the pudding in the oven for 2½ to 3 hours, or until it is set in the center. Let the pudding cool slightly and serve it with the ice cream. Serves 6.

GUIDES TO THE TEXT

GENERAL INDEX

Page numbers in *italics* indicate color photographs
(M) indicates a microwave recipe

INDEX OF 45-MINUTE RECIPES

*Starred entries can be prepared in 45 minutes or less
but require additional unattended time

Page numbers in *italics* indicate color photographs

(M) indicates a microwave recipe

INDEX OF RECIPE TITLES

Page numbers in *italics* indicate color photographs

(M) indicates a microwave recipe

TABLE SETTING ACKNOWLEDGMENTS

To avoid duplication below of table setting information within the same menu, the editors have listed all such credits for silverware, plates, linen, and the like in its most complete form under "Table Setting."

Any items in the photographs not credited are privately owned.

All addresses are in New York City unless otherwise indicated.

Front Jacket

Grilled Teriyaki Shrimp and Vegetable Brochettes: "Sienna" Limoges service plate by Jean Louis Coquet—for stores call Tel. (201) 939-4199.

Frontispiece

Berry and Farmer Cheese Tart (page 2): All items in the photograph are privately owned.

Table of Contents

The Menu Collection (page 6): See Table Setting credits for Fourth of July Cookout below.
A Recipe Compendium—Minestrone; Garlic Bruschetta (page 7): See Table Setting credits for A Breeze of a Lunch below.

The Menu Collection

Table Setting (page 10): See Table Setting credits for Celebrating America's Heritage below.

New Year's Day Fireside Luncheon

Table Setting (pages 12 and 13): Hand-painted ceramic dinner plates and soup bowls designed by Barbara Eigen—Eigen Arts, 150 Bay Street, Jersey City, NJ 07302. "Oasis" stainless-steel flatware—Pavillon Christofle, 680 Madi-

son Avenue. "Guadalajara" Mexican wineglasses—Platypus, 126 Spring Street. Cotton napkins—Wolfman • Gold & Good Company, 116 Greene Street. Brass napkin rings; painted galvanized steel wine bucket; pear candles —Zona, 97 Greene Street. "Melrose" plaid wool fabric; "Tapisserie" printed cotton fabric (both available through decorator)—Brunschwig & Fils, Inc., 979 Third Avenue.
Orange Flans with Candied Zest; Anise Pine-Nut Cookies (page 15): Gien "Olerys" faience plates—Baccarat, 625 Madison Avenue.

An Intimate New Year's Eve

Filets Mignons with Mustard Port Sauce; Red Onion Confit; Pommes Anna; Buttered Snow Peas and Carrots (pages 16 and 17): "Sevilla" porcelain dinner plates designed by Vincent Wolfe— The L/S Collection, 765 Madison Avenue. "American Garden" sterling flatware; Italian silver-luster porcelain candlesticks—Tiffany & Company, 727 Fifth Avenue. Wineglasses designed by Stephen Smyers—Barneys New York, Seventh Avenue and 17th Street. Hand-painted linen tablecloth and napkins by Liz Wain—The Linen Tree, 6137 North Scottsdale Road, Scottsdale, AZ 85250. Flower arrangement—Zézé, 398 East 52nd Street. English silver-luster jardiniere, circa 1810; English eighteenth-century framed silk

needlepoint scenes—Bardith, 901 Madison Avenue. Gilded ballroom chairs— Newel Art Galleries, 425 East 53rd Street.

A Caribbean Buffet

Table Setting (pages 18 and 19): Earthenware banana bowl and leaf plate by Eigen Arts—Mimi's, 1984 San Marco Boulevard, Jacksonville, FL 32207. Glass bowl and pitcher (piña colada punch); cotton napkins—Frank McIntosh Shop at Henri Bendel, 712 Fifth Avenue. Glass pitcher (Jamaican sorrel rum punch); wire-wicker tray—Wolfman • Gold & Good Company, 116 Greene Street. "Bamboo" crystal wineglasses—Justin Tharaud & Son, 23 Maplewood Avenue, Maplewood, NJ 07040, Tel. (201) 762-1422. Polka-dot glasses—Zona, 97 Greene Street. Wicker chairs, circa 1900—Treillage, 418 East 75th Street.
Jerk Chicken; Yellow Rice; Curried Red Snapper; Black Beans; Squash Purée with Olive Oil and Lime; Wilted Cucumber Salad (pages 20 and 21): Glass dinner plates—Frank McIntosh Shop at Henri Bendel, 712 Fifth Avenue. "Fiddlehead" steel flatware—The Pottery Barn, 117 East 59th Street. Cotton napkins; bamboo servers; metal fish platter, glass bowl—Frank McIntosh Shop at Henri Bendel, 712 Fifth Avenue. Earthenware banana leaf platter and round bowl by Eigen Arts—Mimi's,

1984 San Marco Boulevard, Jacksonville, FL 32207. Earthenware baker by Eigen Arts—Felissimo, 10 West 56th Street.

Picnic in the Snow

Barbecue Bean Soup; Prosciutto, Münster, and Cumin Corn-Bread Sandwiches; Pickled Carrots, Turnips, and Peppers (pages 22 and 23): Wood plates and cutting board—Dean & DeLuca, Inc., 560 Broadway. Flatware; vintage wool blanket; vintage backpack—Whispering Pines, 516 Main Street, Piermont, NY 10968. Steel cups; plastic mugs and container; cotton napkins—Bloomingdale's, 1000 Third Avenue.

A Southwestern Dinner

Table Setting (pages 24 and 25): Cassis & Co. ceramic dinner plates; wineglasses; tumblers; heatproof glass bowls; decanter; Wilton Armetale wine coaster; cotton place mats and napkins—Cookworks, 316 Guadalupe Street, Santa Fe, NM 87501, Tel. (505) 988-7676. Michael Aram "Gibralter" silver-plate flatware—Ad Hoc Softwares, 410 West Broadway. Iron candlesticks; candles—Zona, 97 Greene Street. Plants—Canyon Road Flowers, 423 Canyon Road, Santa Fe, NM 87501, Tel. (505) 983-9785. Mexican bench, circa 1900, with tin and glass decoration by Ford Ruthling; iron sculptures by Ford Ruthling—313 East Berger, Santa Fe, NM 87501, Tel. (505) 982-2241.
Mexican Chocolate Torte (page 27): Ceramic cake plate and dessert plate; Rogers Bros. "Zia" stainless-steel cake server—Tumbleweed Traders, 110 Galisteo Street, Santa Fe, NM 87501, Tel. (505) 984-0094.

A Breeze of a Lunch

Minestrone; Garlic Bruschetta; Assorted Dry-Cured Italian Sausages; Escarole and Radicchio Salad (pages 28 and 29): "Este" ceramic soup bowls and plates—Barneys New York, Seventh Avenue and 17th Street. Annie Glass

"ABC" child's glass soup plate; hand-painted wooden balls by Jon Wigren—The Whitney Museum's Store Next Door, 943 Madison Avenue. "Federal" silver-plate flatware; napkin rings—The Pottery Barn, 117 East 59th Street. Wineglasses and tumbler—Williams-Sonoma, 20 East 60th Street. Cotton napkins—ABC Carpet & Home, 888 Broadway. Oak slab table with ebony inlays—Daniel Mack Rustic Furnishings, 14 Welling Avenue, Warwick, NY 10990, Tel. (914) 986-7293. Kites—Big City Kites, 1201 Lexington Avenue.

Celebrating America's Heritage

Table Setting (pages 30 and 31): "Camelot" porcelain soup plates designed by Robert Lee Morris for Swid Powell; silver-plate trays (under soup plates) and candlesticks (on dining table) designed by Richard Meier for Swid Powell—Bloomingdale's, 1000 Third Avenue. "Winslow" sterling flatware by Kirk Stieff—Fortunoff, 681 Fifth Avenue. Water goblets and wineglasses; crystal torch—Tiffany & Company, 727 Fifth Avenue. Linen napkins—Barneys New York, Seventh Avenue and 17th Street. "Turquoise Stars" cotton and rayon fabric from the National Trust for Historic Preservation—F. Schumacher & Co., 939 Third Avenue. Majolica jardiniere, circa 1860; nineteenth-century brass candlesticks—Yale R. Burge, 305 East 63rd Street. Steel and brass chairs; Art Deco steel and marble table—Newel Art Galleries, Inc., 425 East 53rd Street. Flower arrangement—Zezé, 398 East 52nd Street.

Meanwhile . . . Back at the Ranch

Bacon and Sage Panfried Trout; Grilled Chili-Rubbed Lamb Chops; Wild Rice and Toasted Pecan Pilaf; Spinach and Mushroom Salad with Orange Vinaigrette (pages 34 and 35): "Westward Ho" ceramic dinner plates and bowls; cotton napkins; iron horseshoe napkin holder; vintage brown cotton blanket—Whispering Pines, 516 Main Street, Piermont, NY 10968.

"Shire" wood and stainless-steel flatware—Frank McIntosh Shop at Henri Bendel, 712 Fifth Avenue. Glasses; wooden dough bowl—Cookworks, 316 Guadalupe Street, Santa Fe, NM 87501. "Wild West" ceramic platters by Csara; metal napkin rings; stainless-steel serving fork and spoon—Johnson and Benkert, 128 West Water Street, Santa Fe, NM 87501. Cotton potholder—Zona, 97 Greene Street. Wrought-iron barbecue set—Platypus, 126 Spring Street.

A Thoroughly Modern Mother's Day

Table Setting (pages 36 and 37): "Torsade Bleu" porcelain dinner plates; faience service plates—Pavillon Christofle, 680 Madison Avenue. "Double Helix" silver-plate flatware by Ward Bennett for Sasaki—Barneys New York, Seventh Avenue and 17th Street. "St. Remy" crystal water goblets, wineglasses, and Champagne flutes; crystal hearts and bows—Baccarat, Inc., 625 Madison Avenue. Hand-painted linen napkins by Leslie Pontz—Frank McIntosh Shop at Henri Bendel, 712 Fifth Avenue. Flowers—Zezé, 398 East 52nd Street. "Montserrat" glass table on aluminum base by Oscar Tusquets, 1987; lacquered wood and steel chairs by Arne Jacobsen, 1958 (available through decorator)—ICF, Tel. (800) 237-1625. "Shangrila" handmade wool dhurrie (available through decorator)—Rosecore Carpet Co., Inc., 979 Third Avenue.
Rosewater Angel Food Cake (page 39): Ceramic cake plate and dessert plates—Frank McIntosh Shop at Henri Bendel, 712 Fifth Avenue.

A New England Breakfast

Stir-fried Red Flannel Hash; Fried Eggs; Raspberry Corn Muffins; Orange Juice; Coffee (pages 40 and 41): "Bennett's Bridge" hand-decorated earthenware dinner plates, dessert plates, and mugs designed by Sybil Connolly—Tiffany, 727 Fifth Avenue. English bone and silver flatware, circa 1800 (from a set of 6 knives and forks)—

Pantry & Hearth, 121 East 35th Street. Glass pitcher and tumblers; silver-plate coffeepot, sugar, and creamer, circa 1900 (one of a kind)—Wolfman • Gold & Good Company, 116 Greene Street. Cotton tablecloth and napkins by Paula Sweet—Bergdorf Goodman, 754 Fifth Avenue.

A Greek Luncheon

Table Setting (pages 42 and 43): Holmegaard "Trigona" glass plates and bowls—Royal Copenhagen Porcelain/Georg Jensen Silversmiths, 683 Madison Avenue. Gien "Ottoman" faience canapé plates—Baccarat, Inc., 625 Madison Avenue. "Ionic" stainless-steel flatware—The Pottery Barn, 117 East 59th Street. Glass bowls (olives and dip); wineglasses; metal napkin rings—Frank McIntosh Shop at Henri Bendel, 712 Fifth Avenue. Glass beakers—Simon Pearce, 500 Park Avenue (entrance on 59th Street). Murano glass urn and pitcher—Avventura, 463 Amsterdam Avenue. Wood-handled knives; resin candlesticks—Wolfman • Gold & Good Company, 116 Greene Street. Decanters—Pier One Imports, 225 Greenwich Avenue, Greenwich, CT 06830. "Calliope" cotton fabric from the Benaki Collection—Brunschwig & Fils, 979 Third Avenue.

Toasting the Bride and Groom

Table Setting (pages 46 and 47): "Grappa" ceramic salad plates—Avventura, 463 Amsterdam Avenue. "Aster" round earthenware platter; "King William" sterling dinner forks; wineglasses from The Classic Wine Glass Collection—Tiffany & Co., 727 Fifth Avenue. Footed ceramic bowl; ceramic cake stand—Wolfman • Gold & Good Company, 116 Greene Street. Cast-aluminum serving fork and spoon—William-Wayne & Co., 324 East 9th Street. Hand-painted cotton napkins—Vietri, Tel. (800) 277-5933. "Dionysos" linen and cotton fabric from the Benaki Collection (available through decorator)—Brunschwig & Fils, 979 Third Avenue.

Fourth of July Cookout

These pictures were photographed at a farmhouse in Martinsville, Maine. For information regarding rental of the property, contact Cindy Lang, P.O. Box 282, Tenants Harbor, ME 04860, Tel. (207) 372-8906.
Table Setting (pages 48 and 49): "Clearwater" ceramic dinner plates, "Emma" goblets, and hand-blown Pilsner glasses, all by Waterford Wedgwood; "Wainwright" stainless-steel flatware by Reed & Barton; "Betsy" cotton napkins; "Janie" cotton fabric (tablecloth)—The Ralph Lauren Home Collection, Tel. (212) 642-8700. Silver-plate napkin rings—Wolfman • Gold & Good Company, 116 Greene Street.
Maple-Barbecued Chicken; Potato, Corn, and Cherry Tomato Salad with Basil Dressing; Romaine and Cucumber Salad with Garlic Vinaigrette; Black Pepper Pita Toasts (pages 50 and 51): "Sunflower" handmade ceramic bowl by Barbara Eigen—ABC Carpet & Home, 888 Broadway. Silver-plate serving fork and spoon—Wolfman • Gold & Good Company, 116 Greene Street.

Dinner in the Great Indoors

Roast Rack of Lamb; Herbed Tomato Chutney; Basil Couscous with Summer Squash (pages 52 and 53): Porcelain dinner plates by Dan Levy; hand-painted glasses—Bergdorf Goodman, 754 Fifth Avenue. "Sphere" bronze flatware by Izabel Lam—The L • S Collection, 765 Madison Avenue. Cotton napkins and tablecloth; A² resin-and-mirror candlestick; hand-blown glass vase by Anthony Stern—Barneys New York, Seventh Avenue and 17th Street. Flowers—Zezé, 398 East 52nd Street.

Lunch for a Lazy Day

Table Setting (pages 54 and 55): "Mallory" ceramic dinner plates—Avventura, 463 Amsterdam Avenue. "Fiddlehead" stainless-steel flatware; "Pop" hand-painted wineglasses—Pottery Barn, 117 East 59th Street. Glasses; Italian linen napkins—Frank McIntosh

Shop at Henri Bendel, 712 Fifth Avenue. "Mosaic" cotton fabric by Athena Design (available through decorator)—Woodson Wallpapers, 979 Third Avenue.
Ricotta Gelato with Blackberry Sauce: (page 57): "Butterfly" Italian ceramic dessert plates—Frank McIntosh Shop at Henri Bendel, 712 Fifth Avenue.

A Blueberry-Picking Picnic

Chilled Tomato Yogurt Soup; Olive and Jarlsberg Salad Sandwich; Corned Beef and Coleslaw Sandwich (pages 58 and 59): Glass mugs and ceramic trivets—Dean & DeLuca, Inc., 560 Broadway. Glass tumblers—Wolfman • Gold & Good Company, 116 Greene Street.

A Polo Picnic

Picnic (pages 60 and 61): "Montauk" porcelain dinner plates and salad plates—Sasaki, Tel. (212) 686-5080. Scof wood-handled flatware; glasses in rattan holders; English silver-plate tongs; vintage tin picnic basket; woven aluminum and brass basket; galvanized tin tray; folding wooden tables in wicker picnic baskets; rattan and iron folding chairs—William-Wayne, 850 Lexington Avenue. Kosta Boda "Felicia" crystal highball and Double Old Fashioned glasses designed by Anna Ehrner; Kosta Boda "Accent" crystal bowl designed by Bertil Vallien—Galleri Orrefors Kosta Boda, Tel. (800) 351-9842. Cotton napkins and straw napkin rings (from a boxed set of four); cotton tablecloth; blue rush basket—Wolfman • Gold & Good Company, 116 Greene Street. Iron egg holders—Zona, 97 Greene Street. Hand-loomed chenille throw (#72-649392); rattan-wrapped bottle (#72-631226)—Chambers, Tel. (800) 334-9790.
Saffron Vichyssoise; Cold Roast Fillet of Beef; Cucumber Horseradish Sauce; Curried Yogurt Sauce; Assorted Breads; Tomato, Potato, and Mustard Green Salad; Cumin and Coriander Spiced Chick-Pea Salad (pages 62 and 63): Ceramic cups and coasters—Portico Home, 379 West Broadway. Porce-

lain serving dish in sea-grass holder—Wolfman • Gold & Good Company, 116 Greene Street. English silver-plate cold meat fork, horn-handled sauce spoons, and serving spoon, circa 1900; painted wood stool with bamboo legs, circa 1900—William-Wayne, 850 Lexington Avenue. Thermos—Ad Hoc Softwares, 410 West Broadway.

Back–to–School Send-Off

Cornmeal-Crusted Oven-Fried Chicken; Mashed Potatoes with Garlic and Shallots; Minted Sugar Snap Peas (pages 64 and 65): Gien "Feuille de Chêne" faience dinner plates and canapé plate—Baccarat, 625 Madison Avenue. "EXL" stainless-steel flatware—Bissell & Wilhite Co., Tel. (213) 931-1101. Royal Copenhagen "Elyssee" wineglasses—Royal Copenhagen Porcelain/Georg Jensen Silversmiths, 683 Madison Avenue. Ceramic serving bowls and platter—Dean & DeLuca, 560 Broadway. Archipelago linen and synthetic raffia napkins—William-Wayne, 850 Lexington Avenue. Wire vase—Zona, 97 Greene Street. Tiger maple table with ornate painted base by Lark Upson; Meeting House Shaker reproduction stained maple armchairs and side chairs with tape seats and backs—Portico Home, 379 West Broadway. Cotton duck zipper duffel bag and tote bag—L. L. Bean, Tel. (800) 221-4221. All Weather Leather Sherpa pack and totes—Dooney & Bourke, Trump Tower, 725 Fifth Avenue.

A Mexican Fiesta

Guacamole with Scallion and Coriander; Black Bean, Green Pepper, and Red Onion Dip (pages 66 and 67): Glass bowls; beer glasses; Rogers Bros. "Taos" stainless-steel tray; woven basket—Tumbleweed Traders, 110 Galisteo Street, Santa Fe, NM 87501, Tel. (505) 984-0094. Wall sculpture and tin decoration on door and columns by Ford Ruthling—Ford Ruthling, 313 East Berger, Santa Fe, NM 87501, Tel. (505) 982-2241.

Caldo Tlalpeño; Tamales; Jícama, Pineapple, and Watercress Salad with Orange Chili Vinaigrette (page 68): Terra-cotta service plates; Cassis & Co. ceramic dinner plates; Annieglass soup bowls; Rogers Bros. "Taos" stainless-steel flatware; glasses—Tumbleweed Traders (see above). Cotton napkins—Ad Hoc Softwares, 410 West Broadway. Cotton tablecloth; trug—Umbrello, 701 Canyon Road, Santa Fe, NM 87501, Tel. (505) 984-8566. *Mexican Floating Island with Kahlúa Custard Sauce and Sesame Pumpkin-Seed Brittle; Fresh Figs* (page 69): Annieglass plate; terra-cotta bowl—Tumbleweed Traders (see above).

An Elegant Autumn Dinner

Eggplant Ravioli with Lemon Sage Oil and Fried Onions (pages 70 and 71): "Drum Papaya" porcelain plates designed by Geoffrey Beene—Swid Powell, Tel. (800) 808-SWID. "Triade" silver-plate flatware—Pavillon Christofle, 680 Madison Avenue. Kosta Boda "Cleopatra" wineglasses designed by Ulrica H. Vallien—Galleri Oreffors Kosta Boda, Tel. (800) 351-9842. Handmade wrought-iron candlesticks and tole cachepots and wall sconce—Briger Design Ltd., Tel. (212) 517-4489. Flowers—Zezé, 398 East 52nd Street. Tressard "Zebra" cotton fabric (available through decorator)—The Friendly Lyon, 979 Third Avenue. Webbed settee designed by Vincente Wolf—Niedermaier 900, 120 Wooster Street. Framed engravings—Yale R. Burge Antiques, 305 East 63rd Street. "Henley Stripe" wallpaper (available through decorator)—Clarence House, 211 East 58th Street.

A Shaker Thanksgiving

Table Setting (pages 72 and 73): Vintage Dedham pottery dinner plates and salad plates—Malvina Solomon, 1122 Madison Avenue. English glass rummers, circa 1815, and wineglasses, circa 1840—Bardith, 901 Madison Avenue. Eighteenth-century English brass

candlesticks—Bob Pryor Antiques, 1023 Lexington Avenue. "Joseph" pink luster mug, circa 1830; spongeware salts, circa 1880—Thos. K. Woodard, 799 Madison Avenue. Tied bundles of rye—Zezé, 398 East 52nd Street. Mount Lebanon youth table chair; tin window ring candle holders—Dana Robes Wood Craftsmen, 28 East Putnam Avenue, Greenwich, CT 06830. Dried herbs and flowers—Shale Hill Farm & Herb Gardens, 6856 Hommelville Road, Saugerties, NY 12477. *Roast Turkey with Chestnut Stuffing and Cider Gravy; Cranberry Fruit Relish; Scalloped Onions, Leeks, and Shallots; Maple Squash Purée; Herbed Buttered Parsnips; Warm Green Bean Salad with Dill* (pages 74 and 75): Dummy board, circa 1750—Kentshire Galleries Ltd., 37 East 12th Street.

Holiday Weekend Brunch

Maple Walnut Coffeecake (page 76): Herend hand-painted porcelain platter and dessert plates—Scully & Scully, 504 Park Avenue. "Garland Song" ceramic coffeepot, cup and saucer, and creamer—Wolfman • Gold & Good Company, 116 Greene Street. Mahogany butler's tray on stand, circa 1860—Kentshire Galleries, Ltd., 37 East 12th Street.
Cranberry Champagne Cocktails; Cream Cheese and Chive Scrambled Eggs; Shredded Potato Pancakes with Smoked Salmon; Watercress Salad with Warm Vinaigrette (pages 76 and 77): Herend hand-painted porcelain dinner plates—Scully & Scully, 504 Park Avenue. "Windsor Shell" hand-forged sterling flatware by Old Newbury Crafters; Stuart "Iona" crystal wineglasses—Cardel Ltd., 621 Madison Avenue. Cotton damask napkins—Wolfman • Gold & Good Company, 116 Greene Street. Flowers—Zezé, 398 East 52nd Street. Mahogany breakfast table, circa 1805; Regency faux-rosewood side chairs, circa 1810; four-panel leather screen, circa 1870—Kentshire Galleries, Ltd., 37 East 12th Street.

Christmas Dinner

Table Setting (pages 78 and 79): "Harcourt" Sherry glasses—Baccarat, 625 Madison Avenue. Cut-glass rummers, circa 1810—Kentshire Galleries Ltd., 37 East 12th Street. Bavarian nineteenth-century antler and carved walnut candelabrum; nineteenth-century antler and brass candlesticks (on mantelpiece); nineteenth-century carved wood bear with backpack vase (on mantelpiece)—Newel Art Galleries, 425 East 53rd Street. Hand-painted edible sugar place cards and Christmas tree ornaments—Margaret Braun, Tel. (212) 929-1582. "Berwick Glade" cotton and linen fabric (available through decorator)—Brunschwig & Fils, 979 Third Avenue. Antler and brass candelabra (on rear table)—Bob Pryor Antiques, 1023 Lexington Avenue. English nineteenth-century pottery log planter; nineteenth-century majolica pâté pot (both on rear table)—J. Garvin Mecking, 72 East 11th Street.
Chocolate Linzertorte (page 81): English nineteenth-century cut-glass cake stand with cranberry-glass inserts—J. Garvin Mecking, 72 East 11th Street. Brameld creamware dessert plates (from a service for eighteen), circa 1870; English cut-glass bowl, circa 1820—Bardith Ltd., 901 Madison Avenue. "Colbert" crystal wineglasses—Baccarat, 625 Madison Avenue. Heinz copper tray with sterling-silver overlay, circa 1900—Newel Art Galleries, 425 East 53rd Street.

A Casual Christmastime Dinner

Baked Polenta with Shiitake Ragout; Arugula, Radicchio, and Endive Salad (pages 82 and 83): Rosenthal "Versace Barocco" porcelain dinner plates—Bloomingdale's, 1000 Third Avenue. "Homes" reproduction sterling flatware by Lunt Silversmiths—available at fine department and specialty stores. "Vineyard" wineglasses—The Pottery Barn, 117 East 59th Street. "Angelique" stainless-steel baking dish (cover not shown)—Fortunoff, 681 Fifth Avenue. Salad bowl and cachepot; handmade decoupage dinner plates (on wall) by Jered Holmes Ltd.—Hoagland's of Greenwich, 175 Greenwich Avenue, Greenwich, CT 06830, Tel. (203) 869-2127.
Prosciutto-Wrapped Breadsticks with Fig; Cucumber Tapenade Canapés (page 83): English tole trays, circa 1840—S. Wyler, 941 Lexington Avenue. "Spangle" cotton fabric (on table) by Jean Churchill (available through decorator)—Cowtan & Tout, 979 Third Avenue.

A Recipe Compendium

Curried Grilled Chicken Salad (page 84): Moretti wineglass—Avventura, 463 Amsterdam Avenue.

A Lunar New Year's Buffet

Soy-Braised Chicken and Black Mushrooms; Pickled Cucumber; Steamed Red Snapper in Black Bean Sauce; Beef and Bell Peppers with Oyster Sauce and Noodles; Stir-Fried Lettuce and Snow Peas with Sesame Seeds (pages 268 and 269): Octagon bowl; gold buffet plate—Fitz & Floyd, 225 Fifth Avenue. "Golden Procession" platter (with snapper); "Silk Winds" dinner plates—Noritake, 41 Madison Avenue. "Royal Hong Kong" platter (with chicken)—Wedgwood, 41 Madison Avenue. "Golden Juilliard" serving pieces—Oneida, Ltd., Oneida, NY 13421, Tel. (315) 361-3000. "Omnia" wineglasses—Sasaki, 41 Madison Avenue. Chinese screen—Charles R. Gracie & Sons, Inc., Tel. (212) 753-5350 (by appointment only). Flowers—ZeZé, 398 East 52nd Street.

Harvest Moon Dinner

Braised Pork with Anise, Orange Flavor, and Fennel; Steamed Rice; Stir-Fried Chili Shrimp; Baked Butternut Squash with Chinese Mustard and Duck Sauce (pages 278 and 279): Cobalt blue pottery vase and burnt-sienna pottery bowl (for the rice)—Gordon Foster, 1322 Third Avenue.

Dim Sum

Stir-Fried Vegetables with Crisp Rice Noodles (page 286): Crane with pine platter—Fitz & Floyd, 225 Fifth Avenue.
Pot Stickers; Shrimp Toast Rolls (page 286): Shell series cala lily leaf platter and buffet plate—Annieglass Studio, 303 Potrero Street, Santa Cruz, CA, Tel. (800) 347-6133.
Mushroom Turnovers; Curry Chicken Wings; Turkey Won Tons and Chinese Broccoli with Spicy Peanut Sauce (page 287): Celadon oval platter; Celadon bowl—Chinese Products Co., 225 Fifth Avenue. Flowers—ZeZé, 398 East 52nd Street. Harry Lauder Stick Branches—SKH Floral Manufacturing, Tel. (717) 898-6076.

If you are not already a subscriber to *Gourmet* Magazine and would be interested in subscribing, please call *Gourmet*'s toll-free number, 1-800-365-2454.

If you are interested in purchasing additional copies of this book or other *Gourmet* cookbooks, please call 1-800-678-5681.